Interpretive Trends in Christian Revitalization for the Early Twenty First Century

J. Steven O'Malley

Asbury Theological Seminary Series:
The Study of World Christian Revitalization Movements

EMETH PRESS
www.emethpress.com

Interpretive Trends in Christian Revitalization
for the Early Twenty First Century

Library of Congress Cataloging-in-Publication Data

O'Malley, J. Steven (John Steven), 1942-
 Interpretive trends in Christian revitalization for the early twenty-first century / J. Steven O'Malley.
  p. cm. -- (Asbury Theological Seminary series: the study of world Christian revitalization movements)
 ISBN 978-1-60947-018-0 (alk. paper)
 1. Church renewal. 2. Christianity--21st century. I. Title.
 BV600.3.O43 2011
 262.001'7--dc23
            2011031182.

Contents

Part Four: Where in the Name of Christ our Lord Are We Headed?

Appendices: Selected Addresses from Consultation One and Two

Acknowledgments

On behalf of the Center for the Study of World Christian Revitalization Movements, I hereby wish to acknowledge those persons and institutions that have contributed substantially to this research reflected in this volume. Foremost, we are grateful to The Henry Luce Foundation for providing the research grant that has funded the project, and in particular to its theology program director, Lynn Szwaja. We are grateful for our host institution, Asbury Theological Seminary, in which this project is housed and where our first annual consultation convened (2009), as well as the University of Edinburgh and Tyndale Seminary (Toronto), the institutions that hosted the second and third annual consultations in 2010 and 2011, respectively. It is also our privilege to acknowledge with gratitude the work of the several scholars who contributed to the chapters of this volume, as well as all participants in the consultations where the research was generated.

Thanks also are extended to the program committee of the Center, and to its co-chairs, Professors Lester Ruth and Beverly Johnson-Miller. Professor Ruth provided leadership in planning the services of worship at the consultations, and Professor Johnson-Miller prepared a summary of the table discussion at Edinburgh, as well as assisting the editor in reading and offering advice in preparing the chapters of this volume for publication. We are also grateful for Professor Laurence Wood and to Emeth Press, our publisher.

Finally, we give thanks to God for enabling this entire process, as persons from many denominations and nationalities have responded to the invitation to engage the task to which we were commissioned. Our awareness of the ongoing ministry of the Holy Spirit in bringing revitalization around the globe has been enhanced in this study, and it is our joy to share the fruits of that research in the present volume.

J. Steven O'Malley, PhD
Director, Center for the Study of World Christian Revitalization
Movements   and John T. Seamands Professor of Methodist Holiness History
Asbury Theological Seminary

Introduction

The Center for the Study of World Christian Revitalization Movements, a research center at Asbury Theological Seminary, grew out of a deep-seated concern of a small group of faculty members to take the pulse and heart of the various movements of revitalization which are developing in a variety of cultural settings across world Christianity. Consequently, the Center received a grant from the Henry Luce Foundation in March 2007, enabling it to proceed with that research task. In a day when renewal movements seem to proliferate more rapidly than they can be adequately identified, it was deemed to be the right moment for a thoughtful examination and evaluation to discern what is genuine and effective. To that end, we launched a serious probe into the relationship between Christian revival and revitalization of faith communities and the larger cultures in which they are housed.

Along the way, we are drawing upon lessons from the world church, and do so by use of a diverse range of perspectives. One perspective is provided by the site where this project was initiated. Asbury Seminary is rooted in a commitment to the Wesleyan theological perspective, which takes seriously John Wesley's dictum that the world is to be our parish, as we seek to keep step with the trajectory of the movement of God's Spirit in bringing revival among people groups of diverse cultures. The Center continues the work of the former Wesleyan-Holiness Studies Center at Asbury, which documented the history and theology of the holiness revivals of the nineteenth and early twentieth centuries, showing their significant impact on social reform and the higher life movement that generated a host of denominations and initiatives around the globe. The Center was originally established in 1991 and has consistently built a reputation around interdisciplinary scholarship and the formation of revitalized communities in world Christianity

Additional perspectives come into play as well. We are led to give attention to contemporary trends in revitalization that are occurring from the congregational level to the trans-national networks. We are concerned to explore emerging trends in revitalization in a comparative light, using theological and social research insights. To study revival at those levels has required that we summon a wide range of scholars and practitioners to address these issues.

In practical terms, students from many nations across the Global South and East have come to schools like Asbury, as well as Tyndale in Toronto, where our next research consultation will be held. They have come in response to outbreaks of revival that have been initiated within their home cultures. Their experience of Christian faith has typically been developed apart from the cultural norms of Western Christianity. We are compelled to take seriously what God is doing in these locations, so that theological education learns from these initiatives and can be responsive to preparing students in North America, as well as those from the Global South and East, to come to terms with the *missio Dei* that is rapidly and decisively reshaping the global church.

It is significant that this research is being pursued within the arena of theological education. This means we intend to assist those preparing persons called of God for ministry in the early twenty first century to discern new realities not observed in previous generations of Christian leadership, and to minister effectively within those realities. To that end, we seek to track with the Spirit of God, as revealed in the biblical and confessional documents of our Triune faith, in discerning how God is at work amid the crucial human demographic and cultural developments that are redefining the shape of Christianity. Our learning and praxis need to be responsive to these shifts, that include post-denominationalism, transnationalism, urbanization, and globalization. Social scientists are at work in these fields, but here we are asking, how is Christian revitalization occurring in the midst of these realities, and in what ways is it making a difference at all levels of human culture, amid its brokenness? We expect to be finding new ways of doing homiletics, Christian discipleship, and, yes, historical and systematic theology, by seeing how preaching and Christian formation are being practiced in the midst of revival, as it is in the Global South and East. Revival is being manifested in the midst of these shifting social realities. In so doing, it tends to move ahead of and apart from the routinized life of congregations concerned with their own survival and well-being.

A final perspective that concerns this project is to identify new opportunities for mutual learning and action in revitalization that will draw together the major expressions of church. We are finding a lively sense of ecumenical awareness as persons from diverse faith traditions have shared together in our meetings, seeking in our different modes of expression to trace the sovereign movement of God's Spirit in bringing revitalization and hence deeper unity throughout a scattered world Christian constituency. Further, we are discovering that this constituency includes Jesus-movement insiders within other religious faiths and cultures, as the definitive demographic study of Todd Johnson and his colleagues at the Center for Global Christianity in Boston have been discovering.[1]

How do these concerns come to expression in this volume? The Luce Foundation has funded the project, based on a series of annual consultations, and this study is the product of their work. At consultation one, convened at Asbury in 2009, our theme was "Pentecost and the New Humanity: Explorations in World Christian Revitalization". Professor Howard Snyder, founding director of the Center for the Study of World Christian Revitalization Movements, provided the keynote address to a large plenary audience on this theme.[2] Discussion centered around presentations of two historical and two contemporary movements of Christian revitalization enabled us to gather a wide field of data describing what sorts of revitalization is occurring across global Christianity and how it shows similarities and dissimilarities with movements of revitalization from past ages. Table groups, led by doctoral students in Asbury's E. Stanley Jones School of Mission and Evangelization, teased out what they saw or heard that looked like revitalization or contributed to understanding how it is being manifested in traditional and non-traditional ways, including the attending social dynamics. Through probing examination of these dynamics, the consultation became cognizant of the diverse ways in which diverse communities of Christian faith are discovering the urgency of embracing movements of revitalization.

Consultation two, held May 28-June 2, 2010, convened at the University of Edinburgh, Scotland, as the preconference event preceding the international convocation of churches, "Edinburgh 2010: A Centenary Conference". This main event was heralded as the most important world assembly of Christians since the International Missionary Council, which was held at the same location in 1910 and was responsible for launching the interdenominational world mission initiative of global Christianity in the twentieth century. Representing a diverse body of Christian scholars and practitioners of revitalization,[3] our consultation preceding this major convocation was grouped into teams to examine the extensive transcriptions from consultation one[4] The theme of consultation two, "Exploring the Dialectic Between Revitalization and Church" had the task of evaluating the data from consultation one and moving the discussion from a descriptive to a more normative level, showing how revitalization works in distinct ways to impact the church in its various ecclesial and cultural expressions The strategy, based on the data and participants' expertise, was to (1) give a definition of revitalization, (2) construct or reconstruct a model of the church for revitalization, and (3) explain what revitalization means for the internal and external life of the church.

Highlights from this consultation include a keynote presentation from Professor Andrew Walls, arguably the most influential voice of Christian mission in our time, who focused on the mission of St. Anthony of Egypt as a model for perceiving Christianity in its engagement of culture as a revitalization movement. Resources to assist the participants in achieving these results included presentations of four distinctive (and classical) models of church by practitioners of those models,[5] ,and also an introduction to key theories of revitalization. Each team was free to engage these resources in their work with the data. The results generated new insights into the meaning and import of revitalization and church that are distinctive to the data, and reflecting revitalization movements of the early twentieth century. Most of these participants were different persons from those who generated the data in consultation one. With the range of diversity represented in the participants, the heart of the consultation was the robust way they engaged in table discussions. The mix of participants had been designed to ensure each table had distinctive.

A summary of the data from each of these table discussions at Edinburgh is provided by Professor Eunice Irwin in Appendix A of this study.

The notes from the Edinburgh conversation were organized around seminal themes into which the data were assimilated.. The themes from the Edinburgh consultation represent the chapter titles for this volume, and they are presented here through a study entitled *Interpretive Trends in Christian Revitalization for the Early Twenty First Century*. The authors of these chapters are key practitioner-scholars who also served as participants in at least one of the first two consultations .

Part One concerns the nature of revitalization, viewed under the subcategories of defining the characteristics, forces and barriers to revitalization in our day. Part Two illumines the present realities that constitute revitalization movements, as they are inextricably enmeshed in human cultural dynamics. This theme is explored in terms of a plethora of issues that constitute this reality. These include prevailing myths about what revitalization is, pathologies, commonalities and anomalies inherent in revitalization, the interplay of revitalization with forms of worship, the affirmation of women in church and culture, and where the Holy Spirit's moving. Each of these issues we discern among the prevailing realities of revitalization. Part Three concerns how revitalization in the past shapes its present reality. Issues here include the use and misuse of theological constructs from the Christian past, the role of diaspora in redefining human identity amid revitalization, and the interplay between revitalization and longstanding issues of social justice. Part four directs our focus to the future, looking at the trajectory of where is headed in this century. Forces driving this trajectory are the rediscovery of sacraments and liturgy in revitalized churches, relating revitalization to traditional issues of soteriology in Christian faith and experience, the use of the means of grace, ecological issues, and the abiding tension in revitalization movements between the vision for the future and the perennial tendency to generate new expressions of revitalization that seems inherent in Christianity.[6]

At the Toronto consultation in October 2011, the essays in this volume will also provide a grid for engaging six cases concerning contemporary revitalization movements currently developing within that culture. Each of these cases will concern diasporic ministry initiatives that work with particular transnational population groups from the Global South now residing in Toronto, the most ethnically diverse city of North America. Globalization and transnationalism are two of the dominant features impacting twenty-first century Christianity. Most of these immigrants come from the fastest growing sector of Christianity, the Global South and East.

The cases in the Toronto consultation will provide the first field test for the insights and perspectives on revitalization that are housed within these chapters. This connection will also facilitate the development of insights for shaping theological education that will address the major demographic shifts of the twenty-first century. Following this consultation, the Center for the Study of World Christian Revitalization Movements convenes a public forum in a large Chinese congregation in Toronto, which will offer another venue for examining the insights of this volume. Hopefully there will come many other conversation sites for which the insights that fill this volume will provide perspective and meaning. This volume is offered as an invitation and summons for practicing Christians and scholars of revitalization from a wide range of academic and church background to focus their best efforts in understanding and hence extending the work of revitalization abounding around the world today, as the movement of the Holy Spirit in history.

J. STEVEN O'MALLEY, EDITOR

Notes

1. Todd M. Johnson and Kenneth R. Ross, eds., *Atlas of Global Christianity* (Edinburgh: University of Edinburgh Press, 2010).

2. That address is found in appendix one of this study.

3. The consultation included scholars and practitioners from 15 nations and five continents, including 16 from Asia and A frica, 5 from Europe, and 18 from North America. Denominational representation included 3 Catholics, 12 from Asian and African indigenous churches, and 15 from a range of North American Protestant churches, including Pentecostals.

4. Each participant was provided with a 700 page transcription of the table discussion and papers from consultation one, with guidelines for reading the data.

5. Models of church that are conducive to revitalization included a Catholic sacramental model from Judith Kubicki of Fordham University, an evangelical Lutheran model from the dean of a Malaysian Lutheran seminary, a model reflecting a "community of the converted" in the secular setting of contemporary Kiev, and a Ugandan Pentecostal model that interfaced with indigenous African Christianity.

6. In an appendix following these chapters, the reader will find the text of selected addresses delivered at consultation one and two.

Part 1

The Nature of Revitalization

Chapter 1

Dancing with God:
The Forms and Forces of Revitalization

BEVERLY JOHNSON-MILLER, PHD
PROFESSOR OF CHRISTIAN DISCIPLESHIP
ASBURY THEOLOGICAL SEMINARY

Have you ever been to a dance? If so, did you dance? If not, why not? Dancing is fun: joy-filled, playful, and energizing. Dancing typically necessitates music, with harmony, melody, and rhythm. The rhythm provokes movement and moving rhythmically is instinctual. Even people watching sway to the music or tap their feet. Rhythm provides the pulse and movement, the driving force of the dance.

God resides "in the thick of life," "in the mess [as well as] the beauty."[1] "God is public, ...not private. God is at work in the world."[2] Overwhelming evidence points to God's presence and work throughout the globe: in every nation, race, tribe, and people group, in the good, the bad, the beautiful, and the ugly. The presence and revitalizing work of God in the world resemble a dance, having movement, music, rhythm, harmony, and dissonance.

Everyone is invited to participate, but to do so, individuals must hear the rhythm and respond. Both sound and silence constitute the rhythm that makes music flow. The arrangements of silences interspersed with sounds form patterns that create rhythm. The revitalizing work of God results from human responses to such repetitious arrangements of the Spirit's rhythms. The rhythm compels movement: a creative response from the inside out. Human response to the Spirit's pulse employs many evolving forms, styles, and steps.

Participation in the dance of revitalization requires listening for the rhythm and attuning to the sounds and movements of the past, present, and future. "In music the art comes from listening as it should in life. And we have to listen to the rhythm, the person, or the sound before us as well as to the tone, sound, or person after us." [3] Present movement always responds to the past; it sets the stage, inspires, guides, and empowers creative movement to follow.

The forms and forces of God's dance change course and evolve. They move in different directions through varying configurations, like a marching band on the football field or the dance performances at the Beijing 2008 Olympic Game's opening ceremony. Listening, people can recognize the sights and sounds of God's transforming grace and experience the beauty of human movement creatively aligned with the rhythms of the Spirit. Data from the Christian Revitalization research consultations confirm that the forms and forces of revitalization compose the redemptive dance of God in the world ushering in the new creation. [4] Research data illumines how the present revitalization movements responsively and creatively engage the past and future.

The rhythm of the Spirit is *the* force of revitalization propelling many kinds of redemptive movements, and varied forms. A form refers to the "mode in which a thing exists or manifests itself."[5] A force is an "exerted strength or impetus," or the exertion of such.[6] The forms emerge as humans respond to the Spirit. They grow, evolve, change, and even die over time. Death of one form creates space for the birth of new forms and forces.

What forms and forces embody the rhythmic summons of the Spirit? What dance styles emerge as human responses to the Spirit? Consider the significance of revitalizing responses, and how they change over time. What forms and forces are evident in the world today?

Forms and Forces:
Emerging, Intersecting, & Evolving

When it comes to dance, "ANY choreography is governed by a set of IMPLICIT rules. By making those rules EXPLICIT their hidden potential... can be revealed."[7] A close look at the forms and forces of revitalization makes explicit the implicit governing principles, unrecognized possibilities, and fresh frameworks and systems of revitalization.

The forms and forces of revitalization can only be identified within a complex web of systems, organizations, forces, and realities. There is no such thing as a "solo" form or force of revitalization. No individual form or force can stand alone, and the entire network of forms and forces would be impossible to fully describe. Any particular form or force identified cannot be contained in any single category.

All revitalization movements consist of multiple intersecting forces. For example, discontent with the state of the church often intersects with innate spiritual thirst that may also overlap with painful realities in society. Every force has multiple interacting dimensions such as those that initiated the 1960's Jesus Movement: counterculture development, social discontent, disillusionment, increased value of relationships and authenticity, and a fresh theological focus on Jesus.

New forms and forces arise from the evolution of or in connection with historical movements. The Charismatic Movement that penetrated the Catholic Church in the late 1960's directly stemmed from a lay deacon in an Assemblies of God congregation; the pastor of a Four Square church ignited the Jesus Movement.[8] Both congregations descended from the early twentieth-century Pentecostal Movement, which was rooted in the nineteenth-century Holiness Movement. The intersecting of the Jesus Movement with the Charismatic Movement facilitated fellowship between Catholics and Protestants.[9] The charismatic theology and renewal movements of the 1960's–80's contributed to an undoing of colonial mission and a resurgence of ancient spiritual practices.

Descendants of the Pentecostal Movement transcended their theological "fringe" reputation and lower socioeconomic status to become well-educated pioneers of strategic mission organizations such as universities, seminaries, Teen Challenge, World Relief Agencies, Latin America Child Care, and the Global Center for Women and Justice. The Jesus Movement in North America influenced the Jesus House Movement in Germany and Israel. Jesus House Movement participants did not identify with Pietism, however the movement bore strong resemblance and perhaps some historic ties to German Pietism. [10]

Revitalization is the reconstruction of life in the face of death.[11]The emergence of monasticism in the Dark Ages demonstrates that revitalization cannot occur apart from cyclic life and death forces. Acceptance of death of outdated systems creates space for relevant forms. Clinging to dead forms hinders new life, whereas letting go of the old empowers new life. Prophetic voices of individuals such as Howard Snyder challenged the Church in the 1970's to invite, accept, and give birth to new forms.[12]

The forms and forces of revitalization create space for renewed openness to the Spirit. Regardless of the models generated, the Holy Spirit indwells, guides, and remodels them. The spirit of renewal assumes vital forms of human relationship: enlivens old structures, fosters new relationships, draws people to Christianity, awakens people to God's love, inspires authentic worship, mobilizes mission, and enables human flourishing.

Forms: Diverse and Multi-Dimensional

A dance can have many purposes– self-expression, communication, aesthetic engagement, therapy, etcetera. While goals shape forms (i.e. Dance aimed at emotional healing requires forms that express negative emotion), new forces result from emerging forms. In a similar manner, every revitalization movement has multiple dimensions and goals– moving beyond the limitations of tradition, reviving life-giving practices, generating new ways of *being* in faith, enabling spiritual depth and authenticity, and more.

Goals and forms go hand-in-hand, giving rise to meaning, direction, and motivation. The goal of a revitalized church, for example, is to engage in God's mission in the world, renewing culture and faith. Structure and change necessitate goals. Forms of revitalization correspond with four intertwining meta-categories: Tradition Centered, Person Centered, Church Community Centered, and Society Centered. These categories align with primary aspects of Christian revitalization: communion with God, relationship within community, social transformation, and human flourishing. The new creation is God's meta-goal for all humanity.[13]

Each category reflects distinctive aims yet no particular form of revitalization exists exclusively in any one category. Reclaiming Christology, a major theme of the Jesus Movement, certainly aligns with tradition-centered revitalization yet the Jesus Movement was not a tradition-centered form of revitalization. Various combinations of multiple intersecting dimensions exist within every movement (theological, anthropological, cultural, spiritual, academic, intellectual, emotional, and relational), yet each dimension could become a form of revitalization. *Theology (or theological)*, one normative dimension in any form of revitalization, also functioned as the meta-focus in the fourth-century Catechetical Movement and the sixteenth-century Reformation Movement.

The tradition-centered forms aim to proclaim the gospel story, make accessible the tradition's resources (beliefs; symbols, disciplines, and values), teach people to think/reflect theologically, and promote moral and ethical implications of Christian love. Preserving past practices, as well as retrieving specific marginal practices like catechism, a remerging twenty-first century focus, characterize tradition-centered revitalization.

Person-centered revitalization focuses on empowering people to live in the fullness of their values and faith, maximize faith, hope, and love, nurture relationship with God, develop one's human potential, nurture growth into Christ likeness, and nurture experience of the holy. Person-centered revitalization awakens people to the realities of sin, calls people to repentance, attracts new believers, supports lifestyle reform, and cultivates brilliant expressions of faith. The Chinese House Church Movement reflects person-centered revitalization.

Church-centered forms create community in transformational tension with society and help people act, discover, exercise gifts/roles, and worship. They call people to rebuild, unify, restore, and energize the Church for effective participation in God's project of creation. The call of Saint Francis to rebuild the Church established the Franciscan Movement. In recent years, the Guatemala renewal movements formed communities, bringing fresh spiritual experience and vitality to the Church and society.[14] The South Korean Cell Group Movement exemplifies church-centered revitalization.[15]

Society-centered revitalization mobilizes action for the sake of healing, compassion, justice, and evangelism. The evangelistic, holistic, and ecumenical nature of the East African Revival Movement led to the establishment of mission churches in Uganda, Kenya, and Tanzania.[16] Significant society-centered movements often go unrecognized: the twenty-first century Martin Luther King Civil Rights Movement; the twenty-first century Creation Care Movement, the Evangelical Environmental Movement; Latin American

Liberation Movements , and the Catholic Women's Movement of Post Vatican II.

Some revitalization movements fit in multiple categories. *Intellectual academic movements* include the Christian College Movement and Christian Apologetic Movement (i.e. L'Abri). *Trans-denominational initiatives*: Billy Graham Crusade, Ecumenical Movement, Campus Crusade for Christ, Youth With a Mission, and Alpha. *Arts & music*: the Contemporary Christian Music Movement and New Liturgical Movement (i.e Taize). Campus Crusade for Christ is one example of a *Para-Church* movement. *Insider movements:* Vatican II and Indigenous Christian Conferences. Regardless of variety or complexity, all forms advance the restoration of humanity and community.

Forces: Organic and Spirit Empowered

Searching to identify forces of revitalization begs the question: *Can revitalization be initiated in a test-tube*? If we gather all key ingredients identified in the history of Christian revitalization movements, can we manufacture revitalization, or create a controlled *greenhouse* environment for cultivating growth? Could that be the point of revitalization research? Who controls the forces at work in revitalization? If *greenhouse revitalization* is not possible or a good idea, why? What are the forces of revitalization that, even though we cannot or perhaps should not attempt to control, invite and guide meaningful participation? Is there a mechanism of revitalization available to us? How do we discern what is really at play in the birth and growth of Christian revitalization?

The complex web of forces and realities cannot be entirely described, nor can any particular force be classified within a single category. It is difficult if not impossible to identify which forces played what role, and which were the greatest or most crucial or essential forces, yet it *is* possible to identify a wide range of active forces, and how they potentially intersect, evolve, and coincide with particular forms of revitalization. While the Holy Spirit is *the* catalytic force, many other Spirit empowered forces exist. Forces coincide with revitalization goals and dimensions and can be organized according to a variety of generative themes. The organizing categories- Divine Encounter, Social Realities, and Human Need- reflect meta-themes associated with the breadth and complexity of revitalization forces.

Divine Encounter

Divine encounter drives revitalization. Mary's encounter with the Holy Spirit ushered in a new era of salvation. The Samaritan woman's visit with Jesus led to the conversion of many. On the day of Pentecost thousands were baptized and the church was born. Paul's dramatic transformation on the road to Damascus strengthened and proliferated the church.

Divine encounter, grounded in God's love, is the method and message, the beginning and end. All forces are initiated, empowered by, and for the sake of

God, who is love. Divine engagement is the ultimate, overarching, underlying, all-consuming force of Christian revitalization. Stated by one table participant:

> Some revitalization movements can be explained by the social sciences, but is this the actual genesis of these things...that give it its energy? Does this revitalize a whole society or just a part of society? ...What changes, what doesn't change? ...Can you plan it or not? There is something explosive about this that doesn't happen in normal evangelization programs in institutional churches.

> ...We need to consider the presence of God and [God's] heart for [reaching] creation. [God] is the author and genesis of good evangelism and revitalization... How do people respond to God's presence when [God] begins to move? Often their understanding of God strongly influences how the movement grows, spawns, or dies or gets highjacked in the individuals understanding of God... God is the one drawing us and wanting to renew us. Revitalization starts with something more than just ecclesiology and personal salvation, but with the revitalization of creation... and we are God's created beings. So, again, it's God reaching down to us and how we respond.[17]

God's initiative that precedes our response makes human response possible.

The dance of revitalization consists of God's initiative and human response. Dance makes it possible for revitalization to be both fully God's action and fully human action.[18]

> ...We recognized the work of the Spirit contributed to the... Jesus Movement, and that work connects to context, to culture, and the Spirit... In observing that, did you see that there was any human agency involved in recognizing the Spirit... and responding... or is it all from the Divine side? Is it all Divine agency? Are we [suggesting] that in this one particular [movement]... it was all the Spirit's work, or was there any human agency involved?

> My answer to that would be, it is both, but it is spontaneous in the sense that it is the work of the Spirit and using the channels of the people; it is not the people using the Spirit, but the Spirit using the channels.

> Clearly there was human agency and intentionality in lots of ways, some of that was good and effective, some of it was apparent, counter-productive, but clearly there was human agency... [19]

Although human effort cannot replace the work of the Holy Spirit, the Spirit's activity cannot be separated from the context of creation and human response.

The life-transforming work of the Holy Spirit does not occur in a vacuum. The Holy Spirit, the ultimate force of revitalization, cannot be reduced to or abstracted from human reality. Rather, the Holy Spirit moves within and among individuals, communities, and institutions. The concrete presence and acts of the Church in the world are the primary witness of the Spirit. The revitalizing force of the Holy Spirit takes vital forms: enlivening old structures, fostering new relationships, transforming people for mission, enabling human flourishing, etcetera. Contextualization of the Gospel occurs through the Spirit's indwelling in the concrete contexts of human existence.[20]

The force of the Holy Spirit, though often unrecognized, takes concrete form in the life of the Church. The Church, in turn, participates with God to broaden and deepen the move of the Spirit, however this movement cannot be manufactured by or limited to human effort. When the Holy Spirit moves people reconnect to God. Gifts of the Spirit, expressed through the Church, concretely embody God's actions in the world.

Social Realities: Cultural Engagement

Revitalization cannot be isolated from cultural realities. Potent revitalizing forces result from reaction to and adaptation of culture. The seventeenth-century Pietism movement protested against Enlightenment intellectualism, church formalism, ethical passivity, and spiritual deterioration for the sake of Christian piety and purity of life. Pietism brought widespread revival to Protestant churches, a major impetus to Protestant missions.

The eighteenth-century British Sunday School movement emerged in response to a rapidly growing poverty-crime cycle, a result of England's shift from an agrarian to an industrial society. Robert Raikes sought to end the poverty-crime cycle by teaching reading, hygiene, and religion to poor children victimized by industrialism. The Sunday School Movement forged positive social change that proved a potent reciprocating force of revitalization.

The existential thirst that drove widespread social revolt became a catalyst for spiritual revolution. As society awakened to various social-structural limitations, many hippies embraced Jesus as the answer to their cry for authentic, liberating spirituality. In reference to the Jesus Movement, one consultation participant stated,

> I think what we shared in common was incredible disillusionment... It was the beginning of the cracks of modernity, and there was great disappointment in the promises that had been made to us, and so we had largely checked out of the dreams and we constructed... We were wonderfully naïve, but dared to believe it was possible. I think the thing that happened for me [was] I'd already sort of largely abandoned the god I was raised with, and abandoned any expressions of church. There were many like me, but there was still a deep spiritual hunger and longing.[21]

Christianity took on fresh meaning, unencumbered by rigid, meaningless, and superficial traditions. Personal experiential faith replaced detached religious conformity; something very appealing to a generation of young people calling for more love, less judgment and more relationship, less tradition.

Hippies who turned to Jesus forced the Church to deny, resist, critically accommodate, or fully assimilate the theological, philosophical, social-structural attitudes, values, and practices passionately propelled by the societal revolution. Churches that welcomed the social change (Calvary chapel led by Chuck Smith) fueled pervasive revitalization. Social-religious changes pioneered by the "Jesus People" carried forward by Para-Church, Seeker Friendly, Mega, and Emerging Church Movements. Shifts adopted in the larger social context invite fresh perspective and new forms of revitalization.

Social Realities: the Ecclesial Dimension

Ecclesial attachment, as positive interactions within or related to the church, is a dominant, multi-dimensional social force of revitalization. The church, by nature, exists asthe primary location of the presence of Christ in the world, the byproduct of God's mission in the world, a perpetual life-giving community, a sign and conveyor of God's grace, anda constituency of revitalized individuals. Renewal embeds in the heart of the tradition. It is "not that the Church has a mission, but that the mission has a church".[22] Christian revitalization is always about the ecclesiology; it is always about the church. Christian ecclesiology is the generative, organic, teleological, trans-cultural, contextual, counter-cultural, and cross-cultural force of revitalization.

Social Realities – Institutions

In spite of a capricious," "complex," and "controversial" relationship, revitalization benefits from institutions. Revitalization forms fertile institutions, occurs through insstitutions, redeems institutions, and or sets people free from institutions. Under the influence of the nineteenth century Protestant revival movement, Anabaptist and Pietistic separatists shifted from localized and contextualized organizational structures to centralized and institutionalized organization. This spiritual "awakening" led to the adoption of organized Sunday schools, meetinghouses in place of in-home worship,mission committees, mission stations,benevolent institutions, Bible conferences, and educational institutions that reflected the spiritual vibrancy of the revival.

Some German Jesus House Movement participants stayed connected to the state churches, contributing to revitalizing impact within them.[23] House meetings, however, created space for revitalization not possible from within the institutional Church. Themeetings, held in non-traditional contexts such as an "auto dealership," appealed to people who did not want to identify with institutional "limitations" and "suppression."

The Jesus Movement had a lasting institutional impact even though it did not institutionalize.. Calvary Chapels and Vineyard Churches, as well as some mega-churches, are the "children" of the Jesus Movement.[24] Revitalization in South Koria emerged as their churches 'practiced the ethos of the Acts of the Apostles by emphasizing the Christian virtues of fellowship and praying together in the Spirit..'[25] Even "institutionalization can be good news because this Jesus thing is about something we do together. Institutions are God's life raft – they're sure messed up but they are better than nothing… Institutions are not inherently evil. They are a mixed bag, but they are a call to a redemptive purpose[26]

Social Realities: Contextualization

The undoing of Christian colonialism has proved to be a powerful force of Christian revitalization. The widespread East Africa Revival that "emphasized both indigenous evangelism and holistic witness" challenged the Eurocentric and Enlightenment form of Christianity, which "lacked spiritual depth, and fell short of the early Church apostolic vitality of evangelistic discipleship." That revival challenged traditional structures of hierarchy. "The spirit of revival tended to level the gender roles of both men and women. The role of the clergy and laity in the Church was also swallowed up by the new move of one spirit, one faith, and one Body of Christ..."[27] In a similar vein, the aboriginal peoples of North America as well as many Latin America communities are experiencing Christian renewal through their movement to reclaim their native culture.[28] Pentecostal Movements in Latin America spread as they challenged imposed, conservative mission models that failed to respect culture. [29]

Human Need

Revitalization often erupts when a culture induces suffering and marginalization by disregarding human dignity, neglecting human need, or imposing conflicting world-views. Cultural realities of poverty, persecution, social oppression (religious, ethnic, gender, and economic), violence, war, injustice, moral perversion, and political upheaval are potentially powerful forces of Christian revitalization. Hope in the face of serious social challenges and upheaval characterize the South Africa revitalization movement. The recent upsurge of the Chinese House Church Movement exemplifies the potential revitalizing response to social suppression and religious persecution.[30] Needs tied to any dimension of our humanness, be they spiritual, physical, emotional, intellectual, social, existential, or ethical are potential forces of Christian revitalization. Spiritual thirst is integral to our humanness, and all aspects of our humanness are potentially the subject and force of spiritual renewal.

To be Christian is to participate in a life-long process of transformation. The process is dynamic, and is something that cannot be confined by words or defined by conformity. Everything about *who* we are as human beings and everything about *who* we are as Christians points to change. The call of God in Christ is an invitation to growth and change, depth and authenticity, and an ever-evolving sense of meaning.

In the words of the Anglican Bishop of Durham, N. T. Wright,

Learning to live as a Christian is learning to live as a renewed human being, anticipating the eventual new creation in and with a world [that] is still longing and groaning for that final redemption. This Christian way of life is the place in which God's future breaks into the present, in which we discover what genuine humanness looks and feels like in practice. It is the place where we hear the voice of Jesus, calling us to follow him into God's new world. We are called to be part of God's new creation, called to be agents of that new creation here and now.[31]

The call to be Christian is an invitation to human renewal, an opportunity to participate in God's redemptive work.

Joining the Dance

The forms and forces of revitalization invite us to participate in the dance of God. Do you hear the call of God; do you feel the rhythm of the Spirit? Do you recognize the significance of your participation in the dance? As we listen for the rhythmic pattern in the past and present, we can move creatively into the future. The revitalizing dance of God is not limited to one form or style or step. The dance brings joy and beauty, healing and hope. Response to the rhythm of God makes a difference in the world. Response to the rhythm is an act of worship. The dance of God goes on and on. As we journey through life in the overlap between heaven and earth we share in the revitalizing movement of God from creation to new creation.

Notes

1. Thomas Moore, The Soul's Religion: Cultivating a Profoundly Spiritual Way of Life (New York: Harper Collins Publisher, 2002).
2. N.T. Wright, "God in Public" (N.T. Wright Lecture Series, Wilmore, KY: Asbury Theological Seminary, November 14, 2007).
3. Peter Erskine, "The Role of Rhythm in Popular Music," USC Thornton School of Music, April 2010, http://www.youtube.com/watch?v=eXcg_b_R9OY.
4. The insights offered in this chapter are based on research data from the Revitalization Consultations I and II focused on "taking the pulse and heart" of revitalization movements currently developing in cultural settings across world Christianity. The Luce grant enabled the Revitalization Center's research process to embrace a wide diversity of revitalization movements occurring across denominational lines and including the indigenous expressions of Christianity emerging in the global south and east. The research focus ranged from the congregational level to the trans-national networks, and an understanding of contemporary trends in revitalization.
5. Oxford American Desk Dictionary. (New York: Oxford University Press, 1998), 227.
6. Ibid. 225.
7. I.G. Hagendoorn, "Emergent patterns in dance improvisation and choreography," Proceedings of the International Conference on Complex Systems, 2002, http://www.ivarhagendoorn.com/files/articles/Hagendoorn-iccs02.pdf.
8. Ray Bullard of South Bend, Indiana Calvary Temple, Assemblies of God, and Chuck Smith, founder and pastor of the Calvary Chapel, Costa Mesa, California.
9. "Pentecost and the New Humanity: Exploration in World Christian Revitalization Movements," in *Data From: Consultation One*, ed. Steve O'Malley (Wilmore, KY: Asbury Theological Seminary Center for the Study of World Christian Revitalization Movements, 2009), 121:85.
10. "Pentecost and the New Humanity: Exploration in World Christian Revitalization Movements," in *Data Form: Consultation One*, ed. Steve O'Malley (Wilmore, KY: Asbury Theological Seminary Center for the Study of World Christian Revitalization Movements, 2009), 121:21,84.
11. "Exploring the Dialectic Between Revitalization and Church," in *Data Form Summary Outline: Consultation Two- Edinburgh*, ed. Beverly Johnson-Miller (Wilmore, KY: Asbury Theological Seminary Center for the Study of World Christian Revitalization Movements, 2010).
12. Howard Snyder, The Problem of Wineskins (Downer's Grove: InterVarsity, 1975).
13. "Pentecost and the New Humanity: Exploration in World Christian Revitalization Movements," in *Data Form: Consultation One*, ed. Steve O'Malley (Wilmore, KY: Asbury Theological Seminary Center for the Study of World Christian Revitalization

Movements, 2009), 121:20.

14. "Pentecost and the New Humanity: Exploration in World Christian Revitalization Movements," in *Data Form: Consultation One*, ed. Steve O'Malley (Wilmore, KY: Asbury Theological Seminary Center for the Study of World Christian Revitalization Movements, 2009),121:15.

15. Ibid. 121:84.

16. Ibid. 121:15.

17. "Pentecost and the New Humanity: Exploration in World Christian Revitalization Movements," in *Data Form: Consultation One*, ed. Steve O'Malley (Wilmore, KY: Asbury Theological Seminary Center for the Study of World Christian Revitalization Movements, 2009), 121:82.

18. Ibid. 121:3-8.

19. Ibid. 121:56.

20. See discussion on the relationship of the Holy Spirit to context and culture in the Albert Hernandez's Plenary Presentation "Re-Discovering Medieval and Early Modern Conceptions of Pentecost in the Twenty-First Century of "Pentecost and the New Humanity: Exploration in World Christian Revitalization Movements," in Data Form: Consultation One, ed. Steve O'Malley (Wilmore, KY: Asbury Theological Seminary Center for the Study of World Christian Revitalization Movements, 2009), 129:114-115.

21. "Pentecost and the New Humanity: Exploration in World Christian Revitalization Movements," in Data Form: Consultation One, ed. Steve O'Malley (Wilmore, KY: Asbury Theological Seminary Center for the Study of World Christian Revitalization Movements, 2009), 121:55.

22. "Exploring the Dialectic Between Revitalization and Church," in *Data Form Summary Outline: Consultation Two- Edinburgh*, ed. Beverly Johnson-Miller (Wilmore, KY: Asbury Theological Seminary Center for the Study of World Christian Revitalization Movements, 2010).

23. "Pentecost and the New Humanity: Exploration in World Christian Revitalization Movements," in Data Form: Consultation One, ed. Steve O'Malley (Wilmore, KY: Asbury Theological Seminary Center for the Study of World Christian Revitalization Movements, 2009), 121:21-23.

24. "Pentecost and the New Humanity: Exploration in World Christian Revitalization Movements," in *Data Form: Consultation One*, ed. Steve O'Malley (Wilmore, KY: Asbury Theological Seminary Center for the Study of World Christian Revitalization Movements, 2009), 121:85-86.

25. Ibid.121:84.

26. Ibid. 129:5-6.

27. "Pentecost and the New Humanity: Exploration in World Christian Revitalization Movements," in *Data Form: Consultation One*, ed. Steve O'Malley (Wilmore, KY: Asbury Theological Seminary Center for the Study of World Christian Revitalization Movements, 2009), 121:15.

28. Ibid.121:48.

29. Ibid. 121:54.

30. "Pentecost and the New Humanity: Exploration in World Christian Revitalization Movements," in *Data Form: Consultation One*, ed. Steve O'Malley (Wilmore, KY: Asbury Theological Seminary Center for the Study of World Christian Revitalization Movements, 2009), 129:32-33.

31. N.T. Wright, Simply Christian. (San Francisco: Harper, 2006), 223, 225, & 236.

Chapter 2

A Barrier to Revitalization:
Ecclesial Alienation

WILLIAM J. ABRAHAM, PHD
ALBERT COOK OUTLER PROFESSOR OF WESLEY STUDIES
AND ALTSHULER DISTINGUISHED TEACHING PROFESSOR,
PERKINS SCHOOL OF THEOLOGY,
SOUTHERN METHODIST UNIVERSITY, DALLAS, TEXAS

The basic meaning of alienation is straightforward: one is subject to discomfort, unease, and restlessness caused by estrangement from the group to which one belongs.

Originally used to speak of property being transferred to another owner, the term was readily applied to human agents who felt displaced. Hence it came to signify that one is no longer at home; that one ceases to be nourished by associates and fellow-members; that one cannot relax or flourish any more. In modern philosophical and political theory, the term has come to mean a systematic sense of strangeness and separation. Thought is alienated from reality in so far as it ineptly reflects it; I am self-alienated in so far as I cannot comprehend or accept myself; I am alienated from the results of my labor in so far as they become mere products; I am alienated from my desires because they are not authentically my own, but assault me as if they were from without; and I am alienated from my society in so far as I feel regimented by it, rather than part of a social unit that constructs and shapes it. The ensuing results are manifold: isolation, powerlessness, and meaninglessness.

The application to church life is obvious. Folk become alienated from the communities to which they belong or in which they are appointed leaders. They feel isolated and powerless; they no longer find meaning or spiritual fulfillment; they lose their bearings and lose heart. At one level, they are ripe for revitalization and renewal; at another level, they are at great risk because alienation means that they do not have the motivation or energy to get beyond their estrangement. Some are lost forever to the church because the alienation runs too deep and intervention came too late.

Alienation as we see it in the church can take many forms. At a personal level, one may feel hurt, mistreated, misunderstood, rejected, and even abused. Many clergy undergo such experiences at the hands of local congregations or leaders above them. In the outrageous cases of clergy child-abuse, victims may never fully recover. In this case the alienation is essentially personal and interpersonal; it is inescapably person-relative.

It is also possible to become alienated from the administrative practices of the community. One loses faith in the policies adopted; or one loses confidence in the practices of the administration; or one simply gives up on the leadership as corrupt, incompetent, or stupid. In these circumstances folk are likely to complain at length of the "system" or of the "impersonal bureaucracy" whose demands they have to satisfy. The temptation to believe that institutions are essentially unspiritual, represent a fall from grace, and cannot be subject to the activity of the Holy Spirit is very great indeed.

One can also become morally alienated, as happens, when one can no longer comply much less understand the moral convictions, culture, or ethos of the church to which one owes affection and allegiance. In the current scene there is much moral alienation in and around issues related to sexuality. Given the ineradicable differences that have surfaced, alienation in this arena is simply inescapable. Alienation in this instance runs so deep that the division is the order of the day.

Often moral alienation goes hand in hand with theological and intellectual alienation. This can be especially acute if one feels that the Gospel has been set aside or replaced with an alien gospel that is no gospel. More generally, intellectual alienation can be either material or formal. In the first instance, the great truths of the faith may be rejected or ignored; in the second instance, there is a glaring indifference to or disparagement of serious theological reflection or integrity. Often, the worry surfaces powerfully in criticism of seminaries or of theological education in and of itself. It is as if the institutions for training officers have been infiltrated by enemy agents and as if the instruments of assessment for such institutions are carried out by insiders with a vested interest in self-congratulation and self-maintenance.

A common source of alienation focuses on the liturgical and sacramental life of the church. Take the example of hymnody. On one side, the loss of the great hymns of the church has left many older church members estranged and even rejected. On the other side, the inability of the church to adjust to changing styles of communication and sensibility have driven many in a younger generation to leave the church of their parents. One of the great advantages of mainline megachurches is that they are big enough to accommodate the genuinely diverse needs that arise at this level of the church's life. Of course, the challenge is to provide sufficient liturgical integrity in the different forms of worship that are offered.

Yet another source of alienation is the politics of church life. The general atmosphere can be poisoned by fear. Meetings are controlled by caucuses and party-spirit. It can be difficult to find sessions where there is real consensus and genuinely conciliar decision-making; instead one encounters clever manipulation of the process, dissimulation, and an absence of trust among the delegates. Elections to high office can be marked by ambition and status rather than by humility and by a commitment to the good of the whole. It is no surprise that many run in the other direction when they are asked to participate in the various rounds of assemblies and conferences; it can take weeks to recover from them; or folk go home feeling that they have been informally excommunicated from the fellowship.

Those who become alienated from the church are clearly in a perilous state. They are liable to adopt one of several strategies that are dysfunctional and destructive. At one end of the spectrum one can simply opt out psychologically, remain nominally a member, and retreat to the sidelines. The best one can do is to survive, hoping to do so without causing obvious harm to others. One continues to play a role where that is deemed essential or obligatory, but the aim is to keep that role to an absolute minimum compatible with membership. At the other end of the spectrum, one can leave in search of greener pastures elsewhere. Given that few communities are perfect, the possibilities of wishful thinking, uncritical romanticism, and disappointment are always on the horizon. In between, one can yield to cynicism, anger, resentment, pessimism, or even quiet despair. These can spread like poison through a community and, once lodged, can be extremely difficult to eradicate.

There is no one-size-fits-all solution to alienation in the life of the church.

In broad terms it is vital, first, to develop a thoroughly realistic assessment of the life of the church. From the beginnings of creation, human agents have turned against the will of God. The Israelites rejected again and again their covenant responsibilities. Among the first disciples, Judas sold his Lord for a song. Jesus himself made it clear that there would be wheat and tares not just in the church but in the kingdom of God (Matt 13: 24-30). Luke provides a generally upbeat account of the spread of the gospel in Acts, but he resolutely faces all sorts of problems, not least the initial tension between Jews and Gentiles. The New Testament epistles are riddled with contrasting challenges. The warrants for adopting a resolutely realistic account of the church are legion. The trick is to stay realistic as an orienting disposition and to twin it with a complementary disposition of encouragement. Quiet cheerfulness derived from an optimism of grace should be the order of the day, whatever the circumstances.

As a second antidote to alienation, it is important to find the relevant resources in the means of grace to stay the course. God has equipped the church with practices (prayer, meditating on scripture, fellowship, Holy Communion, and the like) that work; approached in the right way in humility and faith, through the unceasing grace of God, they are effective in sustaining us in discipleship and ministry. In their own inimitable way, the means of grace are the unfailing source of renewal both personally and corporately.

Beyond such generalizations, there is no alternative but to think through the sources of one's alienation and find apt prescriptions for resolution either personally or in working with others.

Let me illustrate. For over twenty years I have been working to see serious formation and catechesis become central to evangelism in my own tradition; to date I have found no effective way forward at the corporate level. Yet I continue to pursue this issue in season and out. Frankly, I am skeptical that anything substantial will happen in my circles in my lifetime; yet I refuse to give up on my convictions; I am hopeful a new generation will get the message and deliver the goods.

I have been much more effective in resolving the alienation I have experienced at the level of mission. Thirty years ago, work I had done on catechesis in Southwest Texas found its way into Karaganda, Kazakhstan. At the time all I knew about Karaganda was that Solzhenitsyn had written his famous book, *One Day in the Life of Ivan Denisovich*, while in the vicinity. I could not spell Kazakhstan, much less find it on a map. After visiting Karaganda I was overwhelmed at the needs on the ground. I was also deeply ashamed of the incapacity of our official corporate missionary agencies to recognize the challenge, much less do anything about it. I would lie awake at night, haunted by what I had seen and heard. The alienation was severe.

In time, I took some lay folk with me on a second visit to Kazakhstan. They were equally moved by what they experienced. Out of our alienation we created our own mission society, Oasis International Missions, tackling the host of legal and administrative issues that arose. We now engage in relational missionary work not just in Kazakhstan but also in Nepal and in Romania. Over a ten year period it is astonishing what has been achieved. We keep the work very focused; over time we have streamlined our structures and personnel; our budget keeps expanding to scary proportions; we make it through each year not knowing what the future holds. I am delighted in what my church does in humanitarian relief; I remain ashamed at how little my church does in bedrock evangelistic work of preaching and church planting. Given the challenges we face in our very concentrated missionary work in Kazakhstan, Nepal, and Romania, there is no time for moping about our situation or for resentment about the failures that abound.

Yet the need for critical reflections continues to beckon. As a philosopher and theologian one of my spiritual responsibilities is to think systematically about the theological and practical life of the church. In part this has meant returning again and again to the issue of church renewal as a pressing issue for the church today.[1] In the recent past, I have given much informal attention to the shortcomings in renewal related to The United Methodist Church.

Two sets of events have triggered extensive reflection. The first stems from our failure to implement the new mission statement that was adopted in 1996 at the General Conference. With others I was involved in the process of making the Great Commission (making disciples of Jesus Christ) the mission statement of

The United Methodist Church. At the time I thought that this was a landmark decision. This is not how it has turned out historically. On the one hand, The United Methodist Church completely failed to operationalize this change. I had assumed that this would happen; it never did. On the other hand, the bishops of the church decided to 'improve' on the original Great Commission by adding the phrase 'for the transformation of the world' to the imperative to make disciples of Jesus Christ. To be sure, I could readily mount a defense of this move; but it would be an insincere defense. In reality, the change enshrines the weary and failed policies of the mid-to-late twentieth century leadership of The United Methodist Church who arrogantly and mistakenly held that they were in a position to transform the world. It allows the church to continue to live in deep denial about its incompetence or lack of will in making genuine disciples of Jesus Christ. We have squandered the opportunity of a lifetime to bring significant missional renewal into the heart of the church. Perhaps a new generation will make the necessary operational changes.

The other major event to trigger a second look was the election of a new raft of bishops in 2004 at the Jurisdictional Conferences. A whole new generation of around twenty bishops looked set to face reality and begin to address the loss of members over the previous twenty generation. The hopes inspired by the elections have not materialized. I can think of several factors that explain this outcome. First, the entrenched culture of the College of Bishops of the preceding period prevented any kind of radical change at the top. Perhaps many of the new bishops were simply co-opted very quickly into the culture of denial and ignorance that prevailed. Second, election to the episcopate brings with it in its very being its own unique round of temptations, illusions, and hubris. Somehow, bishops are not dissimilar from regular politicians in that there is a massive gap between what they promise or publicly represent and what they deliver. Third, it may well be that the office of bishop is so beset around and within with strains, limitations, and impossibilities, that my expectations were unrealistic. I may well have invented a hocus-pocus world which ignores the real causal realities that inhere in the communal ethos and practices of The United Methodist Church. Whatever the causes for disappointment, they are worth pondering in order to foster the kind of realism I mentioned above.

It may be helpful to take this kind of analysis even deeper into further reflection on the origins of Methodism itself. Methodism began as a surprising work of the Holy Spirit that swept through Europe and North America in the eighteenth century. The roots of this go back even earlier to the practices of piety that developed around the Eucharistic tradition among Presbyterians in Scotland, Ulster, and thereafter among immigrants to North America.[2] In this instance revival and awakening were intimately related to the careful administration of the communion services that were held within Scottish Presbyterianism. The celebration of the Lord's Supper involved significant preparation that ran from Thursday till Sunday and a follow-up day of thanksgiving on Monday. The services themselves, despite clerical and political opposition, drew such great crowds that they were often celebrated in the open fields. The stories of conversion and new life that arise out of these events are astonishing.

Equally interesting is the demise of this crucial source of renewal in the life of the church. Over time these Eucharistic celebrations were quietly dropped because of intense ridicule by sophisticated outsiders; because of an 'Enlightenment' mentality that despised popular religion and piety; because the time required to attend them did not fit with the developing capitalist economy; because the tacit values involved did not fit with the new Victorian values of privacy, the home, and genteel decorum; and because they were quietly replaced by forms of revivalism that abandoned the centrality of a Eucharistic piety as lodged in a truly theocentric vision of the Gospel. This laundry list of factors clearly point to extremely important matters that future thinking about revitalization should pursue. There is no way we can microwave what happened in the eighteenth century, but very few have caught a vision of the possible connection between robust and lively Eucharistic practice and widespread spiritual awakening.

I continue to ponder these themes and find myself looking at ancillary topics. While there was clearly a major shift in the move from revival to revivalism, it is much too simplistic to dismiss the latter because it focused on other means of grace rather than on the celebration of the Eucharist. I wonder if similar forces did not show up to undermine the remarkable effectiveness of nineteenth-century revivalism. If this is the case, then it is important to tackle the attacks of sophisticated outsiders, to be more forthright about the catholicity of the church in its embrace of popular piety, to find timetables for renewal services that work in our setting, and to resist the hegemony of certain class values when it comes to music and preaching. I am increasingly struck by how many are intimidated by aggressive 'catholic' ecclesiastical claims related to episcopacy and sacraments that drain members of my own tradition of their self-confidence in the Spirit. The really deep problem is a lack of nerve and clarity on what it is to be the church. If I am on the right lines here, then we will need to return to first principles in ecclesiology and work upward from these to instill over time a deep recovery of ecclesial nerve.

It is tempting to think at this point that I have lost the plot and have wandered far from the issue of alienation from the life of the church. How can we begin to make progress on the challenges of the doctrine of the church if we feel estranged, isolated, and powerless in the church to which we belong? The answer to this question is simple. Many currently alienated by the life of the church will in part be cured of their alienation precisely as they recover an accurate and lively vision of the nature and ministry of the church that truly fits the history of awakening and renewal. Hope can in part be rebuilt by developing a vision of the church that relocates the origin and life of the church in the work of the good and life-giving Holy Spirit. Once this happens, those alienated will cease to be intimidated by hardline rival versions of the church, find the norms to adjudicate healthy forms of church life, and secure the motivation to take up afresh the challenges that detain them.

Notes

1. For my more formal treatment see *The Logic of Renewal* (Grand Rapids: Eerdmans, 2003)

2. For details consult Leigh Eric Schmidt, *Holy Fairs, Scottish Communion and American Revivals in the Early Modern Period* (Princeton: Princeton University Press, 1989).

Chapter 3

The Measure of Authenticity: Is Revitalization Centered in a Recovery of Church or in Reclaiming Personhood, Or...?

CHRIS KIESLING, PhD
PROFESSOR OF CHRISTIAN DISCIPLESHIP AND HUMAN
DEVELOPMENT, ASBURY THEOLOGICAL SEMINARY

Twenty-five years ago, enamored with my fiancé, I set out to purchase a diamond that would express my commitment of love and that would ultimately become the gift of an engagement ring. I suppose it would have sufficed to have simply seen the diamond, confirmed that it was the anticipated cut, and relied solely on my own sensibilities and preferences to verify its worth. Nevertheless, I sought out several jewelers to see what I could learn about measures of authenticity. How astonished I was to discover that there was much more to evaluating a diamond than the shape and form perceptible to the naked eye. The worth of a gem could be determined by much more than the subjective appreciation of the shopper. Jewelers, I discovered, measure authenticity on the basis of color, cut, clarity, and carat weight. Distinctions are made utilizing magnification, various sources of light that expose flaws and inclusions, cleavage habits, luminosity of the gem, and weight that is measured even to the exact point (a point representing $1/100^{th}$ of a carat).

In this chapter I aim to provide a similar process of discovery, seeking measures of authenticity from reliable sources whose work in one way or another contributes to a better way of seeing into the revitalization diamond. I draw first from Anthony Wallace's formulation of revitalization movements to offer an initial conceptual framework. I then link this to the psychoanalytic work Erik Erikson provided in exploring spiritual exemplars who ignited historical movements. This provides the background necessary to establish reclamation of personhood as the central feature of revitalization movements. I then argue however, that reclamation of personhood should not be the exclusive measure of authenticity, but that it must be vitally linked to other criterion such as the recovery of church, the transformation of society, and ultimately the vision of new creation.

Although renewal movements can be traced back to the early centuries of the Christian movement,[1] the modern study of revitalization movements is most often attributed to Anthony Wallace. From analysis of over 100 movements on five different continents, Wallace defined a revitalization movement as "a deliberate, organized conscious effort by members of a society to construct a more satisfying culture" (p.265).[2] Two conditions, according to Wallace, typically precipitate deliberate cultural change: first, individuals experience a high degree of stress; and second, widespread disillusionment occurs within an existing cultural system. Wallace did not chronicle the societal conditions that induce individual stress as a felt loss of personhood, but it seems consistent with his conceptualization to imagine social, political, personal, familial and ecclesial forces that inhibit human flourishing. Indeed, in many of the historic and contemporary presentations given during revitalization gatherings the cultural conditions of dislocation, oppression, migration, poverty, neglect, rationalism, institutionalism or routine all create ripe settings for revitalization.

Wallace posited that the origins of a movement could generally be found in a revelatory vision given to a prophetic figure. Compelled by a sense of divine sanction, the prophet then reformulates the central images of self and society that govern the patterns of learned behavior, relationships, and practices of a culture - a process Wallace called *mazeway reformulation.* Drawing from Wallace's sociological formulation, reclamation of personhood is a central element located both in the personality transformation of the prophetic figure and in the outworking of renewed humanity that accompanies mazeway reformulation. Consider for example, the origins of African Independent or African Initiated Christianity (AIC) that Joseph Karanja traced to a group of prophet/healers known as the Arathi among the Gikuyu of East Africa.[3] Compelled by dreams and divine healing, prophets preached about the downfall of colonialism that left many Africans feeling as if they were second class citizens. Offering holiness, baptism of the Holy Spirit, and the accessibility of the Scriptures freed Africans from the paternalistic posturing of Western missionaries and their pronouncements. Likewise, Kwabena Asamoah-Gyadu reported that the founders of African revitalization movements are foremost receivers of revelation from the spirit.[4] The ministry they offer focuses on the charismatic triad of prophecy, prayer and healing. Linking this to a reclamation of personhood requires one simply to recognize that all three aspects of this triad emphasize a direct experience of divine power efficacious to deliver one from disease, affliction, and evil forces as well as secure one's ultimate destiny.

Movements on other continents similarly begin with individuals reporting pnuematic experiences. Bert Waggoner centered the Vineyard movement in the United States in the fearless and relentless pursuit of the Holy Spirit initially modeled by its founder John Wimber. Waggoner regarded the Kingdom of God as the movement's central theological motif containing vision for a new creation and a new humanity, made visible in concrete expressions of the love of God to the lost, sick, outcast, imprisoned and poor.[5]

Similar to Wallace's emphasis on the critical role of the prophet in sparking revitalization movements, Erik Erikson took a keen interest in studying the psychohistories of spiritual exemplars. Erikson posited that the pathologies of a given historical era inevitably become internalized into the psyche of individuals, thus precipitating personal identity crises. Of particular interest were individuals who universalized the resolution of their own identity crises in such a way that they ignited the passion of a generation. Luther for example, trembled before a dominant father (representative of the authoritarian structure of society) whom he often feared disappointing and from whom he found little solace when serving as a priest, long before challenging the papal authority of Rome.

Erikson's perception of Jesus and the way he reclaimed persons is equally intriguing. Just as the budding field of psychoanalysis sought to free those inactivated by ethical stagnation or ill psyches, Erikson regarded Jesus as powerfully activating those who approached him seeking cures. Further, Erikson favored the New Testament term *metanoi* to signify how one might recover from inactivation due to a bad conscience or a sense of being banned by divine judgment, and thus regain the capacity of central position in one's life space. *Inner light* or the *luminosity of awareness,* signified by Jesus's saying that "the eye is the lamp of the body" (Matthew 5:22), was regarded by Erikson as the most direct Biblical reference to the sense of "I".[6] In an interesting address presented at Yale University on the Galilean Sayings of Jesus, Erikson drew attention to the powerful claim of Jesus to be certified by Jehovah to announce that "the Kingdom of God has come upon you." To a people who lacked a collective sense of *We* by which to formulate an adequate sense of *I,* such a pronouncement actualized a ready numinosity, a choice of action, continuity in time, and a central position – all essential elements for Erikson in the construction of identity.[7]

Biblically, further justification could be made by pointing to the parables of the lost sheep, the lost coin, and the lost son (Luke 15) as key metaphors of the gospel that centralize reclamation of persons in Jesus' mission. Or the Exodus narrative that chronicles the deliverance of Israel from the oppression of Pharaoh into being the chosen people of God could be upheld as the predominant socio-political-spiritual reclamation story of the Old Testament. Perhaps it is most theologically comprehensive and balanced to offer a definition of reclamation of personhood by seeking to honor the full work of each person of the Trinity. Hence, I propose that reclamation of personhood, central to Christian revitalization movements, be defined by: the creating work of the Father endowing human beings with His image; the saving work of the Son redeeming us from sin, death and the devil; and the sanctifying work of the Spirit making us holy and gifting us for mission.

At this point I have not said anything about the church. Thus far, it could be assumed that arguing for the reclamation of personhood as the center of revitalization movements dismisses the recovery of church. If so, I could be suggesting a distorted criterion that inadvertently promotes a Christianity in the service of self-preservation or self-fulfillment. Individual awakenings can become privatized affairs, limiting renewal to the personal.[8] This tendency to turn inward and center on the elevation of the self undermined Israel from realizing their calling to be a "nation of priest" and a "blessing to the nations;" and it continues to sabotage the mission of God, especially in cultures that privilege individualism. Wallace's vision named the prophet as key in originating revitalization movements.[9] The prophetic role tends to locate the activity of the Holy Spirit in individual experience and tends to regard religious institutions and traditions as suspect or even stifling. As our table discussions unveiled, the DNA of Protestantism may well create a bias that centers revitalization in personal experience with little regard for the broader streams of Christian history.

However, revitalization movements that do not originate solely in the prophet, but in the role of priest or in the execution of established leadership within the church, present different accounts. For example, Chung Song Mee's appropriation of the Augsburg confession within the Evangelical Lutheran Church stresses the importance of word and sacrament administered through the church for the proclamation of the gospel.[10] Judith Kubicki's Catholic sacramental view stresses the import of the church as an assembly of persons called out and gathered by the Lord.[11] Sacramental perception enables the invisible divine presence to be disclosed through visible mediated realities, the absence of which is held responsible for secular and sociological understandings of the church as mere institution.

Other ecumenical sources surfaced in our consultations that extend thinking about revitalization that occurs through specific ecclesial practices and traditions. Patristic and canonical resources, catechesis, monastic forms of prayer, the observance of Lent and re-initiation into the Paschal mystery, deeper appropriations of one's baptism, and the rhythmic celebration of feast days offer means by which people come into a truer sense of the God in whom "we live and move and have our being," (Acts 17:28).

Turning again to a review of table discussions, the dynamic interplay between Spirit and church in its various forms spawns a host of questions: "What is the work of the Spirit in the creation of the church and in the provision of resources that enables the church's ongoing work?"; "How do revitalization movements fit into the unfolding story of the church?"; "Who defines what the 'true' church is?"; "What changes are required when one stops regarding the church as a having a mission and instead regards God's mission as having a church?"; "What is the Spirit calling the whole church to do?"; "If every gathered meeting of believers is centered in a search for a personal Pentecost, do we lose the broader story in which Pentecost is embedded?"

Theologically, salvation has always initiated a person into the people of God, marked in the older covenant by circumcision and in the newer covenant by baptism. The gift of the Holy Spirit at Pentecost birthed an explosive *koinonia* that eventuated into the establishment of the *ecclesia*, such that the church becomes the body of Christ in the world, the bride of Christ for whom He died and which He longs to purify, and the primary organism by which disciples are made in the furthering of the kingdom.

So rather than regarding reclamation of personhood and recovery of church as mutually exclusive polarities, I propose that we place them as concentric circles. Locating reclamation of personhood as the inner circle provides an answer to our inquiry; but positioning it within additional concentric circles of church and society also allows an incorporation of many of the dynamics surfaced in Consultation II: *Exploring the Dialectic Between Revitalization and Church.*[12] First, it suggests an outward thrust and purpose that takes renewed persons beyond the personal to the communal and the societal, holding an optimistic view for the possibility of revitalization in all ecclesial structures and cultures. Second, it preferences that the institutional church would create structures inclusive of revitalization movements, but also provides a way of conceptualizing the reality that pneumatic experiences often move persons outside of, away from, and/or against the institutional church. Utilizing this conceptualization, various models of church/ecclesial structures can be compared for their adaptability to revitalizing innovations.[13] Third, placing the church within a broader circle of society honors the importance of social location in setting the probable parameters within which a particular revitalization movement is taking shape. Where there is alliance between the institutional church and political power - the second and third circles - a loss of distinctiveness may predict greater difficulty in maintaining spiritual encounter and vitality within a revitalization movement. Conversely, when the church is in a place of persecution, opposition or marginalization from the broader society, conditions may be ripe for revitalization movements to spring forth.

Concentric circles also permit movement to flow in both directions. Revitalization of a parish can affect renewal in the lives of individual members, and shifts in culture will no doubt affect how a local parish functions, setting the parameters around what constitutes meaning in personal renewal. Many of the most formative questions that emerged from table discussions stemmed from an assumption of this inter-relationship between the parts and the whole of a system: "What kind of personal encounter with God is indispensable to deepening church and society?"; "How do various contexts and dynamics govern the way personal experience goes after an encounter with the divine?"; "Is crisis the only condition for revitalization?" "Can Christian groups be unified ecumenically despite different experiences of the spirit?"; "Does revitalization require a certain version of what the church is?"; "How might we embrace the tension between pneumatology and ecclesiology?"

Returning finally to where we began our consideration, Wallace admittedly formulates his view of revitalization moments utilizing an organismic theory perspective.[14] Culture is viewed as a system that seeks to maintain its own integrity through homeostasis, creating a natural resistance to mazeway reformulation. Where reformulation is possible, it occurs because of the network of intercommunication linking one subsystem to another, creating pathways where cells influence (and are influenced by) organs, persons influence (and are influenced by) groups, and the various parts of a system work to influence (and be influenced by) the whole. It is not at all foreign to Wallace's originating conceptualization then to regard reclamation of personhood <u>and</u> recovery of the church <u>and</u> transformation of culture as part of the same mazeway reformulation.

To this end I would add one final caveat. Consultation I carried the title "Pentecost and the New Humanity: Assessing the Work of God." In the opening keynote address, Howard Snyder presented five dimensions of the inner dynamics of Pentecost relevant for revitalization movements today: (1) harvest of the first fruits; (2) time and history; (3) peoplehood and witness; (4) sovereign action of the Holy Spirit; and (5) the eschatological promise of New Creation.[15] Snyder posits that those revitalization movements that are the most culturally transforming embodiments of Christ are those that exemplify all five of these Biblical dimensions. Yet, in presenting these dimensions Snyder offered that whatever global witness there has been of the renewing power of the Holy Spirit in the world today, it pales in comparison to what is to come. "Biblically speaking," Snyder contends, "Pentecost fullness is not just a matter of individual persons, or even the church, being filled with the Spirit, or speaking in tongues. Eschatologically speaking, Pentecost fullness means a new heavens and a new earth: the earth 'full of the knowledge of the Lord as the waters cover the sea'" (Habakkuk 2:14).

Notes

1. Howard Snyder, *Signs of the Spirit: How God Reshapes the Church*. Eugene: Wipf and Stock Publishers, 1997.

2. Anthony Wallace, "Revitalization Movements." *American Anthropologist*, 58, 2, (1956): 264-281.

3. Joseph Karanja, a response to Gordon MacDonald's address "Pietism as Revitalization" given as part of Consultation I – *Pentecost and the New Humanity: Assessing the Work of God* on the campus of Asbury Theological Seminary, 2009.

4. Kwabenah Asamoah-Gyadu, "'We are here to heal': Revitalization Movements as Charismatic Communities in Africa" an address given as part of Consultation II – *Exploring the Dialectic Between Revitalization and Church* in Edinburgh, Scotland, 2010.

5. Bert Waggoner, "Revitalization as Experienced in the Association of Vineyard Churches: A Movement Caught in the Vortex of Powers of the Coming Kingdom and Pulled Toward the New Humanity" an address given as part of Consultation I – *Pentecost and the New Humanity: Assessing the Work of God* on the campus of Asbury Theological Seminary, 2009.

6. Erikson, Erik, "The Galilean sayings and the sense of "I." *Psychoanalysis and Contemporary Thought, 19,* (1996): 291-338.

7. Erikson, 1996.

8. See Vincent Donovan's account of evangelizing the Masai in his book *Christianity Rediscovered: An Epistle from the Masai.* Notre Dame:Fides/Claretian, 1978 where he expresses this concern.

9. Wallace, 1956, 270.

10. Chung Song Mee, "An Evangelical Lutheran Model of Church in Relation to Revitalization in Light of the Needs of the 21st. Century", an address given as part of Consultation II – *Exploring the Dialectic Between Revitalization and Church* in Edinburgh, Scotland, 2010.

11. Judith Kubicki, "Church as Sacrament", an address given as part of Consultation II – *Exploring the Dialectic Between Revitalization and Church* in Edinburgh, Scotland, 2010.

12. For a good summary of table II table discussions see Mark Lewis's article in the July/August 2010 Revitalization bulletin.

13. For a good discussion of this dynamic see Snyder, *Signs of the Spirit, 1997* cited earlier in this article.

14. Wallace, 1956, 265.

15. Howard Snyder, "The Pentecostal Renewal of the Church, A Biblical-Historical Inquiry into the Theme Pentecost and the New Humanity" an address given as part of Consultation I – *Pentecost and the New Humanity: Assessing the Work of God* on the campus of Asbury University, 2009.

Part 2

The Present Realities

Chapter 4

Models and Myths of Revitalization:
Wallace's Theory a Half-Century On

MICHAEL A. RYNKIEWICH, PHD
PROFESSOR OF ANTHROPOLOGY
ASBURY THEOLOGICAL SEMINARY

Theology and Science

In the Middle Ages, Theology was called "the Queen of the Sciences." With the Enlightenment came a new scientific paradigm based on meticulous observation, analysis, and theory building or modeling. The models of science, in the eyes of some, began to compete with the myths of religion. Some chose to discard religion, specifically Christianity in the European tradition. One defensive ploy was to de-mythologize religion so that what remained would be more acceptable to emerging sciences and a new history paradigm that was inspired by science. Another response was to reject science publically while still enjoying the benefits of modern medicine and technology. Christians are often quite ambivalent toward the areas where science and religion touch.

Over time, as Kuhn has demonstrated, science began to accrue some of the characteristics of religion, and the distinction between myth and model began to muddle.[1] As it turns out, all reflection, all explanation of how things work is based on metaphor.[2] Revival and Revitalization has the same Latin origin in the metaphor of bringing an animal or human who is dying or dead back to life again. However, each concept has a tradition, that is, each is a paradigm unto itself. It is when an established paradigm is applied to a new field that research itself is revitalized as new questions are asked, new observations are made, and deeper understanding is gained. The deployment of Revitalization Movement

Theory in the study of Christian Revivals is that way. While the approach has been productive, there are myths in the model as well as myths about the model.

Revitalization Theory in the Social Sciences

During the colonial era, colonialists were sometimes mystified and sometimes frightened by what they saw as radical beliefs and behavior among those who had been colonized. An armed revolt they could understand, but not rituals and prophecies directed to turn the world upside down. These movements were described loosely as 'messianic,' 'millenarian,' 'nativitistic,' 'charismatic,' and even 'revivalistic.' Ralph Linton, an anthropologist, attempted to bring order to the area.[3] Linton distinguished between those that attempted to revive the past and those what wanted to improve the future, as well as those that seemed rational from those that seemed magical. Perspective was lacking.

Anthony F. C. Wallace proposed the term 'revitalization' for any "deliberate, organized, conscious effort by members of a society to construct a more satisfying culture" including similar movements in European and American history. He considered The Vailala Madness in Papua, the Ghost Dance movement among Native Americans in the American West, and the Wesleyan Revival in England as cases of Revitalization Movements. Thus, he subsumed religious and political movements under a larger category of social movements.

Wallace identified certain patterns or stages in these movements.

I. Steady State

II. Period of Increased Individual Stress

III. Period of Cultural Distortion

IV. Period of Revitalization

    1.Mazeway reformulation

    2.Communication

    3.Organization

    4.Adaptation

    5.Cultural transformation

    6.Routinization

V. The New Steady State[4]

Wallace's approach of using 'event analysis' or case studies and examining political, religious, and general social movements with one model proved very productive for the field. That is why in our consultations we want to base our work on descriptions of actual Christian revitalization movements from around the world before moving to analysis and theory formulation.

Myths in the Model

"Steady State." Is there ever a steady state, or are things always changing? Wallace admits to using an 'organismic analogy,' something that was in vogue at the time as scientists in many fields. If society were an organism, then it might experience periods of 'equilibrium' and periods of 'stress.' However, this is, admittedly, an analogy based on the assumption that society operates like a living system. Wallace concludes later that this was "rather abstract and perhaps fails to attend sufficiently to the unique texture of cultural and historical circumstances."[5]

"Period of Increased Individual Stress." The original model was too dependent on an individual psychology as a frame for explanation. Wallace, after all, is known to us as a Psychological Anthropologist. The long-standing issue is whether or not individual stress adds up to the same thing as "societal stress" such that social movements emerge. The mechanisms for the transfer of individual adjustments into a societal trend are not yet explained.

"Period of Cultural Distortion." All of the studies up to Wallace's time were done among colonized peoples whose stress was the distress of oppression. Wallace himself later raises the question of "whether the revitalization model is applicable only to those situations of colonialism in which a subordinate group is impelled to reform its way of life in reaction to pressures imposed by a dominant power."[6] Wallace himself calls for a consideration of the possibility "that revitalization does not merely occur among the fringe peoples of the world but, in fact, happens in the belly of the beast as well."[7] Indeed, the studies presented in the consultations of the Center for the Study of World Christian Revitalization Movements demonstrate that revitalization movements arise in the mainstream as well as among people who are suffering from the effects of globalization. Indeed, such phenomena as the Wesleyan Revival, Pietism and Pentecostalism, as well as movements such as the Jesus People, the Missional Church, and Radical Orthodoxy come out of mainstream culture.

Cannot "relative deprivation"[8] occur among the wealthy of the world as well? The social setting for the rise of the Prosperity Gospel in the United States is not poverty, but rather relative deprivation. This raises questions of who initiates Christian Revitalization Movements, in what contexts, and for what reasons?

"Mazeway Reformulation." If the model was too individualistic, it was also too cerebral, both reflections of the Western context out of which the model emerged. Is it possible to describe spiritual renewal as "renewal of the mind"? Paul does in Romans 12, but one does not have to go far to encounter "the body," or "the mystery" of God in Christ, Christ crucified, and Christ in us. People operate as agents in their own lives as much on feeling as on thinking, but the model does not recognize this.

Finally, not all movements are about "revitalization." Peter Gow considers agency in his account of what the Piro were doing when they converted under SIL's evangelism. The Piro converted, and then forgot about their conversion.

> When I consider what exactly it is that puzzles me about the way in which Piro people forgot about their conversion, I think the answer lies with their failure to use it as a very powerful conceptual tool for thinking about their past. ... I think that Piro people converted to evangelical Christianity primarily because they wanted the SIL missionaries as a new kind of white people, and they wanted to be evangelical Christians because the SIL missionaries wanted them to be so. But, because they did not think of their cosmology as a religion parallel to evangelical Christianity, they could not see that the missionaries were trying to bring them a new religion. Conversion, therefore, made sense to them as a historical action, but not as a historical event.[9]

Their shamanism was more experiential than cognitive (no creeds, no enduring beliefs or myths), more based on what seemed to be working than what was "true" or "right." Their spiritual pragmatism contrasted with SIL's absolutism concerning beliefs. "What they do not seem willing to accept is why that understanding is supposed to matter so much."[10] Thus, their movement toward Christianity was not so much a "mazeway reformulation" as it was the latest in a series of attempts to develop relationships with wise and powerful people in order to help them engage the world as it is. This has been, for the Piro, a continuous search because no shaman's knowledge or power has lasted forever.[11] Thus, the movement to Christianity did not involve unusual deprivation nor mazeway reformulation nor a lasting routinization of the ritual. There are other motivations and other strategies in the world.

Myths about the Model

Wallace's model of "Revitalization Movements" has been widely used in the social sciences as well as in missiology and theology. A number of myths about the model have emerged in practice.

"Wallace's model will tell us how a revitalization movement ought to be organized." A critical difference between Social Science research and the ultimate concerns of theology and missiology is that Social Science research is descriptive and analytic while theology and missiology have additional concerns. We should not expect a "how to manual" out of Social Science models. They are a description of what happens, the good, the bad, and the ugly. They are not statement of what should happen or what we hope will happen or even what the Bible seems to say will happen. That's good. They are the reality-check that theologians and missiologists need.

"Wallace's model should consider the spiritual forces at work in revitalization." The failure of the Social Sciences to recognize and credit spiritual forces, whether the work of the Holy Spirit or the work of other spirits, good or evil, is a given. That will not change. Nor should it change. First, the job of the Social Scientist is to discover social, cultural, and psychological causes for human behavior. Attributing behavior to the spirit world short-circuits the research. Second, God is in mission through human beings, and thus human behavioral patterns still emerge when the Spirit is at work. Discovering those patterns does not rule out the work of the Spirit as much as it recognizes the persistent reliability of the Spirit.

Adapting Wallace's Model to the Globalized World

E. Paul Balisky shows that prophets and evangelists in the recently defeated Wolaitta Kingdom in Ethiopia rediscovered their identity and reoriented themselves as a religious center by sending evangelists south and converting other tribes.[12] Evangelism itself was part of a Revitalization Movement for the sending people as well as for those who received the gospel.

In this urbanized and globalized world, Christian Revitalization Movements no longer originate on the fringes of empire. More than half of the world's population live in urban areas, and those areas are getting increasingly complex. Ethnic groups are not melting into the majority; instead groups maintaining their *ethnic identities* have become the majority. Migrants are not cutting ties with the homeland but are becoming *diaspora* communities with dual citizenships, at least in their minds. The channels between diaspora communities and homelands are full of global flows of goods, ideas and persons, so some in the community have become *transnationals.*

The Revitalization Movements model must be expanded to account for the degree of urbanization and globalization in the world today. Who would have thought that African-American Gospel Music would spread like wildfire through a jaded and staid Denmark thus revitalizing Christianity there?[13] What kind of movement is it that originates in Nigeria with the development of truly indigenous Pentecostal churches but spreads to America and is nurtured by the transnational flow of persons, goods and ideas aided by a daily Delta Airlines flight between Atlanta and Lagos?[14] What kind of research does it take to study persons moving between multiple sites, presenting multiple identities, and operating in multiple social settings?

Revitalization is not limited to the colonial era as is evidenced by the presence of revitalization movements after the colonial era, and by evidence of revitalization movements before the colonial era. Paul B. Roscoe argues that, for the Yangoru Boiken *(East Sepik Province of Papua New Guinea), "It is not so much that people desire* cargo—Western material goods; rather, they desire what access to these goods represents—a state of *halinya*, of 'strength' or 'power.'[15] Further, Roscoe argues that "the earliest movements in this evolutionary trajectory were in no sense a response to perceived stress, deprivation, or cultural distortion but, rather, were attempts to increase well-being in a culture already considered satisfactory."[16]

I have argued, following Ennio Mantovani,[17] that Melanesians are searching for *gutpela sindaun* 'the abundant life.' I would dispute whether any Melanesian people considered their current state or culture "satisfactory," that is, at a "steady state," given the fact that they were always searching the horizon to see what might be coming and whether or not it might be propitious for their well-being.

As Hirsch puts it,

> An event among Melanesians is something to get a 'hold' on: to discover what its outcome will be, what it conceals and what its effects will be (whether they will be propitious or inauspicious). By considering events as images (analogous to performances and artifacts), it becomes possible to perceive that Melanesians acted as though they were powerful when encountering the potentially ominous.[18]

This approach locates the people as agents in their own right, with their own goals and strategies, sometimes pushed to the limit, but always seeking 'the abundant life' and in ways that sometimes look to the outsider like a Revitalization Movement.

Finally, in this Postmodern age with the spread of literacy and the daily flows of information over the internet, the distinction between the subject and the observer has become blurred. This series of consultations is a classic case of subjects, those who create and manage revitalization movements, becoming participants along with trained analysts in social and historical approaches in a meta-dialogue that goes on above the activities of either one. In the past, the question of meaning was left entirely up to the observer who had the privilege of publishing. It has taken the voice of the other to reveal hidden links between colonial metanarratives of power and academic descriptions of resistance movements.[19] Thus, Richard Twiss complains that the concept of "revitalization" implies that something was dead or dying, a judgment that traditionalist Native Americans would not only not accept, but find insulting (Personal Communication). Following Derrida's concept of *difference,* meaning is never complete but always deferred until the next interpreter comes along, therefore interpretation will never be exhausted because of the apparently limitless capacity of human beings to create, recombine and refocus creed and ritual for the lived situation. Neither practitioners nor social scientists operate outside the human condition, and finally, in this age, both voices are being heard in a meta-dialogue about how a society finds the abundant life

Notes

1. Thomas Kuhn, *The Structure of Scientific Revolutions*(Chicago: University of Chicago Press, 1964; see also Ian Barbour, *Myths, Models and Metaphors.* (New York: HarperCollins, 1974).

2. George Lakoff and Mark Johnson, *Myths We Live By* (Chicago: University of Chicago Press, 2003).

3. Ralph Linton, "Nativistic Movements," *American Anthropologist* 45:230-240.

4. Anthony F.C.Wallace, "Revitalization Movements: Some Theoretical Considerations for their Comparative Study," *American Anthropologist* 58: 268-275.

5. Anthony F. C.Wallace, ""Foreword," in Michael E. Harkin, ed., *Reassessing Revitalization Movements: Perspectives from North America and the Pacific Islands* (Lincoln, NE: University of Nebraska Press, 2004), viii.

6. Wallace, "Foreword"., ix.

7. Wallace, "Foreword", ix.

8. "Relative Deprivation" is a social science concept that arose out of the study, *The American Soldier*, particularly the volume by Robin Murphy Williams, Jr., *The American Soldier: Adjustment During Army Life* (1949).. The concept was further refined in a study W.G. Runciman, *Relative Deprivation and Social Justice.* London: Routledge, 1966.

9. Peter Gow, "The Summer Institute of Linguistics Mission in the Piro Lived World," in Michael E. Harkin, ed., *Reassessing Revitalizataion Movements: Perspectives from North America and the Pacific Islands.* (Lincoln, NE: Univeristy of Nebraska Press, 2004), 237.

10. Gow, "The Summer Institute," 237.

11. Gow, "The Summer Institute,".236.

12. E. Paul Balisky, Wolaitta Evangelists: A Study of Religious Innovation in Southern Ethiopia, 1937-1975.

(Eugene, OR: Pickwick Publications, 2010).

13. Mark Lewis, The Diffusion of Black Gospel Music in Postmodern Denmark: How Mission and Music are Combining to Affect Christian Renewal. Lexington, KY: Emeth Press, 2010.

14. William Efiong Udotong, Transnationalism and the Reverse-Mission of Nigerian-led Pentecostal Churches in the United States of America: A Case Study of Selected Churches in Atlanta.Unpublished Phd Dissertation, Asbury Theological Seminary, 2010.

15. Paul B.Roscoe, "The Evolution of Revitalization Movements among the Yangoru Boiken, Papua New Guinea," in Michael E. Harkin, ed., *reassessing Revitalization Movements: Perspectives from North America and the Pacific Islands.* (Lincoln, NE: University of Nebraska Press, 2004),164.

16. Roscoe., 164.

17. Ennio Mantovani,, *Divine Revelation and the Religions of PNG: A Missiological Manual.* (Goroka, PNG: The Melanesian Institute, 2003).

18. Eric Hirsch, "Between Mission and Market: Event and Images in Melanesian Society," *Man* 29 (3), 1994: 689-716.

19. "...the way in which the analytic categories are intimately intertwined with discourses of the colonizers has become far more apparent. The issue of 'whose meaning', therefore, forms the central topic...." Laurence Marshall Carucci, "New Life for Whom? The Scope of the Trope in Marshall Islands Kurijmoj," in Michael E. Harkin, 207.

Chapter 5

Pathologies of Revitalization

Scott W. Sunquist, PhD
Professor of World Christianity
Pittsburgh Theological Seminary

"An almost Christian, if we consider him in respect to his duty to God, is one that halts between two opinions; that wavers between Christ and the world...he is fond of the form, but never experiences the power of godliness in his heart."

~ George Whitefield (Almost Christian)

Discerning Vital Signs

Movements spun off by a renewal movement are frequently misidentified as the renewal movement itself. It is an easy mistake to make, and it is also a tempting move of disbelieving (or even vindictive) scholars to judge the original movement by its secondary effects. What is often ignored is that revitalization movements do produce permutations, imitations, and reductions of the original movement. At other times, the movement itself, which at its inception seems "healthy" and hopeful, turns into something quite different. Heading towards New York City the movement ends up in Bayone, New Jersey. Revitalization involves spiritual power, and as with all power, it attracts the virtuous and the vain, the devout and the deceived. Not all church revitalization is good or true, as Jonathan Edwards so carefully and eloquently reminded us over two and a half centuries ago.[1] It is important not only to analyze the threads of revitalization—preconditions as well as identifying characteristics themselves—but it is also important to be aware of where revitalization movements go wrong. Can we identify spin-offs that imitate or use the movement in unhealthy ways? The ancient Christian writers would say that "discrimination" (what we might call discernment) is the mother of all virtues.[2] No thought or gift is safe without first having discrimination. Can we identify—discriminate—tendencies or pathologies of revitalization movements? I think we can and we learn about these tendencies both from Scripture and from revitalization movements gone awry.

Revitalization and Revolution: An Example from China

The Taiping Rebellion in China, one of the most lethal wars in human history— between 20 and 30 million dead—is not usually identified with revitalization movements. However, in its origin and in many of its elements it had the marks of revitalization and could have become a remarkable revitalization for Christianity in China. In fact some missionaries pinned their hopes on the young Chinese disciple, Hong Xiuquan (1814-1864).[3] After failing his important, but very difficult, civil service exams for a fourth time, Hong read a Christian pamphlet written by the convert Lian A Fa: "Good Word for Exhorting the Age" Xiuquan found it helpful and so he began to read the Bible and was even instructed by other Christians about the faith. He was moved by the clear social teachings, resistance to idolatry and, frankly, the person of Jesus Christ and the hope of heaven. Soon he began to have visions and dreams which he recorded, but all the time he was reading the Bible carefully, along with Confucian texts. The times were oppressive with much corruption in the country and poverty on the increase in the waning years of the Qing Dynasty. Soon Hong, following his visions more than the newly translated Bible developed a "Heavenly Kingdom of Great Peace," to promote his understanding of the Kingdom of God. Hong's Kingdom became a unique Chinese religion based upon a realized eschatology: the kingdom of heaven is here and Hong is the younger brother of Jesus who is elevated to the place of Heavenly King (*Tian Wang*). Soon the Kingdom of Great Peace was creating a great war, spreading its apocalyptic vision on all Chinese. Hong's soldiers memorized the Ten Commandments and many were copying Bibles by the thousands. For a decade the Kingdom attempted to conquer all of China from this base in Nanjing. The movement was strongly Biblicist, opposed to idolatry, foot binding and corruption, and very communal (sharing goods, etc.). Foreign armies had to be brought in to end the Chinese civil war, but only after millions had died for a "heavenly vision."

In retrospect we can see this as a heretical and militant movement, and yet there were many elements of renewal throughout: reading of the Bible, resistance to corruption and concern for the poor. Hong was a strong leader who studied the Bible with missionaries; most revitalization movements have strong leaders who study the Bible. Hong had visions and dreams about the Kingdom of God. Historically, many revitalization movements are initiated by dreams and visions; not only 20th century movements in Africa, but also medieval movements in Europe and Catholic monastic renewal movements and indigenous movements in China. So we ask, what are certain marks of renewals gone awry, or, in medical terms, what are pathologies of revitalization? Here we will look at five pathologies.

First Pathology: Overly Politicized Revival

As our example from China indicates (an extreme example to be sure) it is possible for revitalization to become overly politicized. True revitalization will speak out of local contexts and political realities, in fact it must if it is to avoid another pathology (see "overly spiritualized concerns" below). But when the context becomes the movement, the revitalization movement has become defined by its context and the Gospel imperative has become reduced to a narrow set of concerns. True revitalization will be inclusive, speaking to personal wounds caused by sinful relationships as well as speaking to injustices that are an affront to God's holiness and love for all of humanity. The tendency toward a political reductionism is strong, especially in the West where the Church has often had the power to effect political change. This tendency often results in liberalism, seeking the results of conversion, but not conversion itself. On the other side, of the divide is the tendency to ignore political realities completely and this results in a type of fundamentalism. Revivalism can often turn to fundamentalism and Social Gospel can easily turn toward social work. Liberation theology—often coming out of a revitalization movement from the poor and oppressed—can also become liberation fighters; soldiers filled with anger directed at dictators. When this happens, the political concerns have snuffed out love for the Savior on the cross. Revitalization, we might say, will naturally resist being hijacked by political agendas while still being engaged in social issues. No matter how important or crucial the political issues may seem at the moment, renewal will resist social or political reductionisms.

Second Pathology: Overly Doctrinal Agenda

Revitalization is theological. Over and over again it has been discovered from Scripture (Paul's correctives in Galatians, Romans, Colossians, etc.) and Tradition[4] that vital movements of God's Holy Spirit are not contrary to theology, but in fact are deeply theological. Jesus Christ is honored as God acting in human form, in the very power of the Holy Spirit, and on our behalf in humility. Doctrine is never ignored or skirted in revitalization, but neither does it become rigidly and narrowly dogmatic. What do we mean by this?

There have been revivals that have been narrowly dogmatic—promoting a particular eschatology or theology of predestination—and their impact has been hampered because of its unnecessarily divisive tendency. Revitalization will divide, but it will do so around foundational issues of the Lordship of Jesus Christ and the authority of His Word to read us: to read our death certificate and then to read for us new life. When the message turns from the cross, or when another message is put on the same level as the cross, a movement turns pathological. True revival crosses theological and cultural divides; building bridges from the hearts of individuals and cultures to the heart of God. Revitalization levels the land at the foot of the cross.

Another way of seeing this issue is to note that many revitalization periods in churches have occurred because of the cross-fertilization of church traditions. Cross-fertilizations of theology prevent a particular or distinctive dogma from replacing central doctrines. As a historian I can say most, if not all revitalizations involve such cross-fertilization. Movements of people and inter-cultural Christian life are catalysts to revitalization. Without going into much detail we can note a few such cases. The early Pietist movement did not come about simply by a continued deepening interest in Luther or in the *Book of Concord.* In fact,

> It seems clear that Spener also learned from his more ecumenical travels to Basel, Bern Lausanne, Geneva, Lyons, Freiburg and Tubingen. Spener pulled together a much more eclectic, ecumenical pastoral theology that called for greater devotion around scripture and smaller communities (*ecclesiola in ecclesia:* little churches in the church) that would meet under the oversight of the local pastor.[5]

Turning a little bit further to the east and a few centuries earlier a similar pattern was part of an Orthodox revitalization movement. The sixteenth century renewal of the Russian Orthodox Church under St. Nilus owed its new energy and vision to the time of Nilus (Nilus of Sorka ,or Nil Sorskii, 1433-1508) who spent much time at Mt. Athos learning of the *hesychastic* tradition from the Greeks. His austere life of silence and prayer brought renewal to a church which had struggled for years under Mongol rule. Turning to the Atlantic world in the 18th century, it is easy to see how the Great Awakening, especially the Wesleyan and Whitfield streams benefited greatly from cross-cultural influences from the Continent (German Pietists and Moravians), as well as from North America and its many ethnic churches. If we look at the reading list of Whitefield, the Wesleys (who were steeped in ancient Christian literature) and Edwards, we can see that even their reading brought cross-cultural and theologically diverse movements.[6] Turning to Africa, the great revival of West Africa under William Wadé Harris (1860-1929) was brought about by the multi-cultural Harris. In fact much of his revival was a push against western cultural imperialism, which he had been strongly attracted to in his earlier years. Resisting narrow dogmatism, Harris was uncompromising on his message of Jesus Christ and repentance for sins.

Each of these movements was prevented from becoming overly narrow in their dogmatic formulas because they reached beyond their own cultural and theological landscape. Thus they had the ability to communicate in different contexts, and even to take on something of the concerns of each context. Revitalization always speaks the deep spiritual life into particular contexts.

Third Pathology: Overly Eccentric Identity

A renewal or revitalization movement, oddly enough, can become an idol or ideology. When this happens the process or movement has become the center displacing the real center, the cross of Christ. Revitalization is always centered on Jesus Christ, but Christian zeal for a certain product (renewal) can displace the center. Such eccentricity in revitalization is actually quite common. When combined with large budgets, media, promotion, and the promises of fame or fortune, renewal leaders often de-center their movements. Imitation can be a form of flattery, but in revitalization it is one of the best forms of disruption. Seeking the experience or the sign (which points to the "real"), people sell their souls for something that does not exist. Today we see this in the process of reaching millions through satellite broadcast, or developing an international ministry which often becomes the driving or central concern. It is a subtle but very common deception. It is not just a modern phenomenon, however.

The Wesleys, in the early stages of their own renewal, were troubled by the overly sanguine poetry and prayers of the Moravians in England, even while they benefited greatly from their Christian witness.[7] In the early church we have many writings by ascetics decrying the "extreme" ascetics who seek an experience of God or levels of contemplation rather than seeking God. Revitalization is often side tracked by losing its center. If we go back even earlier than the Desert Fathers, we see that Paul had the problem of Corinthian spiritual eccentricity: seeking to be identified with the right person or program, rather than focusing on grace found in the cross of Christ (I Corinthians 3:1-11).

Pentecostal revivals have at times centered on gifts of the Spirit more than on the Spirit of Christ himself (II Corinthians 3:17). When this happens, the movement tends toward eccentricity and the fullness of revitalization is robbed. Some are excluded for the wrong reasons and others are included for the wrong reasons. Not just Pentecostal or Spiritual forms of Christianity are tempted by eccentricity. Roman Catholic revitalization, often initiated through liturgical renewal or monastic devotion, can become eccentric as forms or rituals replace the reality behind the rituals. Leaning on the wrong support will cause any movement to collapse, although it may take a long time for the truth to be revealed.

Fourth Pathology:
Overly Contextualized or Enculturated Movement

Genuine revitalization will live a healthy life of Gospel radicalism in particular contexts. The Gospel constant will never be compromised by particular contextual concerns, no matter how "successful" any particular contextual expression may be.[8] There will be an intuitive cultural presence of the Spiritual movement, with the Spirit clearly in control. Another way of expressing this is that the Spirit will inhabit the cultural or social context even as He converts that context. Conversion moves one way, and contextualization moves the other; both movements are necessary. Proof that a movement has not become culturally pathological or overly contextualized is seen in how the movement jumps cultures, languages, ages and geography. Today's revitalization of Christianity in China is urban and rural, Mandarin and dialect, Han Chinese and ethnic minorities; it is also pouring out into non-Chinese in Central Asia and the Middle East.

Today, with the *pathological* concern (no pun intended) for product and results in the West, revitalization movements are often hijacked by a concern for numbers. The culture says "You can have the future you want to have, now!" and so the church says *Your Best Life Now, 7 Steps at Living Your Full Potential.*[9] Over-contextualized revitalization movements have two problems: they end up promoting cultural values and hopes as a substitute for Gospel norms, and they also become bound by the very culture they are to convert.[10]

True revitalization requires radical discipleship and as part of that radical discipleship it will call people to let go of personal dreams and they will take on newer and higher purposes not centered on self. The ancients talked about "self-esteem" as one of the primary vices that will separate us from God. Finding our esteem in our self is death. On one level, true revitalization calls a person to willingly and joyfully die to the self who is attached to death. In the 21st century we have many pseudo renewal movements that promise fulfillment before repentance and life before death. However, real revival is not spirituality as therapy, comfort or personal vocation. Revitalization requires and will produce communities of people who are "denying themselves, taking up their cross[es] and following Jesus."

Another way that a renewal can be overly-contextualized is in church structures. A denomination is, among other things, a culture. Revitalization is not limited by denominations or church hierarchies, but it flows through, over and around them. When a movement is held within a particular church tradition that movement has become too small and ineffective. Revitalization is more like a tsunami than a stream in dry season. A stream generally keeps within its banks or structure; a tsunami carries away everything in its path. A particular denominational structure or particular cultural expression (read "contemporary music," or "your dreams fulfilled") is carried away with and by a true revitalization movement. If a particular cultural expression becomes necessary or essential, it is too small a thing compared to something as large and uncontrollable as the Spirit of the Living God. In fact, most of these pathologies are rooted in types of reductionisms of the Spirit.

Fifth Pathology: Overly Spiritualized Concerns

I place this final pathology at the end, because I believe it is the only one that is most likely to regain some health after falling into pathology.[11] An overly spiritualized revitalization will often detach itself from local issues of justice, evangelism, or concern for the poor. Jesus had the problem with people being too "spiritual," tithing every little fraction of their income, but forgetting the weightier matters of justice. Revitalization movements can become so preoccupied with prayer, Bible study, worship and devotions that they ignore the outworking of revitalization in local communities and in the larger society. We might say that this is an overly personalized revitalization. This option speaks of converting individuals rather than praying and working for a renewed community that will have the spiritual power to then bring about the conversion of cultures. This pathology is very common, especially in wealthier cultures where it is possible to isolate yourself from the needy God has brought into your midst. The Revitalization Project has shown that revitalization is intensely contextual and historically holistic. There is no such thing as a renewal that focuses only on spiritual issues, although many have tried.

Revitalization may begin as a purely spiritual renewal, focusing on penance and personal conversion, but it will then, as in the second movement of a concerto, break out into cultural expressions. Renewals are not exclusively personal, nor are they exclusively public; they flow through individuals into their contexts, picking up cultures and "baptizing" them along the way. From the other direction, a movement may also be initiated from social injustices or even from persecution, but if it is a genuine renewal, it will flow back into the personal lives of the people so conscientized. There is a fullness or wholeness to revitalization that will not be denied by the power of cultural norms or (here) by spiritual privacy.

A Humble Attempt to Avoid Pathologies

One of the interesting observations that has come out of the Revitalization gatherings sponsored by Asbury Theological Seminary has been the notion of death. Something has to die before new life, or revitalization can take hold. When all seems healthy and happy there is little chance for revitalization to take place. Who, after all, seeks to bring back life to an organism that seems to be living quite well? New life is meant for what is dead, or what needs to die. When there is no prophet, when there is no will to love, when there is no breath of the Spirit, *then* there is the possibility of revitalization.

Related to this truism, I am reminded of two of the major themes in the important Orthodox work *Philokalia* or "love of the beautiful." A collection of ancient writings from the Desert Fathers up to the 11th century in the Orthodox tradition, these spiritual, theological, and philosophical writings are held together by a few common themes. One of the most important themes is that of humility. Humility is viewed as the mother of all virtues. Without humility we can not read the Scriptures, we can not pray, we are not granted the gift of discernment. Humility is expressed as tears when we pray and then as thanksgiving on the other side of tears.

If there is one antidote to these various pathologies in revitalization it would have to be humility expressed as remorse for sin. The ancients, as well as Wisdom writings, call it the fear of the Lord. The beginning of spiritual renewal or what is called the quickening of the *intellect* (seat of spiritual apprehension), is found in tribulations, knowledge of our own fault, and reflecting on our own death.[12]

Finally, we have a little more insight into the primacy of humility and penance from one of the many movements of revitalization in Europe in the fourteenth and fifteenth centuries. There were numerous interwoven reforming and renewing movements during that time that would eventually both break the structures of Roman Catholicism as well as reform Catholicism from within. One of these movements was called simply the "Modern Devotion," meaning a contemporary devotion. Its main expression was seen in a new structure within the Mother Church, the Sisters and Brothers of the Common Life.[13] I think it can be argued that much of this modern devotion was just that, devotion. Studying the records, devotional writings and diaries, it is clear that it was a very personal, communal, and pietistic movement. However, in strange and mystical ways the Modern Devotion laid the groundwork for devotion and spiritual practices that were foundational for Thomas á Kempis, John Calvin and even Ignatius of Loyola.[14] Through this movement, towns, villages, churches, and priests were transformed through communities of humility. Ignatius ignited one of the most powerful missionary movements of the modern era and his "Spiritual Exercises" were patterned after that of the Modern Devout.[15] Theirs was a contextually appropriate revitalization that crisscrossed European cultures. And what was their core value or virtue? The "Modern Devout" wrote about this in their own memorials, or diaries. "In one computerized survey of word choice in Devout memorial lives… `humility' and `virtue' ranked first. Humility was central to their vision…"[16] This may be the single most important antidote for revitalization pathologies.

Bibliography

Bevens, Stephen and Roger P. Shroeder. *Constants in Context, A Theology of Mission for Today.* Maryknoll, NY: Orbis Books, 2004.

Bickley, Gillian. "The Right Revd Dr George Smith (1815-1871), First Anglican Bishop of Victoria, Hong Kong (1849-1865)…" paper presented at the Robert Morrison Bicentennial in Hong Kong, March, 2007

Edwards, Jonathan. *The Works of Jonathan Edwards, Volume IV, The Great Awakening* (including *A Faithful Narrative of the Surprising Work of God*). New Haven, CT: Yale University Press, 2009

_____. edited by John E. Smith *The Works of Jonathan Edwards, Volume II Treatise on Religious Affections.* New Haven, CT: Yale University Press, 2009.

Hastings, Adrian. *The Church in Africa, 1450-1950.* Oxford: Clarendon Press, 1994.

Irvin, Dale T. and Scott W. Sunquist. *History of the World Christian Movement, Volume II.* Maryknoll, NY: Orbis, 2012.

Osteen, Joel. says *Your Best Life Now, 7 Steps at Living Your Full Potential.* Nashville, TN: Faith Works, 2007.

Origen, edited and translated by Henry Chadwick, *Contra Celsum.* Cambridge: Cambridge University Press, 1965.

Palmer, G.E.H., Philip Sherrard and Kallistos Ware, trans. *The Philokalia, Five Volumes.* London: Faber and Faber, 1984.

Reilly, Thomas H., *The Taiping Heavenly Kingdom, Rebellion and the Blasphemy of Empire.* Seattle: University of Washington Press, 2004.

Spence, Jonathan D., *God's Chinese Son, The Taiping Heavenly Kingdom of Hong Xiuquan.* New York: W.W. Norton and Company, 1996.

Van Engen, John. *Sisters and Brothers of the Common Life, The Devotio Moderna and the World of the Later Middle Ages.* Philadelphia: University of Pennsylvania Press, 2008.

Notes

1. See Jonathan Edwards' reflections on Awakenings and religious affections in The

Works of Jonathan Edwards, Volumes 2 and 4.

2. From John Cassian, "On the Holy Fathers of Sketis and on Discrimination" which is found in Cassian's Conferences, Book I and II, and it is also found in Philokalia, Volume I, pp 94-108.

3. Anglican Bishop George Smith left his wife (8 months pregnant) and two year old son to follow the movement and meet Hong. (see Gillian Bickley's "The Right Revd Dr George Smith (1815-1871), First Anglican Bishop of Victoria, Hong Kong (1849-1865)..." paper presented at the Robert Morrison Bicentennial in Hong Kong, March, 2007). "Bishop Smith's objective was to make the most of what he excitedly took to be a providential opportunity for confirming what he saw as the Christian tendencies of the Taiping leaders, with its promise, as he saw it, of a fruitful means of reaching thousands among the masses of China with the Christian message. This was a hope which the Bishop kept alive. In the first half of 1862, he met rebel leaders, and his description of his meetings was published." Many other missionaries were hopeful that this was the breakthrough to China, most notably the Baptist Issachar Jacox Roberts who taught Hong for two months and later moved to Nanjing to help out Hong's brother, Hong Rengan.

4. We mean here the Great Tradition of the Church, what is often defined as what has been taught by all of the Church, at all times and in all places. The Great Tradition is not exclusively, but not incidentally found in the Nicene and Constantinopolitan Creeds. Before the time of the Early Church Councils, Origen talked of "the Great Church," in a similar way (Contra Celsum (5, 59).

5. Dale T. Irvin and Scott W. Sunquist, History of the World Christian Movement, Volume II, chapter 12.

6. Later divisions between the Wesleys and Whitefield can be considered to be an early expression of this pathology. I think it can be shown that John's mother, Suzanna, encouraged the more rigid position that John later promoted. See Irvin and Sunquist, HWCM, Volume II, chapter 15: "Writing July 18, 1725 she said to John, 'The doctrine of predestination, as maintained by rigid Calvinists is very shocking; and ought utterly to be abhorred, because it charges the most holy God with being the author of sin.'"

7. Wesley's relations were strained with the Moravians in about 1740 and in 1755 he published a pamphlet against the Moravian leader Zinzendorf. When Wesley was 80 years old he visited Zeist, Netherlands (1783) but it was more of a formal than heartfelt conciliation. See the June, 2008 monthly newsletter from the Moravian Archives, This Month in Moravian History.

8. Appreciation should be given to Stephen B. Bevans and Roger P. Schroeder for their excellent volume, Constants in Context, A theology of Mission for Today (Maryknoll, NY: Orbis Books, 2004).

9. Joel Osteen, (Faith Words, 2007)

10. It can be argued that the overly contextualized "Gospel of Health and Wealth" has had great global or cross-cultural attraction. This is true, but when proclaimed in Cambodia (as I have seen) or in Nigeria or Haiti, its attraction is tragic, bordering on demonic, not Christian.

11. An overly spiritualized movement, I assume, will have people reading the Bible and praying a lot, and therefore there is the possibility of repentance and reengagement in society as a renewed community.

12. These are the first three stages of contemplation as described by St. Peter of Damaskos in Philokalia, Volume III, translated by G.E. H. Palmer, Philip Sherrard and Kallistos Ware, (London: Faber and Faber, 1984) p. 108. It is interesting that there are also listed negative signs which show that an intellect is not spiritual. "When, on the other hand, a person lacks patience and humility, the signs of this are doubt with regard to God's help, being ashamed to ask questions humbly, avoidance of stillness, and the read-

ing of Scripture, a love of distraction and of human company, and with the idea—entirely misguided—that one will attain a state of repose in this way." Ibid, pp 139f.

13. See John Van Engen's excellent study, Sisters and Brothers of Common Life, The Devotion Moderna and the World of the Later Middle Ages. (Philadelphia: University of Pennsylvania Press, 2008).

14. I believe Van Engen's understated argument is true regarding the Modern Devotional practices at the University of Paris that were part of the very spiritual air that both Ignatius and Calvin breathed and prayed. See pp 305-320.

15. Van Engen, p. 317f.

16. Ibid, p. 315.

Chapter 6

The Church Alive: Beyond the Commonalities and Anomalies of Revitalization Models[1]

DARYL IRELAND
PhD CANDIDATE,
BOSTON UNIVERSITY SCHOOL OF THEOLOGY

At an international conference with forty participants from 17 countries and five continents, one would expect great diversity; and, indeed, the conversations in Edinburgh from May 29 – June 2, 2010 around the topic of revitalization confirm that different Christian revitalization movements, approached with different analytical tools, from different global perspectives, yield an abundance of interpretations. Anomalies abound. Models based on revivalism tend to anticipate cyclical patterns of revitalization, while the church growth movement expects its linear expansion. Approaching revitalization as the work of sects or a believer's church suggests that renewal provokes persecution, whereas social scientists argue that persecution is frequently the precondition for revitalization. Peculiarities seem to exist in every case of revitalization, and they contribute to the diversity of models. Any commonalities, therefore, appear weak or artificially imposed.

Yet, the constructive task is to look beneath the many models and different interpretations for shared assumptions and common ground. Although no unanimity existed in the consultation, at a variety of times various participants tried to move beyond current models of revitalization. As they did so, they began to outline a new way to speak about the subject. It is the task of this essay to discern, develop, and finally reflect on the usefulness of these changes for the study of revitalization.

A Change in Conception:
The Church is the Revitalization Movement

The distinguishing feature of the new way of imagining religious revitalization is its affirmation that the *Church is the revitalization movement.* At the consultation the idea was occasionally expressed directly, but more often it undergirded the conversations. This concept was not universally embraced, but there was a distinct shift towards melding the Church and revitalization together.

Prior models of revitalization almost universally posited two tiers within the Church. Some theologians, at least from the time of Martin Luther, have imagined a dedicated *ecclesiola,* or little church, revitalizing the larger nominal *ecclesia.* Historians have described the polarizing effects of revivals. Sociologists have tended to separate the Church into sects or denominations, with the prior evolving into the latter as revitalization wanes. Missiologist Ralph Winter has distinguished sodalities from modalities, with dynamic sodalities (e.g., monastic orders) being critical in creating or revitalizing modalities (i.e., the church). These two-tier models of the Church have been at the core of reflection on revitalization.[2]

These models, however, no longer suffice. Even as the language of duality continues to surface, with some people juxtaposing *radical* discipleship to minimal consecration, or trying to distinguish cores (men and clerics) from peripheries (women, children, and laity), such formulations must ultimately be transcended. They appear to emerge more from social science than from theology, or they sound hopelessly imperialistic and modern. Current models are forcing all revitalization movements to conform to predetermined dimensions, and fail to account for global diversity or historical particularity. Models lack subtlety.

Thus, to suggest that revitalization does not happen to the Church, but that it *is* the Church, is to construct a foil to the historical models of revitalization; it is an anti-model if you will. By asserting that the *Church* is the revitalization movement, the Body of Christ cannot be reduced to a particular model. Despite its various historical forms, the Church is embraced as a fundamental unity, and can no longer be divided into groups of stronger or weaker commitments. Similarly, church structures and theological traditions become insignificant; revitalization happens in all ecclesiastical structures and communions. From this vantage point, a church longing for revitalization does not need to mimic certain behaviors, search for particular conditions, or restructure according to the demands of a favored model of renewal. The Church simply needs to become what it already is in Jesus Christ. The Church *is* the revitalization movement.

A Change in Theology: Revitalization is Trinitarian

In order to ground such a claim, it is necessary to articulate revitalization in Trinitarian language. For, unless revitalization proceeds from the eternal life of God, it is easily dismissed or reduced to an optional aspect of the Church. The Church cannot be the revitalization movement apart from the renewing life of God the Father, Son, and Holy Spirit.

Historically, "Where is the locus of revitalization?" has been answered in two ways. Reflection has focused on the Church or salvation. An ecclesiological approach to the subject insists that revitalization takes place in the church.[3] A soteriological approach, on the other hand, argues that the individual human heart is the center of revitalization.[4] Yet in the light of a Trinitarian articulation of revitalization, these theological disputes appear secondary.

Pressing beyond both the church and the human heart, revitalization must be located, first and foremost, in God. Pneumatology offers that possibility, as the Holy Spirit is widely recognized as the initiator of revitalization. However, the contribution of Christology must not be overlooked – for the resurrected life of Jesus Christ offers the only viable basis for the notion "to live again," (re-vitalization). The revitalization of the Church and human hearts has its source in, and takes its meaning from, the resurrected – or revitalized – life of God the Son. Only with such a strong Christological interpretation of revitalization is it possible to develop a truly Trinitarian theology of renewal. To that end, one may resituate the foundation for the study of revitalization by stating: The *Church* is the revitalization movement, because it is from the revitalized life of the Son that the Church – united to Him by the Holy Spirit – draws its renewed life, in accordance with the will of God the Father. When placed thus within the life of God, the source, scope, and purpose of revitalization take on new meanings.

Interlude: Historical Background for the Changes in Thinking about Revitalization

A reader attuned to changes in missiology over the last half-century will recognize the language and the theological moves used by this consultation to describe revitalization. The change in how revitalization is being articulated was directly borrowed from the shift in how mission has been reconceived. As evidence of such a connection, I simply remind the reader that at the conclusion of the revitalization conference most attendees stayed in the city in order to participate in the Edinburgh 2010 mission conference. There is remarkable overlap of scholars between the two disciplines. Those currently involved in reflecting on revitalization have been active promoters of the paradigmatic changes in the theology of mission. Missiology is heavily fertilizing the changes in thinking about revitalization.

In brief outline, missiology underwent a seismic shift in the 1950s and 1960s. The International Missionary Council convened a meeting of Protestants in Willingen, Germany, in 1952. After World War II, and in the face of missionary expulsion from China, mission appeared to be in crisis. In the shadow of such events, Willingen proposed an alternate model of mission. It recognized that the Church is neither the starting point nor the goal of mission. God's salvific work is prior to both Church and mission. Although not used in the meeting, the term *missio Dei* – mission of God – came to encapsulate this shift in theological thinking. Mission was no longer a program of the Church, or even foremost concerned with salvation. Mission was derived from the very nature of the Father, who sends the Son, and who with the Son sends the Holy Spirit. This eternal *missio* (literally, sending) within the Godhead is temporalized as God sends the Church into the world. This reconstruction of mission was a far cry from denominational missions structures, exotic foreign adventures, or penny subscriptions.[5]

The Second Vatican Council, convened between 1962-1965, affirmed these changes in thinking about mission. The Roman Catholic Church expressed the Trinitarian source of mission lucidly: "The pilgrim Church is missionary by her very nature, since it is from the mission of the Son and the mission of the Holy Spirit that she draws her origin, in accordance with the decree of God the Father" (*Ad Gentes*, 2). In the constitution *Lumen Gentium*, the Catholic Church also reworked its definition of the Church. It was henceforth to be, fundamentally, the People of God. Emphases within the Roman Catholic Church that elevated external, legal, and institutional definitions were subverted. The Church was no longer neatly divided between clerics and laity. Such distinctions did not cease to exist, but they were no longer constitutive of the Church. The Church, after Vatican II, was to be conceptualized as *one* Body that incorporated all its members into the mission of God.[6]

By following the lead of such changes in both Protestant and Catholic missiology, scholars of revitalization are resituating their own field of study. Dualistic conceptions of the Church can be jettisoned, and the concept of revitalization can be enriched in so far as its origin and purpose are located in the very nature of God. In addition, by hitching the theology of revitalization to missiology, insights from later post-colonial mission can be incorporated into the study of renewal. It is to these developments that we now turn.

A Change in Place and Time:
Revitalization is Here and Now

The conclusion that the *Church* is the revitalization movement undermines previous models that have all constructed revitalization as happening sporadically within space and time. Traditionally, revitalization was conceived as existing in specific places for a limited duration of time. The Azusa Street Revival, for example, is tied to Los Angeles in 1906 – 1908. Revitalization happened there and then. Those who met in Azusa Street were the "haves" of revitalization, and therefore it was assumed that as people moved from there to

India, China, or Scandinavia they were the carriers of revitalization to the "have-nots."[7] Revitalization was never imagined to be universal, but it was believed to be a temporary phenomenon that moved from here to there.

When the *Church* is the revitalization movement it is no longer possible to create strong boundaries in space and time – as if revitalization only happens here and there, and not everywhere; as if revitalization only happens now and then, and not always. To perpetuate the language of boundaries is to recapitulate the error of colonial missions that assumed that mission moves from the West to the Rest. Linking revitalization to geography, as missiology had formerly done, would be to return to the captivity of colonialism. To use the example of the Azusa Street Revival again, one cannot assume that it was the Pentecostal missionaries who revitalized congregations around the world. Rather, Pentecostal missionaries shared novel expressions of life (e.g., *glossolalia*) with churches already revitalized in Jesus Christ. Therefore scholars should be equally attentive to the signs of revitalization that already existed in India, China, and Scandinavia before the missionaries even arrived.[8] This is revitalization in six continents, the free imputation of revitalization to all congregations everywhere.[9]

The corollary to this change in thinking about revitalization in space and time is a shift in eschatological orientation. Revitalization is no longer imagined to lead to some better place or time, some eschatological description of the future.[10] Millennial visions, whereby the Church is purified and moved closer to God's promised future through revitalization, are now abandoned in favor of discovering God's appointed future already among us. The envisioned future, although veiled, is already here.

Combined, these alterations in the space, time, and direction of revitalization grant new freedom to explore revitalization beyond privileged places and times. Older models that were focused on the geographical and temporal frontiers of revitalization can now be supplemented by studies of Christian renewal that highlight the quotidian aspects of the revitalized Church. The power of revitalization no longer belongs to a select few. It is the gift of God for the People of God.

A Change in Focus: Revitalization is for the World

While revitalization is God's gift to the Church, the Church is not the object of revitalization. It is the *world* that needs to live again. Colliding with narrow theological models that focus on revitalization as something that happens in churches and for churches, this new understanding of revitalization stretches to cosmic proportions.

The social sciences have always maintained an outward focus for revitalization; it rejuvenates an entire culture. It might appear, therefore, that this new approach is merely absorbing the insights of the social scientific models. Yet, this new approach does not come to the world through the social sciences, but through theology. The path, therefore, is very different and the destination is likewise unique. For while the social sciences imagine the revitalization of a society, a theological vision of revitalization encompasses everything in creation – all that is seen and unseen.

The entire *cosmos* longs for renewal. The environment, in particular, needs to be included in revitalization. The despoiling, destruction, and death of the planet are urgent concerns. Furthermore, political institutions, economies, families, the arts, civil societies, and even the Church itself, are all complicit with the forces of death. Everything groans and eagerly awaits revitalization in Jesus Christ.

It has been said among missiologists, "God does not have a mission for the Church, but a Church for God's mission." Echoes of that sentiment can be heard in the reconfiguration of renewal: "God does not have a revitalization movement for the Church, but a Church for the revitalization of the world." This is a remarkable shift in the study of revitalization. It is not just a study about the Church, but an invitation to participate in God's cosmic redemption.

Concluding Reflections

The consultation on revitalization that met in Edinburgh produced some fresh perspectives on the subject. Various strains of thought shared a common assumption: the *Church* is the revitalization movement. Although in no way unanimous or systematic, the conference hinted at significant changes in the approach to revitalization.

These changes hold rich potential for future productive work in the study of revitalization. First, it allows scholars to avoid splitting the one Body of Christ into two groups or tiers of religious commitment, and therefore encourages a more holistic appraisal of revitalization. Second, grounding the conversation first and foremost in the Trinity enriches the concept of revitalization. It also curtails the inclination to engineer the conditions for a revitalization movement, because revitalization is primarily a theological reality, not a sociological one. Third, when revitalization is freed from identification with specific locations and times, it pushes scholarship beyond the "haves" and "have-nots" of revitalization. *All* churches share in the revitalized life of Jesus Christ. This conclusion opens the study of revitalization to the fullness of the worldwide Church in all spaces and times, instead of prioritizing one place or one time over another. Finally, by renaming the object of revitalization as the world, instead of just the Church, the focus of revitalization expands in scope. Revitalization must be explored as part of God's cosmic act of salvation, the redemption of all things in Jesus Christ. These are four significant contributions to the study of revitalization.

In order to gain a secure foothold in the field of revitalization, however, two issues need to be addressed. Scholars must first face the question whether this theological shift is an attempt to lessen the anxiety within churches and denominations that are apathetic and declining. Is this a way to justify theologically the church's lethargy? Is it a form of self-deception, vehemently insisting one already *is* revitalized, even as one is dying? Such a question should provoke important self-reflection, and force an honest assessment of the source of these paradigmatic changes.[11] Second, and more importantly, it will be necessary to address the problems introduced by separating the Church's revitalized essence from its existence. This new approach insists that the Church is fully revitalized in Jesus Christ; in its essence the Church is the revitalization movement. Existentially, however, the Church is not automatically vibrant and alive. It needs to appropriate subjectively the new life given to it objectively. In their historical existence, therefore, churches fall somewhere along a continuum of actually manifesting the revitalized life of Christ. Some churches approximate their revitalized essence more fully than others. On the one hand, this explanation is extremely useful. By appealing to the gap between essence and existence, a person may explain the paradoxical persistence of sterility and apathy in the midst of a Church that *is* the revitalization movement. On the other hand, once a person acknowledges that churches appropriate revitalization to different degrees, then one has returned to creating two-tiers or multiple levels within the Body of Christ. Furthermore, when churches in certain times and set places approximate their essential nature in a remarkable fashion, scholars will likely continue to gravitate towards these existentially definable revitalization movements. The field of revitalization will then remain bound to definite coordinates in space and time, and will proceed with the virtually unmodified assumption that some churches "have" more revitalization, and others "have-not." If this is true, one may wonder if the proposed changes to the study of revitalization have actually anything new to offer. Theologically all churches may be the same in essence, but scholarship on revitalization deals with the Church in the only dimension in which it may encounter it – in the Church's historical existence. Hence, it will be necessary to narrow the gap, or explain the correlation, between the Church in its essence and existence.[12] Only then will the idea that the *Church* is the revitalization movement be capable of truly altering the field of study.

Notes

1. This essay was written in consultation with Dr. Dana L. Robert, the Truman Collins Professor of World Christianity and History of Mission at Boston University, and participant at the second research consultation on World Christian Revitalization Movements held in Edinburgh.

2. Howard A. Snyder, *Signs of the Spirit: How God Reshapes the Church* (Eugene, OR: Wipf and Stock, 1997), 31-67. Snyder describes seven possible typologies of revitalization, all of which depend on some sort of bifurcation of the church. Besides the opposition of the *ecclesiola* to the *ecclesia*, revivals to apathy, sects to denominations, and modalities to sodalities, Synder also demonstrates how revitalization can be approached as a believer's church separating from Christendom, revitalization as a force overcoming cultural stagnation or decline, or – from a Roman Catholic perspective – Catholic Anabaptism as a minority that functions within Christendom. Although each model has made its own distinctive contributions to the field, it is the similar assumption of duality within the church that allows them all to be linked together, and impresses one with opportunity to do something new.

3. See, for example, C. Peter Wagner, *Your Church Can Grow: Seven Signs of a*

Healthy Church (Glendale, CA: G/L Publications, 1979). Wagner suggests that revitalization occurs by modifying several features within the church. Alan Hirsch, *The Forgotten Ways: Reactivating the Missional Church* (Grand Rapids, MI: Brazos, 2006) describes revitalization as the church recovering its apostolic (sent) identity, instead of relying on its ability to attract others to come into church. See also Roger Finke and Patricia Wittberg, "Organizational Revival from Within: Explaining Revivalism and Reform in the Roman Catholic Church," *Journal for the Scientific Study of Religion* 39, no 2. (June 2000): 154-170. Although not theologians, Finke and Wittberg describe revitalization as an ecclesiastical phenomenon: it is the ability of the church to expand its supply of religious products that facilitates revitalization.

4. A clear formulation of this position appears in J. Edwin Orr, *The Flaming Tongue: The Impact of Early 20th. Century Revivals* (Chicago: Moody, 1973), vii: He describes how in a revival one person can be changed, but if enough individuals are changed then a large group forms, and large groups can change congregations, and congregations a city, and cities a country, a country a continent, and a continent the world. In other words, revival is an individual experience, but its aggregate effects can be massive. From a non-theological perspective Anthony F.C. Wallace, "Revitalization Movements," *American Anthropologist* 58, no. 2 (April 1956), suggests that revitalization transforms an entire society, but begins in an individual: "With few exceptions, every religious revitalization movement with which I am acquainted has been originally conceived in one or several hallucinatory visions by a single individual" (270).

5. For a full account of the development of the *missio Dei* concept, see John G. Flett, *The Witness of God: The Trinity, missio Dei, Karl Barth, and the Nature of Christian Community* (Grand Rapids, MI: Eerdmans, 2010). Chapters five and six especially cover the missiological turn of the mid-twentieth century.

6. The Second Vatican Council was deeply concerned about revitalization, and in its published documents sought to fuel renewal in the Church. Determined that revitalization does not stem from the Church changing into something new, but from becoming more fully what it already is, *Unitatis Redintegratio* declared, "Every renewal of the Church essentially consists in an increase of fidelity to her own calling." For the impact of these theological shifts in Roman Catholicism, see Helen Rose Ebaugh, "The Revitalization Movement in the Catholic Church: The Institutional Dilemma of Power." *Sociological Analysis* 52, no. 1 (Spring 1991): 1-12.

7. As an illustration, see Luke Wesley, *The Church in China: Persecuted, Pentecostal, and Powerful* (Baguio City, Philippines: AJPS Books, 2004), 54-60. Wesley seeks to trace contemporary Chinese Christianity back to the Azusa Street revival, because of its expressive spirituality and use of *glossalalia*.

8. As an example of this counter-thrust to traditional ascriptions of revitalization moving from "here" to "there," see Lian Xi, *Redeemed by Fire: The Rise of Popular Christianity in Modern China* (New Haven: Yale University Press, 2010). Throughout the book, Lian Xi argues that indigenous Chinese Christian movements developed expressive spirituality and *glossalalia* largely independent of Pentecostal missionaries by exploring the Scriptures and developing religious practices rooted in Chinese popular religion.

9. For the missiological precursor to this shift, see the first Council for World Mission and Evangelism held in Mexico in 1963: *Witness in Six Continents: Records of the Meeting of the Commission on World Mission and Evangelism*, edited by Ronald K. Orchard (London: Edinburgh House Press, 1964).

10. Revivalism has especially emphasized the eschatological destination of revitalization. Jonathan Edwards, *A History of the Work of Redemption Containing the Outlines of a Body of Divinity in a Method Entirely New*, 2nd. edition (Edinburgh:

Alexander Jardine and Edmund Whitehead, 1799), first situated revivals as heralding the dawn of the millennial age. J. Edwin Orr, *The Flaming Tongue: The Impact of Early 20th. Century Revivals* (Chicago: Moody, 1973) likewise believed that "successive Evangelical Awakenings are each more radically proto-New Testament in emphasis—the Reformers more evangelical than the Lollards, and the Puritans more evangelical than the Reformers, eighteenth century Revivalists more evangelistic than the Puritans and nineteenth century Evangelists more enterprising than their predecessors..." The evolution of such revivals would eventually culminate in the *eschaton* "when there will be a great Revival over the whole earth" (199).

11. Donald McGavran, *Understanding Church Growth*, Fully Revised Edition (Grand Rapids: Eerdmans, 1970), first asked a similar question of the missiological shifts that occurred in the 1950s and 1960s. Was the new definition of mission an escape from responsibility? He worried that, "Some of the plateaued and declining denominations in all six continents, but specially in North America and Europe, owe their stagnant condition to the inroads which the above reduced and twisted view of evangelism has produced in their leaders, both lay and clerical" (31).

12. Orland Costas, "A Wholistic Concept of Church Growth," in *Exploring Church Growth*, edited by Wilbert R. Shenk (Grand Rapids, MI: Eerdmans, 1983) outlined an integrated vision of Church Growth. Although not specifically addressing the gap between the Church in its essence and existence, his work stands as an invitation for scholars of revitalization to think holistically about the Church – both in its essence and existence, refusing to allow the two to function in independent spheres.

Chapter 7

The Dancing Church:
African and Pacific Perspectives

Thomas A. Kane, PhD

ASSOCIATE PROFESSOR OF HOMILETICS AND
LITURGICAL PRACTICE, BOSTON COLLEGE

Revitalization Movements will be enhanced by considering creative worship as a way to animate and renew Christian communities. Movement and inculturation are two ways to open up Christian worship in new ways. We live in an increasingly global society and our congregations tend to be more and more cross-cultural. Dance or sacred movement can be an entry point to these communities as a universal language. The following reflection comes from *The Dancing Church around the World*, a DVD collection of visual materials.

Dance and Renewal

Dance can be a renewing force in our spiritual lives, whether it is for personal prayer, public prayer or celebration. Today we are recovering an holistic sense of the person, acknowledging the body-spirit connections. We are just beginning to explore in simple ways how our body expresses in movement our deepest longings and yearnings and connects us more powerfully with our God. This may still sound very abstract. Good theory but where is the model? What does it look like? Can communities do it? What is the connection between dance, prayer and culture. How can we learn from the peoples of the globe? How can we break down the barriers that divide us?

As a ritual maker and dancer, I struggle to portray the power, the majesty and the prayerfulness of dance in the context of liturgy and culture. Over the years, I have explored liturgy, dance and culture, traveling to two very different parts of the world to experience, study and record worship experiences in Africa and Oceania, primarily Polynesia and Melanesia.

With reports from missionaries about wonderful dancing and thrilling integration into liturgy, I brought that experience back on videotape. After months traveling around the African continent and the deep blue waters of the Pacific, I had incredibly moving experiences about life, family, faith and dancing. Not only was the church dancing, but the Christian faith was so embodied and connected to everyday life. No longer a tourist, my traveling became a pilgrimage and I learned to pray and move in unexpected ways.

My new DVD collection, *The Dancing Church Around the World*, presents actual worship; nothing artificial, nor constructed for the purposes of the project. The DVD aims to acquaint Western audiences with the liturgical developments within the wider Church and to present full, embodied worship, examining various Church contexts: village worship, Cathedral/city worship, worship in the bush and the worship of a cloistered community. Many of the locations were selected because of the creative use of cultural elements in the worship, especially dance.

Inculturation, the bringing together of cultural elements and the symbols of the Christian faith, is no longer a theoretical exercise, but takes shape in a variety of communities where the parish or church leadership has begun opening up the Christian symbols within the local context. This means using the experience and history of a particular tribe or community as the starting place to express the deepest Christian mysteries. Theological reflection is not static and requires the interaction of poets, musicians and dancers with the theologian and liturgist. The work is creative, collaborative and ongoing.

In the beginning was the dance - words on a screen in a darkened theatre, set amidst blue sky and clouds - so begins the new Irish dance sensation, *Riverdance*. The show explores the origins of Celtic dance and connects classic Irish step dancing to world dance and music, including the fiery flamenco of Spain, the high kicking and boot stomping of Russia and the easy flow of African-American jazz dance and tap. *Riverdance* celebrates a world dancing together. This image is particularly striking because it understands dance as a uniting force. Today, not only the world dances, but the church dances. While this may seem shocking to some, it is happening around the globe, especially in cultures where dance is such a vibrant life principle.

We live in a society that yearns to dance, where dance may be a metaphor for life, but the actual practice is a bit conflicted. We may love the dance, but we often don't know what to do with it. Sometimes we have removed dance from our direct experience and disconnected it from the life of the community. We have marginalized the dance of western culture by preserving it as a fine art in the exclusive and privileged world of ballet, or by calling it entertainment, available for the masses in the disco and dance halls of the city, or by seeing it as a museum piece, an oddity, reserved for a *National Geographic* or a PBS special. Dance becomes something to look at, acknowledge, but rarely to participate in. Its power is too threatening, its allure too seductive.

Dance Throughout the World

Dance has its origins in mimetic movement. Our ancestors imitated the world around them, created symbolic and ritual forms of communication. Before speech and before music, the ancients moved to the rhythms.[1] Dance, the most universal of all the arts, is movement ordered by rhythm, time and space, expressing life and its deepest mysteries. Throughout history dance has been significant to all aspects of life. From the beginning most cultures employed dance in their rituals, ceremonies and celebrations. Dance was inescapable, part of everyday life. As societies developed, dance was a constitutive element. It would be impossible to consider society without dance

Throughout the world, various societies danced for the planting and harvesting of crops, for rain and productivity, for rites of passage, for celebrating new life and commemorating the dead. The Hebrew scriptures record the frenzied dance of King David accompanying the ark into the city and the tambourine dance of Miriam after the crossing of the Red Sea.

Dance has had an uneasy history with Christians over the centuries focusing primarily on the body: fear of the body, the need to control the body, suspicion over ecstasy, splitting the person into two with the spirit being good, the body being bad, in need of redemption. However, the dance story is not all bleak - the early Christians used the body to express prayer. Through gesture the body was expressive of reaching out and beyond to God. The *orans* position painted on the walls of the catacombs portrayed holy women praying with arms and torso raised, communicating with God in what some consider a "Jewish style of praying," with heart opened. Early worship also used the body to express resurrection by standing and repentance by kneeling and processions and modest dance or movement forms became a part of Christian worship.

In the Middle Ages, dance was often a significant aspect of religious and academic celebrations. There were May pole dances at weddings and a ring dance for the conferring of doctoral degrees. Imagine doctoral committees dancing in a circle around the successful candidate! Yet the official Church has been fearful and leery of the charismatic power of dance, describing dances as pagan, physical or carnal. In reading the history of sacred dance and Christianity, we can see vividly the repression of the body in worship and the fear of the raw spiritual energy emerging in the Middle Ages.

Processions and popular devotions employed a variety of movement styles and celebrational rituals. Dances were taken out of the churches and strong barriers were placed between the sacred and the secular. As the ban on dance in Churches began sweeping over Europe, the dance moved from inside the Church to outside - to parks, piazzas and plazas. Even today on most Sundays, one can experience the *Sardana*, the folk dance of Catalán outside the Cathedral of

Barcelona. This celebration dance was most probably the closing part of the actual service in earlier days and now it finds its way to the Cathedral steps and eventually to the Cathedral plaza. The place for the dance has changed, but the dance lives on.

This fear continues in our present age. The musical, visual, architectural arts flourished under church and papal patronage. Sadly, the dance did not fare as well. There are remnants today of sacred dance protected by papal jurisdiction. The dance of Los Seises in the Cathedral of Seville is one example. At the recent Eucharistic Congress in Seville, during the exposition of the Blessed Sacrament, the young boys from Seville performed the classic medieval dance with full pageantry to a packed Cathedral of cardinals, bishops and pilgrims with Pope John Paul II presiding.

A Dance Explosion

In the Arts, as Europe developed ballet, North America discovered the roots of modern dance. In performance, Isadora Duncan, the foremother of Modern Dance, explored the spiritual realm and the freedom of the body in her greco-classical mode. Martha Graham, a revolutionary modern dancer and choreographer, explored intensely religious and psychological themes on the stages of America. Graham dances were often powerful rituals with scriptural or classical themes. Her dances continue to touch audiences deep inside. At Jacob's Pillow, Ted Shawn included men in his athletic choreography and opened the possibility for men to explore ritual and movement in what was predominantly "a woman's world."

Dance is a part of our folk heritage and a fine art. Ballet and modern dance companies are performing across North America. Folk dancing and aerobics are taught in adult education classes and social dancing is very much a part of family celebrations and other social situations. In the midst of this "dance explosion" religious groups are working with dance as an art form and as religious or ritual communication. In the United States, the Shakers, the "holy Rollers" and some evangelical church groups have used and continue to use sacred dance or "the holy dance" in their worship. These dances might be a simple circle dance or ecstatic movement brought on by the spirit.

The new-old art of liturgical dance has been renewed. While it is difficult to pinpoint the actual rebirth of sacred dance in churches, we get glimpses as early as the mid 1940s of individual dancers using movement to explore the sacred or spiritual realm. In the United States, some dancers became aware of a deeper spiritual energy within themselves and the possibilities of this new form within the worship of their communities. These dancers brought together their spiritual quest along with their own disciplined training in the dance. Thus began the re-birthing of the sacred dance tradition and the new awakenings of liturgical dance. It is interesting to note that about the same time, there were similar explorations in Europe, especially in France and Switzerland. Dancers began reclaiming sacred dance as part of their Western religious and cultural tradition.

These pioneers introduced dance in worship and engaged the congregations in using the body to express prayer and connection to God.

As religious dance struggles to find its old-new identity, the effort is enriched by the growing interest and study of different types of dance styles in western culture, especially folk dancing, ballet, modern dance, yoga and world dance along with the experimental work of contemporary dancers and choreographers.

Recovery of the Sacred

The recovery of sacred and liturgical dance continues to have a mixed reception in the United States. For many, it is difficult to conjure up a proper image of sacred or liturgical dance. Our own images may disturb us. Dance is either for the trained professional and therefore tends toward performance, or it is manipulative or unworthy of being a part of the divine liturgy. If one were to say liturgical music, one can hear or imagine the sounds of a Mozart Mass, a Bach cantata, Christmas carols, Gregorian chant or contemporary church music. If liturgical dance is mentioned, what does one see in the imagination, perhaps nothing, a blank screen, or maybe a thin pale women in a diaphanous gown gesticulating to the heavens and or taking flight into the heavens. The fact is that we don't have a clear image of liturgical dance. In church circles, a recovery of the word *dance* might be an off putting term, perhaps the use of movement or gesture might be more appropriate.

The growth in liturgical music, an allied art, may help us see the parallel in liturgical dance. The harsh, amateur-sounding guitar strumming of the sixties has given way to a more advanced and enriched style of performance. Church musicians have moved through the "hootenanny stage" to a more blended style of instrumentation. Today liturgical music has matured in lyric and melody with less friction between the organ and the guitar. Composers have also recognized the value of musical heritage and are more attuned to the aesthetic and theological issues within the liturgy. Music, in general, also reflects a more global or world music style. We are beginning to sing in different languages and with syncopated rhythms.

For over twenty years I have pondered this liturgical, aesthetic and political question. Some liturgical dance I have experienced has been prayerful, uplifting and carefully crafted within the liturgical rite, appropriate to the architectural space and the rhythm of the liturgy itself. At other times, I have experienced poorly planned and rehearsed dance, more performance than prayer, more aerobic than artful, more pretentious than prayerful. In the final analysis, liturgical dance is a mixed bag, reflective of where we are in the church and the many struggles we continue to work out liturgically.

I have been encouraged by the seriousness of many leaders in the liturgical dance field, who work for collaborative liturgical planning, insist on fine performance skills and are aware that the dance is a part of the larger liturgy. The bottom line is to minister to the prayer life of the community.

As liturgical dance continues to move through this period of adolescence, the issues facing it are manifold: a more public understanding of dance, an appreciation of the place of liturgical dance within our North American culture, a deepening of the quality of choreography, the appropriate placement of dance within the liturgy, a sensitivity to a deepening multi-cultural church, the involvement of the community and the need for the artistic discipline of the solo or group dancers themselves.

An African Perspective

The African research was done on two different visits in 1987 and 1990. The first visit took almost six months, crossing the continent from East to West. On the second visit, I retraced some steps and explored new areas that opened up. Because there is no generic African worship, it is impossible for any one example of community worship to represent the entire continent. Each segment speaks its own language and culture. Let us take a journey and experience some of the world's Christian communities where dance is part of the every day experience of people, especially in prayer. I have divided the journey into the types of liturgical dance. PROCESSION DANCE is direct and functional movement to and from a specific place, including the Entrance procession, the Gospel procession and the Gifts Procession. PRAYER DANCE includes acclamation and invocations while MEDITATION DANCE is reflective by nature. PROCLAMATION DANCE announces the scriptures. CELEBRATION DANCE begins or completes a ritual activity.

Procession Dance

Ndkamenya, Malawi: The *Ingoma* is a traditional dance of the Ngoni warrior, from the Zulu stock of the "Nguni Peoples" of South Africa, who came north on a conquest trek in the mid-nineteenth century and settled in the northern districts of Malawi. Today, the Ingoma warrior dance is performed throughout the district by different tribal groups, including the Tumbukas. The opening dance of the liturgy has been adapted from village life and transformed into a liturgical procession dance for the Easter season. The procession includes all age groups - beginning with the young girls, who are part of a small liturgical dance group, followed by the members of the Legion of Mary, dressed African-style in white and blue.[3] Men of varying ages up to seventy years of age surround the presider at the altar and dance with a heavy foot step, the same step in the village dance. They dance naturally, without being conscious of their movements; the dance is in their bodies; it is a comfortable thing to do. The movement is into the ground, because the earth is sacred, they are connected to the earth. Africans make little or no distinction between the sacred and the profane. All life is holy, all life is sacred. For them, to dance is to breathe. To dance is sacred. The candle bearer and the book bearer sustain the holding up of the book and candle throughout the entire opening song, which takes about ten minutes.

This opening is a traditional dance form transformed into liturgical dance. This form is called *Mgubo*, the celebration of victory. The text has been adapted and changed from the village victory to Christ's victory over death, Christ victorious in the Easter Season. During the long procession, the entire church sings: *God sent his only Son, to come and save all humankind. And we all say thank you, merciful God. Jesus came to save us by dying on the cross, but rose from the dead, we are saved indeed.*

Yaoundé, Cameroon: The Presentation of Gifts is a full choir dance in which the gifts of bread and wine, banana, fruits, squash and food stables are brought to the presider and then danced around the church and then back and down the main aisle again The movement is repetitive, more complicated than the once down the aisle processions we may know.

Prayer Dance

Kumasi, Ghana (Acclamation): Under the direction of Bishop Peter Sarpong at the Cathedral in Kumasi, the dance at Eucharistic acclamation draws on the traditional greeting of the Ashanti King with special drumming and movements reserved for royal occasions. The women, dressed in special cloth, greet the coming of the Lord/King during the Eucharistic Prayer with hand gestures and a torso curved reverently. The dance is slow and deliberate as the music group sings: *The King has come. Let us ask the King for a blessing. Praises to the King!*

Lilongwe, Malawi (Invocation): At the Poor Clare's House of Prayer, for the Feast of Our Lady of Africa, the Mary statue, carved of ebony wood, draped with a blue dress and pearls around her neck, is placed in a corner of the chapel. At the beginning of morning prayer for the Feast, there is a hushed reverence to the *a cappella* singing as the sisters kneel on the floor and bend over as they sing. At the opening hymn, a sister pounds an actual mortar and pestle for the percussive sound. The sounds of the grinding mix with the sounds of sifting grain as a rhythmic element underneath the singing. These dramatic sounds are the ones young women would have heard in the village, in the early morning light before sunrise and the oncoming heat of day. The percussive elements highlight a unified sifting dance gesture, down, left and right, all combining to underscore the hymn-text.

Yaoundé, Cameroon (Acclamation): This liturgy has been celebrated for about ten years in this parish. Set in the middle of the capital city, the people celebrating are city people. The modest church structure is new. The Eucharistic Prayer of the priest is intertwined with the choir singing and dancing. It begins with the *Sanctus* and continues through the Eucharistic Acclamation. The choir is dressed in traditional African colors: white, red and black. During the *Sanctus*, the choir becomes almost a living iconostasis between the people and the altar. The dancing is highly stylized. The women carry *abui*, white pompoms, symbols of respect, used traditionally to express joy and happiness. The men shake the *apback*, symbolizing the power of God, *chasse-mouche* or fly-swatters. The movement continues throughout the Eucharistic Prayer in a call and response style. Note the integration of voiced prayer, sung chants and danced acclamations.

Proclamation Dance

Addis Ababa, Ethiopia: In the Capuchin Church of Holy Savior down-town, people gather before sunrise to sing the psalms of Morning Prayer. The most significant aspect of the prayer is the *Allegro dance*, one of the oldest liturgical dances in Christendom with its origins in the early church. This dance represents the ecstatic dancing of David rejoicing before the Ark. Large drums are carried and played in a circle dance with a stylized stomping of the feet. Even with an ongoing civil war, in a time of food shortage, the Christian gathers to pray, sing and dance and in these difficult times to offer their dance for peace and reconciliation.

Turbo, Kenya: On Good Friday, there is a dramatic presentation of the Passion, beginning with the betrayal in the garden and concluding with the interchange of Jesus and Pilate. The drama uses the grounds of the Mission, the Parish house and church as the congregation follows the action from place to place. From Pilate's house, everyone then continues in the way of the cross through the village, praying the Stations of the Cross. The entire event takes about three hours; and the journey goes through the village up a hill to Calvary. This drama has an evangelical edge, proclaiming the passion of Jesus Christ. As the procession moves through the center of town, stopping traffic and using the main road, more people hear the proclamation and they join in the prayer walk. At the time of crucifixion, there is real weeping and a genuine sadness descends over the entire congregation.

Celebration Dance

Nandom, Ghana: To celebrate the Feast of Corpus Christi, there is an outdoors mass on the grounds of the Church of St. Theresa in the Northern District. After the post communion prayer, each group in the Parish is invited up to pray, sing and dance before the Blessed Sacrament. The monstrance is placed on the altar and for the next four hours or so, there is a variety of adoration styles. The Dagatti people are basically agriculturists, living on the Southern Burkina Faso border, whose Ghanaian dance forms are quite strenuous and complex. The foot patterns go deep into the ground with an isolated movement of the torso, the back bent over a bit and there is a sudden impulse to the shaking of the head. The dancing is ecstatic. People are aware of the Eucharistic Presence, yet they give themselves over to the dancing. Time seems suspended as priests, sisters and parish groups spend most of the day praising God with song and dance for the gift of the Eucharist.

Special Celebrations

Kinshasa, Zaire: The popularly called *Zaire Rite*[4] is the first new Roman rite in many centuries. As celebrated in St. Alphonse Parish, Kinshasa, Matete, the opening procession involves all the ministers doing a *step together step* dance, servers carry spears as symbols of the chief and the main presider carries the *symbole du chef* (the sign of the chief, a carved stick with horse hairs). As the procession nears the altar, the presider kisses the altar north, east, south, west, representing the universe, signifying the global quality of praise. The Gloria is a *circle dance* around the altar with all ministers, men and women, following the presider who incenses the altar. The steps are highly patterned and there is stylized hand-clapping. Note that dance is not something added on to the rite, but a constitutive element. Without the dance, there can be no rite, which is very comprehensive in describing the elements for the celebration. Each participating tribal group must work with their own symbols and find the balance in expression. The rite is more than a liturgical order or set prayers, but rather the entire complex of words, actions and cultural symbols.

During the opening prayer the congregation uses the *orans* gesture, spreading out their arms with their hearts opening to God. The people respond with a longer phrase than *Amen*. The homily is also energetic as the congregation participates, shouting out certain phrases or singing a song or acclamation. The order has also been re-worked according to the older liturgical tradition. The Introductory rites have been simplified. After the homily, there is an invocations of saints and ancestors, a litany of forgiveness, the sprinkling rite and the sharing of peace.

Lilongwe, Malawi: *Misa Chimalawi* is the result of many year's work by the Poor Clare sisters. Still in an experimental stage, this mass is not often celebrated publicly. The structure of the Mass combines Roman liturgical form and rich, traditional Malawi symbols. At the beginning, there are prayers before entering the sacred space. Once inside the enclosed sacred space, the sisters invoke the saints and ancestors to be present in the celebration. The presider is dressed in the style and colors of a Chief. Highlights include the firepole dance as part of the responsorial psalm; the presentation of bread and wine along with the symbols of a cloistered life: prayer books, song books, farm implements, the fruits of the field, flowers, chickens and rabbits raised within the cloister. These are received and placed near the sacred fire. In place of incense, flour is sprinkled on the objects, the traditional way to make things holy, as a blessing

A Pacific Experience

The journey to the South Pacific took place in 1995 and 1996 and included many islands in Polynesia and Melanesia. During the return trip, I showed the original, raw video footage to a variety of communities for discussion and feedback. These responses along with some new footage helped shape the final edited version.

The people of the Pacific dance! They learn movement as little children. Dancing with hand gestures is perfectly natural. Thus the inclusion of dance in the liturgy can be very natural, too. One of the interesting features of Pacific liturgical dance is that many dances done in Church come directly from the culture with little adaptation. This is more often the case than not. While there may be a new dance adapted from the rich assortment of movement patterns, most pacific people themselves make the connections and design natural movements to fit the liturgical moment, based on traditional dancing styles. The dances use hand gestures and a gentle swaying of the body. In some cultures, the congregation itself would remain seated on mats throughout the ritual. Standing up or changing positions, except for communion, would be disrespectful.

Inculturation is becoming a hallmark of the Vatican II Church and many Pacific Islands are beginning to developing a Pacific Theology by exploring the interaction between their island way of life and the age-old traditions of Christianity. It is a lively and exciting time to be Church in the Pacific.

Procession Dance

Suva, Fiji: For the patronal feast of St.Peter Chanel, the seminarians at Pacific Regional Seminary have employed a traditional Royal Kava dance. In its original form, the dance is a presentation of a bowl of kava to a royal personage, such as the chief. In this Gifts procession dance, the seminarian in full Fijian attire, dances the chalice and paten to the Archbishop. While the chant has been rewritten for the liturgical act of presentation, the dance movements are the same as the Royal Kava dance.

Gizo Island, Solomon Islands: For the Ordination of the Bishop Cyril O'Grady, the Solomon Island boys from the local high school, played the pan pipes, swaying in rhythm to the hypnotic tunes. These traditional musicians led the procession from the downtown Cathedral to the open field where the liturgy was celebrated. The traditionally clad pipers contrasted to the servers, a few in warrior dress, but most in red cassocks and white surplices.

The women from Kiribati presented the bishop-designate to the Apostolic Nuncio with a rhythmic and patterned dance. The women surrounded the candidate, weaving intricate cross patterns with their steps as the men stayed on the outside edge, singing and gently drumming.

The Papal letter was also presented to the Apostolic nuncio by three warrior-messengers. The contrasting image was startling: three boys in grass skirts and fresh white paint on their black bodies interacting with a white and gold vested Roman bishop with towering mitre. Here was a meeting of two very distinct cultures!

Throughout the South Pacific: In many parts of Western Samoa, the Fiji Islands, Kiribati (actually a part of Micronesia, whose peoples have migrated to other islands) and Papua New Guinea, women play an important role in bringing the Scriptures to the congregation. After the opening prayer, it is quite traditional for the women to dance in the Word with a group of four to six. The dance styles, costumes and chants are as varied as the cultures.

Prayer Dance

Suva, Fiji (Acclamation): In preparing a new Alleluia acclamation dance, a group of seminarians, designed an Alleluia in the *Haka* style (usually associated with the Maoris of New Zealand). The arm movements were strong, almost chopping like karate, yet joyful, combining arm gestures from different island traditions. The dance was natural and graceful to introduce the reading of the Gospel.

Proclamation Dance

Southern Highlands, Papua New Guinea: The Obene people live deep in the bush in the mountainous region of the Southern Highlands. The community is an outpost station in the diocese of Mendi. In the community there are a number of dance groups. Wearing traditional Obene attire, one dance group greeted the arrival of the priest and performed a welcome dance to the church. This group also assisted in blessing the new church space with a special dance. Within the liturgy there were other groups of men and women who perform a processional dance with full circle turns with guitars and all.

The water used in the baptisms during the liturgy was *bamboo water*. This water was carried through a bamboo piping system from the top of the hill all the way down into the village square near the church. The water was flowing and living water. Because the village is not near a stream, they use this form of *bamboo water* because for them it is living water. They call *plastic water* (water in a plastic container) dead water. This water would not be suitable for baptism.

During the marriage ceremony, the couple pledges their love by placing their hands on the village rock with the priest's hand on top as a seal. This is the rock of covenant and is used for all contractual matters. It is a symbol of the sacredness of contracts and the special place of marriage within village life.

Meditation Dance

Nanaculli, Oahu, Hawaii: Because there has been a repression of Hawaiian culture for a number of years, the Hawaiian people are very interested and determined to revive the ancient customs and religious symbols. The Hawaiian hula has always been an expressive religious dance and not just for the tourist industry. On *Aloha* Sunday, the parish of Saint Rita prepares the liturgy in an Hawaiian way.. After communion, a group of women dance a hula meditation. Each hand gesture has a meaning and the movements are gentle and beautifully constructed. By its very nature, the hula is religious. The joining and recognizing of traditional Hawaiian culture within the church rituals is just a start - a way to honor a culture and a people that almost disappeared.

Rarotonga, Cook Islands: The Cook Islands are also in the midst of a cultural revival. The Maoris or the indigenous peoples of the Cooks are trying to relocate their Polynesian identity. The dancing in these islands is the most noticeable cultural force. In general, the English language and the New Zealand influence have taken over. At the Cathedral, there is just the hint of a start toward the use of more cultural elements and of the possibility of dance in the church. At a First Communion celebration, the boys and girls learned simple hand gestures for a post communion song. The gestures are very elementary but powerful. The children are committed to their movements with a certain ease. The next step will be to move into simple congregational movement and possibly solo dance meditation.

Celebration Dance

Mendi, Papua New Guinea: For the celebration for the new bishop of Mendi, Stephen Reichert, the various Huli tribes came to the city after a three or four day trek. On the Saturday before the ceremony, the tribes gather for a singsing. This is celebration dance in one of its truest and most original forms. With multi-colored painted faces and plumage from the birds of paradise, these tribal people are stunning and fierce in appearance. This was a first for Mendi as hundred of tribal people, men and women, marched in unison onto a large grassy plain. Each group then assembled, performing in place. Some pounded their drums and did a form of jump dancing, other groups marched around as if in a military parade. They were celebrating the new bishop and showing themselves off to the people of Mendi who wore western-style shirts and pants. It was a high pitched celebration. Many of the assembled groups would participate in the Liturgy the next day by dancing the word procession, the alleluia dance, or the gifts procession. Words on this page could never capture the incredible sight of these Huli tribes in feathers and paint engaged in Catholic worship. See the video! Our church is truly catholic and embraces the world.

Leava'a, Western Samoa: The feast of Pentecost is an example of the creative liturgical work of Cardinal Pio Taofinu'u. The cardinal is Samoan and recognizes that the future of the church in Samoa and possibly the world depends on an evangelization that speaks the language and culture of the people. To this end, the cardinal has been working on a liturgy that expresses itself with the rich symbols and folkways of Samoa. The *fa'a samoa* (Samoan way) is still very strong in the islands. As part of the celebration, the cardinal has involved a number of dance groups and various chiefs.

Three moments stand out. The first is during the penitential rite, when the eldest chief and his wife are covered with fine mats as a symbols of reconciliation. This custom follows traditional village life for the seeking of forgiveness. The couple remains under the mats during the singing of the *Kyrie*. They are then greeted with the sign of peace and the paschal candle, which the priest then processes throughout the church. The second is during the liturgy of the word when the talking chief, present on the altar through the entire liturgy, speaks to the people and then gives the talking stick and the symbol of the chief to the cardinal. The Cardinal with the appropriate symbols in hand then advances to the lectern for the reading of the gospel and the homily. The third is the gifts procession where flowers are presented around the altar and to the presiders and associates. This also includes traditional Samoan dancing with oiled bodies and the unique hand gestures of Samoa, finishing with the bringing in of a roasted pig as a sign of community celebration.

A Response

Today in North America, we continue our exploration through images, stories and symbols to understand the relationship of liturgy to culture and to discover how the body can be used more expressively. This entails studying the life experience, history and symbols of the community as the starting place to express the deepest Christian mysteries. The work presumes the creative input from poets, musicians and dancers to shape the material with liturgists and ritual makers. We must move forward with confidence of a faith that is embodied and does justice.

It is clear that Africa and parts of the Pacific are still considered mission land. Yet, there is more freedom with experimentation and less surveillance because liturgy is considered the new evangelization. The Catholic liturgy invites and beckons the uninitiated, speaking the language of Christ from within the culture. Many of these newer churches are post-Vatican 2 which means they only received an inculturated church. Many communities, especially in Papua New Guinea, did not have to *unlearn* from the past. This is not to say that the work of the church and the spread of the gospel is finished. Inculturation speaks Christ, but not in Western clothes, with Western words.

Art and ritual can elevate and expand our spiritual horizons. Symbols can express what the heart feels and the tongue cannot articulate. Let this experience of *The Dancing Church* invite you to a ritual world of symbols and dance. Just as poetry transcends the use of everyday language, even though the words are the same, so too does dance transcend ordinary body movement to elevate and uplift the spirit. One does not need to have a complete understanding of the poem to experience the transcendent. Likewise, an understanding of every movement is not necessary for the dance experience to be felt and appreciated. *The Dancing Church* can raise questions and open new possibilities for worshipping God and celebrating the spirit.

Through an understanding of dance and the ways various cultures have employed symbols in their own societal and religious ways, we need to begin reflecting on how we can embody our own worship and open up ritual activity to the entire congregation. As technology shrinks the world and we become more a global community, the practices and customs of the world will touch us in new ways. For so long we have given our resources and our missionaries for the building up of world and church and now, perhaps for the first time, we must learn to receive. It may be difficult or embarassing to open our hands and arms. Now is the time to receive from the world church. Now we learn from others very different than ourselves to receive a new spirit of Pentecost which will challenge and transform, bringing fire and light to our lives, our faith and our worship. Let there be dance!

Notes

1. Suzanne Langer, *Philosophy in a New Key*, Cambridge, MA: Harvard University Press, 1957.

2. Women play a significant role in the Church life of Africa, as lay ministers and in a variety of liturgical ministries.

3. The official title is the Roman Rite for the Dioceses of Zaire. Many dioceses have not yet implemented this new rite, especially in Eastern Zaire.

Chapter 8

Music, Liturgy, and Culture Driving Revitalization

ROBERTA R. KING, PhD

ASSOCIATE PROFESSOR OF COMMUNICATION AND
ETHNOMUSICOLOGY, FULLER THEOLOGICAL SEMINARY

> I waited patiently for the LORD;
> he turned to me and heard my cry.
>
> He lifted me out of the slimy pit,
> out of the mud and mire;
> he set my feet on a rock
> and gave me a firm place to stand.
>
> He put a new song in my mouth,
> a hymn of praise to our God.
> Many will see and fear the LORD
> and gave me a firm place to stand.
>
> Psalm 40:1-3 (NIV)

Central to Biblical scriptures and the Christian faith lays the intervention of God in the lives of His people wherein a divine call-&-response in musical form—'a new song'--occurs between individuals, communities, and the triune God. 'New songs' serve as distinguishing markers of God's intervention and ongoing relationship with His people. Psalm 40, for example, reveals key dynamics between music, liturgy, and culture located within the revitalization process. The opening three verses encapsulate in succinct and pithy form the heart of the divine encounter, a sacred call-&-response, with its two-fold movement between life-stages of 'orientation-disorientation-new orientation' as so often expressed throughout the Psalms.[1] They point to the dialogical nature of Psalmic literature that "expresses (and implies) both sides of the conversation of faith."[2] Such conversations arise out of life-experiences, the highs-and-lows and the struggles-

and-joys of daily living. What one individual experienced as divine encounter with God becomes a new song. In Psalm 40, comprised of both a psalm of thanksgiving (40: 1-10) and one of lament (40:11-17),[3] we find that song testifies not only of personal experience with God but also speaks to the local community and beyond. Ultimately, this 'new song' becomes incorporated into the liturgy and life of the worshiping community.

Similarly, church historians have long recognized music, and especially "a new song" as a major, distinguishing characteristic of revitalization in the Church[4]. The Protestant Reformation, for example, gave birth to a multitude of innovations that in addition to new church structures and theological positions included Luther's 'fresh' approach to music. For Luther, music was intended to serve the church as a vehicle of prayer and praise.[5] Recognizing the powerful communication values inherent in music, Luther encouraged participation of all people in singing and wrote numerous hymn texts in the vernacular language set to local, popular musical styles of his day.[6] His understanding of music as an expression of faith and a gift of God thus birthed both new song and ultimately new liturgical *praxis*. In addition to Luther's fathering of Protestant Church music,[7] the significance of music has continued on through countless revivals and their leaders such as Methodism with Charles and John Wesley in England, George Whitefield in America, Dwight L. Moody's Revivals with Ira Sankey's musical leadership, Aimee McPherson with the Azusa Street Revival, the Pentecostal-Charismatic movement, and on through to Billy Graham and Cliff Barrow's partnership in the late twentieth century.

Thus, music, liturgy and culture are interconnected and play pivotal roles in the life of the Church. In this chapter, I ask the question, "How does God work among His peoples through the dynamic intersections of music, liturgy, and culture in relation to revitalization movements?" I seek to identify and lay out an initial framework for analyzing and understanding these arenas as they energize faith communities and promote revitalization, most particularly in relation to global-local contexts of the twenty-first century. I begin by offering five foundational principles concerning the intersection between music and culture, followed by an exploration of representative renewal movements in relation to music, liturgy, and culture.

Music and Culture

Music and culture are inextricably linked. Indeed, music cannot exist without a cultural context from within which to arise. Nor, according to ethnomusicologists, do any cultures apparently exist without music. With the rise of increased global interactions, the study of the intersection between music and culture (the discipline of ethnomusicology) offers a means to exegeting music-and-culture in relation to a people's daily life. Five fundamental principles drawn from ethnomusicology, though not exhaustive, provide an initial set of analytical frames for understanding the multi-dimensional complexity of music.

Music as Life-Processor

Just as theologians are concerned with reading the Biblical text in one hand and a newspaper in the other, so music serves as an equivalent to local and global newspapers. Furthermore, it has the ability to bring the two elements together into spaces of dynamic, relational interaction. Within these spaces people are afforded the opportunity to weave together the strands of their lives in ways that reveal deep levels of their thought-life, their emotions, and related behavior.[8] This can occur simultaneously on individual and group levels within an experiential domain. When a 'new song' emerges among people who have encountered God, it is a dynamic expression of their Christian experience where a transformation has occurred and a 'new orientation' to life is expressed. One must ask further, though, "Isn't all music meant to be the same?"

Music as Universal Phenomenon with Immense Cultural Diversity

Many people say that "Music is a universal language." Yet, this saying is all too often interpreted to mean that music has universal meaning. However, in reality, "Music is universal; its meaning is not."[9] This aspect of music and culture was not understood when missionaries of the eighteenth and nineteenth century ventured into Africa and beyond for they brought with them "from their places of origin religious belief systems and accompanying musical practices."[10] This resulted in many misunderstandings of the Gospel and minimized effective contextualization of the Christian faith. Yet, more recently, as the Church in the Global South has grown and believers have found their own voices, cultural diversity has manifested itself exhibiting great vitality and vibrant celebration.[11]

Music as a Vehicle of Communication

Music also facilitates communication in similar ways as language. Accompanying all of life in multiple social contexts, music communicates profoundly as it simultaneously incorporates multiple signal systems, both verbal and non-verbal. For example, forms of African music extend western definitions of classical music in that music, dance, drama, dress, and musical instruments are all encompassed in the definition of music. These elements are combined together to create multi-sensory events that communicate appropriately and profoundly within their cultural contexts significantly contributing to the development of meaningful communication. Music is more appropriately defined by cultural groupings of people who determine the combination of elements incorporated into it and how it develops meaning.

Music and Cultural Context

Likewise, cultural contexts are essential in determining the function of music events, from baby dedications to weddings and funerals as well as worship. They also play a significant role in determining meaning of musical sounds. Music-*as*-sound cannot be studied "isolated from the human behavior that produced it."[12] Thus, a people interpret music and the occasion in combination with their cultural expectations and assumptions. The mere singing of a song stripped of any additional cultural cues can create unintended interpretations. For example, in singing a celebratory worship song in a West African language at Fuller seminary in California, non-African students mistakenly identified it as either a funeral or pagan cultural rite.

Additionally, both the cultural context and specific life-experiences determine meaning in song. This becomes significant not only across cultures but also within cultures. In Côte d'Ivoire, neighboring Senufo Christian believers who have closely related languages discovered misinterpretation of songs that had grave theological consequences. Nyarafolo believers, for example, in borrowing neighboring Cebaara Christian songs, discovered that non-believers assumed the outsiders' songs had no significance for them. When new Christian songs were composed in the vernacular Nyarafolo language, local people exclaimed, "You mean that God is for us, the Nyarafolo? We thought he belonged to the Cebaara!" Thus, similar but not contextually specific musical sounds of the Cebaara delivered an unintended message to Nyarafolo non-believers. God was not for them; rather, he belonged only to the Cebaara. The critical issue of identity associated with musical style and cultural context were at stake.[13]

Music and Identity

An increasingly important principle of ethnomusicology for today's global world observes that "people realize and express identities, both personal and collective, through music. Therefore we can know something of an individual's identity through the music they create, employ, and enjoy."[14] Believers who attend worship services that employ Christian contemporary music, for example, are making a statement about who they are, what speaks to them, and what draws them closer to Christ. Likewise the same occurs for those who prefer nineteenth century hymns. Further, through the chosen musical style, people are also identifying the group to which they wish to relate. As Shelemay argues, "Although identity is experienced differently by each individual, it is almost always constructed in relation to groups that we wish to be part of."[15] This can have both positive and negative ramifications.

With these principles in mind, let us consider how God moves through music, liturgy, and culture in relation to revitalization dynamics, both in local and global contexts.

Music and Revitalization Movements

The late twentieth century on into the early twenty-first century has seen a number of revitalization movements arise around the globe. Yet again, we see cultural musics playing prominent and significant roles, both locally and globally.

Local Movements in Globalizing Contexts

Since all musics originate in specific contexts, we turn first to local contexts. It must first be stated that it is rare, if hardly ever true, that any society is without influence from surrounding cultures. Yet, each dynamic context has developed unique ways of creating music that is both culturally appropriate and meaningful. Highlights of three such movements contribute to developing a framework for understanding the dynamics of music in relation to revitalization.

The Jesus Movement

On the West coast of the United States in the midst of a volatile, disorienting era of the 1960s and 1970's young people forced and conscripted to fight what for many was an unjust war in Vietnam, and to deal with a world in flux. They disdained a church seemingly short on relevant answers, and there emerged prophetic voices who expressed themselves through the vernacular, popular music of the day. Larry Norman, a leading rock musician of his era, encountered Jesus, dropped out of his successful band, *The People,* and chose to 'preach' his personal testimony and scathing critique of politics and society through the musical vernacular of his day. Cited by many as the "Father of Christian Rock," Norman sang to an angry "audience more influenced by Bob Dylan and The Beatles than by Billy Graham or the Gaither Trio[16]." Where Christians spoke one language, "Norman not only spoke the Church's message to the culture, but he created culture in the process – works of arts that by any standard were masterpieces."[17] Norman's musically prophetic voice contributed to launching new liturgical formats where music-in-the-service-of-liturgy became music-as-worship. Song texts were no longer restricted to horizontal singing with theological information about God, but were transformed into vertical songs-of-encounter in experience-driven, worship with God. Participation and authentic singing of praise and adoration to God ultimately contributed to inspiring two church movements, Calvary Chapel and the Vineyard.

Marked by a return to reading and studying the Scriptures, the Jesus Movement generated "textual communities"[18] through 'new song' in an era of media innovations. Fromm, in his astute study focused on Calvary Chapel, convincingly argues that new song first speaks on an individual, testimonial level, "in which the story of a believer's conversion provides a history and example that serves as a guide and sign for others who may follow in the path".[19] As people respond to sung testimony where communities form, not only the song's story of conversion contributes to forming dynamic communities, but the musical genre itself becomes embedded within the identity of the church in its liturgical (worship) *praxis.* As Fromm notes, " . . . the song not only tells the story of the church, it effectively embodies its message and its collective identity by virtue of what it is, not only what it says."[20]

Emerging African Christian Voices

Meanwhile, half a world away from Southern California, located in a rural, West African, agrarian society constituted of back-breaking field work and enslavement to spirits demanding regular life-sacrifices, a musically-gifted, young sorceress thoroughly knowledgeable in indigenous proverbs, song, and storytelling, encountered Jesus. Nonyime, a Cebaara Senufo believer in northern Côte d'Ivoire, found herself singing of her new freedom in Jesus, a faith encounter testimonial in cultural musical style. Laced with the deeply, nuanced knowledge of an insider astute in local singing since childhood, Nonyime spontaneously contextualizes her story-style songs that profoundly impact participants in the music event. When the first translated Scriptures became available, their story was orally voiced through indigenous song styles making God's Word alive and accessible to a predominantly non-reading audience. Dull church services, wherein most people slept during the incomprehensible singing of western hymns and preachers longed to speak *before* the singing, now came alive. Churches soon found people gathering around the event-oriented music, especially during Christmas celebrations. This new ritual event took place outside, lasted all through the night, required circle dancing and a lead singer proclaiming the gospel message calling out people's names to come to Jesus. Non-believers often found themselves drawing closer to the lead singer in order to hear the gospel message proclaimed in the songs. The church experienced explosive growth in an area that had been highly resistant to the gospel message[21].

Key dynamics of these oral communication events repositioned music criteria as incorporating, indeed requiring, dance and drama in performance spaces that foster encounters with the living God set within local community contexts.[22] In general, new rituals and broadened definitions of music (music, dance, and drama) are representative of the multiple places where the burgeoning church in the Global South is voicing their *dynamic expression of Christian experience.*[23] African urban contexts, such as Abidjan, Accra, and Nairobi, are drawing from the vitality of local, culturally appropriate musics and worship events that create African Christian identity intimately connected with the church's outreach and impact in the larger, global community.

A Southeast Asian Approach

Finally, among Salako believers on the island of Sarawak, Malaysia, *Transformative Worship*[24] is taking place through a fresh engagement with culture that is igniting not only renewal within the church, but also the local, surrounding society. In the process, emerging worship rituals embody holistic experiences that incorporate affective communication levels of sensing 'a touch from God' and simultaneously providing spaces and forums that process identity formation.[25] Key markers for this renewal movement include songs facilitating God's encouragement to believers in the midst of persecution, prayer and song that serve together as a portal to God, and the dynamic interchange between "song worship, spoken prayer and prophecy" intricately tied together so that worship "flow(s) together in a fascinating interplay of prose, poetry and song."[26]

Tan argues further that *Transformative Worship* incorporates three worship phases, similar to those of Brueggeman. She identifies them as *Come, Commune, and Renew for Action.*[27] The liturgy deepens believers' relationship with God and empowers them for living via a new orientation.

Global Movements and the Diffusion of Local Musics

Globalization and the expansion of technological development leaves hardly any society untouched. In contrast to local contexts, "deterritorialization," the interflow of commodities, goods, people, culture and ideas throughout the world, fosters the removal and transcendence of previous cultural boundaries and identities.[28] Deterritorialization exacerbates concerns for identity that are forging new arenas where the diffusion and reception of local musics breathe new life into churches, societies, and whole nations. This reflects, "today's world musical cultures . . . moving closer to each other and thereby affecting each other symbiotically." [29] Some scholars now view the musical world "not so much as a group of musics but as a large network of musical interrelationships"[30].

An obvious example is in the diffusion of the Contemporary Christian Music genre in adapted and variegated forms both within the United States and worldwide. New songs birthed out of a Christian rock mode have generated a "Great Worship Awakening" taking place in the postmodern church. [31] Accelerated and driven through the media such as radio, TV, audio cassettes, mp3s and the internet, new songs have ignited local movements with emergent streams of music and liturgical *praxis.* From Seeker Services to the Vineyard worldwide, from Praise and Worship to the dynamic Hillsong movement from Australia, sung worship is speaking to new generations in redesigned liturgical formats.

A less obvious yet extremely vital movement is located in the diffusion of Gospel music on a global scale. From Denmark[32] to Japan where the Gospel message has experienced resistance, songs of vital testimony are bringing together people seeking a dynamic spirituality. From a newly formed gospel group in Eagle Rock, California to Nigerian church planting in the Ukraine, and the emerging market of African Gospel music,[33] the singing of lament and celebration in response to God's interaction in people's lives is experienced while performing gospel music. Gospel music with its roots in African traditions and recognized as originating out of the pain and suffering of slavery in the United States seemingly resonates with people in crisis on multiple levels. Racked with confusion, persecution, conflict, economic difficulties, the struggles of immigration reshaping societies, and the insecurity of terrorism in the twenty-first century, people identify with the suffering, balanced with joyful testimonies, expressed in music and texts laced with Biblical imagery, encounters with God, and hope. Christians and non-Christians alike are flocking to opportunities to participate in the singing, both in the church and in society at large.[34]

Key Dynamics of Music and Liturgy Driving Revitalization

In the twenty-first century, when people from everywhere are moving into new contexts everywhere, key dynamics of cultural musics and liturgy that drive revitalization reflect the continuity and change of people struggling with life as they experience fresh encounters with the triune God. A hallmark of engagement with God is the birthing of new songs from within specific cultural contexts that ultimately lead to innovations in liturgy. These *"dynamic expressions of Christian experience"* often begin with personal encounter with God where the individual encountered, often a singer or musician, cries out in prayer and song with a renewed focus on God's Word and the work of the Holy Spirit in their lives. In the midst of their disorientation,[35] a divine call-&-response takes place. God lifts them out of the 'mud and mire' of their lives, sets their 'feet on a solid rock' and puts a 'new song' of praise and worship on their lips. The 'new song', as personal response to God's transformative work in one's life, expands to others who 'see and fear the Lord' and ignites revitalization in the Church that transforms individual lives and societal structures.

Notes

1. Walter Brueggemann, *The Message of the Psalms: A Theological Commentary* (Minneapolis: Augsburg Publishing House, 1984), 19-22.

2. Ibid., 5.

3. John Goldingay, *Psalms*, ed. Tremper Longman, 3 vols., vol. 1, *Baker Commentary on the Old Testament: Wisdom and Psalms* (Grand Rapids, MI: Baker Academic, 2006), 128.

4. Kenneth Scott Latourette, *A History of the Expansion of Christianity*, 7 vols. (Grand Rapids: Zondervan Pub. House, 1970).

5. Paul Nettl, *Luther and Music* (New York: Russell & Russell, 1948), 6.

6. The hymn, "A Mighty Fortress is Our God," was written in German and is recognized by most scholars as based on a popular tune of the day, deemed by some as a barroom tune.

7. "Just as the Reformation was set in motion by a great individual who, as an individual, visibly crossed the threshold from the Middle Ages to the modern period, Protestant church music in the actual age of the Reformation was decisively shaped by this Reformer. Therefore, at the beginning of any history of Protestant church music we must place the figure of Martin Luther" in Friedrich Blume, *Protestant Church Music: A History* (New York: W. W. Norton & Co., 1974), 5.

8. See Roberta R. King, *Pathways in Christian Music Communication : The Case of the Senufo of Cote d'Ivoire*, American Society of Missiology Monograph Series (Eugene, OR: PICKWICK *Publications*, 2009), 165-75.

9. Jeff Todd Titon, Ed., *Worlds of Music: An Introduction to the Music of the World's Peoples.*, 5th ed. (Belmont, CA: Schirmer Cengage Learning, 2009, 2002), 3.

10. David W. Stowe, *How Sweet the Sound: Music in the Spiritual Lives of Americans* (Cambridge. MA: Harvard University Press, 2004), 226.

11. See Thomas A. Oduro, "Church Music in the Life of African Christian Communities" in Roberta R. King, Jean Ngoya Kidula, James Krabill, and Thomas Oduro, *Music in the Life of the African Church* (Waco, Texas: Baylor University Press, 2008), 81-100.

12. Alan Merriam, *The Anthropology of Music* (Evanston: Northwestern University Press, 1964), 32-33.

13. See Roberta R. King, "Toward a Discipline of Christian Ethnomusicology: A Missiological Paradigm," *Missiology: An International Review* 32, no. No. 3 (2004).

14. Timothy J. Cooley, "Europe/Central and Southeastern Regions," in *Worlds of Music: An Introduction to the Music of the World's Peoples, Fifth Edition,* ed. Jeff Todd Titon (Belmont, CA: Schirmer Cengage Learning, 2009), 209.

15. Kay Kaufman Shelemay, *Soundscapes: Exploring Music in a Changing World,* 2nd ed. (New York: W. W. Norton & Company, 2006), 421.

16. From notes on the Larry Norman exhibit at the David Alan Hubbard library at Fuller Theological Seminary (Pasadena, CA), May-June 2011

17. Ibid. Additionally, "His songs have been translated into over a dozen languages and recorded by over 300 artists. Larry Norman's friends and fans included Bono, Frank Black, Malcolm Muggeridge, and Francis Schaeffer, among others."

18. Charles Fromm, *Textual Communities and New Song in the Multimedia Age: The Routinization of Charisma in the Jesus Movement, PhD Dissertation* (Pasadena: Fuller Theological Seminary, 2006).

19. Ibid., 346.

20. Ibid., 347.

21. See Roberta R. King, *Pathways in Christian Music Communication: The Case of the Senufo of Côte d'Ivoire,* American Society of Missiology Monograph Series (Eugene, OR: Pickwick Publications, 2009).

22. Ibid. In particular, see Figure 6: Transaction Music Communication (pp. 40-41) and Chapters 10 and 11 on the "Pathway of a Songs" (pp. 165-192).

23. These examples are not exhaustive of what is happening on the African continent. Similar reports are coming in from the Sudan, Cameroun (the Mafa people), the Maasai in Kenya and Tanzania, all-night *keshas* (prayer and song) in Nairobi, Kenya, and among the African Independent Churches such as has the Harrists in Côte d'Ivoire just to name a few.

24. Sooi Ling Tan, *Transformative Worship Among the Salako of Sarawak, Malaysia. PhD Dissertation.* (Pasadena: Fuller Theological Seminary, 2008).

25. Ibid., 187-89.

26. Ibid., 211-12.

27. Ibid., 217-34.

28. Arjun Appadurai, "Global Ethnoscapes: Notes and Queries for Transnational Anthropology," in *Recapturing Anthropology: Working in the Present.,* ed. R. G. Fox (Santa Fe, NM: School of American Research Press, 1991), 192.

29. Tan, *Transformative Worship Among the Salako of Sarawak, Malaysia. PhD Dissertation.*: 14.

30. Bruno Nettl, *The Study of Ethnomusicology: Thirty-one Issues and Concepts,* 2nd Edition ed., (Urbana: University of Illinois Press, 2005), 435.

31. Robb Redman, *The Great Worship Awakening: Singing a New Song in the Postmodern Church* (San Francisco, CA: Jossey-Bass, 2002).

32. Mark W. Lewis, *The Diffusion of Black Gospel Music in Postmodern Denmark: How Mission and Music are Combining to Affect Christian Renewal,* ed. J. Steven O'Malley, Asbury Theological Seminary Series in World Christian Revitalization Movements in Intercultural Studies (Lexington, KY: Emeth Press, 2010). This is an

excellent and astute study on the relationship between music and revitalization.

33. See Jean Ngoya Kidula, ""Sing and Shine": Religious Popular Music in Kenya" (University of California Los Angeles, 1998).

34. For a more thorough development see both Lewis, *The Diffusion of Black Gospel Music in Postmodern Denmark: How Mission and Music are Combining to Affect Christian Renewal.* and Kidula, ""Sing and Shine": Religious Popular Music in Kenya."

35. Brueggemann, *The Message of the Psalms: A Theological Commentary*: 21.

Chapter 9

Christian Revitalization and the Affirmation of Women in Church and Culture

MERCY AMBA ODUYOYE, MA
HONORARY DOCTORATE, YALE UNIVERSITY
DIRECTOR OF INSTITUTE OF
AFRICAN WOMEN IN RELIGION AND CULTURE
TRINITY THEOLOGICAL SEMINARY, GHANA

The hues and shades of Christianity in Ghana defy categorization. The coastal lands of call Ghana, have known Christianity since its introduction by the 15th century Portuguese merchant adventurers and their chaplains. The same applies to most of the coastal lands of Africa excluding the Mediterranean coast, which has nursed Christianity from its inception. Christianity took root on the west coast of Africa through the efforts of European missionaries. In this essay, I refer to the missionary inspired establishment of mainline churches as "Western Christianity," basing this name on the great divide of the church into Western Catholic and Eastern Orthodox. This almost uniformly western Christianity generated what became known as African Independent/Indigenous/Instituted Churches (The AICs). The AICs marked the beginnings of Christianity with a distinct flavor of African culture. This has been thoroughly documented by many scholars.

The AICs revitalized the impact of Christianity in Ghana as it did elsewhere in Africa. It became the Christianity that highlighted the presence of women in the church as prophets and founders of Christian congregations and churches. They were showcased for utilizing African cultural practices in their liturgies and music and forms of prayer. The leadership of women was lauded but always alongside very evident effects of a cultural glass ceiling. Generally speaking, women were more at home in these AIC churches than in the Western churches where their most positive agencies were in the guilds of women, like the Methodist Women's Fellowship that began in Ghana in 1931 and remains vibrant today.

In my opinion, the revitalization of Christianity that took Ghana, if not the world, by storm originated from the charismatic Christianity that erupted in Nigeria during the 1970s. The Deeper Life and other groups, founded as tertiary educational institutions, exemplified this spiritual eruption. This charismatic movement began by young men from the western churches who carried with them the ethos of western Christianity, excluding women in leadership. Still today, some argue against the ordination of women in the sacramental ministry. Hundreds of prayer groups and prayer camps sprouted into churches. These practices seeped into Western churches and their hallmark of deliverance ministry energized churches of all types. This very vibrant Christianity incorporates cultural beliefs and practices that affect all, both women and men, young and old, formally educated or otherwise.

Does this movement of Christianity affirm women in the church? Does it affirm women in the Ghanaian culture? I would like to use the yardstick of leadership as evidence of the affirmation of women in the church. Leading into this, let me underline some factors revitalizing Christianity in Ghana. The exponential growth of those who label themselves as Christians is evidenced by the proliferation of churches, prayer camps, open-air crusades, and conventions. The mass media, especially radio and television provide witness to this. Numerous CDs of sermons are readily available to be purchased and routinely played, not to mention the widespread "gospel music" frequently heard at traditional funerals and festivals. All of these practices evidence the vitality of Christianity in Ghana.

Incorporating current issues such as economic prosperity, peoples' fears and yearnings, their music, and their mother tongue prayers, produced a vibrant Christianity in Ghana. This Christianity enhanced the role of the spirit world, of witches, demons, and the devil. It awakened belief in ancestral curses, evidence of the power of the religious-cultural emphasis on communitarian links and legacy as undying- a sort of spiritual DNA that sets the children's teeth on edge when the fathers eat sour grapes. This removes personal responsibility for woes and places the worshipper in the hands of the deliverance minister who has power to break the ancestral curse and set individuals free to enjoy the prosperity ordained by God. This theology revitalized faith, drove many into the churches, and kept them there, portraying Christianity as a most energizing faith.

The people called Christians, irrespective of their type of church "fellowship," respond positively to the theological leadership and ministrations of church leaders. Anointing oil for healing and protection from evil, the calling down of blessings, and other various offerings are common practices. Exorcism in the name of Jesus and cleansing with water are popularly associated with deliverance. The revitalized Christianity asks people to alter their names if it is associated in any way with traditional deities or beliefs. "Positive" names are then created from religious concepts like blessing, thanksgiving, grace but using the mother tongue versions. Traditional ritual symbols undergo modification sometimes losing the essence of the intended symbolization. The main contention since the days of the Western missionaries has been the role and significance of ancestors in Ghanaian culture. All of these practices are areas of current research by theologians and sociologists; some are women. Women exist among the revitalization leadership as pastors, counselors, and initiators in charismatic communities.

The revitalized Christianity seemingly disregards the theological debates of the Early Church, the period of European enlightenment, and even the struggle to craft a relevant theology for the African context. The revitalized church thrives on song, dance, deliverance, counseling and empowerment, spiritual powers and manifestations, as well as miracles and overt signs of the efficacy of prayer and rituals. Those who study would rather focus on demonology than on theology.

The revitalized Christianity in Ghana seems to be an even more powerful example of control than western education with regard to effectively alienating Ghanaians from traditional African culture. What affirms women in the traditional culture is sidelined by westernization as it is by all forms of Christianity that have captured Africa. Leadership of women in the traditional religious, political, and social systems was dismissed, and the revitalized church used the centrality of marriage in the culture to preach and enforce submission of women not only to husbands, but to all men. The most obvious presence of women in revitalized Christianity is a figure of compliance.

Submissive Women

From my work place, I see clearly and hear loudly a prayer group that meets all morning under a mango tree from Monday to Friday. They may be there Saturday, Sunday, every evening, and in the night too, for that seems to be the pattern elsewhere. Mercifully, I am not around during these times to be forced into their experience.

I am still smarting under an experience I had when, out of solidarity and a real sense needing to be with my church community, I took part in a three-day revival service. I knew the pattern: the style of revival in my church included charismatic, anointed, miracle working" ministers. However, I never thought that the preacher would make his way to my seat in the middle of the congregation of nearly 150 women and men to hit me on the forehead with the palm of his hand! What for, I do not know, but I did not like the blatant invasion of my person with impunity. Apparently, this happens all the time at these gatherings. Whenever I narrate my experience, I get more examples of women whose space was invaded in this manner.

Under the mango tree at my work place, I have counted between eight and twenty women with two men whose leadership role is obvious from the call and response that emanate from their direction. These two men, I imagine, are earning their living as leaders of the group. I wonder about the women supporting these economic activities. To an observer, Christianity in Ghana is a religion in which women are the main clients and men the "service providers." What influences do these two male Christian leaders have on the women they so obviously control? In what way do they affirm women?

Although I lack research data, the experiences I share speak for themselves, and hopefully will assist you in deciding whether or not this type of Christianity empowers women. Let us examine what constitutes affirmation of women and the role of Christian revitalization in this process. I am using leadership roles as an index of affirmation. Another index is the ability and the space for one to take initiative. The inculcation of self-esteem, self-worth, and self-respect is also an index because one's contribution is both openly appreciated and carefully considered in deliberations of what affects the whole community.

Leadership

I would like to present the concept of leadership that informs my perspective on the subject at hand. To lead is to inspire the love for meaningful life and its attainment. A leader is a source of encouragement, and brings out the best in others such that they become achievers rather than just spectators, producers, and consumers. To lead is not merely to acquire subordinates, but rather to stimulate an empowering community. Leading is working to enable those around to overcome their shortcomings such as lack of skills and knowledge and the absence of self-worth. A leader is an originator: one from whom life-giving and life-enhancing words, deeds, and attitudes proceed to affirm and empower the whole community. A leader enables others to take control of their lives. Where God reigns, leaders are servants of their communities.

The leaders of contemporary Christianity in Ghana are the counselors, healers, deliverers, exorcists, wonder workers and preachers. Some of these leaders are found among churchwomen who also usually have high social profiles. More often however, the women leaders are usually those incorporated into the patriarchal system, having been selected according to criteria set by men regarding the measure of a good woman. In this way, the status quo is kept in tact and the ancient Roman *pater familias* and the Ghanaian patriarchal system keep their seats unruffled. Most of these leaders avoid discussion of systemic issues. They concentrate on personal salvation and prosperity: for women, this usually means having a husband and children, doing everything to keep them healthy and wealthy, even at the cost of impoverishing oneself and undermining one's health.

The leaders of contemporary Christianity in Ghana are not just the high profile TV preachers and crusade personalities. In addition is a whole host of assistants you have to go through to get to them. These "gate-keepers" exercise their own authority. Leaders of contemporary Christianity in Ghana include the

"Gospel Singers," men and women whose rhythm and rhyme ring in people's heads all day long. The influences of songs and sermons on tapes are not to be underestimated.

In the churches are several specialized organizations: interest groups with appointed leaders ensuring compliance not only with church codes but also with individual wellbeing. Some of these leaders are women and some are young people. All participants, from the founders of Christian communities to the lowest of the hierarchy, exercise authority according to church orders.

Once Jesus was asked, "By what authority do you do these things?" I want to examine this in relation to the role of authority and authoritative statements and action in the revitalized Christianity of Ghana.

Authority

All Christians have the Bible as their primary source of authority. The challenge is in how the Bible is read, interpreted, and utilized. Churches have distilled what is immediately applicable and, by tradition, have compiled usages and disciplines to guide their members. Some churches reserve the right to discipline their members who are recalcitrant or who default in their duties. The community's approval or disapproval has a powerful effect, as membership of the church is an integral part of the members' personal identity.

Churches have a way of demonizing beliefs they disagree with rather than allowing open dialogue to seek the truth. In Christianity, popular biblical texts and stories from the past ages and contexts are slapped on to the Ghanaian scene without any attempt to discover the universal truth they may embody. The Bible and denominational traditions are not the only source of authority for religious leaders. The beliefs and practices, values and mores of the cultures of Ghana constitute another source of authority. Religious leaders exploit this source. Where the source makes women the victims, religion often either actively promotes the cultural victimization or remains silent. Where there are religious underpinnings that leaders deem contrary to Christian faith and practice, they speak against or seek to change them without even consulting women.

Teaching Women Compliance

Let us now try to examine the methods used by leaders to influence women. What methods are used to get women to comply in such a way that they seem to participate happily in their own oppression? In my view, there is a lot of indoctrination that goes on in religious and cultural communities including churches. Indoctrination happens where there is no room for questions, debate, or dissension. There are very few opportunities for debating what leaders present. There are no debates, and selective readings of scripture aid this method. Those who ask questions or point out tension are frowned upon, and one quickly learns to say "hallelujah, amen" and clap when told to do so.

The church has a way of keeping women complacent by presenting them with the patriarchal image of the ideal woman. Idolizing marriage and procreation has had the effect of keeping women complacent. This, they are taught, is their "raison d'etre," and whatever hinders this state should be avoided else they have no honor. Thus, women go with the cultural stance that marriage is the glory of a woman, which has the effect of keeping women bound to those who pay for their livelihood. Women get the strongest affirmation from the revitalized Christianity, as from the culture, through motherhood and selfless service to the community.

In the church, excluding women from sacramental ministry and the practice of deliverance tells all women that they have no place in the arena of such leadership, rather leaving them solely responsible for the charitable works that the church as a whole should be minding.

Many Christians, especially women, are ceding their call to pray to professionals who are mostly male ordained ministers and pastors. In this way, women are kept as clients. What most leaders teach lacks sensitivity to injustice and discrimination having a negative effect on people's lives. They focus on personal well-being and charity to the incarcerated poor. All this is very laudable, but they keep women from recognizing their own incarceration. Women's participation in God's mission of justice and compassion is restricted to charitable works that women themselves often initiate and enjoy offering. Charitable works become a great source of affirmation and keep women very active in the churches.

The method of marshalling proof texts to support the subordination of women alienates women from leadership roles in the church. Weddings promote mainly the subordination of wife, while Paul teaches mutual submission of husband and wife. The emphasis on submission as working for one another's wellbeing is usually forgotten, whereas the cultural notion of submission as silencing, enslaving, and demeaning is highlighted. Viewing submission as worshipping the master smacks of idolatry, but this factor is ignored.

Some pastors have tried affirming women by the myth of Eve having been created from the rib of Adam. Their exegesis claims that Eve was not created from the head of Adam so she cannot be the boss, nor was she created from his foot, so she cannot be trampled. She was created from his side (rib) so the two could walk side by side. Beautiful as this imagery is, the counseling that accompanies it can hardly lead to the practice of partnership in marriage.

For a long time, churches used the strategy of controlling women by keeping them out of the study of religion, theology, and especially ministerial formation. The inadequate teaching offered to them from pulpits kept them gullible and disqualified them from leadership roles. The Bible Schools that are revitalizing theological education are open to all who can afford it, and many women avail themselves of this opportunity. They study with a view of becoming pastors in the charismatic–Pentecostal churches and some even start prayer groups that quickly become independent worshipping congregations. This church-planting success enables some women to distance themselves from the disempowering space of male-dominated churches. These female-led churches demonstrate that not all women succumb to the subordination indoctrination.

Women are not just empty vessels being filled with what religious leaders cook up. All women are not the same. Many who are discerning filter out the disempowering teachings of religious leaders in sermons and gospel songs.

Critical Responses of Women

How does all this impact women, and how do they respond to the influences of the revitalized Christianity of Ghana? First, generalizing about women is, itself, oppressive. Women are individual human beings who cannot be expected to respond to church leadership in the same way. Many who participate in uniformed churchwomen's groups demonstrate autonomy by pursuing their own special interests and concerns, and exercising leadership skills. Although denominational women's groups may be captive to denominational norms, the non-denominational groups like Aglow demonstrate women's leadership, perspectives, concerns, and methods. These non-denominational groups share empowering words that cultivate leadership and nurture the worth and power of individual women as unique daughters of God. They encourage women to believe and access the grace of God for themselves through prayer and appropriation of Bible study to their daily lives. They are more or less a "women's church" revitalizing Christianity to the advancement of women.

In 1989 African women in religion formed The Circle of Concerned African Women Theologians in response to the practice of excluding women from theological education, especially education offered at church institutions. The Circle of Concerned African Women Theologians covenanted to research, write, and publish on questions of religion and culture that effect women. If untaught persons cannot teach, they were going to ensure that they learn to write, speak and teach.

While the majority of these women theologians were not actively seeking ordination, they all made it known that they agreed with Keener's statement: "It is a dangerous thing to turn people from their call, or oppose their call if it is genuinely from God."[1] They read the Bible and studied its ancient cultures as well as their own African cultures. They made the latter their main field of specialization in order to offer relevant alternative interpretations that are liberating and empowering. Today there are many women teaching theology in African universities and elsewhere. Many are ordained and many more are living intentionally rather than complacently and compliantly.

In 1999 the Circle in Ghana created the Institute of Women in Religion and Culture to concretize this approach in Ghana. They located the project at Trinity Theological Seminary where several churches form their ministers. This was a deliberate move in order to accompany women as they seek to distill what is positive from the churches' teachings and its leaders' influences, whether through sermons or "gospel songs." Religious leaders teach, counsel, and even intimidate, but religious women have learned to skim and strain for what they

---

[1] Craig Keener, *Paul, Wives, and Women: Marriage and Women's Ministry in the Letters of Paul* (Grand Rapids: Baker Publishing Group, 1992), 120.

can use for self-empowerment and the affirmation of their humanity and talents. The Institute is set up to support churchwomen in this effort. It is often assumed that religion, as a whole, is a negative force in women's lives, however this is not an accurate assessment. Religion is a double-edged sword and women who follow Jesus' counsel to be as wise as serpents and docile as doves know how to make religion work for them. They can see through the leaders, both women and men, who are out to exploit and by the grace of God they are led to do God's will and not necessarily what pleases their leaders.

Women do discriminate, eliminating what they deem as negative influences while appropriating what works. Women know that they have to work out their own salvation and that, in the end, they stand before God as individuals to give account of their stewardship. It is no small claim to say, "I am made in the image of God. I have to exhibit creativity as one bringing into being what God can look upon and pronounce good." This is an affirmation seldom heard from street preachers of the revitalized Christianity sweeping Ghana, but it is always heard in "Women Aglow" meetings. Aglow- a women's prayer movement that is vigorously committed to Christianity, enthusiastically charismatic, and uses symbolisms in its preaching and praying- offers monthly national prayers on public television. It is one of the most women-affirming movements in Ghana, revitalizing not only Christian women but also the entire Christian community by drawing members from the whole spectrum of the Christians in Ghana. At times even Muslim women are amongst the vast crowd, especially when the focus is on praying for Ghana

Affirmation

Do the aforementioned examples demonstrate that the current revitalization of Christianity affirms women in the cultural sphere? The booming Christianity only affirms African culture to the extent that it provides a foil for its ministry of deliverance, its' preaching of economic prosperity, and abundance of human fertility, especially geared towards women. By looking at the aspects of culture that empower women we may be able to discern the role of the revitalized Christianity as it relates to women.

This Christianity is promoting a marriage culture that is different from the larger culture. African culture does not portray wives as attachments to husbands. These revitalized churches advertise conventions as being conducted by "Prophet and Mrs. ..." In some contexts, the wives are showcased as heads of the women's wing of the church in much the same way as did the traditional socio-political organizations. Women here may be co-founders of the church and hold key positions second to the husband's. Unlike the African culture, they promote marriage as between two persons, whereas the traditional culture encourages the participation of the natal families. Often the church community replaces the extended (natal) families in the lives of couples, putting the woman completely in the hands of the man. Whether this affirms the woman is debatable.

In the area of economic independence my sense is that women fare worse under the tutelage of this Christianity. The marriage enjoins community of property, but makes the husband the sole executor of how it is administration. This is contrary to the traditional matrilineal system in which there is no community of property between spouses and to the patrilineal in which the wife has no private property. It is therefore a mixed bag leaving women even less affirmed than does the traditional custom. It is attempts at national legislation that are moving women out of this morass. Yet even in this instance waking up the traditional religion has promoted the demonization of women and subjected many to deliverance from evil spirits. These evil spirits have allegedly been using women to secure the demise of their spouses so that these wives might inherit the property according to the national legislation.

An area affirming of women is their participation in the music industry. Traditional culture has many female singing groups that play their own instruments. They entertain themselves, perform at rites of passage, and are much appreciated for the interpretation of music into dance. The revitalization of Christianity appropriates this tradition and makes it possible for women to participate in keeping it vibrant. Some women become "celebrities" by singing their original Christian songs on television and radio. In Western Churches these new music groups are usually mixed and composed of young people using western music ensembles.

Conclusion

By now it has become obvious that I am struggling to glean aspects of the revitalized Christianity that affirm women. Women's very presence in these churches, far outnumbering men, indicates that they are being served by this mode of worship and the accompanying ministrations. There needs to be research that targets women to respond to this question. Once, a group of African women theologians visiting an afternoon service of a very vibrant Pentecostal-charismatic church in Ghana was given the privilege of asking questions during the service. Regardless the question, the pastor answered. On one occasion, in this majority-women congregation of over a thousand, such questions were raised: "Where are the men? Why is this place full of women?" The pastor's answer was "you know how this country is, it is women who have a lot of problems. Therefore, it is the women who need to be here." The question "Why is it only women who have problems?" was answered with a smile and the shaking of the head, and on that note the question and answer period came to an end. My response to the issue of "Christian" revitalization and the affirmation of women in church and culture of Ghana is the same: a smile and a shaking of the head.

Chapter 10

Lessons for Revitalization from the Broader, Missional Phenomenology of the Holy Spirit as Found in the Data

VELI-MATTI KÄRKKÄINEN, PHD
PROFESSOR OF SYSTEMATIC THEOLOGY
FULLER THEOLOGICAL SEMINARY

"Revitalization Movement is the work of the Holy Spirit."[1]

"Only the Holy Spirit can bring revival. It is the witness of the Spirit that makes Jesus known."

"The work of the Holy Spirit goes on whether we recognize it or not."

"The spirit of renewal takes vital forms of human relationships – enlivening old structures, fostering new relationships, converting people to Christianity, deepening us to the love of God, inspires authentic worship, enables/mobilizes the people of God for ministry/mission, meaning/purpose, creative future, hope/ healing, enabling people for human flourishing,"

Our theological and spiritual sensibilities testify to the intimate and robust relationship between the Holy Spirit and revitalization of the church and her mission. How else could it be? The *vita nova* (new life) brought by about the Creator Spirit and the constant re-*vita*lization of the church are the functions of the one and the same Divine Spirit. When speaking of the church, we are speaking of the community of him who was baptized with this same Spirit in the

Jordan and thereby empowered for the ministry of forgiveness, healing, freedom, and restoration – and indeed, of him who was finally raised up to new life through the power of his Father's Spirit. At the Day of Pentecost, the Risen One poured out his Holy Spirit "on all flesh" in accordance with the promises of the Holy Scriptures. This pouring out of the Spirit heralded the beginning of the End, in anticipation of the righteous rule of the Triune God.

Hence, as we reflect on the pneumatological resources, conditions, and implications of the revitalization of the church, we are not only looking at the daily, constant dependence of the community of Christ on the energizing, empowering, and sanctifying work of the Spirit, but we are also looking into the past as well as into the future. Behind the church is the work of creation. In front of the church is the coming eschatological fulfillment. The Triune God who is the only Lord of the Church, will manifest his faithfulness to his creation by redeeming and sanctifying the whole cosmos in the new creation; in this missionary movement the church is graciously invited to participate. The same resurrecting energy, mightily working in the life of the Resurrected Servant of the Lord, will constantly renew, revitalize, and re-equip the community of his followers.

With this wide, inclusive, and "cosmic" vision in mind, the discussions were formulating a most comprehensive "definition" of what revitalization may mean:

> Revitalization originates from and is rooted in the triune God; it takes place where people in specific (historical, cultural, social and spiritual) contexts experience God's enlivening and reawakening Spirit leading to a fresh encounter with the living Christ. This gives rise to repentance, new life, spiritual revival, healing, reconciliation, love, hope and holistic salvation. It often takes place amidst dissatisfaction with the status quo, vulnerability, suffering and pain, deep yearning, radical discipleship including persistent prayer, scripture study, worship and an unquenchable anticipation of God's renewing presence. It is the rejuvenated partnership of God and the people of God towards life, faith and justice. It is the prophetic impulse for social and spiritual transformation in every generation.

Significantly this "definition"[2] reminds us of the particularity of the work of the Spirit. One doesn't have to subscribe to any particular type of post-/late-modern epistemology to be warned of the universalizing tendency of modernity that leads to abstract notions of the Spirit. True, the Spirit of God is universally present, there is not one "square inch" where the divine Spirit is not to be found (to paraphrase the famous Kuyperian slogan). That however does not mean that therefore, the Spirit's ministry in, for, and through the church would be the same everywhere and at all times. The Spirit of God is particular, "contextual," sensitive to difference and to the Other. Thus, the experience of the Spirit is deeply personal even when its reverberations flow into the community and other peoples' lives. The Spirit's enlivening, releasing, reconciling, and restoring energies are being experienced in ever new ways in new occasions and in response to various needs. This kind of Spirit-created sensitivity to the specific, particular needs of the people of the suffering of the world will guide the church to follow in the footsteps of her Master. Significantly, in one of the group reflections an important saying from the Vatican II document *Gaudium et Spes* (Pastoral Constitution on the Church in the World) came to our minds: "The joys and hopes, the grief and anguish of the people of our time, especially of those who are poor or afflicted, are the joys and hopes, the grief and anguish of the followers of Christ as well" (# 1).

The particular, specific ministry of the Spirit also means that there is no set formula of revitalization, nothing like "one size fits all"; rather, all church forms, structures, and traditions may be renewed, refreshed, revitalized:

> Revitalization is possible in every ecclesial structure that exists. Whatever model we employ the community is called to ongoing discernment of the Spirit that promotes conversion inspired by repentance, lament, and self-denial. Such renewal provokes radical opposition, demonic activity, and fear. A revitalized model provides the possibility for the appropriation of the gifts of the Spirit that is context specific and person relative. Renewal fits into a complex cycle of life that stretches back to Abraham and Sarah and spans the history of the Church.

Hence, we also discovered that "Revitalization is a common ground term that allows for inclusion of Catholic and Orthodox as a well as Protestant mainline, evangelical and Pentecostal."

What is also striking about the "definition" above is that it rightly breaks the artificial boundaries between "spiritual" and "earthly" tasks of the church, say, between prayer and work for justice. This artificial and counterproductive dichotomy between the "spiritual" and "secular" must be resisted. It does not belong to the divine economy. The work for the poor and marginalized is as much "spiritual" work in the eyes of the Lord as the work in proclamation and sacraments; they are just different ways of serving the cause of the Head of the Body. Hence, true revitalization and renewal is related to the "heart of the tradition" but is not limited to it: "Renewal [happens] in the heart of the tradition – but [is] also found most profoundly in the poor and marginalized of society – a profound conversion that responds to God's work among the poor.... Is revitalization most profoundly seen in and among the poor? ...Do the poor have a special privilege to access to the truth about God? " And: "Worship among the poor bring us an efficacious presence that cannot be found in any other way – a distance made of access by the poor."

The Spirit of God is not only the Lord of the spiritual but also as much of social and political. Neither in Hebrew nor in Greek is the idea of the "spirit" (*ruach*; *pneuma*, respectively) limited to what the post-Enlightenment Western culture thinks of in relation to the term "Spirit" or, even worse, "Ghost"! Those connotations imply something abstract, esoteric, numinous. In the Old Testament the Spirit of God is the life-giving vitality. Spirit in the Bible is "grounded" rather than numinous, "concrete" rather than abstract, "particular" rather than generic. Speaking of the *ruach Yahweh*, the Psalmist makes this robust statement:

> When thou hidest thy face, they are dismayed; when thou takest away their breath [*ruach*], they die and return to their dust.

When thou sendest forth thy Spirit [ruach], they are created; and thou renewest the face of the ground. (104:29-30 RSV)

In keeping with this biblical horizon, this delightful and bold statement was formulated as yet another "definition" of what revitalization may mean:

It is finished! Comprehensive renewal of all creation has already occurred by the act of the Father in the life, death, and resurrection of the incarnate Son by the Spirit. The Church's revitalization is participation in that reality as gift and promise, through the life of the Spirit, now.

These biblical and theological considerations inspired us to consider the role of the environment and ecology in a Christian vision for revitalization of the church. If we take seriously the biblical insight that all life is the function of the Divine Spirit and that the same Spirit will "renew the face of the" earth, that relationship seems to be obvious. We were wondering if "There has been an overemphasis on the atonement while we sideline creation," and asked, "Do revitalization movements contribute anything to the distressed earth?"

An important aspect of the Spirit's revitalizing ministry has to do with charisms, spiritual gifts, and the charismatic structure of the church. One of the reasons why the church in the twentieth century has come to a more profound appreciation of the charismatic element is the rise and continuing proliferation of the Pentecostal/Charismatic movements. Their vitality, vigor, and missionary expansion – although at first resisted by other churches as yet another form of "enthusiasm" – is a living testimony to the significance of yearning for and opening up for numerous kinds of gifting and energies brought about the Spirit. That aspect of the Spirit's ministry was of course known already in the First Testament. In the lives of judges, prophets, and some other heroes, the capacities and limitations of mere human gifting were surpassed by the miraculous powers of the Spirit.

Christ, the Anointed One, was not only a master Teacher but also an itinerant healer and exorcist. In anticipation of the coming to existence of the church, even before pouring out of the Spirit, he sent the disciples to preach, heal, and release people from under the powers. In the power of the Pentecostal pouring out the Spirit, the newly founded church spread the gospel even to the "ends of the earth" under the mighty empowering of the Holy Spirit. The promise in the beginning of the book of Acts was fulfilled in the life of the apostolic church (1:8): "But you shall receive power when the Holy Spirit has come upon you; and you shall be my witnesses in Jerusalem and in all Judea and Sama'ria and to the end of the earth." We came to the conclusion that the church at large could well take a lesson from Pentecostalism in this respect. Said one of us at the consultation: "I cannot see a deeply renewed church without harvesting the developments in the Pentecostal stream – that is the assignment of the next fifty year project!"

One of the lessons to be learned from Pentecostals – as well as from the early church of the book of Acts – is the importance of evangelism and reaching out. The role of evangelism in church life, or lack thereof, was seen in the deliberations both as a continuing challenge and an issue to be carefully reflected upon. Merely getting new members, "evangelizing" them and adding to church numbers, hardly earns the name of revitalization. On the other hand, many of our churches, we fear, have lost the kind of expansive, evangelistic orientation that seems to be typical of times of renewal and revitalization. We heard testimonies from African contexts in which Christians in many churches, whether traditional or younger communities, have incorporated everyday evangelism and "soul-winning" as part of their renewed life. "When the Spirit moves it pushes people out of their comfort zones." Thinking of the book of Acts, we were also reminded of the fact that at times the evangelistic impulse was so fervent as to elicit opposition, even persecution. "Revival does not only happen among Christians. Even non-Christians were touched by the move of the Spirit." This still happens in many parts of the world among Christians, for example in India. What about us who live in the comfort and abundance of the Global North? Are we willing any more to suffer anything for the gospel? As one of us pointedly noted, we Westerners have to be reminded of the fact that the "Spirit was not given to the church for her entertainment." When observing the life of many churches in affluent the United States and Europe, one wonders if entertainment rather than service and suffering for Christ has taken the foremost place in the minds and hearts of Christian men and women.

Yet another area in the life of the church that has everything to do with revitalization and mission is the Spirit's charismatic endowment of leadership. Several of us gave testimonies to the fact that "When spirit arises people come into leadership from children, youth – spirit inspired leadership." In the book of Acts the leadership-oriented function of the charismatic Spirit is evident in various places and moments. On the one hand, the first church leaders were men and women of the Spirit, and on the other hand, the church at every critical juncture of the missionary expansion looked upon the Spirit as the ultimate leader. In the life of the first Christian church focusing on "foreign" mission, this model came to the fore in a most wonderful way:

> While they were worshiping the Lord and fasting, the Holy Spirit said, "Set apart for me Barnabas and Saul for the work to which I have called them."
>
> Then after fasting and praying they laid their hands on them and sent them off.
>
> So, being sent out by the Holy Spirit, they went down to Seleu'cia; and from there they sailed to Cyprus. (Acts 13:2-4)

Similarly, the Apostle Paul's missionary team was willing to change plans as "the Spirit of Jesus did not allow them" to follow their first instincts but rather led their way to Europe (Acts 16:9).

With all of these testimonies to the Spirit's presence and power before us, we were led to ask the obvious question: Why are many churches, ours included, often not experiencing the revitalizing presence and power of the Holy Spirit? We reflected on that issue time after time in our deliberations and did not even imagine being able to give any kind of conclusive answer. Who could? One of the reasons, however, that we thought might be an answer to this question is the lack of yearning for the Spirit. It seems that there is often a connection between a deep, sincere, sustained hunger for the Spirit and the Spirit's gracious, manifested presence among the community. If nothing else, the yearning for the Spirit expresses the humble confession by men and women of the dearth of our own resources. Daily dependence and prayer for the coming of the Spirit over and over again over the community of Christ is a statement about how deeply we are in need of the Divine Spirit. As one of us put it succinctly: "Prior to experiencing revitalisation there must be revival before revitalization." Revival means coming to an end of our own capacities, repentance from everything that hinders the Lord from working his purposes in our lives, and openness to every new resource and opportunity. That kind of revived church may be open to something else we also thought might be important: "open vision," vision that knows no limits and is not conditioned by our own limitations. Open-ended vision best facilitates "a context that promotes questions that leads to new possibilities."

When and if the Lord of the Church graciously grants us the times of refreshment and so helps us respond to our calling, at no point is the church in a place to think that her manifold ministries and capacities would come from her own resources. Even less is there ever an occasion for the church to congratulate herself for excellence. The fountain of vitality, energy, and patience to follow Christ comes from the Spirit: "an authentic revitalization movement will bring the Church to acknowledge its own poverty. Through the power of the Spirit such a movement will enable the Church to bring the liberating presence of Christ for the healing of human brokenness." Those who are able to bring healing and restoration to the suffering ones are usually men and women who have experienced weakness and brokenness in their own lives. The self-righteous and haughty are seldom used by the Spirit of God to lift up those who are heavy-hearted or down-stricken. The followers of Christ should always keep in mind afresh the apostolic promise: "Likewise the Spirit helps us in our weakness; for we do not know how to pray as we ought, but the Spirit himself intercedes for us with sighs too deep for words" (Rom 8:26). Even the possession and exercise of spiritual gifts is no reason to boast. Indeed, as it dawned on us in the conversation, when we speak of a charism as miraculous as *glossolalia*, speaking in tongues, it is also a "deconstructing force, sign of the death of the subject." The Spirit is speaking, through the Christian, mysteries to God.

Notes

1. Note: the citations in this paper are taken from the unpublished summary of the data from consultation two table conversation, dated May 28-June 2, 2010.

2. The reason the term "definition" is in quotation marks is obvious: it is not given to us to come up with any kind of closed "definition" of the manifold and mysterious work of the Spirit who *ubi vult spirat* (John 3:8; "blows where it wills").

Part 3

How the Past Shapes the Present

Chapter 11

Discovering Lost Stories - A Driving Force for Revitalization or Idolatrous Imprisonment? A Case Study of Mizo Revivals in Northeast India

LALSANGKIMA PACHUAU, PhD
DEAN OF ADVANCED RESEARCH PROGRAMS AND ASSOCIATE PROFESSOR OF THE HISTORY AND THEOLOGY OF MISSION, ASBURY THEOLOGICAL SEMINARY

Revivals, Renewals, and the History of Christianity

The topic of this chapter begs a historiographical reflection on revitalization or renewal movements in Christian history. We are constrained to ask the treatment of revival or revitalization movements in Christian history. Given their importance in the life and growth of Christian communities, what roles have historians assigned to revival movements in their historical accounts of Christianity? How important are these movements in the minds of historians? In recent years, we are witnessing to a surging interest due largely to their roles in the emerging new Christian communities in the global South and East. For a long time in modern historical accounts, revivalists are seen as fringe groups and revival movements are either marginalized or trifled.

A recent article in *the New York Times* provides us with a helpful introduction to the subject matter we are considering. It is a story of the recollection of the once-forgotten riot of 1921 in Tulsa Oklahoma, which the article termed as "what may be the deadliest occurrence of racial violence in United States history."[1] So brutal was the episode, it says, "that this city, in a bout of collective amnesia that extended more than a half-century, simply chose to forget it ever happened." The story, as "unearthed by historians" a decade ago, revealed that an estimate of "300 people were killed and more than 8,000 left homeless."[2] It is reported that "The riot will be taught for the first time in Tulsa public schools next year but remains absent in many history textbooks across the United States."[3]

Changes in social attitude toward particular matters, incidents or issues often lead to changes in the writing of, or the importance given to their history. When high school history textbooks in China were revised in 2006, the changes reflect a radical shift to the new economic reform. Reporting a new High School history book, a reporter wrote, "Socialism has been reduced to a single, short chapter in the senior high school history course. Chinese Communism before the economic reform that began in 1979 is covered in a sentence. The text mentions Mao only once — in a chapter on etiquette."[4] We are witnessing to a major shift in global historiography. From colonial historiography to nationalist historical writings, historians in many formerly colonized nations have moved on to postmodern, subaltern and postcolonial historical methods.[5] The history of the writing of Christian revivals and renewal movements seem to be following the same pattern. Much of the renewal movements that enlivened Christianity in history have either been ignored or overshadowed by other stories. In much of their appearances in historical accounts, they are often over-rationalized to the extent that their true characters were lost in the accounts.

Discovery of vital stories of the past has the potential of recovering strength and vitality in the present. Such revitalization then changed the course of history. In Western history, the renaissance movement of the 15th to 17th centuries, for instance, typifies what it meant to be renewed by the recovery of the past. As Lucy Wooding has rightly stated, "The Renaissance was, broadly speaking, a movement of cultural revival which sought to rediscover and redeploy the languages, learning and artistic achievements of the classical world."[6] While there can be romanticization of the past, it is the strength of the past that paves new ways for the future. Classics came into being through rekindling of interest in past glories. In this sense the potentiality of future glories is hidden in how one makes use of the past. Reflecting on the New Prophecy movement otherwise called Montanism, Howard Snyder draws some essential characteristics of Christian renewal movements the first of which is the importance of the "recovery of an earlier dynamic, or for 'better times' in the life of the church." He states, "This is how renewal movements arise. A perception grows that the church has declined from its early purity or power, and that somehow the vitality and perhaps the patterns of the early church must be recovered. This is often called 'primitivism': the wish to recover the vitality of the early (or primitive) church."[7] Stressing the work of the Holy Spirit in the present times, such movements then try to turn the church into a dynamic radical community to the extent of being countercultural. Tension with institutional leadership and existing conventional patterns becomes inevitable. The church's capacity to absorb the new movement and its ability to maintain creative tension between institutional order and the renewal innovations often proved to be the strengthening of the church.

One can argue that the Protestant Reformation initiated by Martin Luther was largely rooted in, and spawned by, the Renaissance movement. More than anything else, it was the sense of recovery of the original (biblical) faith that connects the Renaissance and the Reformation characteristically. Its claim of recovering the biblical faith and a new sense of spiritual connectedness with the early church was a chief feature of the Reformation. By recovery, however, we should also quickly point out that every process of such recovery for new life involves reinterpretation and re-appropriation. A combination of change and continuity, even in tensed condition, are necessary characteristics of history.

If renewal of Christianity through personal faith in the Reformation was dwindled by the emergent Protestant scholasticism, the recovery of personal faith and spirituality was the centerpiece of the Pietist movement. As much as the Reformation claimed renewal of Apostolic faith and thus gave birth to a new faith tradition, Pietism attempted to recover what was being lost from the Reformation in the course of the next century. Because of its renewing role of modern Western Christianity and its pioneering part in the modern missionary movement, the Pietist movement carved out a place for itself in modern Christian history. Similarly, the Evangelical Revival also came to occupy a similar place in Christian history in connection with the founding of Methodism by John Wesley. If not for the new denomination instituted, the revival itself (called the Evangelical Revival) would not have been accounted for in history. The emphases on the institutional contribution overshadow the spiritual revival aspect of Wesley and Methodism as much as the rationalized versions of Pietist accounts eclipse the renewing dimension of the movement.

Several factors may account for the neglect of revivals by Christian historians. Broadly speaking, the influence of the Enlightenment with its unwavering emphasis on human rationality seemed to be a major root-cause for the sidelining of the revival accounts. Because the revivals claim the mysterious work of God's Spirit which is unexplainable to the human reasoning faculty, they tend to stay outside the rationally-driven mainline historical accounts. At the heart of the issue is the difficulty in rationalizing the mystery of the Holy Spirit. Protestant Christianity in the age of the Enlightenment slipped into the disuse of the power of the Holy Spirit. A nineteenth century German New Testament scholar David Friedrich Strauss called the doctrine of the Holy Spirit, "the Achilles heel of Protestantism."[8] Most Protestant theologians seemed to prefer a rationalized doctrine of the Holy Spirit, and some such as B. B. Warfield, go so far as propounding "a cessationist viewpoint." If not for great revival leaders such as John Wesley, George Whitefield and Jonathan Edwards, and especially their stresses on the experience of the Holy Spirit, the church's doctrine of the Holy Spirit would stay merely as a theoretical doctrine, and not as an empowering source for Christian life.[9]

If the nineteenth century was to be remembered as the "Great Century" of world missions, the twentieth century may be remembered for the ecumenical movement and the rise of worldwide Christianity. The first half of the century was occupied by the story of missionary cooperation and the beginning of the ecumenical movement, whereas the second half witnessed the tremendous growth of Christianity in the global South and East. If one is to characterize this sprouting Christianity in the non-western regions which Philip Jenkins dubbed as a new "Christendom," the most common factor is the charismatic nature of Christianity. A number of Pentecostal scholars have identified this rise of non-western charismatic Christianity to Pentecostal movement that came out of Azusa Street revival of 1906.[10] As important as Azusa Street revival was for the rise of Pentecostalism, a number of historians have come to recognize what may be called sporadic revival movements in the first two decades of the twentieth century around the world. While the Pentecostal movement successfully capitalized on these movements, there are other lines of development. The remainder part of this paper will trace one of these lines, namely the line of development from the Welsh revival to India's northeast state of Mizoram. Recovering this little-known story[11] may help us in uncovering new characteristic of revitalization movements.

It is logical to think of revival or renewal as something experienced by Christians who have slumbered in their spiritual life. Perhaps, it is the prefix "re" (meaning "anew") that naturally lead to this understanding. It is, however, the same phenomenon experienced as "revival" in the West that leads to the conversion of many in the global South and East during the recent past. In the African continent alone, from the story surrounding the works of William Wade Harris in western Africa in the second decade of the twentieth century, that of Simon Kimbangu in the third decade in Congo, and such other movements as the Methodist revival from 1918 in Rhodesia (now Zimbabwe), East African revival in the 1930s and others, we have seen great revivals leading to scores of conversion from non-Christian religion to Christianity. Among several such examples to be cited in Asia include those in Korea in 1907 and Western India in 1905, the recurring revival movements among the Mizo people is now a century old.

The Case of the Mizo Revivals

With an official census record showing 86.97 percent of the state population as Christian, the state of Mizoram (or land of the Mizos) is the second most Christianized state in India. As most historians have shown, Mizo Christianity is the product of a series of revivals. While most agree that revivals characterized Mizo Christianity, whether the revival is a single movement or a series of movements has been debated. Some use the term "waves" and "stirrings" to describe the high tides of the movements, while others describe them as different movements recurring at different times in different places. The Mizoram Presbyterian Church published a volume on revival (or "*Harhna*" in Mizo) in 2006 to commemorate the centennial of the first or beginning of the revival movement in 1906.[12] The volume identifies 16 major revival occurrences among the Mizos, two of which are outside of Mizoram. Seven of the 14 in Mizoram are regional while the remaining seven touched in one way or another people of all regions within the state.

It is customary to name the first-four waves (1906 -, 1913 -, 1919 -, 1930s) as the first, the second, the third, and the fourth revival consecutively. No other subsequent wave is named the fifth, and the first-four are considered historical. Some historians concluded that after the fourth in the 1930s, the revival never really died down in Mizoram, and therefore, the fourth may be said to be continuing with several high tides until today. One significant outcome of these four waves is that it helped to convert the entire Mizo community to Christianity. New converts came in scores during each of the four and the third wave was particularly known for the rapid increase in new converts.[13] By the 1950s, all the Mizos are considered to have converted to Christianity.

What do the Mizos mean by 'revisit' (or *harhsa* in Mizo, which is most accurately translated as 'awakening')? Mizo historian Vanlalchhuanawma's descriptive definition captures the people's understanding of revival quite well. He said, the term "refers to a phenomena [sic] marked by a state of excitement accompanied by enthusiastic activities of singing, body movements, preaching and even social action."[14] It is an expression of spiritual joy conveyed in singing and dancing to the accompaniment of the drums. From the third revival, we began to see "new songs" in new indigenous tunes accompanied by dancing. The first Christian use of traditional drums was also dated around the same time. At the heart of these new singing of praises is the communal character of the revival movement. The new songs and dance are understood to be performed corporately.

Some of the chief characteristics of Mizo revivals may be identified as historical lessons of revivals from the experience of a non-western Christianity. We will use these features as point of reference to further recount the story of Mizo revivals.

The Significance of the Holy Spirit in the Spiritually-Centered Worldview of the Mizo people

Like many non-Western societies of today, the Mizo worldview continues to be spiritually-centered. The hold of a traditional spirit worldview in which the world is believed to be peopled by multitude of benevolent and malevolent spirits is strong. The line between natural and supernatural is blurred in this worldview and the belief in the mysterious activities of the spirits in the life here and now is strong. In such a context, acceptance of the empowering presence and activities of the Holy Spirit is not only sensible, but received as foundational to human existence. The success and recurrence of the revival movement among the Mizos as well as many non-Western societies is to be located in this worldview which is less influenced (or less tainted) by the rationally-driven worldview of western civilization.[15]

Revival Movements as Inculturating Agencies

In a typical Mizo Protestant church service (of most denominations) today, a mix of western hymns and indigenous tunes (revival songs) are sung to the beat of traditional drums. Each church building has a set of two drums. While the larger of the two drums is used to accompany western hymns, the two drums are used together for indigenous revival songs. Most indigenous revival hymn singings are accompanied by simple revival dance as expression of spiritual joy. These three indigenous symbols of Mizo Christianity are products of revival movements. Their acceptance and use in the church had taken years in process, and most western missionaries did not accept the drums in the church until the last missionary left the state in the late 1960s.

The first revival among the Mizos (beginning in 1906) came as an extension of the Welsh revival of 1904-5 through similar movement in the Khasi hills of Northeast India. Christians seemed to have borrowed expressions of their spiritual joy from the Khasi and the missionaries and the characters appeared to be imported ones. The manner of dancing as an expression of spiritual delight and ecstasy began to change from the second wave and by the third wave in the early 1920s it had dramatically changed. Singing at the beat of the drum accompanied by corporate dancing in circle began which can be traced to indigenous practices at the time. From the fourth wave, any mention of revival includes the new revival songs, the native drums, and the revival dance.[16]

Tension between Church Leadership and Revival Enthusiasts

Beginning with the third revival, tension began to develop between missionaries and some native church leaders on the one hand, and revival enthusiasts on the other hand. In fact, the disagreement on the use of drum and the disliking of the new songs in some circles were to be traced from here. The fourth revival (from the 1930s) was known for its excessive characters and divisive outcome. Strangeness and the mysterious characters of the Holy Spirit seemed to be confused. There were several strange "manifestations" of the Spirit recorded. The highhanded attempt to control the movement by the missionary-controlled church leadership was responded negatively by some revivalists. As a result, a major division was experienced through which the first Pentecostal Church among the Mizos came into being. The division continued and multiplied new groups and denominations while the large majority of revivalists continued to remain within the mission churches. What Howard Snyder termed "institutional/charismatic tension"[17] seems to be relevant to a western-orderliness/indig enous-spirituality tension. Revivalists who are also loyal to mission churches adhered to the leadership demand for orderliness and the "messy" revival expressions in tension. In the long run, there developed a creative tension between the institutional orderliness and the less-organized revival characters of indigenous spirituality that both enliven and sustain the church.

In the new global Christian setting, the historical experience of Christians in the global South and East may have lessons to pass to Christians in the West. Among the lessons are the call to be open to the reality and empowering presence of the Holy Spirit and the Spirit's work in interweaving Gospel and culture while leaving cultural and civilizational orderliness in tension with the open-ended "messiness" of that work.

Notes

1. A. G. Sulzberger, "As Survivors Dwindle, Tulsa Confronts Past," *The New York Times*, June 19, 2011 (http://www.nytimes.com/2011/06/20/us/20tulsa.html?_r=1&emc =eta1 accessed June 20, 2011)

2. Ibid.

3. Ibid.

4. Joseph Kahn, "Where's Mao? Chinese Revise History Books," *The New York Times*, September 1, 2006 (http://www.nytimes.com/2006/09/01/world/asia /01china.html?th&emc=th, accessed July 2, 2010).

5. For a good discussion on recent global historiographical shifts, see Iggers, Georg G., Q. Edward Wang, and Supriya Mukherjee. *A Global History of Modern Historiography*. Harlow, England: Pearson Longman, 2008.

6. Lucy Wooding, "Christian Humanism: From Renaissance to Reformation," *History Review* 64 (September 2009): 14.

7. Howard Snyder, *Signs of the Spirit: How God Reshapes the Church* (Eugene, OR: Wipf and Stock Publishers, 1997), 24.

8. Quoted in George S. Hendry, *The Holy Spirit in Christian Theology* (Philadelphia: Westminster Press, 1956), 2.

9. For a discussion on the tension between cessationist theology and the revivalist theology of the Holy Spirit, see Timothy C. Tennent, *Theology in the Context of World Christianity* (Grand Rapids: Zondervan, 2007), 170-177.

10. For instance, see Jack W. Hayford, *The Charismatic Century: The Enduring Impact of the Azusa Street Revival* (New York, Boston, Nashville: Warner Faith, 2006).

11. Not only is this line of revival movements missing from such recent studies as Mark Shaw's (*Global Awakening*, IVP, 2010), the infrequent mention of the influence of Welsh Revival of 1904-1905 stopped with the movement in Khasi hills and the movements among the Mizo people are ignored.

12. R. L. Thanmawia et al., eds. *Harhna: Mizoram Revival Centenary Souvenir* (Aizawl: Synod Revival Committee, 2006).

13. For detailed discussion of this point, please see Lalsangkima Pachuau, *Ethnic Identity and Christianity: A Socio-historical and Missiological Study of Christianity in Northeast India with Special Reference to Mizoram* (Frankfurt am Main: Peter Lang, 2002), 71-81.

14. Vanlalchhuanawma, *Christianity and Subaltern Culture: Revival Movement as a cultural Response to Westernization in Mizoram* (Delhi: ISPCK, 2006), 1.

15. For further discussion, see Lalsangkima Pachuau, "Mizo Sakhua in Transition: Change and Continuity from Primal Religion to Christianity," *Missiology:An International Review* 34 (January 2006): 51-53.

16. For a detailed analytical discussion of this point, see Pachuau, *Ethnic Identity and Christianity*, 131-141.

Chapter 12

Christian Theological Constructs and Revitalization in Africa

J. Kwabena Asamoah-Gyadu, PhD

Vice President and professor of Religion and Pentecostal Studies, Trinity Theological Seminary, Ghana

The history of Christianity in Africa south of the Sahara has within the last century, been a history of a series of revitalizations both within and without existing church traditions. The first reactions to Christianity of the Western missionary kind occurred towards the end of the twentieth century when certain African Christian elites protested against the administrative dominance of white missionaries over church life. David Vincent Brown of the Niger Delta, a pioneer in this endeavor, seceded from the foreign Baptist mission churches to form his own Native Baptist Church at the end of the nineteenth century. He demonstrated his revulsion against Western European hegemonies in the church in Africa by symbolically dropping his 'foreign' name for a more indigenous one and so became known as Mojola Agbebi. The church he went on to found took to the vernacular in the expression of Christianity and his initiative was replicated throughout the sub-region of West Africa including Ghana. Here, a Methodist Minister, the Rev. Samuel Solomon also became known as Attoh Ahumah. He went on to form the Christ's Little Band within the Church, a movement that is still dedicated to the singing of vernacular songs/lyrics in the Methodist Church Ghana. Ghana's Nigritian Church was formed through the inspiration of Agbebi and Ahumah. Nationalist churches, as these initiatives came to be known were significant but they never became as mass movement because, in principle, they pursued the same theological agenda as the Western mission churches.

Christian Revitalization and Oral Theology

This chapter pays attention to the second major response to missionary Christianity in Africa, and that is, the formation of independent churches with a pneumatic character. I will give a brief history of Christian independency in sub-Saharan Africa and discuss those theological constructs that gave Christian revitalization its unique African character. One of the most important theological contributions that these independent churches have made the reconstruction of Christian theology in Africa, for example, is the attention they have drawn to the importance of oral or grassroots theology. In contrast to systematically documented and articulated theology, oral or grassroots theology comes from the living experiences of people. It is expressed through spontaneous sermons and prayer, through locally composed choruses, and through those testimonies that may be described as outflows of relationship with God in Jesus Christ. Oral theology testifies to the power of God as experienced in healing, protection and deliverance. Ghanaian theologian Kwame Bediako in the following statement talks about the significance of oral theology:

> We ought to speak positively of oral, spontaneous, implicit or grassroots theology, as a theology which comes from where the faith lives, in the life situation of the community of faith. Accordingly this grassroots theology is an abiding element of all theology, and therefore one that is essential for academic theology to be in touch with, to listen to, to share in, and to learn from—but never to replace.[1]

The story of Christian revitalization in Africa, the sources of oral theology, properly began with the African independent/initiated churches (AICs) from the early years of the twentieth century. These were the first indigenous mass movements with a clear Christian orientation in Africa. The AICs known in Ghana as 'Spiritual' churches and in Nigeria as 'Aladura' (people of prayer) churches changed the theological face of Christianity in Africa with their pneumatic orientation to the faith.

Within the first decade of the twentieth century indigenous itinerant prophets burst onto the Christian scene of the West Africa sub-region and gathered large followings through dramatic conversions mainly from African traditional religions to embrace Christianity of a certain kind. The leading prophets in these endeavors were Garrick Sokari Braide of the Niger Delta, Joseph Babalola also of Nigeria, William Wadé Harris of Liberia and Simon Kimbagu of the Congo, if one is to include Central Africa. As David Shank has argued, these prophets did not appear essentially as opponents of the White Western missions but indeed rather as authentic African efforts to take to their own people 'a de-westernized, African appropriated Christian message in contrast to that of institutional missions.'[2] They denounced the worship of local idols and in their ministries, demonstrated the power of God to heal and deliver from the demonic by invoking the name of Jesus and the cleansing power of the Holy Spirit. The 'blood of Jesus' that we read so much about, especially in the book of Hebrews, was upheld as superior to the blood of goats and calves that African's were used to using in their sacrifices. To that end the movements of Christian revitalization that were born out of the evangelizing efforts of these indigenous prophets were, theologically speaking, qualitatively different, from the work of the Nationalist churches. The sorts of theological constructs arising out of the Christian orientation and religious discourses of the AICs are what we want to delineate and examine in this chapter.

Revitalization and the Edinburgh Conference

At the Edinburgh 1910 World Missions Conference it had been feared that Africa would develop as an Islamic continent. When the Conference reconvened in 2010, it was clear that sub-Saharan Africa had already become overwhelmingly Christian. How did this happen?

- First and foremost, by the middle of that century, most historic mission denominations had come under African leadership leading to major strides in Christian mission.

- Second, the translation of the Scriptures into the vernacular had facilitated the spread of the gospel led by such indigenous clergymen as Bishop Samuel Ajayi Crowther of the Niger Delta Mission fame.

- Third, the various streams of pneumatic movements, beginning with the older African independent churches (AICs), have, since the early years of the twentieth century, helped sub-Saharan Africa to defy the odds by gradually developing into a major heartland of Christianity.

Prophets William Wadé Harris and Garrick Sokari Braide of West Africa, Isaiah Shembe of South Africa, Simon Kimbangu of Central Africa, and several other such charismatic prophets had led masses of people to abandon traditional gods in favor of the worship of the God and Father of the Lord Jesus Christ. This is what Ogbu Kalu had to say about the work of the prophets in relation to the rise of modern Pentecostalism:

> These prophets tilled the soil on which modern Pentecostalism thrives. They were closer to the grain of African culture in their responses to the gospel and so felt the resonance between the charismatic indigenous worldviews and the equally charismatic biblical worldview. In 1910, the year that European missionary leaders gathered in a conference on The Mound, Edinburgh, to map the future of mission in Africa and the rest of the world, Wade Harris trekked from Grebo Island through the Ivory Coast to the Gold Coast baptizing, healing, teaching new choruses, and charismatizing the religious landscape. The charismatic fire that he lit became more important for the future of Christianity in Africa than the grand Edinburgh Conference of 1910 that shut out African voices.[3]

The result of the ministries of these prophets was the rise of the independent church movement, some of which even began to use militaristic idioms to describe their mission. This includes the Musama Disco Christo Church or 'The

Church of the Army of the Cross of Christ'. In his book *The Go-Between God: The Holy Spirit and the Christian Mission,* John V. Taylor who was himself a missionary to East Africa in the 1950s observed that:

> In Africa today it seems the incalculable Spirit has chosen to use the Independent Church Movement for another spectacular advance. This does not prove that their teaching is necessarily true but it shows they have the raw materials out of which a missionary church is made—spontaneity, total commitment, and the primitive responses that arise from the depths of life.[4]

What Bishop Taylor had in mind at the time of writing was the AICs. Their characteristics of 'spontaneity, total commitment and the primitive responses that arise from the depths of life' have remained important parts of Pentecostal spirituality in modern Africa. The AICs are no longer paradigmatic of African Christianity and I have discussed the reasons for their decline elsewhere.[5] However, their religious and theological emphases of practical salvation, charismatic renewal, innovative gender ideology, and oral and interventionist theologies, have found new leases of life among contemporary revitalization movements in Africa. The fact that their theological ideas have survived the changing African Christian landscape is an indication that the AICs, as the first mass revitalization movements, held within their ambits what African Christians generally considered important in their faith.

Theological Constructs and Revitalization

The various revitalization movements that Africa has known within the last century have emphasized the important fact that the church of Jesus Christ stands in need of constant renewal. Renewal comes from the Holy Spirit and so in what follows, we will consider ways in which this renewal theology has been made to address African religious sensibilities. To arrive at an understanding of revitalization theology in Africa, attention needs to be paid to the fact that this is a theology that is lived out in the everyday public and private activities rather than articulated in a systematic way. This is theology that is expressed in the song, prayer, testimony and dance, rather than in a written creed. So for example, it the revitalization movements that drew attention to the fact that when the Psalmist says 'I will make a joyful noise unto the Lord', it literally means one can play drums, dance and shout in church without feeling that we are being disorderly in the presence of the Lord. Thus until the rise of these African revitalization movements African drums and locally composed choruses were virtually unknown in the worship lives of the historic mission denominations. There are various ways in which their Christianity has enabled the church in Africa rethink modes of theological appropriation and discourse inherited from Western traditions.

Reinterpreting Soteriology

First is the soteriological emphasis. In Christian terms, Salvation refers to God's rescue function in Jesus Christ. This has been a key theme in Christian revitalization in Africa with this 'rescue function' been extended to include healing and deliverance from danger. This is in keeping with Old Testament thought in which the salvific works of God included the deliverance of Israel from Egypt, their defeat of Goliath at the hands of David, and other such practical ways in which God established himself as a God of power in the lives of his people. An important passage in this understanding of salvation is Psalm 116:1-9,

> I love the Lord, for he heard my voice; he heard my cry for mercy.
>
> Because he turned his ear to me, I will call on him as long as I live.
>
> The cords of death entangled me, the anguish of the grave came upon me;
>
> I was overcome by trouble and sorrow.
>
> Then I called on the name of the Lord; 'O Lord save me!'
>
> The Lord is gracious and righteous; our God is full of compassion.
>
> The Lord protects the simplehearted; when I was in great need, he saved me.
>
> Be at rest once more, O my soul, for the Lord has been good to you.
>
> For you, O Lord, have delivered my soul from death, my eyes from tears, my feet from stumbling,
>
> That I may walk before the Lord in the land of the living.

This testimony is continuous with the way in which Jesus reached out to people through healing from disease, deliverance from the demonic, and transformation through reinterpretations of religious traditions that made the law a burden rather than a blessing.

The model of salvation mediated by historic mission Christianity tended to emphasize the moral dimensions of it to the neglect of those aspects in which God in Christ is seen to touch people at the practical level in the power of the Holy Spirit. In the African context, religion is a survival strategy. People went to religious shrines in order to enquire about unhappy testimonies, seek solutions to health issues, improve their business and generally reverse their unhappy destinies. What the prophetic movements and the resulting revitalization movements did was to provide a Christian ritual context within which practical salvation—those needs that formerly took people to shrines—could now be offered within a Christian setting. The focus of prayer within revitalized Christianity consisted of pleas for the restoration of health and well-being, thereby rendering the new movements more amenable to masses of Africans who felt that the mission churches were too theoretical, even unbiblical, in their approach to salvation.

Reinterpreting Christology

There is a relationship between the soteriology and Christology articulated through the ministries of African revitalization movements. A great deal has been achieved in the attempt to bridge the gap between oral/grassroots theology and academic theology since the days when scholars like John S. Pobee and John Mbiti had agitated over such an enterprise. Today, books like African Evangelical scholar Kwame Bediako's *Jesus in Africa* and several others have used oral/grassroots theology extensively and in the process, demonstrated its viability as a valid theological form.[6] The greatest advantage of such informal theology is that it is born out of real encounters with Jesus Christ, how African

Christians understand their walk with him, and how they as ordinary people express the faith. The rise of the many revitalization movements in Africa is itself an indication of grassroots responses to the initiative of God in Christ. The composition of Gospel music is an example of grassroots/oral theology and one of the defining characteristics of contemporary African Christianity and public life. As an example, Ghana's Bernice Offei has recently composed a song called *Mogya,* 'Blood', and the lyrics read in part:

> The blood, the blood, I've been saved by the precious blood …
> The blood, the blood, through which we are made complete …
> Because of the power of his blood, we've received forgives of sins,
> Everlasting life, healing and salvation
> The blood, the precious blood which was shed at Calvary
> The blood that never loses its power
> It is our mighty weapon
> The devil is defeated
> God's children have won the victory.

In the theological thinking underpinning the lyrics of this song, the blood of Christ has not only delivered from sin, but 'everlasting life, healing and salvation' are seen to belong together. They are all found in the power of the blood, which is also described as 'our mighty weapon' through which the devil is defeated and God's children have the victory'. The theological basis of this music is Hebrews 9:12-14. The religious import of blood is not alien to African religions. African concepts of human existence are unequivocally in harmony with the Levitical idea that blood is life. Blood therefore occupies a very significant place in African beliefs and thought forms, especially in sacrificial rites. Blood possesses a mysterious spiritual power, and is regarded as the animator and stabilizer of human life.' Indeed one of the most important annual traditional festivals in the Eastern Region of Ghana, the *Odwira,* 'Cleansing', which is celebrated to cleanse or purify the soul of the nation from ritual filth, revolves around the symbolic slaughter of a lamb that is 'without defect' and the sprinkling of the blood on houses and people around the traditional area.

The Ghanaian Pentecostal woman, Afua Kuma, is another useful example of the sort of contribution that oral theologies make to the dynamic presence of revitalized Christianity in Africa. Although without formal education, we can describe her as a 'grassroots theologian' who has played a significant role 'in the development of Christian thought' and whose theology 'is foundational for [African] Christian theology in the 21st century.' In Afua Kuma's prayers, Jesus is imaged as *Obaatanpa* (Capable Mother/Guardian), *Kronkron* (Holy One), *Otumfo Nyankopon* (Almighty God), *Ohene* (King) and *Nyansabuakwa* (Custodian of Wisdom). These titles have been borrowed fro traditional appellations for Ghanaian chiefs as well as from biblical discourse. Consider her application of the Akan expression *Obaatanpa* to Jesus. This image is derived from the natural and biological roles of women as mothers with exceptional qualities of emotional attachment and care for their children. The expression is however not restricted to the feminine gender. It is also used for guardians or benefactors, male or female, and also for any human institution that performs the functions of providing care and emotional support. The theological import of Jesus as *Obaatanpa* lies in the fact that although the Jesus of history comes to us as a male, our conception of him as Jesus of faith transcends gender. The Jesus of faith is *Obaatanpa* because him both genders come together.

In another of Afua Kuma's 'prayers and praises', Jesus is imaged in his supremacy as having no equal in the universe:

Mere chiefs and kings are not his equals,
Though filled with glory and power,
Wealth and blessings, and royalty
In the greatest abundance
But of them all, he is the leader,
And the chiefs with all their glory follow after him (Laryea 2000:20).

This particular prayer of Afua Kuma connects with St. Paul's reference to Jesus as one 'for whom all things were created' (Colossians 1:16-20). In the African imagination, one who is greater than the chiefs who sit on the stool of the ancestors as custodians of power, authority and tradition must be supreme indeed. This has profound implications for the experience of Christian conversion in Africa. If Jesus is the 'leader' of all the authorities and if the chiefs with all their glory follow after him, then it is in order that conversion means the dethronement of all rival authorities in the traditional religio-cultural sphere. This was a key message of the prophets whose work inspired the formation of AICs. Such dethronements of rival authorities include the worship of ancestors in whose stead the chief rules. Indeed Christian G. Baëta suggests that in Africa's revitalization movements, we see people who like the Thessalonians 'turned to God from idols to serve the living and true God' (I Thessalonians 1:9).

Reinterpreting Pneumatology

What defines African revitalization movements is their very dynamic understanding of the Holy Spirit. The leader of a revitalization movement is usually first and foremost a charismatic person who has encountered the Spirit of God in transformative ways that were alien to understandings of the Spirit in the historic mission denominations. Thus the Spirit of God was seen not simply in terms of something to be confessed in a creed but as the power of God at work—either in direct action or empowering people to speak in tongues, healing, or bring revelations to others. In the pneumatology of African revitalization movements the Godhead is envisaged as present and powerful through the Holy Spirit, who reveals the will of God and the destiny of the individual, guides through dangers, and fills men with new powers of prophecy, utterance, prayer and healing. This could be said to be in keeping with the biblical material as shown by Christopher J.H. Wright:

Power, then, is effective action, making a difference, influencing events, changing the way things are or will be. It is not surprising, then, that the Spirit of God in the Old Testament is commonly linked with power, for the biblical God is nothing if not effective in action in bringing about change!...The Spirit of God is God's power at work—either in direction action or in empowering people to do what God wants to be done.[7]

That the AICs were from the outset popularly referred to as 'Spiritual' churches is very instructive. They were so called precisely because of the keen emphasis that they placed on the activity of the Holy Spirit and the integration and normalization of charismatic renewal experiences in Christian worship. In a sense African revitalization movements made a distinction between 'I believe in the Holy Spirit' and 'I have experienced the Holy Spirit'. One was continuous with the other because belief in the Holy Spirit, it was expected, would manifest in the same acts of power that he was associated with in Scripture.

Conclusion

The practical implications of the soteriological, Christological and pneumatological emphases of African revitalization movements for theological education in particular are profound. It has been said that Africa's revitalization movement reveal what the African, when left to make his own choices, considers as important in Christianity. In drawing up curricula that prepares candidates for ministry in Africa, it is important to consider the pneumatic nature of her revitalization movements. These movements—whether as AICs, independent charismatic churches, or renewal movements within historic mission denominations—have become the representative face of Christianity in Africa. They constitute a paradigmatic shift as far as indigenous appropriations of the Christian evangel are concerned and in terms of mission, we ignore their messages of the importance of the Holy Spirit in Christian life at our own peril.

Notes

1. Kwame Bediako, Jesus in Africa: Christian Theology and the African Experience (Akropong, Akwapim: Regnum Africa, 2000), 23.

2. David A. Shank, Prophet Harris: The 'Black Elijah' of West Africa, Abridged by Jocelyn Murray (Leiden: E.J. Brill, 1994), xi.

3. Ogbu U. Kalu, African Pentecostalism: An Introduction (Oxford: Oxford University Press, 2008), x.

4. John V. Taylor, The Go-Between God: The Holy Spirit and the Christian Mission (London: SCM, 1972), 54.

5. J. Kwabena Asamoah-Gyadu, African Charismatics: A Study of Independent Indigenous Pentecostalism in Ghana (Leiden: E.J. Brill, 2005).

6. Kwame Bediako, Jesus in Africa: Christian Theology in the African Experience (Akropong, Akwapim: Regnum, 2000).

7. Christopher J.H. Wright, Knowing the Holy Spirit through the Old Testament (Downers Grove, Illinois: Intervarsity Press, 2006), 36.

Chapter 13

Diasporas and Revitalization

Steven Ybarrola, PhD
Professor of Cultural Anthropology
Asbury Theological Seminary

The United States has been seen by social scientists and lay people alike as the great immigration experiment. Today, however, that experiment is being played out in various parts of the world as people are on the move as never before, with approximately 214 million people living outside their countries of origin.[1] States in Europe who used to export people to their foreign colonial outposts are now the recipients of large-scale immigration, often from those former colonies; the colonial boast that the "sun never sets on the British empire" goes a long way in explaining the great cultural diversity now found within the UK. In addition, countries that were once exporters of labor (e.g., Spain) are now recipients of workers from various parts of the globe. A good number of these immigrants to Western counties are Muslims, who are challenging social norms and cultural understandings, and are thereby testing the limits of multicultural policies in those countries.

People migrate for a variety of reasons, including economic necessity, educational and business opportunities, to escape repressive political regimes and military conflicts, and to share the Good News of salvation in Christ with members of the host society. More than ever we need to understand the changes that take place in individuals and communities as people immigrate into different sociocultural contexts, and the implications this migration has for the revitalization of God's church.

Diasporas and Transnationalism

People rarely migrate alone or in isolation; the social forces that lead individuals to emigrate generally affect large segments of a society. "Chain migration," where individuals follow after those they know who have previously migrated, is a very common migratory pattern, and can, along with other patterns (e.g., resettlement of refugees), lead to the development of immigrant communities, or diasporas, in the host country. The anthropologist Mike Rynkiewich defines a diaspora as, "the dispersal of a people from a homeland to a host country or countries, the formation of a community within the host country that identifies with the homeland, and the maintenance of links between the Diaspora community and the homeland and/or the maintenance of links among the Diaspora communities themselves."[2]

Diasporas are not a new phenomenon; indeed, the term itself was originally used to refer to the dispersal of the Jews from their homeland in the 1st and 2nd centuries A.D.[3] In the recent past, social scientists spoke of ethnic enclaves in reference to migrant and minority communities in a society. An early, and now classic, work on ethnic enclaves in the United States was *Beyond the Melting Pot*, an analysis of such communities in New York City by the sociologists Nathan Glazer and Daniel Patrick Moynihan.[4] However, beginning in the 1990s social scientists began to reassess migrant communities in light of the changes brought about by globalization (e.g., increased communications technology, the ease and affordability of travel, the flow of capital across state borders). These changes made it much easier for immigrant communities to stay in contact with people and products from their homeland, creating what came to be known as "transnational" communities. As Steven Vertovec puts it,

> The meaning of transnationalism which has perhaps been gaining most attention among sociologists and anthropologists has to do with a kind of social formation spanning borders. Ethnic diasporas—what Kachig Tololyan (1991, p.5) has called "the exemplary communities of the transnational moment"—have become the paradigm in this understanding of transnationalism.
>
> …[D]ispersed diasporas of old have become today's "transnational communities" sustained by a range of modes of social organization, mobility and communication.[5]

To illustrate this change, allow me to give a personal example. In 1898 my grandfather left a very small village in the Pyrenees Mountains in the Basque Country near the border of Spain and France, and migrated to the United States. He arrived in New York, but quickly made his way to California where many Basques had migrated, creating a diasporic community. He eventually bought some land in northern Montana and started a sheep ranch. My grandfather never returned to his natal village, and to the extent that he maintained contact with the family back home, it would have been a very slow and infrequent process. I, on the other hand, have traveled to the Basque Country on many occasions, even living there for 15 months while conducting my dissertation research. I have visited our family in the Pyrenees several times, and am able to be in contact with them almost instantly via the internet or by phone. We could even have a "face-to-face" conversation using Skype if we so desired. The changes in communications technology and the relative ease of travel means that I have been able to maintain much closer contact with my relatives (and other friends in the Basque Country) than my grandfather, who passed away in 1952, ever could.

Diasporas, Transnationalism, and Revitalization

Today some of these diasporic transnational communities in the West are composed of those who are coming from the "global South and East" in order to be intentionally missional in their host societies. This "reverse mission" (or "echo mission") has as its goal nothing less than the revitalization of the church and society in the West. Afe Adogame notes, "The rationale for reverse mission is often anchored on claims to divine commission to 'spread the gospel'; the perceived secularisation of the West; the abysmal fall in church attendance and dwindling membership; desecralisation (sic) of church buildings; liberalization; and on issues around moral decadence."[6] The question is, how effective will these missional communities be in this endeavor? There is some evidence that they can be quite effective. For example, the largest evangelical church in the Ukraine (and one of the largest in Europe) is pastored by Sunday Adelaja, a Nigerian. On the other hand, many Western countries are experiencing a backlash against what is perceived to be an "invasion" of foreigners with very different cultures, creating what Andrew Walls calls a paradox: "The developed world...needs immigrants, but does not want them."[7] This backlash can be seen in the recent laws against the wearing of veils or head coverings by Muslim women in countries like France, and the British Prime Minister stating that multiculturalism in the UK had failed.[8]

All societies and cultures have ways of categorizing individuals and groups, and then assigning meaning to those categories. In the United States, as in other countries, an ideology of race developed over time that is used to place different categories of people into a social hierarchy. By ideology of race I mean "a way of thinking about, speaking about, and organizing relations among and within human groups" (Scupin 2002, 12). As a result, when people from other parts of the world come to the U.S. they are defined, to an important degree, by this ideology, which affects the opportunities they will have in the new society. Therefore, when migrants come with the intention of evangelizing the members of the host society, they too will be viewed through this racialized lens, which will have an impact on their missional effectiveness. A recent study of Nigerian Pentecostals in Atlanta, Georgia, seems to bear this out; though the Nigerian Christians migrated to the United States to be intentionally missional to the broader society, thus far their congregations are comprised almost exclusively of members of the Nigerian diaspora.[9]

There is, of course, nothing wrong with establishing churches that minister primarily to diaspora communities. In some cases, due to language and cultural differences, these churches are inevitable and serve an important function. For example, Korean churches in the United States are important cultural institutions for the Korean diaspora, and have been effective in reaching non-Christian Koreans. These churches provide a place where Korean believers can worship in their mother tongue, using familiar forms, and where non-Christians can speak their native language, eat their ethnic foods, and participate in other cultural activities. As a result, the latter are exposed to the gospel, and many convert to Christianity. This is what the missiologist George Hunter refers to as "belonging before believing." [10] However, for churches attempting to practice reverse mission, establishing diaspora churches will not do.

Perhaps the 1.5 and 2nd generations [11] will be more effective in reaching members of the host society. Having a more "hybrid" identity (i.e., identifying with both their diasporic community and the host society), these individuals have a greater ability to act as bridges between the two cultures. In reference to these generations of Koreans, the Duke Divinity School professor Kate Bowler states, "Second-generation Korean American Christians are forging new connections between their generational, ethnic, and religious identities. In short, they find new ways to be all three: Koreans, Americans, Christians" [12] The question that has yet to be answered is, will these subsequent generations maintain the missional zeal and vision of the preceding generation(s), or will they succumb to the secularizing influences of the broader culture? If the former, then we'll have the opportunity to witness the long-lasting impact of reverse mission on the revitalization of the church in the West.

The transnational nature of missional diasporas also raises some interesting issues. As Udotong's research demonstrates, the Nigerian Christians in Atlanta maintain very strong ties to their church and leadership back in Nigeria. The fact that there are direct flights from Atlanta to Lagos, Nigeria, makes the flow of goods and people from "home" much easier and more frequent. Combined with the ease of communication, this means that the Nigerian churches in Atlanta are constantly being infused with the vision and direction of the church leadership in Nigeria. Thus, the missional focus is continually being reinforced, and the necessary material needs for that mission are being supplied. In addition, there are networks of Nigerian missional communities within the United States that are partners in evangelization and ministry.

There are, however, potential problems with such close association with the leadership at home and the networks abroad. One of these has to do with an old but important missional concept—contextualization; how do the transnational ties affect the integration of these diaspora churches and communities into the host society and culture, as well as the contextualization of the gospel? As I've stated elsewhere,

> In some ways, "reverse mission" may suffer from some of the same problems as mission from the West—too strong of an identity with, and influence from, the home church or mission organization, which keeps the mission effort from being more effective as it is viewed as something foreign in the new context.... A challenge for Christians in diaspora, especially those who are intentionally missional, is to maintain the vision

and zeal they bring with them to evangelize the West, something that the continual infusion and support of their home churches and communities can facilitate, while at the same time adapting their church forms, worship styles, and even theology to the cultural context in which they find themselves.[13]

Another issue that Christian diaspora communities must be aware of is the impact they can have on the local church in the host country. Let me use as an example a case that I'm familiar with--the relatively small evangelical churches in the southern Basque Country. Until recently these churches were largely populated with people who had come to the Basque Country from other parts of Spain, and their descendants; there are very few ethnic Basques in these churches.[14] However, beginning around the turn of the new millennium, people started arriving from various parts of Latin America. The men primarily work in construction and the women work as domestic helpers. A certain percentage of those arriving had been converted to Protestant (mainly Pentecostal) Christianity in their home countries, and began attending the evangelical (mainly non-Pentecostal) churches in the Basque Country. As the number of Latin American immigrants to Spain increased, so did their numbers in these churches. Today they represent a majority in most of the evangelical churches in the southern Basque Country. When I attended one of the larger churches in the provincial capital Donostia (San Sebastián) in 2009, I was amazed at the number of Latin Americans (mainly from Colombia and Ecuador) in the church. I estimated that at least 90 percent of the congregation was represented by these immigrants. This means two things: 1) the Latin Americans were attending the church in fairly large numbers (at least for the size of the church), and 2) the indigenous believers had left. When I asked a missionary if there were some churches where there were fewer Latin Americans and more indigenous believers, he responded that anywhere there was a sign over the door that read *"Iglesia Evangélica"* (Evangelical Church) it would be full of Latin Americans.

It will be interesting to see how this eventually plays out in the Basque Country. Already there are signs that diaspora churches are forming; there have been pastors/missionaries who have come from Brazil to start churches that minster almost exclusively to the Brazilian immigrant population. I asked one of these pastors/missionaries if he was there to minister to the Brazilian diaspora, and he replied quite emphatically that he was there to reach all of the people in the Basque Country. But, like the Nigerian Pentecostals in Atlanta, so far his congregation is made up of the Brazilian diaspora community.

The question arises, is the Latin American Christian diaspora revitalizing the church in the Basque Country, or merely displacing the indigenous believers? Currently the non-diaspora churches are led by indigenous pastors, but Latin Americans are taking over much of the lay leadership (as would be expected, given their large numbers). It will be interesting to see if they begin to take over the pastoral leadership as well. A missionary told me that he overheard one of the Latin Americans telling another that they were just biding their time until they could take over the church. If and when this happens, how will these churches differ from diaspora churches? They will be led by Latin Americans with congregations primarily made up of members of the diaspora community.

Again, there seems to me to be nothing inherently wrong in forming churches to minister to members of particular diasporas, but when these overwhelm and displace local indigenous congregations then it would appear that something other than revitalization is taking place.

Thus far I have discussed Christian diasporas, some that are intentionally missional (i.e., Nigerian Pentecostals in Atlanta), and others that are not (i.e., Latin Americans in the Basque Country). There are, of course, many non-Christian diasporas that have developed in the West, as well as other parts of the world, and these provide another opportunity to revitalize the global church. Some of these diasporas represent populations from limited access countries (e.g., in the Middle East, North Africa, and China) where missionaries are not allowed; therefore, the people have had limited opportunities to hear the Good News of salvation through Christ. Individuals who have migrated are frequently in a "liminal" state, being uprooted from their home communities and situated in a new sociocultural context, and are, therefore, often more open to new and different ideas. Studies of non-Christian religious diasporas in the United States indicate that the members tend to be more ecumenical than they are in their home context.[15] Clifford Geertz, in what must have been one of his last writings on "religion," notes,

> Being Muslim abroad..., outside the *Dar Al-Islam*, is...a rather different matter than being one at home. Going among non-Muslims induces in many, probably in nearly all, a certain amount of conscious reflection, more or less anxious, on what being a Muslim in fact comes down to, on how properly to be one in a setting not historically prearranged to facilitate it. There can be and are, of course, a number of outcomes: an ecumenical "watering down" of belief to render it less offensive to a religiously pluralized or secularized setting; a "double-minded" dividing of the self, and the self's life, into but vaguely communicating inward and outward halves; a turn toward a much more assertive and self-conscious Islamism in response to the perceived faithlessness of the new setting. And just about every possibility in between....[16]

Another outcome not mentioned by Geertz is conversion to Christianity, and this is what concerns us here. God is bringing populations to us that we are unable to reach in their home countries, except through great personal risk. This provides an opportunity to reach out to the members of these diasporas with radical hospitality and love, sharing the gospel in deed as well as word.[17] As past examples have taught us, those who become Christians in diaspora from these limited access countries often develop a desire to be missional among their own people, and as insiders they have a much better understanding of how to do this than do those from outside the group. If Christians take seriously the task of reaching out to members of these diaspora communities, and do not shirk this responsibility out of fear or national xenophobia, then there is the real possibility of revitalizing the church in these seemingly unreachable parts of the world.

Conclusion

Diasporas have a tremendous revitalizing potential for the global church today. In the increasingly secular and post-Christian West, missional diasporas from other parts of the world can help bring life back to the Western church and society through their evangelistic efforts, as well as their reliance on the work of the Holy Spirit. The Western church needs to be reminded that we serve a *living* God, and that he desires to do a new work among us. Missional diasporas bring with them that vision and understanding of God. However, for these missional communities to have a greater and lasting impact, two things are necessary. First, the church and society in the West must confront and overcome their racial and cultural sense of superiority in order to be more receptive to the message these missionaries bring. [18] Secondly, these diaspora communities must be intentional not only in their mission, but also in their understanding on a deeper level of the sociocultural context in which they are living and evangelizing; if they do not, then they will be viewed as a foreign entity, and relegated to the "exotic" and inconsequential margins of society.

Diasporas also provide perhaps one of the best hopes, at least for the foreseeable future, for revitalizing the church in parts of the world where Christians are either a persecuted minority or virtually non-existent. As I learned from being on a mission team that took Bibles and Christian literature behind the Iron Curtain in the 1970s, God finds a way to get his Word into those places that seem closed off to the gospel. Today one of those "ways" may be through reaching out to non-Christian diaspora communities from limited access countries.

Notes

1. 2008 Revision of the United Nations' Trends in Total Migrant Stock (http://esa.un. org/migration).

2. Michael Rynkiewich, "Pacific Islands Diaspora Studies," in *Pacific Islands Diaspora, Identity, and Incorporation,* eds. Jan Rensel and Alan Howard, in preparation.

3. See Stephane Dufoix, *Diasporas,* (Berkeley: University of California Press, 2008) for a thorough discussion of the history and contemporary application of the diaspora concept.

4. Nathan Glazer and Daniel Patrick Moynihan, *Beyond the Melting Pot: The Negroes, Puerto Ricans, Jews, Italians, and Irish of New York City,* (Cambridge, MA: M.I.T. Press, 1963).

5. Steven Vertovec, "Conceiving and Researching Transnationalism," *Ethnic and Racial Studies,* 22(2) (1999): 449.

6. Afe Adogame, "Reverse Mission: Europe--a Prodigal Continent?," *2gether Scotland Website* (http://www.eauk.org/scotland/2gether/reverse-mission-europe-a-prodigal-continent.cfm).

7. Andrew Walls, "Mission and Migration: The Diaspora Factor in Christian History," *Journal of African Christian Thought,* 5(2) (December 2002): 10.

8. http://www.msnbc.msn.com/id/41444364/ns/world_news-europe/t/british-pm-multiculturalism-has-failed/

9. William Udotong, *Transnational Migration and the Reverse Mission of Nigerian-Led Pentecostal Churches in the U.S.A.: A Case Study of Selected Churches in Metro Atlanta*, (Dissertation, Asbury Theological Seminary, 2010).

10. George Hunter III, *How to Reach Secular People*, (Nashville, TN: Abingdon Press, 1992).

11. 1.5 generation refers to those who migrated as children with their parents, whereas 2nd generation refers to the children of immigrants who were born in the host country.

12. Kate Bowler, "Generation K: Korean American Evangelicals," (*Books and Culture*, May/June 2011, online: http://www.booksandculture.com/articles/2009/mayjun/generationk.html).

13. Steven Ybarrola, "An Anthropological Approach to Diaspora Missiology," (Evangelical Missiological Society North Central Meeting, February 26, 2011).

14. For more on the history and current situation of the evangelical church in the Basque Country, see Steven Ybarrola, "Identity Matters: Christianity and Ethnic Identity in the Peninsular Basque Country," in *Power and Identity in the Global Church: Six Contemporary Cases*, eds. Brian Howell and Edwin Zehner, (Pasadena, CA: William Carey Library, 2009).

15. Ninian Smart, "The Importance of Diasporas," in *Gilgul: Essays on Transformation, Revolution and Permanence in the History of Religions*, eds. S. Shaked, D. Shulman, and G.G. Stroumsa, (Leiden: E.J. Brill, 1987).

16. Clifford Geertz, "Shifting Aims, Moving Targets: On the Anthropology of Religion," *Journal of the Royal Anthropological Institute*, 11 (2005): 12,13.

17. See Brian Howell, "Multiculturalism, Immigration and the North American Church. Rethinking Contextualization," *Missiology*, XXXIX(1) (2011):79-85, for a recent discussion of using radical hospitality, compassion, and justice in reaching out to, and serving, immigrant diasporas.

18. See Tite Tienou, "The Invention of the 'Primitive' and Stereotypes in Mission," *Missiology*, XIX(3) (1991): 295-303, for a discussion of how the non-Western "Other" came to be viewed as "primitive." See also Robert Priest and Alvaro Nieves, *This Side of Heaven: Race, Ethnicity, and Christian Faith*, (New York: Oxford University Press, 2006).

Chapter 14

Revitalization Movements, Social Change, and Justice: Brazil's Toca de Assis in Global Perspective

Sílvia R. A. Fernandes, PhD
Associate Professor of Social Sciences
Universidade Federal Rural do Rio de Janeiro,
Rio de Janeiro, Brazil

Bryan T. Froehle, PhD
Professor of Practical Theology
School of Theology and Ministry
St. Thomas University, Miami

Studying trends among Pentecostals, Reformation-based traditions, Catholics, and other major groupings of world Christianity can no longer be done in isolation. This is particularly true with regard to Christian revitalization. While the end of modernity may spell the demise of expectations for a single global metanarrative, the fragmentation, hybridity, and globalization characteristic of postmodernity meld previously disparate stories and trajectories. Borders have become more porous, and the story of one region or Christian confession has become more parallel and overlapping. Today more than ever, revitalization studies of any single case in any one context offer insight for cases embedded in other contexts, including other Christian traditions. This chapter explores world Catholicism in light of a particular Catholic revitalization movement in order to explore broader interpretive trends tied to questions of social change and justice in world Christian revitalization.

A Common Global Reality

World Christian Revitalization

The rise of the global south within contemporary Christianity may be ascribed to demographic trends and colonial legacies, buts its effects are world historical, broadly transformative in nature. Any emerging understanding of world Christian revitalization must now be global and comparative.

In the case of world Catholicism, the shift to the global south is clear. Within the past 50 years, the proportion of Catholics in Africa increased four-fold, from 3 percent to 12 percent of all Catholics worldwide. Catholics in North America (the USA and Canada) remained about 7 percent of all Catholics in the world, but Europe, which had 49 percent of all Catholics in 1950, had only 27 percent by 2000. Today, the Americas—North and South America taken together—have 49 percent of all Catholics worldwide. In 1900, the four countries with the largest numbers of Catholics were in Europe. Today those countries have been supplanted by Brazil, Mexico, the Philippines, and the USA.[1]

More important than mere numbers are the changes in Catholic worshipping communities. In the time after the Council of Trent, and with roots reaching centuries before, Catholic worshipping communities had been territorially defined parishes assembling in officially-established parish churches.[2] The result in many cases has been a kind of sacramental dispensary, a kind of "service station" model of Catholic parish life. A community's prior existence was generally assumed, but a community focus was not part of the understanding of the Tridentine parish model. The Second Vatican Council (1963-1965) and the resulting revised Code of Canon Law (1983) changed this self-understanding: most parishes continue to be correlated with a specific geography, but now as communities of the faithful.[3] Arguably, it has taken the lived experience of the past five decades, particularly the combined effect of the global south in Catholic life and population declines and shifts in the global north, for this new self-understanding to take root.

Today, using the Vatican's term of "pastoral centers" to refer to any established worship site, one can observe an historical difference between the North Atlantic and most of the rest of global Catholicism. In the former, pastoral centers have been coterminous with parish churches. In the latter, there are many more worship sites than parish churches, whether chapels, shrines, mission stations, or other small, stable worshipping communities.[4] Their management is by definition less formal and ordinarily smaller and more community-based. As Catholicism in the global south becomes the modal form of world Catholicism, the Tridentine form of Catholics parish has simply ceased to be an adequate understanding of Catholic practice.[5] Further, Catholic experience in the global south is not likely to become more similar to that of North Atlantic Catholicism (that is, North America and Europe). The observable pattern today, in fact, is the reverse. The former Catholic heartland is changing in a direction that will make it grassroots faith communities more similar to the global south as its parishes suppressed and merged, often while keeping former parish churches as worship spaces for separate worshipping communities.[6]

At the same time, the agents of Catholic expansion from the nineteenth century restoration through the twentieth century – European apostolic religious orders of women and men[7] – have diminished rapidly even as Catholic population continues to grow worldwide. Catholic creativity, pastoral ministry, and religious virtuosity are now expressed in many different ways in addition to the apostolic religious orders. One of these is the creative re-founding of Catholic religious communities and a new turn toward identity and mission even as contexts change and members of apostolic religious orders diminish far below any possible replacement level.[8] Others are the emerging religious communities and new ecclesial movements.[9] In terms of specifically ecclesial ministry-related vocations, numbers of diocesan priests have been relatively stable or increasing globally, and numbers of this in the restored permanent diaconate and lay ecclesial ministry, especially catechists, have been on a remarkable upward trajectory.[10]

Social Change

Social change processes are today deeply intertwined with globalization and the realities of late capitalism. The end result is a re-allocation of global privilege and poverty. Rather than the state being an engine of social change, global systems of exchange and sheer economic power have become the critical drivers of distribution. The end result is new forms of inequality and a new distribution of poverty. Above all, economic globalization has been about integrating impoverished, urban and urbanizing sectors around the world in the interest of profit. In this sense, fewer and fewer persons are truly marginal to the global economy.[11] Even more: by mid-century, and well before on many continents, the process of urbanization will be completed on a world historical scale.

There simply is very little of humanity left to urbanize. The "idiocy of rural life," as Karl Marx put it, will effectively be ended for the vast majority of humanity over the next few decades.[12] This memorable line of Marx is a famously misinterpreted one: it refers to the isolation of rural life, not rural people's intelligence. This is precisely what is ending. Communications technologies, transportation, and above all new forms of economic and social life have effectively eliminated the isolation once typical of nearly all humanity.

Urbanization is in some ways more a reality of the global south than the global north. The world's most vast urban areas are now in the global south, and highly dense forms of urbanization will likely continue to distinguish the global south into the future.

Forms of cultural or institutional life are forever catching up to new realities, and the same is true of world Christianity and certainly Catholicism. As urbanization continues to mark the world, lag effects continue to emerge. Catholic parish forms and religiosity, with its territorial base, monocultural assumptions, processions and devotions, have historically had a more rural than urban origin and flavor. Pentecostal forms of worship and church life, with their flexibility and shape-shifting character, have grown up with urbanization trends worldwide. The Azusa Street experience, in fact, was of an urbanized, displaced peasantry coming to a new expression of religious hybridity as various people groups came together for the first time. [13] Today, whether in areas once dominated by a Catholic religious monopoly or in spaces where a diversity of Christian confessions have existed from the beginning, Christian life and worship is marked by the presence of poverty and inequality in a massively urbanized, global context. Even as middle sectors grow, the presence of the poor remains and in some cases becomes more palpable. While the built environment of cities in the global south contains a large and growing number of soaring apartment buildings and neighborhoods of the relatively privileged, reality for a global majority will likely continue to be much closer to self-constructed housing in self-constructed neighborhoods.

Justice

Today's Christian understanding of justice flows from the Christian experience of revitalization – continuing, Spirit-led re-founding and renewed theological self-understanding in changed contexts. The logics of justice are a complex but critical interpretive trend in world Christian revitalization. Through the twentieth century, much of the logic of justice was focused on the state, around political freedom and on bringing the power of the state to the side of the underprivileged or oppressed. This focus has not so much disappeared as been supplanted by a keen realization of the limits of the state in an era of globalized economic power. During the struggle for democratization in much of the world during the last decades of the twentieth century, the state was foregrounded in terms of justice. Between 1972 and 2010, however the number of countries with functioning political democracies increased from 40 to 123. [14]

Today, other logics have emerged, more relational, smaller scale, and limited. Within the Christian theological conversation, a focus on social ethics continues, but discourse around virtue, both personal and civic, has notably grown and deepened. [15] As civil society has grown in density and non-governmental organizations have developed, even efforts toward justice have been marked by a certain entrepreneurial, personal, individualist turn. Yet these are nonetheless logics of justice, ones capable of living side by side with other logics of justice, neither denying nor supplanting the other. [16]

The Case of Toca de Assis

Walking through the streets in downtown Rio de Janeiro, Brazil, passersby will see young women and men dressed in simple, look-alike robes, barefoot or in flip-flops, caring for the homeless, talking to street children, cutting hair or the fingernails and toenails of those living on city streets. They are the toqueiras and toqueiros, members of an emerging Catholic religious community commonly called Toca de Assis ("Shelter of Assisi"). This Catholic revitalization movement began in 1994 and counts some 24 houses of men and 33 houses of women, mostly in Brazil, but also in Portugal and Ecuador.17 About 2 or 3 members live in a typical men's residence, and up to six members live in a women's residence, largely because there are relatively more women than men. Most of the communities are located in lower middle class areas, in buildings owned by the church or given by donors. While the number of members has been only irregularly reported thus far and cannot be considered definitive, reports suggest that in 2010, the women's branch had 445 members and the men's branch had 264.18 Regardless of the exact number of members, the growth of Toca during less than two decades has been remarkable when compared to available figures for members of religious orders in Brazil. In 2008, for example, there were only 2,975 Catholic religious brothers in the whole of Brazil.19 Furthermore, Toca is so new that many of its members could be considered the equivalent of novices or as having only temporary vows. This makes it even more interesting to compare numbers of toqueiras to figures for women religious in Brazil: 926 postulants (those aspiring or considering becoming a novice), 699 novices (those in initial formation as a religious), 2,193 with temporary vows, and 24,901 with perpetual vows.[20]

Context: Brazil and Catholic Religious Life

Brazil has more persons who identity as Catholic than any other country in the world. There are also more persons who identify as Pentecostals than any other country in the world, and not surprisingly, Brazil has one of the largest proportions of Catholic charismatics in the world as well. Over 57 percent of Brazilian Catholics surveyed claim a charismatic identity, according to a 2006 study.[21] The country also has by far the largest number of reported Christian Base Communities, the grassroots pastoral form related to liberation theology, according to some sources as many as 80,000 such communities.[22]

Within the Catholic Church in Brazil, there has long been an on-going mix between charismatic and liberationist streams of spirituality and practice at the grassroots. Some base communities are tied to near-exclusively liberationist models rooted in diocesan-wide or parish-based pastoral strategies, but many are not entirely dissimilar from the spirituality and practices of *Toca*.[23] Contemporary emerging religious communities[24] and religious movements alike overlap in many ways and often illustrate such a mixing. It is in this environment that *Toca* emerged.

As a result of declining membership in the apostolic religious orders within the Conference of Religious of Brazil (CRB), a discussion has emerged about a "new foundation of religious life" within Brazil as well as within Catholicism more generally.[25] Diminishing numbers of new entrants have been particularly notable among women religious, who had commonly had membership figures at a level of about 3-4 times as numerous as men religious throughout the twentieth century.[26] In the context of Catholic religious orders, *Toca* is particularly notable since it contains large numbers of deeply committed people in their 20s and 30s, a strong appeal among adolescents, and a radical, high-demand approach to religious practice. Their life is an innovative hybrid of thirteenth century Franciscan-influenced garb and ascetic practice with contemporary music and charismatic prayer experiences fused with Eucharistic Adoration. [27] In this way, one can imagine a community that began in a charismatic experience but influenced by Franciscan models and spirituality might eventually take on the formal trappings of the Franciscan third order regular rule of life and constitutions. [28]

Storyline

In the mid-1990, a young member of a nineteenth century religious order, the Stigmatines, was studying for the priesthood in Campinas, a midsize city in Brazil and birthplace of the Catholic Charismatic Renewal. Building on a blend of charismatic spirituality and strict religious demands, he brought together the first members of what was then called the Fraternity of Covenant *Toca de Assis*, in reference to an animal's burrow or lair ("toca") – a shelter, in other words – dedicated to the poverty of Francis of Assisi ("de Assis"). Beginning with three other men in 1994, *Toca* grew to 80 by 1996, the year when the founder of *Toca*, Roberto Lettieri, was ordained. [29] In 2002, he left the Stigmatines and became an ordinary priest of the Archdiocese of Campinas[30] as he set about developing the emerging religious community under the oversight of the Archbishop of Campinas. [31]

From the beginning, it was impossible not to notice the young people who joined this new common life. They devoted about three hours a day for prayer — usually on their knees before the Eucharist in quiet meditative prayer—and embraced the care of the homeless without taking even minimal precautions to prevent possible disease. More problematically in a society that was only just beginning to experience prosperity after years of hyperinflation, the largely young, middle class youth that *Toca* attracted joined in large numbers, abandoning their studies and work, trusting in donations to sustain their very simple lifestyle of prayer and direct service. Further, in a society where young people commonly live with their parents until marriage, *toqueiras/os* moved out of their homes and frequently had little time left to connect with their families given their all-consuming devotion to prayer and care of the homeless. New members of *Toca* have tended to be from among emerging adults. Often new members join as soon as they are 18 and able to live as they choose, no longer bound by legal restrictions to study or live under the care of their families. [32]

While some sectors of the Catholic Church in Brazil began to express concerns of what they called *Toca*'s "religious fundamentalism," others became increasingly attracted to the radical practice of this religious community. More and more youth learned about the movement as its work was discussed each day on TV *Canção Nova* ("New Song"), a charismatic Catholic broadcaster with which *Toca* has had close ties from the beginning. [33] Though details are unclear, the Archbishop of Campinas, acting within his charge for the oversight of *Toca*, ended the relationship of the founder, Roberto Lettieri, with the community in early 2009. [34] While this has created a major challenge for the community, it continues to enjoy the strong support of many segments of the Catholic Church in Brazil.

Toca as a Practice of Life

Toca is fundamentally about doing. Both women and men wear the same brown robes in the style of the Franciscans. Men are tonsured in the style of medieval monastics and friars, and women members have a similarly austere, very short cropped hair style. Loosely flowing robes and very short hair result in an ambiguity of gender, something that outsiders to the community often find problematic.35 At the center of the Toca experience is a spirituality focused on the care of the homeless and rejection of consumption, including the rejection of academic knowledge. Instead, toqueiras/os emphasize asceticism and intense moments of prayer before the presence of Christ in the Eucharist. Along with previous work obligations and regular family visits, members who were students also abandon their studies, arguing that "all knowledge comes from God" and is to be sought through their practices of prayer and service.

Toca's way of life has notably less asymmetry in gender relations elsewhere in church life or in society in general – though men and women live in separate houses, they dress similarly, worship similarly, and develop joint activities in pastoral ministry with the homeless. Members' class origins tend be similar as well, across the board: most come from the middle classes, quite unlike that of most Brazilian Catholic religious orders today, whose younger members tend to be drawn from the poor and working classes.[36]

The spirituality of Toca has evolved since its founding, becoming more fixed. Today, members emphasize three pillars: the practice of Eucharistic Adoration, poverty, and chastity. At first, mention of Francis of Assisi was relatively sparse, but it has clearly increased over time, and Francis is today a patron saint for the movement. Unusual for a Catholic religious institute, Toca claims four figures as patrons, two men and two women. The others are the lay Dominican fourteenth century Catherine of Siena, the twentieth century Italian Capuchin Franciscan Padre Pio, and the Portuguese lay mystic Alexandrina.[37] The choice of these saints as patrons is suggestive – two of the patron saints received the stigmata and Eucharistic adoration was central to the spirituality of another – thus embodying central elements of the revitalization logic of toqueira/o spirituality, the active asceticism of care of the homeless, poverty, and mystical prayer.

The houses of Toca de Assis are increasingly assigned specific functions such as caring for the poor in the streets, forming new members, or being houses of contemplation. When the group first began, Toca would routinely care for more a hundred homeless people in a single location. Today, care is taken that a single community care for no more than 40 people, thus preventing the relatively small cell groups from being overwhelmed and losing focus on their core religious mission.[38]

Members' Reflections

A critical characteristic of *Toca* remains the expectation that the middle class young people who join it, most of whom are of university age, will leave behind their studies when they join. This anti-intellectual stance has been widely discussed by others but not explained.[39] The key to understanding this stance is perhaps best found in its musical compositions with their strong emotional lyrics and rhythms, the strong internal strictures on the use and possession of goods, and *Toca*'s critique of the way the surrounding culture values knowledge over practices of service or prayer.

Members are well acquainted with these debates. One *toqueiro* interviewed for this research argued that there are two sides to the high value given the pursuit of education in today's society. The first is positive because "wisdom comes from God" but nonetheless there is also a negative aspect: "science without God can turn against God." The view that knowledge or studies may be potentially more negative than position was expressed by many other interviewees, most commonly with the observation that *toqueiras/os* should appreciate the simplicity of life and that real learning should be acquired through experience. In many ways, the attitude of abandonment taken by *toqueiras/os* can be understood as a rejection of therapeutic notions of "self-care" common in contemporary individualist, postmodern society.[40]

The narratives of members thus reject study or any activity solely due to personal desires. In the words of a 25 year old *toqueira*, a member for nine years:

> We are not about training professionals. If a person enters with a degree, she will bring that talent to the community. If you enter as a psychologist, you will assist in human development... We appreciate the simplicity of life above all and so do not look for academic studies, but rather just basic training. Members who did not complete high school should finish the basics. But most things we learn with experience.[41]

Other members see the call of the toqueiras/os as simply incompatible with the pursuit of knowledge since their activities make anything else impossible. As a thirty year toqueiro who has only finished secondary school said: "Our calling is very demanding and cannot be reconciled with study." Comments from a well-educated, 28 year old toqueiro recalled the worldview of the early leaders but also refer to Toca's increasing sense of a need for further training.

> In the beginning when we started, really, everyone would drop everything, leave everything and come to *Toca*... If a person was a student, studies were simply left behind. In the beginning, it was something new, different, and there were many poor people to be cared for. Today, I'd say... it is necessary to have the first, even second degree... Those who had entered before had not done that [but now] this has to end.[42]

In presenting this vision he continues:

> But this is not the essence, not the principle... To touch the wound of Jesus, you need not be trained. To give love and charity, you need not be a doctor but you can study and have a degree. However, I think the general principle is to learn to love.[43]

Toqueiras/os find that their narratives of poverty and daily spiritual practices pose critical questions for possession of goods, even by the community. Some members argue that some collective goods are important for their ministry to the poor. Such narratives about poverty are more complex for Toca since, unlike the question of pursuing or abandoning one's studies, these directly involve core organizational institutional discourse, everyday practices at an individual and collective level, and something highly valued by every member.

The ideas of poverty as "inner struggle," "daily struggle," "empting oneself," or "abandonment to Providence" express in a poignant way the individual attitudes regarding the practice of an austere life in this revitalization movement. As one *toqueiro* put it:

> We seek to live total poverty in total detachment so that in our homes there is nothing [set aside] for anyone and everything belongs to everyone. So with this sandal here, if I lie down to rest and someone else's breaks and he needs to leave, he will take this one... Here in Rio we do not walk barefoot because it is too dirty in the streets, but in other cities we walk barefoot, so there is not even a need for these sandals... Nothing belongs to anybody and everything belongs to everyone.[44]

Respondents strongly emphasize faith in divine providence and many stories are commonly shared regarding the miraculous. Many describe situations when there was not enough food or supplies, but just then, suddenly, a donation was received. Such stories help underline both that God tests their faith and that if they persevere, God will provide.

Toqueiras/os also associate the idea of poverty with freedom. They commonly state that the more one embraces poverty, the more one experiences true freedom. In this and other ways, their values challenge the social logic of the culture of choice within the surrounding society. Not surprisingly, they tend to present narratives detailing their struggles with desires. In a pluralistic society driven by new technologies and consumer goods, the choice of poverty leads to a certain calming of the ego. As a 25 year old *toqueira* put it:

> The human tendency is to want to have, to have security, you know... Therefore, we do not get too attached to one place. We live in Providence, take what people give us, and so take a little of their own free will... You discover a freedom in God, not in the freedom that the world gives, but to do what is necessary with maturity.[45]

A 20 year old *toqueira* from a middle class family echoed this perspective: "I've often had to ask for money in the street to buy a bus ticket. It makes me feel free."[46]

Interpretive Trends and *Toca de Asis*

Toca illustrates critical trends in world Christian revitalization as well as contemporary world Catholicism. Further, when contrasted to the relative decline of religious orders, particularly existing apostolic orders with complicated institutions and educational competencies demanded of their members, and the resulting isomorphic tendencies,[47] one can observe an approach to Christian revitalization that combines radical ideals with a kind of post-modern deconstruction of contemporary church life. This combination of elements is not dissimilar from other revitalization movements elsewhere in world Christianity.[48]

Social Change

Revitalization movements are by nature full of the living and dangerous memory of Jesus Christ and in this sense inevitably eschatological with a strong sense of being somehow a *kairos*, or God's appointed time.[49] Such an orientation toward practice and memory reflects both the contemporary epistemological turn toward practice[50] as well as the increasing confrontation of rich and poor, the comfortable and the rejected, in globalized forms of late capitalism. At the same time, while these developments reflect the larger conversation about the cultural turn toward postmodernism,[51] it also refers back to traditional understandings of the relationship between the Christian and the poor.

The experience of poverty offers a situation from which the scriptures are heard in a particular way. Consider how the experience of poverty helps today's believers identify with the poor of Palestine—carpenters, shepherds, fisherfolk—described in the Scriptures. It would be hard to describe ancient Israelite society or the lifestyle of Jesus and the apostles as resembling anything like a wealthy consumer society. But it is comparatively easy to think of the life experience of Jesus's world as resembling life among the impoverished in the massive cities of the global south—peoples at the margins of empire and, often, the margins of survival. Similarly, it is relatively straightforward to take calls for justice, so characteristic of the message of Jesus and the ancient Jewish prophetic tradition from which he comes, quite literally in situations of such poverty. Such calls for justice – right relationship, in a scriptural sense – are not only for simple structural change witness by the voice of liberation theology and ecclesial base communities.[52] They are also personal and relational, both horizontal – with other persons – and vertical – with God. Perhaps it is not surprising theologically or sociologically that *Toca* would both embrace the poor but also the divine, and both in a very embodied way – in the person of the homeless and in the actual bread of the Eucharist before which they meditate with such a sense of being in God's presence in a special way. Their wider, charismatic-influenced prayer styles emphasizing body movements, raised hands, and the collective effervescence of shared music and dance similarly reflect an embodied sensibility.

In all this, *Toca* represents a contemporary form of Christian revitalization that is very different from older forms of Catholic practice in spite of embracing certain ancient forms such as dress, tonsure, and Eucharistic adoration. First, they are profoundly urban, deeply engaged in the challenges of poverty and homelessness in megalopolis. This is a real shift for Catholicism, which has accumulated a wealth of practices oriented to peasant societies and rural life. Although rural people were among the last to accept the message of the early Church — "pagan" means "country person" in Latin — Catholicism has a weak track record in engaging the working classes of the early modern period. Catholicism's success within the working classes of the cities of the United

States during the twentieth century suggest that Catholicism is not necessarily doomed to fail in revitalization efforts within today's vast megalopolises, but it will require considerable new creativity and perhaps even learning from other Christian traditions that do not carry the sensibility of earlier cultural milieu.

Justice

Contemporary revitalization movements frame questions of justice very differently than movements of decades past, and *Toca* is no exception. Nonetheless, it contains a certain suspicion of contemporary economic and cultural practice as well as a commitment to egalitarian relationship with the poor understood in both a spiritual and practical sense. Simultaneously oriented toward the person and community, *Toca* offers resonance more with meso-level questions of civil society and civic relationships then macro, systemic issues.[53] This is generally consistent with a changed context: what once made sense to embrace as state-based corporativist or socialist solutions are increasingly understood in terms of civil society. At the same time, Christianity and religion in general, including the Catholic Church, have migrated toward civil society from official society, more as an elective commitment than a natural quality of all members of a society.[54] This emerging, new form of ecclesial self-understanding has emerged in the social imaginary only quite recently. It is clearly a cause and consequence of the globalization of so-called modernization processes, but at the same time is much deeper than that. In this way, specific concepts of justice and connected to broader forms of social change in the nexus between religion and society.

Toward a Comparative and
Cross-Disciplinary Perspective

World Christian revitalization evokes distinctiveness in the specificity of their practice but at the same time provoke questions of context and perspective. As the Brazilian National Catholic Bishops' Conference (CNBB) observes, this question is particularly timely today.[55] Although Brazilian Catholicism enjoyed hegemony over many centuries, this has long since disappeared in the growth of Pentecostalism and new religious movements no less than the rise of those who claim no religion and the migration of religion from "officialdom" to "fandom." All these developments demand new interpretations of revitalization movements in Brazil Catholicism and beyond.[56]

Further, it is not as if the Brazilian case can be narrowly construed as merely representative of the "global south," or of the "Christian West" for that matter. Rather, Brazil represents broad world trends, critical for the interpretation of world Christian revitalization. Such trends are best understood comparatively and in a cross-disciplinary light, uniting insights of sociology, practical theology, cultural studies, political economy, and much more.[57] This is particularly the case today because the process of cultural diffusion has not produced a single modern "meta-culture", but rather a variety of relatively autonomous and yet interlinked modernities on the one hand, and on the other, a set of broader global imperatives, pressures and constraints[58]. These dual processes are critical for identifying interpretative trends within world Christian revitalization today.

Within Catholicism, the revitalization movement(s) that constituted the Second Vatican Council (1963-1965) was fundamentally a dialogue with Western society. Arguably this was also a time when modernist thinking, including the modernist vision called communism, was at its peak. Bishops, too, were in their majority from the West, and the issues they dealt with were characteristically North Atlantic ones—the concerns of Europe and North America.[59] As such, the Council was largely about engaging an increasingly secular world and the last council of European Catholicism. In today's postcolonial reality, no experience of any region is a sideline or an exceptional case. Instead, all experiences are hybrid, and all reflect elements of the other.[60] Today, world Christian revitalization can only be understood contextually, in terms of multiple modernities, or as a postmodern framework where there is no longer a single, dominant metanarrative.[61] A single confessional or disciplinary approach is no longer sufficient to understand trends in world Christian revitalization.

Today, all world contexts offer something to advance the innovation processes necessary for the adaptation and development of world Christianity. The challenges faced in each world megacultural region and in every single people group are distinctive, but there is much to be learned across each context.[62] This is as true for Christianity in general as for Catholicism in particular. The experience of *Toca* offers much to the study of world Christian revitalization.

Note on Authors

Silvia Regina Alves Fernandes is associate professor of social sciences at Universidade Federal Rural do Rio de Janeiro (UFRRJ) in the city of Rio de Janeiro, Brazil. Her publications include Jovens Religiosos e o Catolicismo – Escolhas, Desafios e Subjetividades (Rio de Janeiro, Brazil: Quartet, 2010) and other books and *articles on Catholicism in Brazil.* Bryan T. Froehle is professor of practical theology and director of the Ph.D. program in practical theology at St. Thomas University in Miami, Florida. His publications include Global Catholicism (Maryknoll, New York, USA: Orbis, 2003) and scholarly articles on the emerging shape of Catholicism in Latin America and around the world.

Notes

1. Bryan T. Froehle and Mary Gautier, *Global Catholicism* (Maryknoll, New York, USA: Orbis, 2003).

2. John A. Renken, "Parishes, Pastors, and Parochial Vicars," in John P. Beal, James A. Coriden, and Thomas J. Green, eds., New Commentary on the Code of Canon Law (Mahwah, New Jersey, USA: Paulist, 2000), 674.

3. James Coriden, *The Parish in Catholic Tradition: History, Theology and Canon*

Law (Mahwah, New Jersey, USA: Paulist, 1997).

4. *Annuarium Statisticum Ecclesiae 2008* (Citta del Vaticano: Libreria Editrice Vaticana, 2010), 28. The term "pastoral center" goes to the first edition of this statistical yearbook of the church in 1969.

5. This refers to the era of the Counter-Reformation Council of Trent (1545-1563), which includes numerous other historical periods from the sixteenth century baroque to nineteenth century restorationism and twentieth century modernism.

6. The case of the Diocese of Poitiers is just one example of the kind of radical restructuring that is taking place in Europe. No matter how it is undertaken, the end result will likely be many more worship sites than parishes. See Reinhard Feiter and Hadwig Müller, eds., *Was Wird Jetzt aus uns, Herr Bischof? Ermutigende Erfahrungen der Gemeindebildung in Poitiers* (Ostfildern, Germany: Schwabenverlag, 2009). The majors reasons for suppressing the Tridentine parish system, which assumed one full-time priest pastor per parish, has been due to declining numbers of priests and related shifts in demography and religious practice.

7. The term "apostolic" here refers to an apostolate, a term for a particular kind of ministry such as education or health care. Apostolic religious orders, unlike older contemplative, monastic orders such as the Benedictines, are fundamentally about doing active ministry within educational or social service institutions, or other contexts, in the larger society. Historically these have been undertaken primarily as corporate or sponsored works by the religious order itself, but today it has been become more and more common that members take on particular individual ministries with the approval of their religious superiors.

8. See the work of Gerald Arbuckle, SM, *Out of Chaos: Refounding Religious Congregations* (Mahwah, New Jersey, USA: Paulist, 1988). Patricia Wittberg, SC, *Pathways to Recreating Religious Communities* (Mahwah, New Jersey, USA: Paulist, 1996).

9. Regarding emerging forms of religious orders or religious (consecrated) life within Catholicism in the United States, see Center for Applied Research in the Apostolate (CARA), *Emerging Communities of Consecrated Life in the United States* (Washington, District of Columbia, USA: CARA, 2006). CARA, *Recent Vocations to Religious Life* (Washington, District of Columbia, USA: CARA, 2009). For a discussion of new forms of religious movements throughout world Catholicism, see Michael A. Hayes, *New Religious Movements in the Catholic Church* (New York, New York, USA: Continuum, 2006).

10. The yearly, Vatican-published *Annuarium Statisticum Ecclesiae* has presented statistics on such topics as these since 1969.

11. Janice Perlman, *Favela: Four Decades on Living on the Edge in Rio de Janeiro* (Oxford, United Kingdom: Oxford University Press, 2010). This is the successor book to Janice Perlman, *Myth of Marginality, Urban Poverty and Politics in Rio de Janeiro* (Berkeley, California, USA: University of California Press, 1980).

12. The source of this quote appears in the first chapter of Karl Marx and Friedrich Engels, *The Communist Manifesto* (New York, New York, USA: Tribeca Books, 2011). For a discussion of its meaning see "Notes from the Editors," *Monthly Review* 55.5 (http://monthlyreview.org/2003/10/01/3735). As recently as 1800, only about 3 percent of the world's population lived in cities. See Population Reference Bureau, http://www.prb.org/

13. Cecil M. Robeck, Jr., *The Asuza Street Mission and Revival: The Birth of the Global Pentecostal Movement* (Nashville, Tennessee, USA: Thomas Nelson, 2006).

14. See Freedom House: http://www.freedomhouse.org/template.cfm?page= 25&year=2010. A total of 192 countries are full members of the United Nations. Taiwan,

Vatican City, and Kosovo, all established, autonomous, self-governing states, are not members, nor are the Palestinian territories. There are approximately 61 territories in the world, such as Puerto Rico, that continue to exist in a colonial status.

15. James Keenan, SJ, *Virtues for Ordinary Christians* (Kansas City, Missouri, USA: Sheed and Ward, 1996); James Keenan, SJ and Daniel Harrington, SJ, *Jesus and Virtue Ethics* (Lanham, Maryland, USA: Rowman and Littlefield, 2005). See also N.T. Wright, *After You Believe: Why Christian Character Matters* (New York, New York, USA: HarperOne, 2010). For an overall narrative of the transformation in Catholic self-understanding, see James Keenan, SJ, *History of Catholic Moral Theology in the Twentieth Century: From Confessing Sins to Liberating Consciences* (New York, New York, USA: Continuum, 2010).

16. In this sense, the pressing issues of justice raised by the theology of liberation continue, even deepen, as the complexity of the world ecological crisis is understood. In Brazil – and elsewhere – the insights of liberation theology have continued to develop in rich and fertile new ways, even as new logics of justice have also emerged, often combined with earlier logics in new, unexpected ways. See, for example, Mark Hathaway and Leonardo Boff, *The Tao of Liberation: Exploring the Ecology of Transformation* (Maryknoll, New York, USA: Orbis, 2009).

17. These numbers are much lower than the figures reported in 2008 – 1,236 women and 550 men – but it is unclear how accurate such counts have been, since *Toca de Assis* is only beginning to systematize its membership data. Many of the numbers reported in the past seem to have included those with informal ties to the community such as the equivalent of "postulants" in traditional Catholic religious order terms, persons who have not yet committed as long term members. The membership data reported was provided by the leadership of *Toca de Assis* on March 17, 2010.

18. Data provided the Office of *Toca de Assis* on March 17, 2010.

19. *Annuarium Statisticum Ecclesiae 2008* (Citta del Vaticano: Libreria Editrice Vaticana, 2010), 95. This figure may include some who are members of men's religious orders and who are or will be preparing for ordination, rather than only those who join and remain non-ordained members on a lifelong basis. The reason why figures for religious brothers may be more analogous than men religious in general is that it is only recently that *Toca* has begun to explore the idea of having priests among its membership. This possibility has, not surprisingly, brought some considerable discussion within the membership in terms of the community's mission or charism.

20. *Annuarium Statisticum Ecclesiae 2008*. (Citta del Vaticano: Libreria Editrice Vaticana, 2010), 394. The Holy See reports only figures for members of papal-jurisdiction religious institutes. These larger and more numerous established communities are the most important source of those in forms of Catholic consecrated life (persons who have formally taken vows of poverty, chastity, and obedience). *Toca*, however, is an emerging religious order and as such is under the jurisdiction of a diocesan bishop, namely the Archbishop of Campinas, in whose archdiocese the community first began.

21. Pew Forum, *Spirit and Power* (Washington, DC, USA: Pew Forum, 2006). See http://pewforum.org/Christian/Evangelical-Protestant-Churches/Spirit-and-Power.aspx.

22. This claim may well be overstated, but is largely repeated throughout the media. See for example Larry Rohter, "As Pope Heads to Brazil, A Rival Theology Persists," *Der Speigel*, May 7, 2007 (http://www.spiegel.de/international/0,1518,481434,00.html). Regarding the base communities (in Portuguese, *comunidades eclesais de base*, that is, literally, "grassroots church communities") and their ecclesial implications as revitalization movements in themselves, see Leonardo Boff, *Ecclesiogenesis: The Base*

Communities Reinvent the Church (Maryknoll, New York, USA: Orbis, 1986. For a comparison between pentecostal and base communities, see Cecilia Loreto Mariz, *Coping with Poverty: Pentecostals and Christian Base Communities in Brazil* (Philadelphia, Pennsylvania, USA: Temple, 1994). For contemporary comparative studies see Manuel A. Vasquez and Marie Friedman Marquardt, *Globalizing the Sacred: Religion Across the Americas* (Piscataway, New Jersey, USA: Rutgers University Press) and Timothy Steigenga and Edward Cleary, OP, *Conversion of a Continent: Contemporary Religious Change in Latin America* (Piscataway, New Jersey, USA: Rutgers, 2008) For a recent comparative study of charismatic Catholicism in Latin America, see Edward Cleary, OP, *The Rise of Charismatic Catholicism in Latin America* (Gainsville, Florida, USA: University Press of Florida, 2011). For an explicit examination of the base communities and Brazilian politics, see Alfred P. Montero, *Brazilian Politics* (Cambridge, United Kingdom: Polity Press, 2005), 109.

23. Marjo de Theije and Cecilia L. Mariz, "Localizing and Globalizing Processes in Brazilian Catholicism: Comparing Inculturation in Liberationist and Charismatic Catholic Cultures," *Latin American Research Review*, 2008, 43: 1, 39.

24. By definition in the Catholic tradition, a member of a religious institute (a religious order or religious community, in common parlance) formally vows the evangelical counsels of poverty, chastity, and obedience. This is not the case for the broader category of new ecclesial movements within contemporary Catholicism.

25. Prudente Nery, "Refundação da Vida Religiosa" in *Vida Religiosa em face do Terceiro Milênio* (Rio de Janeiro, Rio de Janeiro, Brazil: Cadernos da CRB, 1997), 23.

26. Silvia R.A. Fernandes, *Jovens Religiosos e o Catolicismo – Escolhas, Desafios e Subjetividades* (Rio de Janeiro, Brazil: FAPERJ/Quartet, 2010). See also Patricia Wittberg, SC, *The Rise and Decline of Catholic Religious Orders* (Stony Brook: State University of New York Press, 1994).

27. Cecilia Loreto Mariz, "Comunidades de Vida no Espírito Santo: Juventude e Religião" (Communities of Life in the Holy Spirit: Youth and Religion), *Tempo Social*, 2005, 17:2, 253-273.

28. See *the Rule and Life of the Brothers and Sisters of the Third Order Regular*, the revised rule and constitutions approved in 1982 by the Holy See. (http://www.franciscanfriarstor.com/archive/theorder/Holy%20Rule/index.htm).

29. Cecilia Loreto Mariz, "Comunidades de Vida no Espírito Santo: Juventude e Religião" (Communities of Life in the Holy Spirit: Youth and Religion), *Tempo Social*, 2005, 17:2, 255.

30. The official document reporting Lettieri's departure from the Stigmatines is in *Historia dos Estigmatinos no Brasil 2001-2004* (Sao Paulo: Santa Cruz Province, Congregação dos Sagrados Estigmas de Nosso Senhor Jesus Cristo), 165 (http://www.estigmatinos.com.br/Biblioteca2/HEB-10.pdf. Lettieri has since separated himself from the leadership of *Toca*, but remains in a ministry of prayer and under the oversight of Archbishop of Campinas. See http://tocadeassisoficial.blogspot.com /2010/08/carta-de-dom-bruno-respeito-da-situacao.html.

31. In the Catholic Church, new religious communities are first set up within a diocese, under the care of the bishop of the place where they originate, and only later do some before organized as fully international orders under papal oversight. See John P. Beal, James A. Coriden, and Thomas J. Green, eds., *New Commentary on the Code of Canon Law* (Mahwah, New Jersey, USA: Paulist, 2002).

32. Cecilia Loreto Mariz, "Comunidades de Vida no Espírito Santo: Juventude e Religião" (Communities of Life in the Holy Spirit: Youth and Religion), *Tempo Social*, 2005, 17:2, 255-256.

33. Cecilia Loreto Mariz, "Comunidades de Vida no Espírito Santo: Juventude e Religião" (Communities of Life in the Holy Spirit: Youth and Religion), *Tempo Social*, 2005, 17:2, 254.

34. See http://tocadeassisoficial.blogspot.com/2010/08/carta-de-dom-bruno-respeito-da-situacao.html.

35. Flavia Slompo Pinto, "Hexis Sagrada: Constructos da Juventude Vocacionada na Fraternidade *Toca de Assis*" (unpublished research report, 2007).

36 . Cecília Loreto Mariz, "Comunidades de vida no Espírito Santo: Juventude e religião" (Communities of Life in the Holy Spirit: Youth and Religion), *Tempo Social*, 2005, 17:2, 253-273.

37. All but Alexandrina have been formally canonized as saints within the Catholic Church. Alexandrina has been formally proclaimed as a "blessed," which is a step on the way to canonization as a saint. For more about her, see *A Tribute to Blessed Alexandrina, A Living Tribute to the Eucharist* (http://www.blessed-alexandrina.com/page_booklet_english.htm).

38. Data obtained in 2008-2010 field research by Sílvia R.A. Fernandes, "Franciscanism in Socio-historical Perspective: Modernity and Religious Vocation from *Toca de Assis*," (Rio de Janeiro: Fundação de Amparo à Pesquisa do Estado do Rio de Janeiro, FAPERJ). FAPERJ is a government-funded agency for scientific and academic research in the Brazilian State of Rio de Janeiro. It funded the original research on *Toca* conducted by Sílvia R.A. Fernandes and used in the development of this essay. The original research on Toca de Assis was also supported by CNPq, the National Council for Scientific Research of Brazil, through its grant program for student research. The authors thank those students (Luisa Barbosa, Leandro Gama and Elizabeth Souza) as well as Geziel Souza and Bruno Marino, for their role in this project.

39. Mariz, Cecília Loreto and Paulo Victor L. Lopes, "O reavivamento católico no Brasil e o caso da Toca de Assis" in Faustino Teixeira and Renata Menezes, eds., *Catolicismo Plural – Dinâmicas Contemporâneas* (Petrópolis, Rio de Janeiro, Brazil: Vozes, 2009), 75-108. See also Rodrigo Portella, "Medievais e Pós-modernos: A Toca de Assis e as Novas Sensibilidades Católicas Juvenis" in Cecília Mariz, Brenda Carranza, and Marcelo Camurça, eds. *Novas Comunidades Católicas – Em Busca do Espaço Pós-moderno"* (Aparecida, Sao Paulo, Brazil: Idéias Letras, 2009), 171-194.

40 .Cecília Loreto Mariz and Paulo Victor L. Lopes, "O Reavivamento Católico no Brasil e o Caso da Toca de Assis" in Faustino Teixeira and Renata Menezes, eds., *Catolicismo Plural – Dinâmicas Contemporâneas* (Petrópolis, Rio de Janeiro, Brazil: Vozes, 2009), 102.

41. Marta (pseudonym) interviewed by Silvia R.A. Fernandes on August 23, 2010.

42. Lazaro (pseudonym) interviewed by Silvia R.A. Fernandes on July 18, 2010.

43. Lazaro (pseudonym) interviewed by Silvia R.A. Fernandes on July 18, 2010.

44. Stefano (pseudonym) interviewed by Silvia R.A. Fernandes on November 24, 2010.

45. Marta (pseudonym) interviewed by Silvia R.A. Fernandes August 23, 2010.

46. Amelia (pseudonym) interviewed by Silvia R.A. Fernandes November 8, 2010.

47. Isomorphism, movement toward sameness, is the sociological process observable in like organizations, for example schools or hospitals, that lead to similarity with other schools or other hospitals even when the sponsorship – religious, secular, whatever – is

quite different. See Patricia Wittberg, SC, *From Piety to Professionalism and Back? Transformations of Organized Religious Virtuosity* (Lanham, Maryland, USA: Lexington Books, 2006), 272.

48. See the trends and cases discussed elsewhere in this volume.

49. Johannes Baptist Metz, *Faith in History and Society: Toward a Practical Fundamental Theology* (New York: Crossroad, 2007), 88. See also Elizabeth A. Johnson, CSJ, *Dangerous Memories: A Mosaic of Mary in Scripture* (New York, New York, USA: Continuum, 2004).

50. Pierre Bourdieu, *Outline of a Theory of Practice* (Cambridge: Cambridge University Press, 1977); Michel de Certeau, *The Practice of Everyday Life* (Berkeley: University of California Press, 2002.)

51. Gerald A. Arbuckle, SM, *Culture, Inculturation, and Theologians: A Postmodern Critique* (Collegeville, Minnesota, USA: Liturgical Press, 2010).

52. N.T Wright, *After You Believe: Why Christian Character Matters* (New York: HarperOne, 2010).

53. Catholic religious orders may themselves be seen both as Christian revitalization movements and as precursors of the contemporary conversation about civil society. See Bryan T. Froehle, "Religious Orders" in Helmut Anheier, Regina List, and Stefan Toepler, eds., *International Encyclopedia of Civil Society* (Heidelberg, Germany: Springer Publishing, 2010), 1300-1307.

54. For a discussion of this migration, see Charles Taylor, *A Secular Age* (Cambridge, Massachusetts, USA: Belknap Press, 2007). Karl Rahner, SJ anticipated this development in his observation that "The devout Christian of the future will either be a mystic, one who has experienced something, or he will cease to be anything at all." See Karl Rahner, "Christian Living Formerly and Today," *Theological Investigations* 7 (London, United Kingdom: Darton, Longman & Todd, 1971), 15. The source for this insight can be traced to Ignatius of Loyola and Ignatian spirituality more generally. See Harvey Egan, *Karl Rahner, Mystic of Everyday Life* (New York, New York, USA: Crossroad, 1998).

55. Jesus Hortal, "A Igreja e os Novos Grupos Religiosos," *Estudos da CNBB* (São Paulo, Brazil: Paulinas, 1993), 68.

56. See the discussion of fandom in Tom Beaudoin, *Witness to Dispossession* (Maryknoll, New York, USA: Orbis, 2008). See also Christopher Deacy and Elizabeth Arweck, eds., *Exploring Religion and the Sacred in a Media Age*, a special issue of *Literature and Theology*, August 26, 2010. Regarding particular studies of the growing worldwide phenomenon of increasing proportions of those who report no religion, see Grace Davies, *Religion in Britain Since 1945: Believing without Belonging* (London, England, United Kingdom: Wiley-Blackwell, 1994) and Ariela Keysar and Barry Kosmin, *Religion in a Free Market: Religious and Non-religious Americans, Who, What, Why Where* (Ithaca, New York, USA: Paramount, 2006).

57. Silvia R.A. Fernandes, ed., *Mudança de Religião no Brasil – Desvendando Sentidos e Motivações* (São Paulo: Palavra e Prece, 2006) and Regina Novaes, "Juventude, Percepções e Comportamentos: a Religião Faz Diferença?" in *Retratos da Juventude Brasileira – Análises de uma Pesquisa Nacional* (São Paulo: Fundação Perseu Abramo, 2005) and Danièle Hervieu-Léger, *O Peregrino e o Convertido – a Religião em Movimento* (Lisboa: Gradiva, 2005).

58. Ulrich Beck and Edgar Grande, "Varieties of Second Modernity: The Cosmopolitan Turn in Social and Political Theory and Research" in *The British Journal of Sociology* 61: 3 (London, United Kingdom: London School of Economics and Political Science, 2010), 410-443.

59. Melissa Wilde, *Vatican II: A Sociological Analysis of Religious Change*

(Princeton New Jersey, USA: Princeton University Press, 2007).

60. Homi Babha, "Cultural Diversity and Cultural Differences" in Bill Ashcroft, Gareth Griffiths, and Helen Tiffin, eds., *The Post-Colonial Studies Reader* (London, England, United Kingdom: Routledge, 1995), 206-209. Kwok Pui-Lan, *Postcolonial Theology and Feminist Theology* (Louisville, Kentucky, USA: Westminster John Knox Press, 2005).

61. Charles Taylor, *Modern Social Imaginaries* (Durham, North Carolina, USA: Duke University Press, 2003).

62. Bryan T. Froehle and Mary L. Gautier, *Global Catholicism* (Maryknoll, New York, USA: Orbis, 2003).

Part 4

Where in the Name of Christ our Lord Are We Headed?

Chapter 15

Liturgy and Sacraments: Driving Revitalization by Positioning Worshippers in Vital Communion with the Triune God

JUDITH M. KUBICKI, PHD
ASSOCIATE PROFESSOR
DEPARTMENT OF THEOLOGY
FORDHAM UNIVERSITY

Introduction

A new Spirit hovers over the Christian Church. This Spirit, ever ancient and ever new, inspires an enthusiasm to respond in new and life-giving ways to Christ in this twenty-first century. It is an experience of revitalization. There are many ways to explore this reality and several have been pursued in the consultations that have already taken place, one at Asbury Seminary in Kentucky and the second in Edinburgh, Scotland. This essay hopes to build on that work and offer additional points for reflection and/or conversation from the disciplines of liturgical and sacramental theology. The traditional practice of liturgy and the sacraments is part of the Church's heritage and can potentially provide rich resources for promoting revitalization.

During the Edinburgh consultation in May 2010, this definition of revitalization surfaced in table conversation:

> Revitalization originates from and is rooted in the Triune God; it takes place where people in specific (historical, cultural, social and spiritual) contexts experience God's enlivening and reawakening Spirit leading to a fresh encounter with the living Christ.... It often takes place amidst dissatisfaction with the *status quo*, vulnerability, suffering and pain, deep yearning, radical discipleship including persistent prayer, scripture study, worship and an unquenchable

anticipation of God's renewing presence."… It is the prophetic impulse for social and spiritual transformation in every generation.

A key element in this definition is the clear recognition that, like all movements of the Spirit, revitalization is initiated by God, not by human beings. This movement of the Spirit, because it is communicated to human beings, necessarily is expressed and experienced in a particular historical, cultural, and social milieu. Nevertheless, the initiative is always God's, not ours. In other words, any dissatisfaction, yearning, or desire for God's presence comes from God, not us. This acknowledgement of the action of God in our lives has always been understood as inviting—indeed demanding—a response. Spiritual writers have often described the Christian journey toward communion with God as an ongoing response to the promptings of God's Spirit in the everydayness of our lives. This response is often ritualized in liturgical rites.

Certainly this journey toward communion with the Triune God is, in fact, the goal of all human life. It is the straining forward and yearning for the final fulfillment of all things in Christ already won for us by the life, death, and resurrection of Jesus. This is the eschatological dimension of the Christian life. We have committed ourselves to this journey and to this ongoing response to the Spirit since the moment we were plunged into the waters of baptism. As a result, our Christian life is a participation in the Paschal Mystery of Christ (that is, his life, death, and resurrection) that will finally culminate in communion with the Triune God.

In addition to the question of "where" we are headed (vital communion with the Triune God) is the question of "how" to get there. Briefly considering some aspects of mystery of the Incarnation can provide a starting point for answering the "how" question. As the Prologue to the Gospel according to John so eloquently expresses it: "And the Word became flesh and made his dwelling among us" (Jn. 1:14). And a few verses later, "No one has ever seen God. The only Son, God, who is at the Father's side, has revealed him" (Jn. 1:18).[1] God took on human flesh in order to communicate God's love and will for us. In other words, God revealed God self to us through the human bodiliness of Jesus Christ. God continues to speak to us through our own human bodiliness. We learn to know our Creator and respond to God's invitation as embodied persons. Thus it is by means of our own seeing, hearing, tasting, touching and smelling that other human beings and all of creation communicate the beauty, love, and truth that is God.

Human Beings and Ritual

Anthropologists have long been interested in the study of ritual as a feature of human behavior. To study liturgy as ritual, whether in its historical or contemporary manifestations is to study liturgy in its empirical reality as a species of significant human behavior.[2] It is by means of ritual behaviors that we forge our identity both as individuals and as members of communities. The term ritual, however, can be applied to a wide range of activity, including those that are not strictly religious in nature. Margaret Kelleher defines ritual as "a social symbolic process which has the potential for communicating, creating, criticizing, and even transforming meaning.[3] We observe rituals in times of joy and sadness, victory and defeat, life and death. There are civil rituals, family rituals, ethnic and sport rituals. Oftentimes these are particularly observed— sometimes unselfconsciously—at holidays and rites of passage.

As Christians, both individually and communally, we engage in ritual behaviors as a means of weaving and reweaving our relationship with the Triune God. This is the case when we gather for worship. However, the term "worship" can be more broadly applied not only to formal services or rites of a particular religion, but also to the way one lives one's life. When the term applies to formal services, Christian worship provides the framework for entering into dialogue with the Triune God. In this case, worship can both express and mediate the divine-human relationship.[4] This occurs because worship involves both human beings who desire to have a relationship with God and a God who fulfills that desire.[5]

Since worship often includes a broader usage than formal religious rites, this essay will use the term "liturgy." The term more specifically includes the element of ritual activity as part of its function. "Liturgy" may be defined as the formal public worship of Christian assemblies. It is a type of ritual action whereby Christians gather to remember, express, and renew their identity and their relationship with the Triune God. Finally, liturgy described as ritual action highlights the fact that we are engaged in a symbolic process since all ritual is comprised of the interplay of a wide constellation of symbols.[6]

Liturgy as Symbolizing Activity

As with all rituals, the building blocks of liturgy are symbols. These include not only objects, but also movements and postures, light and darkness, color and form, texture and space. Language can be symbolic, as well as such non-verbal expressions as music and art. The philosopher and semiotician, Michael Polanyi, offers several insights about symbol that apply to our consideration of liturgy. The first is that there is an important distinction between signs and symbols. Signs function on the level of cognition, providing us with information. Symbols, on the other hand, function on the level of recognition, providing not information, but integration. This integration functions both within the individual or a group of individuals. Understanding symbols as mediation of recognition rather than information explains how symbols can mediate meaning within particular cultural and social milieu in which the symbolizing activity occurs.[7] The crucial element is that symbols, and therefore liturgy, are not intended as sources of information. Rather, participation in the liturgy offers an opportunity to recognize and integrate one's place within the experience of Christian faith.

The work of French theologian, Louis-Marie Chauvet, corroborates Polanyi's insights about symbol and applies them to his sacramental theology. He locates his theology of symbol at the heart of mediation, by language, by culture and desire. Indeed, for Chauvet, all reality is mediated through the symbolic network of the culture that fashions us.[8] Chauvet points out that the word "symbol" derives from the Greek word "symballein" which means "to throw together." "Symbolon" involved the ancient practice of cutting an object in two. Partners in some agreement or contract would each retain one part of the symbolon. Separately, the half possessed no value. However, when joined with the other half, the symbolon confirmed the agreement between the two partners. Notice that it was the agreement between the two partners that established the significance of the symbol. It was only because of that agreement that the symbol served as expression of a social pact based on mutual recognition in the rejoining of the two halves. This is what enables a symbol to serve as mediator of identity.[9] Chauvet's point in recalling this ancient practice is to highlight the fact that symbols mediate reality by negotiating connections. These connections allow human persons both as individuals and as members of a social group to make sense of their world and to find their identity by discovering and negotiating relationships.[10]

What slowly emerges is the way in which liturgy (and in particular the celebration of the sacraments) possesses the potential to negotiate identity and relationships because it is symbolizing activity. When we gather for liturgy, we engage in ritual behavior that involves the interplay of symbols. Those symbols are rooted in creation and speak to a "human be-ing-ness" that is bodily. Comparing this interplay of symbols may perhaps be more easily understood by comparing it with a fundamental principle of quantum physics:

> Quantum physics describes the universe as a place where everything is interconnected or interrelated. Connections are realized by energy concentrated in bundles called "quanta" that flow throughout all of reality. Indeed, this energy is the primary essence of reality. It is an astounding and fresh way to look at the cosmos! The notion that all of reality is interdependent and that its relatedness is accomplished by means of the flow of energy provides an apt metaphor for understanding the symbolic activity that occurs in the liturgy. Like the bundles of energy described in quantum theory, liturgical symbols interact with each other, transferring and increasing energy, shedding light, and unfolding meaning.[11]

Liturgical symbols include such elements of creation as water, fire, bread, wine, and oil. They also include architecture, texture, color, sound, silence, music, the scent of incense, sacred vessels, the crucifix, altar, books, vestments, the presider, and the assembly. Postures and gestures such as processing, standing, and bowing are also liturgical symbols. These symbols enable us to both express and shape our Christian faith and position us in vital communion with the Triune God. This is possible because symbols enable both dialogue and transformation.

The Dialogical and Transformative Nature of the Liturgy

Edward Kilmartin has traced the Second Vatican Council's emphasis on the primacy of the divine action in the writings of Odo Casel. This early twentieth century Benedictine made it clear that the liturgy is the action of Christ not the

Church. The Church cooperates with the action of Christ, entering into his redeeming work and responding to God's initiative.[12] Thus the liturgy structures its participants in a relation of dialogue with God. The writings of the Second Vatican Council affirm this dialogical understanding of the liturgy. This does not simply mean that the structure of the liturgy is set up dialogically, although it certainly is (at least in Roman Catholic practice). Rather, it means that on a much more profound level, our impulse to gather for worship is itself a response to God's invitation.[13] Within the rites themselves, Christian first listen to God's Word before making a response. This response can take the form of sung prayer, proclamation of the Creed, or participation in the Eucharistic Prayer and Communion. This dialogic structure is meant to promote our ongoing relationship with God both within and outside the liturgy as we move toward the eschatological goal of full communion with the Triune God.

Because it is symbolic and repetitive, liturgy also has the potential to be transformative. If we apply Chauvet's theory of symbol, we can see how the dynamic of transformation might be in process in an ongoing way. Engaging in the symbolizing activity of liturgy, human persons open themselves to new opportunities to make sense of their world and to find their identity within it. Symbols can change our point of view and our values by shifting our center of awareness. In their innermost nature symbols, especially aesthetic or art symbols, reveal both who we are and the various possible and actual appearances of the world within the Christian faith context. This experience, furthermore, opens us to the possibility of intentional self-transcendence: we can become different persons, we can grow and change, if we allow ourselves to be carried away by new faith meanings and orient ourselves in new ways to our place within our faith world.[14] Symbolic activity makes this possible.

Chauvet explains that by engaging with symbols and dwelling in the symbolic order, subjects build themselves by building their world. This "building" suggests the process of change that is inherent in the process of transformation. Within the liturgical setting, Christians weave or reweave alliances with God and each other in such a way that they can recognize themselves as members of the social group,[15] that is the Church, and find their identity as Christians.[16]

Because liturgical symbols mediate relationships, engaging in the liturgy can direct our responses, not only within the ritual action, but also to our daily living. As the Jesuit theologian Avery Dulles explains, the symbols of the liturgy have the power to stir the imagination, release hidden energies in the soul, give strength and stability to the personality and arouse the will to consistent and committed action.[17] All of this can potentially promote the transformation of both individuals and communities as they live and ritualize the Christian journey.

In speaking specifically of the role of ritual music in Christian liturgy, Don E. Saliers asserts its power to transform those who participate by forming, over time, the imagination and affectivity of the congregation.[18] In making this assertion, Saliers is building on the work of Susanne Langer who describes ritual as the articulation of feeling, not in the logical but in the physiological sense. In other words, one of ritual's characteristics is the *articulation* of feelings. Its purpose is not simple emotion, but a complex permanent *attitude*.[19] Attitude is the point here since it is in the attitudes of the mind and heart that a Christian experiences transformation. Langer continues:

> This attitude, which is the worshipers' response to the insight given by the sacred symbols, is an emotional pattern, which governs all individual lives. It cannot be recognized through any clearer medium than that of formalized gesture; yet in this cryptic form it *is* recognized, and yields a strong sense of tribal or congregational unity, of rightness and security. A rite regularly performed is the constant reiteration of sentiments toward "first and last things"; it is not a free expression of emotions, but a disciplines rehearsal of "right attitudes."[20]

This description of ritual or liturgy as the rehearsal of right attitudes captures the idea of both transformation and repetition. It is by repeatedly articulating these right attitudes that authentic transformation can occur.

Indeed, this is the focus of the sacraments of the Church, celebrated in renewed ways in the midst of the worshipping community since the reforms of the Second Vatican Council. Whether we speak of the primary sacraments of Initiation celebrated by most if not all the churches, or the additional sacraments of healing, ministry, and Christian marriage celebrated by some, each of these sacramental signs celebrates God's action in Christian life. That action is formalized in rituals wherein the interplay of symbols serves to negotiate Christian identity and Christian community.

Conclusions

The Triune God continues to invite humankind into a deeper and deeper relationship, one that will be consummated at the end of time when we are taken up in the *perichoresis*, the dance of the Three Persons of the Trinity. In the meantime, the created world and our human bodiliness are the place where that relationship is worked out. One way this is formalized is through ritual activity we call liturgy. It is a primary means for engaging in dialogue with the God who pursues us first. Chauvet's assertion that all reality is mediated through the symbolic network of the culture that shapes us highlights the significance of symbolic activity. The symbols of the liturgy—when celebrated with integrity, authenticity, and munificence—can position worshippers in such a way that their Christian identity as Church as well as individuals is enlivened with meaning and with hope. This enlivening, which is the fruit of the work of the Spirit, will spill over into a life of mission that can witness to the faith in new and vital ways. It will nurture the revitalization of our churches, positioning us in vital Communion with the Triune God. The structure of ritual behavior includes its celebrating symbols to express and shape identity and relationships. These elements, as well as their faithful repetition over time, provide the possibility that we will grow into communities that are moving toward a more and more intimate relationship with God. This is the life of grace. The liturgical celebration of the sacraments is one of its integral paths.

Notes

1. *New American Bible*, revised edition, 2011.

2. "Mark Searle: Ritual" in *Foundations in Ritual Studies: A Reader for Students of Christian Worship*, eds. Paul Bradshaw and John Melloh (Grand Rapids, MI: Baker Publishing Co., 2007), 9.

3. Margaret Mary Kelleher, "Ritual," in *The New Dictionary of Theology*, ed. Joseph A. Komonchak, Mary Collins, and Dermot A. Lane (Collegeville, MN: The Liturgical Press, 1991), 906.

4. Judith M. Kubicki, Liturgical Music as Ritual Symbol: A Case Study of Jacques Berthier's Taizé Music, Liturgia condenda 9, (Leuven, Belgium: Peeters, 1999), 3.

5. Margaret Mary Kelleher, "Worship," in *The New Dictionary of Theology*, ed. Joseph A. Komonchak, Mary Collins, and Dermot A. Lane (Collegeville, MN: The Liturgical Press, 1991), 1105.

6. Kelleher, "Worship," 1106 and Kubicki, 4.

7. Michael Polanyi and Harry Prosch, *Meaning* (Chicago: the University of Chicago Press, 1975), 73.

8. Louis-Marie Chauvet, *Symbol and Sacrament: A Sacramental Reinterpretation of Christian Existence*, trans. Patrick Madigan and Madeleine Beaumont (Collegeville: MN: The Liturgical Press, 1995), 41, 84-85.

9. Louis-Marie Chauvet, *Symbol and Sacrament*, 112.

10. Kubicki, *Liturgical Music*, 101.

11. Judith M. Kubicki, *The Presence of Christ in the Gathered Assembly* (New York: Continuum, 2006), 125. My applying the insights of quantum physics to theology is derived from Diarmuid O'Murchu, *Quantum Theology: Spiritual Implications of the New Physics*, revised (New York: Crossroad, 2004), 29-30.

12. Jerome M. Hall, We Have the Mind of Christ: The Holy Spirit and Liturgical Memory in the Thought of Edward J. Kilmartin (Collegeville, MN: The Liturgical Press, 2001), 11.

13. Kubicki, The Presence of Christ, 36.

14. See Kubicki, *Liturgical Music*, 122-123 and Robert E. Innis, "Art, Symbol, and Consciousness: A Polanyi Gloss on Susan Langer and Nelson Goodman," *International Philosophical Quarterly* 17 (December, 1977): 475-476.

15. The term "social group" here is used in its more technical, sociological sense. It is not meant to suggest the belonging to a church is simply an experiencing of social networking in some superficial sense.

16. Chauvet, 86, 106-107.

17. Avery Dulles, *Models of Revelation* (Garden City, New York: Doubleday and Company, Inc., 1983), 58.

18. Don E. Saliers, "The Integrity of Sung Prayer," *Worship* 55 (July 1981): 293.

19. Susanne K. Langer, *Philosophy in a New Key: A Study in the Symbolism of Reason, Rite and Art*, 3rd edition (Cambridge, MA: Harvard University Press, 1967), 153.

20. Ibid.

Chapter 16

Salvation and Revitalization

MICHAEL PASQUARELLO, PhD
GRANGER E AND ANNA A. FISHER
PROFESSOR OF PREACHING
ASBURY THEOLOGICAL SEMINARY

Following the witness of Scripture, Christians have confessed that the nature of the Triune God as self - sharing love, desire, generosity, joy, and delight. God's work of salvation - the restoration of our human life to the divine image in Christ - implies an invitation to participate in the joy and delight of knowing and loving God, ourselves, and all other creatures, in God. Thus it is through the preaching of the Gospel that the Holy Spirit pours out the gifts of justifying and sanctifying grace from which all worship, preaching, renewal, evangelism, and mission spring and to which they return as an offering of joyful praise to God.[1] This is the mystery of grace communicated in the message of the crucified and risen Jesus by which the Spirit engenders the joy of a new birth into a new history which is constituted by the worship of God and participation in God's holiness.

Moreover, it is this deep sense of joy, the fruit of being known, desired, and loved by the Father in Christ through the ministry of the Spirit that sustains the church in its vocation of believing, proclaiming, and bearing witness to a gospel that communicates, and is communicated by, the wisdom and power of the cross. Daniel Hardy and David Ford argue persuasively that we have no reason to preach the gospel other than sheer love, enjoyment, and appreciation of and for God; that the most "useful" or "relevant" form of Christian communication is praise - centered rather than problem - centered.

> Recognizing and responding to God inevitably leads to evangelism and mission as acts of love and celebration, longing for others to share in something whose delight increases by being shared. Yet expressions of praise easily become overbearing and triumphalistic, as does evangelism. When this happens, there is a contradiction of the message. The history of evangelism is extremely painful; full of examples of the message being falsified by the way it is spread. The crucifixion of Jesus is the only essential guard against this. It contradicts all glib praise and preaching. It continually demands the repentance, re-conversion, suffering and even death of the evangelist. This is not just a matter of method, as the temptations of Jesus show the classic traps of evangelism - the use of worldly incentives, spectacular events and manipulative power. The alternative is the way of the cross, from which the true ethic [ethos or character] of evangelism springs: an ethic of radical respect which refuses any coercive communication, preferring to suffer and die, but which also refuses to compromise on what is communicated.[2]

Such dramatic announcement and communal celebration is indeed the work of evangelism, the "publicity" or astounding news that in the calling of Israel and the life, death, resurrection and exaltation of Jesus Christ, God has defeated the false gods and disobedient powers of this world and enthroned him as Lord of heaven and earth.[3] Untied with Christ by the indwelling of the Holy Spirit, the church's remembrance and celebration of the Gospel is both a witness and blessing to the nations; a compelling invitation and summons to join creation's true end of praising God.

However, any discussion of salvation and revitalization in our time will need to consider the pervasive influence on the church of a globalized economy as well as the wisdom and habits of technology; what might be called "the technology of ministry" or "the technology of the spirit." By this I mean more than the use of technology in ministry, but rather the pervasive technological mind and spirit that dominates our life as modern people; that we are self made creatures who are capable of self completion. While debates over the use of technology in worship and ministry tend to revolve around matters of style and strategies for producing relevance and success, they seldom address the larger issues that are at stake; that we have been called to worship no gods other than the God of Israel and Jesus Christ. If the ministry of the church is reduced to a matter of style and method that can be designed and instrumentally used to achieve goals determined in advance, then our fundamental calling as human creatures to know, love, and enjoy communion with God and each other will be compromised and our desires disposed toward idolatry. Put simply, salvation, sanctification, and the renewal of the church are the work of God. This is not a matter of constantly looking out for the "Next New Thing," but is rather the gift of God to whom we attend and upon whom we wait in practices traditionally known as "means of grace."[4] The narrative of Scripture will help to illuminate this more clearly.

An Example from Scripture: Simon "Mega"

The witness of the Book of Acts describes the real life effects of an explosion of joy created by the resurrection of crucified Jesus. At the end of the first recorded Christian sermon, Peter announces, "There is no doubt now, this Jesus whom you have killed on a cross, God has made him Lord and Christ. So stunned by this news, the response of the crowed was to cry out, "If this is true, then, what should we do?"

Being the good preacher that he was, Peter had an answer, "Turn to God and be baptized in the name of Jesus Christ and your sins will be forgiven. Receive the gift of God's Spirit which is promised to you, and to your children, and many others who are far away." In other words; this is good news for you, but its news that is not just for you, the people of Israel; this news is for all the nations of the world. Luke tells us that 3, 000 people were added on that day, and that the presence and power of the risen Jesus was so real and palpable among them that it caught the eye of friends and neighbors who gladly responded to what they had seen and heard. This is described by one of the loveliest phrases found in Scripture - praising God with glad and generous hearts - so much, in fact, that God's goodness spilled over into the world. As a result, writes Luke, everyday more were being added to their number; washed, cleansed, and made part of God's new history in Jesus Christ and sealed for the age to come by the Spirit.

In the narrative of Acts, as in our time, the risen Jesus continues to call and create a community of believers who, in life and death, are gladly united in offering themselves to him as the One whom God has raised up and made Lord and Christ of all things. And what Acts seems to show is that such a commitment is not simply a matter of personal choice or preference, equivalent to choosing a pair of running shoes, or a new type of computer, or changing to a different brand of coffee, or shopping for a particular kind of car. It's much more a matter of being chosen, called, and claimed through the person and work of Christ who, by the outpouring of the Holy Spirit, continues to extend the life of the new creation revealed in the wisdom and power of the Gospel as proclaimed and embodied by the witness of the church.

I want to move forward in this story to the first half of Acts 8 which is about Simon Magus, also known as Simon the Magician. In remembering the story of Simon it is important to note that the Book of Acts narrates the amazing spread of the Word through the presence of the risen Jesus to the nations by the power of the Spirit to advance the story of redemption that began with Israel. According to the witness of Luke, there is no doubt that the church and the Spirit must be seen together since the mission of gathering and restoring God's people is led, initiated, impelled and guided by God through the Holy Spirit. This is no less true of the preaching and witness in Acts so that the truthfulness, courage, and prophetic insight of Christian speech and action from Pentecost onward can only be understood within and in light of a larger story of divine speaking and acting that empowered the ministry of Moses, emboldened the Prophets, and was fulfilled in the life and words of Jesus of Nazareth whose death and resurrection signaled the victory of God's future over all rebellious powers and other competing claims.

Because of the resurrection of crucified Jesus the prophetic Spirit is powerfully at work in the world and manifested through the life and mission of the church. Luke's story makes clear that Peter's preaching on the day of Pentecost is not simply the result of human ingenuity, method, style, or skill. Moreover, it is significant that Luke's portrayal of Stephen in Acts 7 as close to that of Jesus himself - Stephen was "full of God's grace and wisdom" which he displayed through his whole manner of living and dying. This is a sign of prophetic authority at work by the power of the same Spirit who spoke through the prophets, John the Baptist, Peter and the apostles, Stephen, and then Philip, Barnabas and Paul, so that news of the arrival of God's rule through the witness of the church continued to spread from Jerusalem to the wider world in spite of overwhelming resistance.

Here it is important to note that it was the death of Stephen which was followed by the persecution of the church that extended the Word of God to Samaria, where we meet Simon Magus. According to Luke, when Philip proclaimed Jesus as the Messiah in Samaria, the people listened attentively, seeing that what he said and the signs he performed were of the Holy Spirit rather than Philip's own power. Simon, on the other hand, was a man well known for his power in the use of magical arts; for his capacity to dazzle and impress the nation of Samaria with his spectacular wizardry. Declaring himself as great, the people shouted: "this is the Power of God, the one called great" which, in Greek, literally means *mega*.

According to Luke, however, when Simon saw how the people were attentive to Philip because he "proclaimed the good news of the kingdom of God and the Name of Jesus Messiah," he too believed, was baptized, and attached himself to Philip, eventually bringing money to purchase the power of the Spirit from the apostles and Peter. "Give me this power too, so that whomever I lay hands on will receive the Holy Spirit." To such a request Peter could only respond, "May your silver go with you to destruction, because you thought that God's gift could be acquired with money!"

Luke shows us a wonder worker whose greatness in spiritual power and technique has been surpassed by the humble and joyful spread of the apostle's witness to the crucified and risen Jesus; a way of living and speaking shared by a Spirit-filled community that possess a power of goodness no amount of money can acquire. When seen in light of Simon's past success, however, this presumably would have appeared as a new form of spiritual power worth purchasing, as a way of establishing immediate authority within the leadership of the Christian movement, and as a means of expanding his personal influence and realizing his ambition for greatness; to be "mega".

Peter was right in discerning that Simon's heart was not right. Because the life of the Spirit is the gift of God's generous, self - giving love, the ministry of the crucified and risen Jesus cannot be advanced by competitiveness, possessiveness, mastery, manipulation, or control. Neither is what makes it attractive either technique or power, nor the effects and results these produce. It is in hearing the news of God's goodness by which the Spirit evokes joy and delight in knowing and loving the Lord who is proclaimed. This is the evidence of God's reign in his life and ministry; the amazing power of God's goodness revealed through his loving obedience in suffering, death, and resurrection. According to Luke, it is not the results or effectiveness of the apostolic preaching that is important but rather the truth and goodness of Jesus that is joyfully proclaimed and embodied by the church through the Spirit's abundant and gracious empowerments. Moreover, if this is true, then the Spirit is not an impersonal or neutral force that can be domesticated and programmed to advance human plans for promoting evangelism and renewal.

It is interesting to observe the contrast between Simon and Philip, whose humble witness displays a wisdom that evinces God's reign of generous love revealed in Jesus through the Spirit's power. Bearing witness to God's gift of salvation is not solely dependent on faith or baptism, but is also manifested through one's conduct, desires, dispositions, and devotion to God. Based on the witness engendered by Pentecost, this will be seen as a matter of truthful worship in the Spirit. As Peter declared to Simon, "There is no portion or share for you in this word, for your heart is not right before God." He names Simon's wickedness as the desire to manipulate the gift of God for his own purpose and advantage, even in the name of helping others. In the reign of God proclaimed by the church it is joyful attention and obedience to the good news of the crucified and risen Jesus that assures consistency between the message and the messenger; between what is preached and those who hear and obey in the new life bestowed by the Spirit.

Luke shows us that while the Spirit directed Philip's attention and words away from himself to Christ, Simon proclaimed his own greatness by performing miracles as demonstrations of divine power in order to extend his influence over others. On the other hand, Philip spoke for the praise of God, calling attention to the presence and power of God's reign revealed in Jesus. Acts seems to show that the Holy Spirit is a gift bestowed upon those who are attentive and responsive to God's work in Christ, who in building his church extends God's reign throughout the world.

Remembering the Gospel of God's Glory

In our time, faith and ministry are easily misconstrued as a kind of technology of the supernatural that can be subjected to human control; something that provides the know-how to get things done when physicians give up, when counselors fail, and when the economy disintegrates. If one learns to pray [or preach] according to the correct rules, formulas, or program and has 'enough faith' a miracle can be produced. It is not surprising that Simon quite naturally saw the Gospel as a better means of expanding what he had mastered in the magical arts; as something that could be possessed; as a commodity useful for gaining attention and for extending his power and fame. Yet his is a way of getting which contradicts living faith as a joyful response of gratitude to God as a sacrifice of praise and thanksgiving for which we have been created and which seeks to invite God to do what he will in the midst of our daily life. We come to God not to get our way but to get his; not to acquire a means of impressing others by our use of spiritual power but rather to let God make an eternal impression on us with his gift of salvation to the world. At the heart of the matter, then, will always be our need for diligence in discerning which God it is we are worshiping and whose glory we are seeking.

Daniel Hardy and David Ford have written extensively of God's glory, the goal of the universe into which humanity is taken up in being turned to the praise, acknowledgement and affirmation of the Triune God. As they observe, "What is God's glory? Its logic is that of overflowing, creative love, which freely perfects its own perfection and invites others to join this life through praise."[5] Moreover, God's fullness and glory disclosed throughout creation and the narrative of Scripture have been revealed definitively in Jesus Christ by the Spirit's witness: "For the Word became flesh and dwelt among us, and we beheld his glory, the only begotten Son of the Father." The revelation of God's self-affirmation radically transforms Christian faith and understanding through the scandalous notion of God's glory appearing in a crucified man, thus making the cross central to the practice of orthodoxy: "right praise or glory." So Hardy and Ford assert,

> All the lines of Christianity converge on the Christ-centered worship of God. Renewal has always come through people whose first interest in life has been adoration and realistic attention to God. Any experience of Christianity that does not participate in this has missed the point.[6]

The divine purpose celebrated in Scripture is the movement by which God communicates and renews the fullness of his life and glory revealed through Christ by the gift of the Spirit within the economy of creation and redemption. The weak foolishness of the cross provides new criteria of who God is and how God acts in the world through the proclamation of the Gospel and its demonstration in the Spirit's life - giving power, thus revolutionizing our perception of the radiant glory of Christ indwelling the church for the salvation of the world.

> Blessed be the God and Father of our Lord Jesus Christ, who has blessed us in Christ with every spiritual blessing in the heavenly places, even as he chose us in him before the foundation of the world, that we should be holy and blameless before him. He destined us in love to be his sons through Jesus Christ, according to the purpose of his will, to the praise of his glorious grace which he freely bestowed upon us in the Beloved. In him we have redemption through his blood, the forgiveness of our trespasses, according to the riches of his grace which he lavished upon us. For he has made know to us his purpose which he set forth in Christ as a plan for the fullness of time; to unite all things in him, things in heaven and on earth (Eph. 1:3-11).

God's glory or purpose shines nowhere more resplendently than when our life is reconstituted as thankful recipients of God's gracious action in Christ and the Spirit within the church's practice of prayer, praise, and proclamation. Through this doxological activity the Spirit joins us to the Son who, in assuming our human flesh, has manifested and communicated the radiance of the Father's life and holiness within a contingent, sinful, dying world. Amazingly, it is this particular form of glory, *doxa*, the blessing and self-giving of the Triune God who saves, sanctifies, and renews through the "utterly un-glorious" cross of Christ into whom human life and speech are drawn and perfected by the working of the Holy Spirit.[7]

Notes

1. Here I am indebted to David F. Ford and Daniel W. Hardy, *Living in Praise: Worshipping and Knowing God*, rev. ed. (Grand Rapids: Baker Academic, 2005).
2. Ford and Hard, *Living in Praise*, 190.
3. Hutter, *Bound to Be Free*, 37-40.
4. See here Brian Brock, *Christian Ethics in a Technological Age* (Grand Rapids: Eerdmans, 2010); *Missional Church: A Vision for the Sending of the Church in North America*, ed. Darrell L. Guder (Grand Rapids: Eerdmans, 1998).
5. Hardy and Ford, *Praising and Knowing God*, 8.
6. Ibid., 8.
7. Saliers, Worship as Theology, 40-41.

Chapter 17

Songs of the Saints as Resource for Shaping Revitalization

SWEE HONG LIM, PHD
ASSISTANT PROFESSOR OF CHURCH MUSIC
SCHOOL OF MUSIC
BAYLOR UNIVERSITY

After this I looked, and there was a great multitude that no one could count,
from every nation, from all tribes and peoples and languages,
standing before the throne and before the Lamb,
robed in white, with palm branches in their hands....
Then I heard what seemed to be the voice of a great multitude,
like the sound of many waters and like the sound of mighty thunderpeals,
crying out,
"Hallelujah!
For the Lord our God the Almighty reigns."
Rev. 7:9, 19:6, NRSV

For Anthony Wallace, the revitalization movement is an abrupt paradigmatic change to the *in situ* cultural setting resulting from a negative reaction of the status quo.[1] Such changes are usually initiated and sustained by members of the movement with a sense of purpose. Given that Christian spirituality is usually intertwined with music, it is equally likely that the Christian revitalization movement will also involve church music. As such, might it be possible for the revitalization movement to also be shaped and sustained by what is sung or experienced in the endeavor of worship via song? If this premise holds true, then music is more than just a by-product of a revitalization movement, but an integral part. In fact, it might be that the function of singing in and of itself reinforces the vitality of the movement and crystallizes the identity of its adherents (participants) even as they coalesce and become the corporate social organism of the movement that sustains and drives its desire for change of the status quo. It is to this end that this essay seeks to investigate the relationship of congregational song to some of the significant revitalization movements in recent church history.

While much work has been invested in documenting revitalization movements as historical phenomena, not much has been done to investigate the dialectical relationship between the character of the revitalization movement and its musical practice. A possible exception is the collection of essays entitled *Music in the American Religious Experience.*[2]

Therefore, this essay will briefly examine three significant revitalization movements and the role music plays in them. These include the eighteenth-century Methodist revival of John and Charles Wesley, the Azusa Street movement of 1906, and the present day Emerging Church movement. The common tread in all three movements is their contribution to the dramatic shift of the status quo in terms of Christian worship, spirituality and the presence of congregational songs in that process.

The Methodist Movement

Methodism was birthed by the desire of two brothers, John and Charles Wesley, and their friends, for a deeper spiritual experience within the Anglican Church in eighteenth-century England. The lyrical effort of Charles Wesley was intrinsic to Methodism. It is a known fact that Charles Wesley created between 6500 to 9000 hymns. However, lesser known is the fact that this musical corpus was not merely a doxological instrument for Christian worship but appropriately termed as the lyrical theology of Methodism. This corpus plays a part in sustaining the movement and forming the identity of its adherents.

The spread of Methodism from Britain to North America was accompanied by congregational song. Created by the founders, John and Charles Wesley, these hymns were more than a musical resource for worship. Compiled into a hymnal such as *A Collection of Hymns for the use of People Called Methodists,* this musical corpus served a greater function of establishing and sustaining the identity of all who chose to be Methodists. In the Preface to this 1780 hymnal, John Wesley persuasively asserted the need of this hymnal for his followers as he wrote,

> For many years I have been importuned to publish such a hymn-book as might be generally used in all our congregations throughout Great Britain and Ireland. I have hitherto withstood the importunity, as I believed such a publication was needless, considering the various hymn-books which my brother and I have published within these forty years last past; so that it may be doubted whether any religious community in the world has a greater variety of them. But it has been answered, "Such a publication is highly needful upon this very account: for the greater part of the people, being poor, are not able to purchase so many books; and those that have purchased them are, as it were, bewildered in the immense variety. A proper Collection of hymns for general use, carefully made

out of all these books, is therefore still wanting; and one comprised in so moderate a compass, as to be neither cumbersome nor expensive... Such a Hymn-Book you have now before you. It is not so large as to be either cumbersome or expensive; and it is large enough to contain such a variety of hymns as will not soon be worn threadbare. It is large enough to contain all the important truths of our most holy religion, whether speculative or practical; yea, to illustrate them all and to prove them both by Scripture and reason; and this is done in a regular order. The hymns are not carelessly jumbled together, but carefully ranged under proper heads, according to the experience of real Christians. So that this book is, in effect, a little body of experimental and practical divinity. As but a small part of these hymns is of my own composing, I do not think it inconsistent with modesty to declare, that I am persuaded no such hymn-book as this has yet been published in the English language. In what other publication of the kind have you so distinct and full an account of scriptural Christianity? Such a declaration of the heights and depths of religion, speculative and practical? So strong cautions against the most plausible errors; particularly those that are now most prevalent? And so clear directions for making your calling and election sure; for perfecting holiness in the fear of God?[3]

Here Wesley clearly spelled out that his hymnological efforts were not mere accompaniment to the movement he had initiated. Rather, his musical corpus was to give spiritual form and nurture to all who made use of it and to enable such persons to live out their faith and be guided in their vocation. Without a doubt his intent was that the regular singing of these works would embed its theological essence in them and thereby sustain the growth of Methodism and form the people called Methodists.

An earlier Wesleyan hymnological effort that is even more pointed in its focus at shaping the theological ethos of the movement is the *Hymns on the Lord's Supper*. This work published in 1745 consisted of 166 hymns that asserted a Wesleyan understanding of the Lord's supper. Here, John and Charles Wesley crafted a poetical collection based on Daniel Brevint's book, *The Christian Sacrament and Sacrifice* published in 1673. In 1941, John Earnest Rattenbury was able to extrapolate a Wesleyan eucharistic theology through this body of hymns and his findings were subsequently published. In that book, *The Eucharistic Hymns of John and Charles Wesley,* Rattenbury asserted that Charles Wesley was indeed a theologian, one who "created, crafted and communicated doctrines in a more creative and original medium than more formal theologians do"[4]

Widely known for their work with the poor in England, it is not surprising that a Wesleyan theological position on this concern is also found in their lyrical works. However, it was not until 1993 through the efforts of Wesleyan scholar, S T Kimbrough, Jr., that these hymns were collated into a monograph entitled, *Songs for the Poor.*[5]

Under the auspices of Charles Wesley Society, Kimbrough was also able to collate and publish additional collections of Charles Wesley's hymn texts. These include *Hymns for the Nativity of our Lord* (1745), *Hymns for our Lord's Resurrection* (1746), *Hymns for Ascension-Day/Hymns for Whitsunday* (1746), and *Hymns on the Trinity* (1767).

Without a doubt, congregational song plays a highly significant role in reinforcing the tenor and identity of Methodism as a revitalizing movement. Even now, familiar Wesleyan hymns such as "And Can It Be," "O For A Thousand Tongues," and "Love Divine, All Loves Excelling," remain the herald call of Methodism worldwide and accentuates its theological center of God's grace and unfailing love.

Azusa Movement

In the early twentieth century, Pentecostalism gained a foothold in Los Angeles through the remarkable ministry of William J. Seymour, an African American preacher, who was mentored by Charles Fox Parham, a former Methodist pastor who had participated in the holiness movement. The epicenter of this new movement of revitalization was a gathering of believers in a former African Methodist Episcopal Church on Azusa Street. From this birthplace, the movement spread beyond the shores of the United States to Europe, Latin America, Africa and Asia, even as its leadership saw the gifts of the Holy Spirit as the basis for ministry and missions. In that prevailing American culture of racial segregation, the Azusa experience was characterized by racial harmony under Seymour. In its mission, both Caucasians and African Americans accepted his pastoral and spiritual authority. Vinson also noted the acceptance of African American hands being laid on Caucasian seekers in their desire for the baptism of the Holy Spirit.[6]

In chronicling the birth of Pentecostalism through the Azusa Street event, Robeck had this observation,

> On Monday, April 9, 1906, the group walked the two blocks to the Asberry home, reaching there just before 7.30pm. A number of people had already arrived and were waiting expectantly for the meeting to begin. All of them were African American. They filled the "double parlor," with a few people in adjacent rooms. Seymour began the meeting, first leading them in a song. The group offered three prayers and then gave their testimonies. This first part of the meting may have taken a half hour or more. It was now time for Elder Seymour to speak, and he announced, as was expected, that he would be using Acts 2:4 as his text. He began to tell them about what had happened to Edward Lee only an hour before their arrival. No sooner had he completed the story when someone in the group began to speak in tongues. As Shumway told the story in 1914, "The whole company was immediately swept to its knees as by some mighty power." They began to pray, and before the evening was over, several others had spoken in tongues as well. Among them was Jennie Evans Moore. Shumway notes that Jennie Moore quickly made her way to the piano and "improvised a melody, with accompaniment, to which she sang in her new ecstatic 'tongue'."[7]

Here again, we observe the rarely noticed but highly essential role of music in this revitalization movement of the early twentieth century. Robeck observes that the repertoire of the Azusa mission did not differ much from the songs sung in other holiness-based churches of that era, still, the songs took on new meaning. Here he cites the song "The Comforter Has Come" as an example where the people "now read the text with new eyes, reinterpreting the message based on John 14:16. They were celebrating not so much the comfort as the empowerment of the Holy Spirit."[8] With its emphasis on the ministry of the Holy Spirit and the second coming of Christ, it is not surprising that songs such as "Baptized with the Holy Ghost" by F. E. Hill and "Jesus is Coming" by F. A. Graces that focused on these concerns gained much traction and were published by the *Apostolic Faith*, the mission paper of the church. The publishing of these new hymns, Robeck noted, "was a way of conveying an important doctrinal and pastoral reminder to the faithful."[9] Here again, we can see the use of song to reinforce the theological position and identity of the movement in enfolding its adherents into a community. Suffices to say, this revitalization movement did give birth to new music and in turn such music reinforced the character of the movement. Such is the dialectical relationship between the movement and music.

Emerging Church Movement

In the postmodern era of the twenty-first century, the Emerging Church movement with personalities like Rob Bell, Chris Seay, Doug Pagitt, and Brian McLaren in the United States and Johnny Baker, Ian Mosby, and Peter Rollins in the United Kingdom, have ushered in a new form of church life. This movement seeks to center itself in local groupings and away from centralized institutionalized structures like the organized church but more like the church in its pre-Constantinian years. Not surprisingly, this contemporary expression of revitalization is reinforced and by a corresponding musical practice that sustains this intent and drives its expressions of worship. Many of these congregations have worship teams that create their own songs that are sung in their worship events. This minimizes the churches' reliance on contemporary Christian songs that are produced elsewhere. Aside from writing their own songs, these congregations have proceeded to re-make traditional hymns because they find current contemporary Christian music sometimes trite and lacking in theological depth.[10] In this process, select traditional hymn texts are either reworked with additional lyrics and/or their tunes are embedded with a pervasive rhythmic drive. An example of this would be "Jesus Paid It All" as played by the worship band, Kenosis, of Mars Hill Church, Michigan.[11]

Given the diverse theological positions of this revitalization movement, there is no single theological theme that dominates its lyrical content. However, what is clear is the intent for "rooting of this more holistic theology in our people... a theology that works in mind and heart, understanding and imagination, proposition and image, clarity and mystery, explanation and narrative, exposition and artistic expression."[12] In his open letter to songwriters, McLaren, points out what is presently lacking in contemporary Christian worship songs. He asserts,

> Too many of our lyrics are embarrassingly personalistic, about Jesus and me. Personal intimacy with God is such a wonderful step above a cold, abstract, wooden recitation of dogma. But it isn't the whole story. In fact – this might shock you – it isn't, in the emerging new postmodern world, necessarily the main

point of the story. A popular worship song I've heard in many venues in the last few years (and which we used to sing at Cedar Ridge, where I was a pastor) says that worship is "all about You, Jesus," but apart from that line, it really feels like worship and Christianity in general have become "all about me, me, me."[13]

He then advocates for a musical corpus that can articulate the postmodern understanding of eschatology. It reflects a paradigm that is not based on unsubstantiated predictions of the future but "plants in us a vision of a world very much different from and better than ours." For him, this is the need for the postmodern generation "to have in their imaginations images of the celebration, peace, justice, and wholeness towards which our dismal, conflicted, polluted, and fragmented world must move. This is much, much bigger than songs about me being in heaven. It's not about clouds and ethereal, other-worldly imagery."[14] Further on in that letter, McLaren tacitly reveals the power of music to shape, reinforce and sustain the beliefs and direction of the Emerging Church revitalization movement. It remains to be seen if this missional call will be fully heeded by adherents of this revitalization movement given its disparate nature. Early indications do reveal a slight shift of postmodern lyrical content primarily among the efforts of songwriters such as David Crowder, Chris Tomlin, Keith Getty, among others.

Conclusion

In summary, I have presented three significant case studies that show the use of congregational song as a resource for the shaping of revitalization movements. Without a doubt, all these movements strive to offer their adherents the possibility of experiencing the in-breaking of the kingdom of God in the present through song. All three movements are equally convinced that music has a transformative function beyond its doxological properties. For these movements, music is given the task of implanting doctrine and crystallizing the ethos of spiritual values, the formation of identity and thereby enabling the establishing of a community, an *ecclesia*, that will sustain and propel the revitalization movement forward. In all three studies, music is not just the handmaiden of liturgy but the theological essence of the movement, and the prime impetus for the revitalization movement. It serves as a critical resource for its adherents in terms of a lyrical theology sustaining the direction of the revitalization process and to give form and reinforcement to the identity of the movement in the face of competing ideologies and cultural contexts.

Notes

1. Anthony Wallace, "Recurrent Patterns in Social Movements," in *American Anthropology*. 52. 265.

2. Philip V. Bohlman, Edith Blumhofer and Maria Chow, eds., *Music in the American Religious Experience*. (Oxford: Oxford University Press, 2005).

3. John Wesley, ed. *A Collection of Hymns: For the Use of the People Called Methodists.*

(London: Wesleyan Methodist Book-Room, 1780), Preface.

4. John R. Tyson, *Assist Me to Proclaim: The Life and Hymns of Charles Wesley.* (Grand Rapids, MI: William B. Eerdmans Publishing, 2007), 253.

5. S T Kimbrough, Jr., ed., *Songs for the Poor: Help Us Make the Poor Our Friends.* (Madison, NJ: Charles Wesley Society, 1993).

6. Vinson Synan, "The Lasting Legacies of the Azusa Street Revival," in *The Enrichment Journal.* Internet. See http://enrichmentjournal.ag.org/200602/200602_142_Legacies.cfm. Accessed 25 May 2011).

7. Cecil M. Robeck, Jr., *The Azusa Street Mission and Revival: The Birth of the Global Pentecostal Movement.* (Nashville, TN: Thomas Nelson, Inc., 2006), 67-69.

8. Robeck, 146. An audio sample of the song can be found at http://youtu.be/MU98khZAz2g. Internet. Accessed on 25 May 2011.

9. Robeck, 147.

10. Brian D. McLaren, "An Open Letter to Worship Songwriters" in http://brianmclaren.net/archives/blog/open-letter-to-worship-songwrite.html. Internet. Accessed 27 May 2011.

11. An audio sample can be heard in http://www.marshillchurch.org/media/kenosis-destructor. Internet. Accessed 27 May 2011.

12. McLaren, "An Open Letter."

13. McLaren, "An Open Letter."

14. McLaren, "An Open Letter."

Chapter 18

Practices for Sustaining Revitalization in Local Communities: Perspectives from Africa

PHILOMENA NJERI MWAURA, PHD
FORMER PRESIDENT, INTERNATIONAL ASSOCIATION OF
MISSION STUDIES, NAIROBI

Introduction

The concept of revitalization together with its related terms namely; "revival", "re-awakening", "reformation" and "renewal" is employed by social scientists and theologians to denote a process by which society responds to stress and varieties of deprivation through formation of social/religious movements that are usually spearheaded by prophetic/ charismatic personalities who initiate the call for social, spiritual and moral transformation. Although these terms have been used to sometimes describe similar phenomena, it is important for the purposes of this article is to attempt a definition of the terms and how if need be, they will be used in this article. In his book, *Dynamics of Spiritual Life*,[1] Richard Lovelace defines revivals as "broad-scale movements of the Holy Sprit's work in renewing spiritual vitality in the church and in fostering its expansion in mission and evangelism". Revival revitalizes the church giving it new life and creating opportunities for a renewed openness to the Holy Spirit. It takes place where there is weakness, brokenness, pain, vulnerability and hunger for the presence of God.[2] Revival usually results in an increase in the number of conversions and a deepened commitment to the central areas of Christian life. As Duncan and Kalu observe revivals are an "endemic aspect of Christianity".[3]

At several points in the history of Christianity, movements emerged emphasizing certain aspects in the gospel like its charismatic resource, ethical imperative or gender ideology resulting in a new expression of the gospel. And as Mark Shaw further points out, revivals incorporate structural, spiritual and social transformation.[4] Reformation relates to purification of doctrine and church structures as happened with the Protestant Reformation in the sixteenth century and also incorporates spiritual revitalization. Renewal is the process by which God's Holy Spirit works through willing and spiritually receptive believers restores the church to health and vitality. It also incorporates updating of the church and making it responsive to its environment. It is evident that these terms are related for they connote a situation in the church when the Holy Spirit moves among an alienated people bringing them back to God, renews human relationships, deepening awareness of God's love, inspires authentic worship and mobilizes the people of God for mission. The term revitalization will be used in this paper broadly to cover the experiences depicted by the above defined words. It is deemed to be more encompassing.

The twentieth century and especially its closing decades witnessed a resurgence of Christianity all over the world but especially in Africa, Asia and Latin America where it underwent a dramatic growth. This growth is attributed by scholars to various factors such as the development and spread of the modern missionary enterprise, indigenous agency where the local people shared the good news of salvation in Jesus Christ, translations of the Bible into indigenous language where people heard the Holy Spirit speak to them in their own language resulting in inculturation of the faith; social political and economic upheaval in colonial and post colonial Africa, the effects of neo- liberal globalization and the work of God moving in history.

Ever since the establishment of Christianity in Africa there have been varied responses that scholars have viewed as manifestations of religious independency and innovation. They portray the development of a Christianity which is rooted self-consciously in African culture and which contributes to a richer world-wide interpretation of the gospel. These African responses to Christianity have been described as African Initiated Christianity and for the purposes of this article they fall within what have been labeled by scholars as revitalization movements. This article explores how revitalization in African initiated Christianity has been embedded in a particular matrix of factors which form the context of God's redemptive interaction with a broken and desperate world. We identify prayer and healing which are usually conducted in the context of worship under the power of the Holy Spirit as elements which foster belief, deepen faith and are instruments that prepare people to receive God, give their lives to Him and also that sustain revitalization of the Christian community. We shall begin by exploring the types of Christian revitalization movements in Africa with specific reference to Kenya.

Typology of Revitalization Movements

Since the beginning of the twentieth century, there are at least four types of revitalization movements which occurred at different times from the early implantation of Christianity into Kenyan soil. They include the following:

The Roho Movement

This movement has three different trajectories visible in western Kenya among the Luo and Abaluhya communities and in Central Kenya among the Agikuyu. In western Kenya, the movement initially started among the Luo when Johana Owalo an Anglican preacher started the Nomiya Luo Mission later church in 1912. By 1960 the Holy Spirit is alleged to have descended on Nomiya adherents who started speaking in tongues, prophesying, revealing sins and jumping in ecstasy after which they were expelled and formed their own indigenous churches. When Owalo was establishing the Nomiya Luo Mission Alfayo Odongo Mango became a Christian the same year. He attended an Anglican school and was baptized in the Spirit in 1916 and received a special calling in a vision. Like William Wade Harris and Garrick Braide in West Africa, Mango operated like a prophetic figure proclaiming the end of colonial rule. He preached against traditional practices, preaching repentance and the power of God and the Holy Spirit to conquer traditional spirits. He is alleged to have had charismatic gifts of healing and visioning. Mango drew a large group of youth around him and was eventually expelled from the Anglican Church. He and seven of his followers were later murdered over local land disputes and thereafter, the Roho people began a vigorous missionary movement called Dini ya Roho (Religion of the Spirit). They emphasized the power of the Holy Spirit and dressed in white robes with red crosses. [5] Among the Abaluhya, the Holy Spirit movement began after a Pentecostal revival in the Friends Africa Mission (FAM) in Kaimosi when in 1927 after a period of ardent prayer for revival an outpouring of the Holy Spirit was experienced with momentous consequences on the character of Christianity in Western Kenya. The revival was characterized by long prayers, public confession of sins, singing and sincere quest for forgiveness of sins in order to attain salvation. It also stressed receiving the Holy Spirit as a sign of sanctification. Speaking in tongues was later stressed as a sign of receiving the Holy Spirit. The FAM missionaries rejected the new experiences and the revived Christians were expelled from the church thereafter starting the whole range of Roho (spirit) Abaluhya churches that are precursors of others.

Meanwhile, another spiritual movement was in gestation in the Pentecostal Assemblies of Canada Mission at Nyang'ori. Zakayo Kivuli an itinerant Pentecostal preacher underwent an experience of receiving the Holy Spirit after praying for physical healing and God commanded him to be an evangelist. He received the gift of healing and his home became a place of worship and in every prayer meeting there ware conversions, repentance, cases of baptism, receiving the Holy Spirit and healings of various kinds. Controversies over these activities led to his being expelled from the church leading to his founding of Africa Israel Church Nineveh in 1942.

In Central Kenya, revival occurred in the Africa Inland Mission in Kijabe in 1926 and experience of the Holy Spirit among young Gikuyu in different parts of Central Province where manifestations of the Holy Spirit included an emphasis on prayer, speaking in tongues, prophecy, visions and confession of sins. Out of these experiences arose Arathi (prophets in Gikuyu) who started a prophet-healing movement that later translated into the current range of Akurinu churches whose members are known for their white turbans, white robes and drumming and reliance on dreams. African Instituted churches emerged as a direct result of the activities of the itinerant preachers and individuals who were expelled from the mission churches.

The Nationalist Movement

The second type of revitalization movement is the Nationalist movement which started in the late 1920s and 1930s as a response by Africans to missionary paternalism and tensions created by colonialism and its attendant oppressive policies and practices. These are similar to the Ethiopian movements in South Africa or the African churches/movements in West Africa. These moments had the goal of promoting African indigenous leadership and evangelizing Africa by Africans. The movements yielded churches that still have a large following mainly among the Agikuyu in central Kenya, the Rift Valley, Coast and Nairobi province.

Renewal Movements in the Mainline Churches

The third Type of revitalization movement consists of the Renewal Movements in the mainline or historic churches. Through these movements, the mainline churches experienced the same renewal witnessed in the Roho movement and churches resulting in not only halting the migration of their adherents to AICs and other Pentecostal movements but also in the revitalization of the liturgy and membership who could also testify to the amazing work of God in their lives. A classic example is the East African Revival Movement locally known as Balokole (saved ones in Luganda) which originated in Rwanda in 1929 in the Anglican Church and spreading like wild fire into Uganda by 1930 to Kenya, Tanganyika and Southern Sudan impacting greatly on mission denominations. It was fundamentalist and puritan and aimed at reviving "backslidden" Christians in their commitment to the Christian faith. This was a mass movement that enjoined the support of the hierarchy. It was also hostile to traditional practices. Many adherents preferred to face death rather than to take traditional oaths during the Mau Mau war of liberation in Kenya. Though the revival remained within the Protestant churches, some extreme revivalists were expelled and subsequently formed their own churches.

The Neo-Pentecostal or Charismatic Movements

The fourth type of revitalization movements is the Neo- Pentecostal or Charismatic movements that today are said to be the growing edge of Kenyan Christianity. They emerged in the late 1960s and gained momentum in the 1990s to the present. According to the *Pew Forum on Religion and Public Life*,[6] Pentecostal and Charismatic movements account for more than half of Kenya's population and have impacted on both Catholics and Protestants Christians. This movement has created an enlarged space for women who have become visible in religious and public life. The churches in this movement besides their Pentecostal doctrine, ethic and polity have certain distinguishing characteristics like aggressive use of media technologies, in evangelism, emphasis on holiness and prosperity, attraction for youth and a lay oriented leadership.

Prayer and Revitalization of the Church

A characteristic feature of all the revitalization movements discussed is the centrality of prayer in the lives of believers and in the entire church as people of God. Prayer fellowships held weekly, monthly and comprising few or larger numbers of believers and interested people, provide opportunities for deeper personal relationships, prayer and praise and a degree of openness to receiving the gifts of the Holy Spirit. The meetings are also characterized by spontaneity, participation, and a salient purpose is recognized as the edification of the members of the body of Christ for spiritual warfare and witness in the world

Prayers are said for praise of God, confession, expressions of sorrow for wrong doings by individuals or groups, intercession, petitions for help, for healing, for guidance and blessings, for individuals, or nations, thanksgiving for blessings received and contemplation. The centrality of prayer in the revitalization movements especially the spiritual and Charismatic ones find resonance with traditional African cosmology. In Africa, prayer is an expression of African spirituality alongside rituals and symbols. Prayers are offered for the above cited reasons and above all for purification of life and to ward off evil. According to Mbiti, they "speak to the question relating to moral evil, suffering, sickness, misfortunes, death, broken relationships, witchcraft, infertility…" Mbiti further observes that "prayer drives out fear and cultivates confidence which in turn generates spiritual health and well being".[7] African Christians like their traditional counterparts still live in an enchanted universe where the forces of good and evil are ever present.

The experience of the Holy Spirit is therefore necessary as a constant support and power against the ever present evil. Praise and worship is a necessary prerequisite to prayer. Denis Maina, a leader of the St. Francis Prayer group in Ruaraka Parish in Nairobi observes that "praise and worship is active prayer, it involves body, mind and spirit. Prevents the mind from unnecessary wondering, it predisposes one to be attentive to the word of God which leads to transformation".[8] This prayer group has ministries to schools, church youth, homes and colleges. They have seen young people transformed due to their testimonies, preaching, and counseling and intercessory prayers. The transformation evident in this prayer ministry is that Christian spirituality is deepened and lukewarm Christians are revitalized and led back to lead a Christ like life under the guidance of the Holy Spirit.

Healing and Revitalization

Healing is one of the gifts of the Holy Spirit occupying a significant place in the Christian revitalization movements especially the Spiritual and Charismatic movements. The strong emphasis on healing has frequently been associated with their very of existence. In these movements, the belief and practice in healing has been rediscovered. Some churches have healing homes and many members allegedly joined the churches when they or their relatives or friends had fallen ill and were healed. Healing is effected by the power of the triune God through the prophets who are usually given the power to heal at their call. Charismatic prophet healers like William Wade Harris of Ivory Coast, Zakayo Kivuli of Western Kenya and the "anointed men and women of God" in the newer Charismatic churches have experienced calls characterized by compelling visions, repeated dreams and sometimes illness that finally led to their total surrender to the call of Christ. AIC prophets for example begin their ministries by calling people to repentance and to abandon traditional practices like sorcery, witchcraft and sacrificing to ancestors. A sign of being called is being endowed with gifts of the Holy Spirit like healing power and prophetic insight about people's problems.

The prophet-healers see themselves as operating under Jesus' command to teach, preach and heal. They feel compelled to witness to Christ's love and his victory over principalities and powers, over Satan, sickness, witchcraft, sorcery and anything that reduces the vital forces of life. The approach to healing is a complex affair that digs deep into social, spiritual and mystical roots of illness. AIC healing addresses the deep rooted cultural fears of witchcraft magic and other phenomena grounded in the African view of the world. Sickness is understood partly as a consequence of sin and there is therefore great emphasis on confession of sins, repentance and reconciliation. Healing is also done in the communal context of dancing, prayer, celebration for the gift of life and God's victory over sin and evil. It is understood not only as a search for physical well being but also wholeness understood as salvation. Healing therefore has social, spiritual, psychological, physical and cosmic dimensions. Healing in these movements is deeply grounded in the African perception of illness and well being. It is one of the areas where the Christian faith has found a home in Africa and contributes to the numerical growth of the church as well as its vitality in terms of faith commitment and outreach.

Conclusion

In this chapter, we have tried to demonstrate that revitalization in the Christian movements in the 20th century Africa and especially in Kenya is embedded in a constellation of themes within and outside the church. Those within the church are factors such as worship, prophecy, healing and prayer which build the people of God, restore their well being and equip them for mission. Revitalization is about creating a community of hope; it gives life to the church and energizes it. It is evidence of God moving into history. Revitalization may occur where there is spiritual lethargy and the church is compromised to worldliness. Social, economic, political and cultural upheaval may contribute to its occurrence but ultimately, revival is the work of the Holy Spirit. Prayer and healing are central to African spirituality and their resonance with biblical spirituality make them an important spiritual resource deployed for the service of the church. For any revitalization to be sustainable, it needs to lead to inculturation of the Christian faith. The AICs and the Pentecostal/Charismatic churches are examples of an inculturated faith that respond to the needs of African in their context.

Notes

1. Richard Lovelace, Dynamics of Christian Life, cited in Mark Shaw, Global Awakening: How 2oth- Century Revivals Triggered a Christian Revolution, Downers Grove Illinois: Intervarsity press p. 14.

2. Report of the of the second Revitalization Consultation, Edinburgh 2010.

3. Graham Duncan and Ogbu U. Kalu, "Bakuzufu: Revival Movements and Indigenous Appropriation in African Christianity", in Ogbu u. Kalu (ed.) African Christianity: An African Story. Trenton New Jersey, Africa World Press, 2007 p. 278.

4. Mark Shaw, Global Awakening: How 2Oth –Century Revivals Triggered a Christian Revolution, Downers Grove Illinois: Intervarsity Press, p. 15.

5. Allan Anderson, African Reformation: African Initiated Christianity in the 20th Century. Trenton, New Jersey: Africa World Press,2001, p. 155.

6. Pew Forum on Religion and Public Life, Survey conducted on Pentecostalism in ten countries including Kenya 2006. Source, http://pewforum.org/survey/pentecosatal. Accessed 6th March 2011.

7. John S. Mbiti. "God, Dreams and African Militancy" in J.S Pobee (ed.) Religion in a Pluralistic Society: Essays in Honour of C. Beata. Leiden, E.J.Brill, 1976, p.515.

8. Denis Maina, Oral Interview, Nairobi, 10th July 2011.

Chapter 19

Renewing the Church, Restoring the Land: The Larger Ecology of Revitalization

HOWARD A. SNYDER, PHD
DISTINGUISHED PROFESSOR OF WESLEY STUDIES, TYNDALE SEMINARY

Does revitalization touch humans only, or also their environment? Clearly if renewing forces are at work, they will touch people in all their relationships, including those with the land—with the physical creation as well as the spiritual and social dimensions of their lives.

This essay addresses the question of ecological issues in relation to revitalization. It does so in two directions: The impact of contemporary ecological concerns on issues of renewal, and—more fundamentally—what the dynamics of revitalization can teach us about revitalization in its largest dimensions, and in particular in relation to the earth, the physical environment.[1] The essay draws upon information and insights that arose out of the first two consultations of the Center for the Study of World Christian Revitalization Movements, held in 2009 and 2010.

In fact, this question was not significantly addressed by the first two revitalization consultations. It thus remains as a largely unexplored agenda item. The extensive "Thematic Summary of Table Discussion Notes" from Consultation II (15 pages; 8,700 words) shows that concerns about creation and ecology did arise incidentally. The summary contains four references to the renewal of creation, but in general the issue was not addressed. There is just one mention of "ecological issues" and of "stewardship," and three mentions of "earth" as a revitalization or discipleship concern. These words do not occur at all in the Summary: environment, environmental, Jubilee, Sabbath, or land (with the exception of one biblical reference).

It is clear, then, that the place of the renewal of the created order has not really been on the radar screen of the revitalization discussions to date. At one point the Summary flags what it calls "Ecological Issues," citing three items that arose in some of the discussions:

1.   There has been an overemphasis on the atonement while we sideline creation.

2.   Do revitalization movements contribute anything to the distressed earth?

3.   In our stewardship are we answerable to creation? (Summary, p. 7)

Although these items were identified, they were not dealt with in any depth.

The conclusion, then, is that the renewal of creation—and more generally the interconnection between church renewal and the created order—remains a pressing agenda item in any comprehensive study of revitalization. The present essay specifically addresses this concern.

The question is this: What is the place of ecological issues within the dynamics of church revitalization? Or, to put it more fundamentally and pointedly: What is the relationship between the renewal of the church and God's intent to "renew the face of the earth" (Ps. 104:30); to "make all things new" (Rev. 21:5)? Theologically, it is the question of the relationship between the doctrine of creation and the concerns of soteriology, ecclesiology, and missiology.

Ecological Pressures and Realities

Over the past two decades, the reality of climate change has increasingly affected human society, including economics and politics. As I was writing the first draft of this essay in February, 2011, reports of global food-price increases due to commodity shortages was a major news story. What caused the price rises? There are many factors, but underlying them all are huge environmental issues, mostly related to climate change: Major forest fires in Russia; flooding in China, Pakistan, and elsewhere; drought or other "natural disasters" in many lands.[2] The world has always experienced fires, floods, typhoons, hurricanes, and so forth. But now a growing international consensus among climatologists, oceanographers, and others tells us that climate change is causing more frequent, less predictable, and more extreme so-called natural disasters.[3]

Among the growing series of climate studies, a February 16, 2011, report by Justin Gillis on the *New York Times* noted that "An increase in heavy precipitation that has afflicted many countries" in recent years "is at least partly a consequence of human influence on the atmosphere." Climate scientists used "elaborate computer programs that simulate the climate to analyze whether the rise in severe rainstorms, heavy snowfalls and similar events could be explained by natural variability in the atmosphere. They found that it could not, and that the increase made sense only when the computers factored in the effects of greenhouse gases released by human activities like the burning of fossil fuels."[4] All major scientific studies point in the same direction, except some that are heavily funded by the fossil-fuel industry.

Without getting into politically charged debates about global warming and other environmental issues, we can at least note—and verify—that ecological concerns and extreme weather events increasingly occupy the attention of the news media, governments, and the business community. This will increase: Year by year, for example, a larger and larger proportion of news reporting will relate to extreme climate events such as floods, tornadoes, hurricanes, and devastating storms of snow, wind, and rain. Predictably, the consequences will be severe especially for the poor and will threaten political and economic stability in many countries.

As I will show, these concerns are directly relevant to revitalization. This brief summary of ecological issues is cited mainly to set the context. For from a biblical and theological perspective, pervasive ecological issues are not primarily a matter of current events. More basically, they concern the biblical perspective on the relation between the land and humanity. And this in turn has important implications for revitalization.

The Biblical Picture: God, People, Land

While much can be learned from studying a range of revitalization movements through history, Christians insist on the primacy of the biblical revelation in understanding and interpreting revitalization. Normative insights from Scripture must inform our efforts to be catalysts for deep revitalization.

I focus here on one biblical perspective in particular, which is fundamental in understanding revitalization in its larger dimensions. This is the biblical teaching about creation and especially the relationship (grounded in both creation and covenant) that God maintains between himself and humanity and the land. This is a three-way relationship—God, People, Land—not a two-way relationship between God and humankind only.

We note first the importance of the "everlasting covenant" God makes with the earth (or land) and "all creatures," as recorded in Genesis 9:8-17. With repeated emphasis Genesis 9 speaks of the covenant God makes "between me and the earth" (9:13); an "everlasting covenant between God and every living creature of all flesh that is on the earth" (9:16).[5] The covenant described here is remarkably comprehensive and enduring, for Genesis 9 uses the same "everlasting covenant" language that is found in later biblical covenants that God establishes. In the background here is of course the pre-Fall description of perfect *shalom* between God, humans, the land, and all living creatures pictured in Genesis 1 and 2.

The rest of Scripture presupposes and builds upon this three-way relationship. For example in Deuteronomy 8:10 Moses says to Israel, "When you have eaten and are satisfied, praise the Lord your God for the good land he has given you" (TNIV).

This simple statement is profound. In the first chapters of Deuteronomy, God reveals to Israel what it means to be God's people as they enter the promised land. Moses reminds the people of all he had taught and all that had been revealed at Sinai and through the desert wanderings. Moses is about to depart, and he carefully reinforces the revealed truth about who God is and what it means to be God's people in God's land.

The story in Deuteronomy, and in fact throughout the Old Testament, is the story of God, people, and the earth. It is the story of God's action through a chosen people to restore harmony to creation by their being a blessing to all earth's peoples (Gen. 12:3). This is the larger narrative that lies behind Deuteronomy 8:10.

This one small verse holds all the seeds of the biblical understanding of holistic (wholistic) or comprehensive mission. Note the structure of the verse. It speaks of three realities: God, the people, and the land. And it shows the proper relationship between the three:

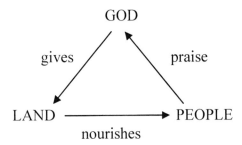

This verse not only mentions God, the land, and God's people. It specifies the *relationship* that God intends between these three realities, these key "subjects." Three fundamental actions are indicated: (1) God *gives the land* to the people; (2) the land *provides food for* or nourishes the people; and (3) the people are to *praise* or worship the Lord. These actions form a perfect triangle, the relationship that God intends between himself, his people, and his land.[6] God gives the land, the land sustains the people, and the people are to praise God in response.

In this instance the arrows move from God to the land, from land to the people, then back to God, completing the wholistic relationship—perfect *shalom*. In other biblical passages, however, the arrows point in the opposite directions. God forms and blesses his people; the people are to enjoy and faithfully care for the land (Lev. 25 and many other passages); and the land shows forth the glory of God (Psalm 19:1 and many other passages). Here the relationships are:

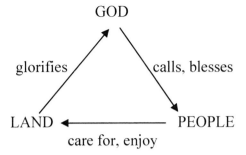

Here is the *God-intended relationship* between Yahweh, his people, and the land. Since in Hebrew, "land" and "earth" are the same word, this is actually a picture of the God-intended relationship between God, humankind, and the created order. This is the relationship, the *shalom,* which God intends but which has been disrupted by sin. In the Old Testament, we learn that through Israel God has begun a plan to restore creation to his original intent. God intends *shalom,* a harmonious, reconciled interrelationship between himself, his people, and the land. The arrows thus point both ways in perfect ecology. So God's intent may be pictured as follows:

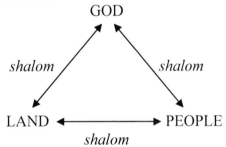

In the biblical narrative, God creates "the heavens and the earth" (Gen. 1:1); he creates humans and places them on earth; and God plants a garden for the enjoyment and sustenance of the human community. This is a perfect picture of *shalom,* the proper mutual relationship between God, humanity, and the earth.

This perfect ecology of *shalom* is beautifully captured in a key Old Testament image of Israel at peace: "They shall all sit under their own vines and under their own fig trees, and no one shall make them afraid" (Mic. 4:4). In a measure this happened under King Solomon, when "Israel lived in safety, . . . all of them under their vines and fig trees" (1 Kgs. 4:25). But this didn't last, and later with Israel's destruction and exile this image becomes an eschatological promise of the kingdom of God in fullness, as in Micah 4:4 and also Zechariah 3:10, "On that day, says the Lord of hosts, you shall invite each other to come under your vine and fig tree." Here is true *shalom,* peaceful and fruitful harmony between God, people, and the land. Sitting under your own vines and fig trees is an image of creation healed.[7]

The story of the Bible is thus the story of God's perfect intent, then the disruption caused by human rebellion, and finally God's way of restoring the harmonious relationships that were disrupted and diseased by sin.

This land theme is perfectly interwoven throughout the Old Testament narrative, recurring over and over. A particularly powerful example is Ezekiel 29–39, and especially Ezekiel 36, where the God – People – Land relationship is central to the vision of Israel's renewal. The parallel with Deuteronomy 8:10 is striking: "Then you shall live in the land that I gave your ancestors; and you shall be my people, and I will be your God. I will save you from all your uncleannesses, and I will summon the grain and make it abundant and lay no famine upon you" (Ezek. 36:28-29 NRSV). The passage goes on to speak of the abundance and fruitfulness of the land.

How does God undertake this mission of healing? We see in the Old Testament that God forms a special redemptive people and gives them a special land—the promised land. God's concern, however, is not just his chosen people, Israel, but in fact all the nations of the earth.[8] Israel is chosen in order to show forth the truth of God and thus be a blessing to all peoples. God tells Israel, "If you obey me fully and keep my covenant, then out of all nations you will be my treasured possession. Although the whole earth is mine, you will be for me a kingdom of priests and a holy nation" (Ex. 19:5-6 TNIV).

So Israel is to be God's priestly people among the nations, a contrast society to show who God is and what God intends. The mission of Israel, then, involves not only Israel's relationship with God but also her relationship with the earth and all its peoples. God is not just the God of Israel; he is the God of all the nations, of the whole earth.[9]

The larger Old Testament picture, then, looks like this:

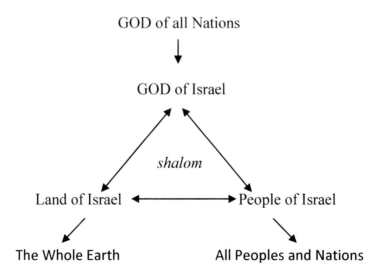

As the plan of salvation unfolds in the Old Testament, we thus come to understand four essential truths:

1. Yahweh is God of all peoples, not just of Israel.
2. God's plan includes the whole earth, not just the land of Israel.
3. God's plan includes all nations and peoples, not just the Hebrews.
4. God has chosen Israel in order to bring *shalom* to the whole creation.

In the Old Testament we see, then, how comprehensive God's plan is. And yet we do not see the fulfillment of this plan.

But Israel's prophets promised that God would in time send a special servant-king, the Messiah, who would actually accomplish God's redemptive plan. Through the Messiah, God would himself bring perfect *shalom*, as pictured so beautifully in Isaiah 11 and many other passages. The first covenant would be superseded by a New Covenant through which sin would be atoned for, God's Spirit poured out, God's law written on human hearts, and God's purposes finally fulfilled. God's kingdom of justice and *shalom* would come in fullness. This was prefigured already in Abraham's encounter with Melchizedek ("King of righteousness"), who was "king of Salem," (a form of *shalom*) (Gen. 14:18-20).

What do we find then in the New Testament? God's plan is stated in many ways. Paul says that through Jesus Christ God is reconciling the world (*kosmos*) to himself (2 Cor. 5:19). God has a plan or "economy" (*oikonomia*) "to bring all things in heaven and on earth together under one head, even Christ" (Eph. 1:10 NIV). The Lord Jesus Christ has been given the power "to bring everything under his control" (Phil. 3:21 TNIV).

Clearly God's plan of salvation as pictured in the New Testament is continuous with the Old Testament revelation. In the older Testament, we see God's concern for all peoples and the whole earth. So also in the New: God is concerned with all peoples and with the whole earth.

In *The Mission of God: Unlocking the Bible's Grand Narrative,* Christopher Wright shows that this is precisely what the Apostle Paul was proclaiming in his mission (comparing Acts 13:17-19 and 17:24-26). Using a triangular graphic similar to the one above, Wright shows how the gospel message expands the Old Testament economy of God, Israel, land to include all humanity and the whole earth (just as prophesied). "All that God did in, for and through *Israel* . . . had as its ultimate goal the blessing of all nations of *humanity* and the final redemption of all *creation.*"[10]

The continuity between the Old and New Testaments here is crucial. It needs emphasizing, due the tendency in much Christian theology to Platonically over-spiritualize God's saving plan. The New Testament pictures not a divine rescue from the earth, but rather the reconciliation of earth and heaven—of "all things, whether on earth or in heaven"; things both "visible and invisible." God is "making peace through [Jesus'] blood," shed on the cross (Col. 1:16-21). God's plan in both Testaments is to bring *shalom* to all creation. In this sense Christians are still "being saved," because ultimately no one experiences *shalom* in its fullness until the whole creation enjoys *shalom*.

Seeing this progression through both Testaments helps prevent a reduced or distorted understanding of salvation, and thus of the potential scope of revitalization.

The climax comes in Revelation 21 and 22 where we read of the Holy City descending to earth. "God's dwelling place is now among the people, and he will dwell with them. They will be his people, and God himself will be with them and be their God" (Rev. 21:3 TNIV). Here is God's plan finally realized, and it is a plan "for the healing of the nations" (Rev. 22:2).

The larger biblical picture, then, is of God's comprehensive plan of salvation:

THE TRINITY

The God of all creation

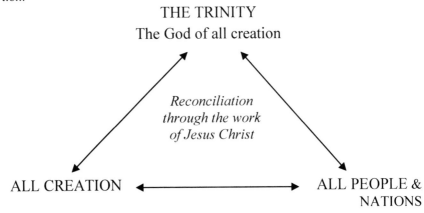

Scripture thus reveals that the wholistic mission of God is to bring comprehensive reconciliation to the whole creation. This is the *missio Dei* which God is accomplishing through Jesus Christ in the power of the Holy Spirit. From this wholistic *missio Dei*, the church derives its mission.

A key learning from revitalization studies is that churches often fail to fully embody their initial energizing vision and therefore need to experience renewal. Due to a variety of factors and dynamics, movements tend to "run down" or be diverted from their original focus, becoming stagnant or perhaps co-opted by other concerns or projects. Thus the need for revitalization.

The point of this essay is that much depends on the initial vision. The key thesis here is this: The biblical vision in both Testaments incorporates the interrelationship of God, People, and Land. Thus any vision or experience of revitalization that does not deeply and integrally incorporate the biblical vision of land/earth will be less than fully biblically comprehensive or "holistic" than it otherwise would be. Any such vision or experience of revitalization will not only be less comprehensive; it will be less dynamic and less relevant to its social-cultural context—especially in today's increasingly globalized society.

A biblical vision and experience of revitalization depends upon and draws much of its energy from the God – People – Land nexus. Without God's presence and action, of course, revitalization is merely humanistic, merely another social movement. Without people—including a real respect for human worth and especially for the poor, women, and children—revitalization movements can become dehumanizing and oppressive crusades.

In our present context however, especially within the Christian church, typically *land* is the missing factor in the God – People – Land relationship. Land itself: The actual physical created order with its abundance of creatures with which human life is inextricably intertwined and upon whose welfare human flourishing depends.

Holistic versus One-Sided Revitalization

If in fact the biblical vision is one which incorporates God's relationship not only to humans but with the whole creation, then by definition any vision or experience of revitalization will be one-sided—or lopsided, "ec-centric"—if it is blind to creation's essential role in the dynamics of renewal. Respect for and actual engagement with land/earth is essential for at least four reasons.

First and most fundamentally, if land is missing from the revitalization vision, the vision is not fully biblical (as already argued). This has implications in multiple directions, including ecclesiology and mission.[11]

Second, if land is missing, the full potential dynamic of revitalization is undermined. To take an example: If a church revitalization movement has a vision for helping the poor, its diagnoses and endeavors will be much less effective if it fails to understand and engage the environmental issues that usually are a major factor in situations of poverty (deforestation, desertification, pollution, and related issues, often being prime factors).

Third, if land is missing in the revitalization equation, the movement will tend to be too easily satisfied with its own internal or institutional success, becoming self-focused, excessively other-worldly, or both. Focus on the land involves us in our common humanity with all peoples and cultures, our mutual interdependence, and out increasingly global interconnects.

Fourth, including the land fundamentally in the revitalization calculus makes the revitalization more prophetic, more socially and ecologically relevant today as environmental issues in multiple ways touch all aspects of our lives. In a world where climate and other ecological issues are more and more the focus of public concern, what do Christian efforts at revitalization have to say? What answers do they provide? Christian revitalization stands mute before many of today's growing global concerns if it misses the full implications of the God – People – Land interrelationship.[12]

With this perspective in mind, I highlight several implications for the study and the experience of comprehensive revitalization today.

Keys to Comprehensive Revitalization Today

If the biblical vision of *shalom* throughout the God – People – Land interrelationship can be brought into creative dialogue with the fruit of revitalization studies, the result could be profound and deeply applicable to church life. The following points seem particularly critical.

1. Careful attention should be given in revitalization studies to the nature of the vision that animates particular revitalization movements. The issue here is much broader and deeper than mere "mazeway reformulation" (in Anthony Wallace's terms). It is the larger question of the vision that animates and motivates people to engage in major, sustained, and sometimes very risky initiatives of revitalization.[13]

2. Revitalization studies should investigate the ways "land" has or has not figured in revitalization movements. The "land" theme may be present and dynamic in either a literal or metaphorical, symbolic sense, or perhaps in some combination of literal and metaphorical. Studies in widely diverse cultural contexts and time periods should prove useful here. Cross-referencing between Christian and other revitalization movements—for example, those concerned with agrarian reform, or with addressing particular ecological concerns—might well provide insights applicable to Christian revitalization today.

Writing this essay in India, I am reminded of Mahatma Gandhi's prophetic vision of harmony with the land and the value of simplicity. His vision was very similar to the Old Testament vision of shalom. Gandhi's vision and movement is an example of movements that should be cross-referenced in Christian revitalization studies.

3. It will become increasingly important to employ an ecological understanding or conceptualization in studying revitalization. Theologically and biblically, the link between the New Testament theme of oikos/oikonomia (household/economy) and contemporary ecological understandings should continue to be explored.

In my book *Salvation Means Creation Healed* I suggest that the biblical narrative is in fact both historical and ecological, yielding a model that can be conceptualized as follows. Here ecology and narrative *together* form the key elements of God's redemptive plan:

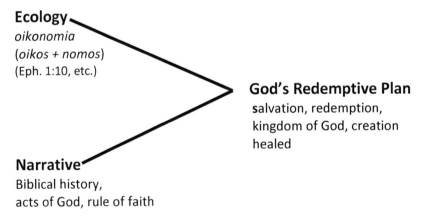

Ecology
oikonomia
(*oikos + nomos*)
(Eph. 1:10, etc.)

God's Redemptive Plan
salvation, redemption,
kingdom of God, creation
healed

Narrative
Biblical history,
acts of God, rule of faith

This model provides a biblical-ecological theology of redemption and renewal that sees *all* elements of human experience and culture—food, art, technology, music, language, literature, economics, political structures, clothing, soil, minerals, architecture, agriculture, energy, climate, communications, symbols, education, customs, sexuality, entertainment, science, plant and animal life, ethics, and moral values—as all *inextricably* interrelated—not just in theory, but in fact.[14]

Incorporating some such conceptualization as this, with a vivid awareness of the spiritual-physical-social-cultural inter-dynamic which *in fact* exists in the world, could expand and revitalize the study and experience of revitalization itself. In other words, we need to study not just the history, sociology, and anthropology of revitalization movements but also their *ecology* in this expanded and fundamental sense.

4. Students and practitioners of revitalization should continue to mine the biblical material and the theological implications of the land-and-creation theme for the dynamics of revitalization today. The previous discussion already points in this direction. Other dimensions here include biblical studies of the theme of land, the relation of land in Scripture and theology to other themes of creation, and what the Bible teaches about God's relationship to the created order in terms of sustaining, providentially guiding, and making all things new in Jesus Christ. Trinitarian theological explorations in multiple cultural contexts are relevant here, as are the New Testament themes of the "coherence" of all things in Jesus Christ and of the significance of Jesus' physical resurrection for God's intent to make all things new (e.g., Eph. 1:10, Col. 1, Romans 8, Rev. 21-22).

Here both ancient and contemporary biblical and theological studies can be brought into service in the ongoing study of the dynamics of revitalization.

Conclusion

Among many other things, an ecological land-and-creation perspective holds out great promise for bridging Scripture and the Christian tradition and witness, on the one hand, and contemporary global-and-local society, with all its combined economic and ecological concerns, on the other. A vision for renewing the church and restoring the land—as fundamental and interwoven themes—is a rich conceptual and practical resource for revitalization today.

Notes

1. The issue originally posed in projecting this essay was: "The realities and possibilities of ecological issues as an emerging force in Christian revitalization."

2. Climatologists report that the disastrous 2010 flooding in Pakistan was in large part a consequence of the exceptionally extensive forest fires far to the north, in Russia—which in turn were fueled by drought.

3. Among the many sources relating to such issues, see chapter 6, "The Groans of Creation," in Howard A. Snyder with Joel Scandrett, *Salvation Means Creation Healed* (Cascade Books, 2011).

4. Justin Gillis, *New York Times* website, February 16, 2011.

5. Citations here from the NRSV. This passage seems to be based on a pattern of sevens: "Covenant" is mentioned seven times, as is "earth"; and the combination "every living creature" (four times) with "all flesh" (three times) also yields the number seven.

6. Philosophically and theologically, we note the importance here both of the three "subjects" (God, people, land) and of relationship, or relationality—not one or the other, but both.

7. Likewise the devastation of vines and fig trees becomes an image of judgment: The enemy "shall eat up your vines and your fig trees" (Jer. 5:17); "I will lay waste her vines and her fig trees" (Hos. 2:12)—which of course illuminates some of Jesus' actions and parables. (Citations from the NRSV. See also 2 Kgs. 18:31, 1 Mac. 14:12).

8. "The nations" is a key theme in the Old Testament, for God's plan is to bless all nations and include them in his redemptive work.

9. The theme of "the nations" is commonly emphasized today in missiology, but in most instances *the land* is largely overlooked as part of the equation and the discussion.

10. Christopher Wright, *The Mission of God: Unlocking the Bible's Grand Narrative* (InterVarsity, 2006), 395 (emphasis in the original).

11. For example: a fully comprehensive vision of revitalization will almost by definition engage the spiritual gifts, interests, energies, and professional skills of people who are involved with or have a concern for the full range of land issues, including economics.

12. My essay "The Pentecostal Renewal of the Church: A Biblical-Historical Inquiry into the Theme: Pentecost and the New Humanity," which was the keynote address at the October 2009 consultation at Asbury Seminary sponsored by the Center for the Study of World Christian Revitalization Movements, provides further biblical and historical background for these points.

13. The question of the animating vision in renewal movements is discussed in my essay "The Pentecostal Renewal of the Church," previously cited.

14. Howard A. Snyder with Joel Scandrett, *Salvation Means Creation Healed* (Cascade Books, 2011).

Chapter 20

What Is It About Christianity That Is Ever Generating Revitalization and Reform Movements?

J. STEVEN O'MALLEY, PHD
JOHN T. SEAMANDS PROFESSOR OF METHODIST HOLINESS
HISTORY AND DIRECTOR, CENTER FOR THE STUDY OF
WORLD CHRISTIAN REVITALIZATION MOVEMENTS,
ASBURY THEOLOGICAL SEMINARY

As a church historian, my contention here is that it is Christian memory which is largely responsible for Christianity to be constantly generating revitalization and reform movements.

Remembering who is our God, and how God has acted redemptively in our past, chiefly in the saving work of Jesus Christ as witnessed in apostolic testimony, is basic to expecting and facilitating new manifestations of that redemptive life, in the ministry of the Holy Spirit, among the people of God.

Much has been written about the role of narratives and metanarratives in defining the core of a faith tradition. I have been intrigued by the amnesia of much of the constituency of the world Christian movement when it comes to linking with the vital stories that offer concrete evidence of God's redemptive activity in their lives and those of the communities of which they are a part. It may be that one of the differences between revitalized communities of faith – or, in the Johannine language of my Pietist heritage, those marked by reborn persons--and non-revitalized ones concerns those who remember Whose they are through pneumatic encounters that persist and, at a minimum, remain subliminal in their awareness and faith formation. Here there is continuity with Israel remembering or forgetting the promises of her God, both personally and corporately. Remembering those promissory manifestations of the divine also becomes the basis of becoming re-membered in terms of personal and communal wholeness.[1] Conversely, a non-revitalized person or community may be sited by the feature of being estranged from such an awareness, and for whom religion functions more at the realm of obligation or vacuous habits of observance. For such persons and communities, the deeper meaning of remembering is displaced by a propensity to recall or recount past events, but they are not profoundly definitive of what or Whose they are.

It is my contention in this essay that acts of remembering carry a higher and more decisive redemptive meaning in the context of Judeo-Christian faith than is the case in other belief systems. That feature reflects the tendency of Christianity constantly to generate revitalization and revival movements at the grassroots level, whether theologians and historians duly acknowledge that reality or not. Without documenting where alternative religious options may be deficient in this regard, this premise rests on the profoundly covenantal nature of biblical revelation, where God becomes intimately and personally invested in the encounter with persons who bear the created image of the God of Christian faith. Human beings are not the distant objects of God's decrees, but personal participants and companions in the mystery of God's interpersonal, and Christians would add, Triune, community.

The biblical faith is profoundly imbued with a prophetic character embodied within the framework of God whose redemptive promises and judgments are revealed through the sealing of covenant, beginning with the promise to Abraham and the house of Israel. A redemptive use of the past is one which catches the wind of the biblical sense of prophetic or *kairos* time in the midst of the mundane. The ancients fought to overcome the wheel of fate, as mystery religions and philosophy cults alike sought innovative though futile ways to ward off the burden of that wheel's grinding rotation from birth to death. By contrast, the trajectory of the biblical promise first given to Abraham is to form in subsequent generations a vanguard of the new humanity, revitalized in the image of God, that had been despoiled by the curse of Adam's disobedience. The goal and object of the salvation history that narrates this promise is Jesus Christ, whom Christians confess to be the only begotten Son of God, made incarnate as the second Adam for humanity's redemption. This promise-fulfilling *missio Dei* proceeds to become manifest in the successive generations of the children of Adam, and its finds consummation in the gathering of the scattered and errant children of God.

The crux of the matter for movements of revitalization is the awareness that not all of humanity will be so regathered. Herein lies the distinction between Christian orthodoxy and universalism. For proponents of these movements, there is, as is acknowledged and attested by the biblical record, an ongoing faithful remnant of the true children of God. They become identified in their personal receptivity to God's mission in Christ for humanity and creation as a whole, which separates them from the darkness of evil reigning in this world. Their common allegiance to Jesus Christ is masked in diverse marks of ecclesial expression. For many, including representatives of apostolic as well as recent evangelical and Pentecostal Christianity, this remnant is identified in the sign of the baptism or infilling of the Holy Spirit, whereby the living Christ becomes formed in persons drawn to salvation in Him.

The corollary of this propensity for remembering among Christians is the inevitability that theonomous memories, being gifts from God, are also promptings for personal repentance, involving lament that our present lives are not what those moments of Christocentric ecstasy or visitation in some fashion, promised. The negative implication of sacred memory is that the past becomes a basis for shame and hence becomes repressed through alternative forms of behavior, often idolatrous, that serve to mask that repression. For those lacking a vital Christian memory, there is also the possibility that shame and conscience are dulled or even missing altogether.

If these occurrences are plausible on a personal level, may they not also be acknowledged as operative at a corporate level as well – as corporate remembering or corporate amnesia? This loss of corporate memory and identity formation is typically masked by the tendency of faith communities—including families, congregations, or denominations—to adopt substitute allegiances. Chief among these is the propensity of homilies to substitute form for substance, or to be self-serving creations that may be entertaining, inspiring, trend-setting, eloquent, or inane, but they do not really connect or convey and draw worshippers into the presence of the living God of Scripture and Christian tradition.[2] As Kierkegaard might have said, not one of them is in the character of the New Testament faith, any more than is this essay. In short, revitalization is needed when there is a prevailing sense that "we are missing something". The climate for its manifestation is a felt need, a sense of malaise with the status quo, or possibly anxiety about life.

It is undeniable that revitalization has perennially occurred within Christianity, apart from and sometimes in spite of attempts to manipulate and manage it for ecclesial programmatic use. In that sense, it is a sovereign movement of the Holy Spirit whose path can be traced from one historical expression of the faith to another, as the trajectory of history continues to unfold. Our concern is not to point a way for churches to tap into this revitalization thread for self-serving purposes. It is to discern how the *missio Dei* has made use of particular expressions of revitalization to advance the larger purposes of God in bringing to fruition a new humanity that will manifest God's nature in its personal and corporate life.

What seems to be requisite is a moment of breakthrough, internal or external, that may be expressed as a sense of participation in salvation history. Remembering the past can be either a sign of atrophy, encrustation, and loss of a forward vision, or it can be a mark of a recovery of perspective that enables us to break out of our confined, visionless, and routinized form of religion. The former is indicated by efforts to preserve historical records to enshrine the sanctity of an ecclesial institution or tradition in all its embalmed glory. Then our task in tracing the marks of revitalization in Christianity would be to "learn, and yet to learn, while life goes by," and so pass our days as students, thereby claiming greatness, and finally to "die embalmed with praise" when our project has ended. Or, our work might be to "but to lose and to forget" our sense of self-importance as interpreters of is grand revitalization theme.[3] Then, and only then, might we who are the inquirers become small in the Presence of the One who brings life and revitalization. Then our task becomes one of "unlearning" what are our preferences and prejudices about how a proper revival of Christianity ought to proceed – "unlearning" all else, save God and the sovereign move of the Holy Spirit.

Having a tradition with an unfulfilled promise, that is patiently but expectantly awaiting fulfillment, is to position our communities to recover the authentic sense of the biblical faith of God's covenant people. Coming to that awareness cannot be fabricated, but it may be discovered as a latent gift to be claimed. My historical interest lies in discovering and tracking particular strands of revitalization which had their onset in a particular "breakthrough" moment. That leads to exploring the antecedent influences which contributed to that moment, as well as the outcomes that flowed from it, in the sense that they bear the mark of that breakthrough moment in some identifiable way.

A case in point is the "United" side of the United Methodist Church, whose formation in 1968 resulted in what at that time was the largest Protestant denomination in North America. In the years following the union that produced that entity, the memory of the minority party and its distinctive witness to the faith, which had endured for two centuries, gradually slipped into oblivion.

That memory had emerged in a breakthrough moment of Christian revitalization among German immigrants and their descendants in the Middle Colonies of pre-Revolutionary North America, before the arrival of Methodism. It was Pentecost Sunday in 1767, and the scene was a large barn meeting—called a *grosse Versammlung* (big meeting)-- consisting of Mennonites, Dunkers (German Baptists), and other sectarians and religious seekers. The preacher was a Mennonite, Martin Boehm, who had experienced what Pietists called the "new birth", a profound conversion to Christ. It occurred for him in the wake of a trip to Virginia to attend a revival that had begun there in the wake of George Whitefield's itinerant preaching among Anglo colonists. Scarcely had Martin Boehm finished his testimony when a member of the audience, a burly German Reformed missionary pastor from Baltimore named Philip William Otterbein, rushed forward and embraced the Anabaptist with the words *"wir sind Brüder"* ("we are brothers").

This event was remarkable for bringing into fellowship leading voices of two adversarial church traditions that had been in painful enmity in Europe from the early days of the Protestant Reformation, then two centuries earlier. Roughly one-third of the German Holy Roman Empire had been decimated in the socio-religious conflict known as the Thirty Years War (1618-1648). And now, in the New World, a revival was precipitated by a moment of reconciliation between two heirs of that conflict. It was an encounter that could scarcely have occurred in the Old World. From that moment there grew a growing fellowship of "unsectarian"[4] witnesses to a new work of God in bringing to fruition a movement of revitalization among the German immigrant groups that would leverage their doctrinal and ecclesial differences around a "higher unity" in Christ, as identified in the common marks of the new birth. They disclaimed an ecclesial identity, given the politically abrasive way that "church" (*Kirche*) was remembered in their European experience. They were a revitalization movement, born of a breakthrough moment of reconciliation, occurring on the date that the calendar of the old Christendom had designated as the commemoration of the apostolic miracle of Pentecost. Now that festival signified, through this breakthrough moment, a launching of a long-desired age of the Spirit, when the old structures of a blood-scarred, politicized Christendom could be laid aside and a new unity in the Spirit would set humans free for holiness and transparent spirituality in fulfillment of the prophetic hopes of the biblical writers.

Yes, it was a heady moment, occurring just a decade before an analogous breakthrough moment at the battle of Lexington Massachusetts, resulting in colonial independence from England. The latter event was achieved by gunfire and patriotic resolve; the former, by the baptism of the Spirit, evoking memory of the Pentecost of old, with its tongues of fire, that had given birth to the young Jesus movement.

From this breakthrough moment, a line can be traced that runs both backward and forward in time. Otterbein had been educated at the earliest center of Reformed Pietism in Germany, the Herborn Academy. Here the irenic Heidelberg Catechism of the German Reformed (1563) was heralded. It was composed by theologians commissioned by the Palatine Prince Frederick III as a veritable breakthrough moment transcending the divisive Lutheran and Reformed doctrinal polemics then poisoning the religious and social life of the Empire.[5] Herborn was also the birthplace of the symbolic-prophetic method of biblical exegesis, developed in concert with a Ramist pedagogy that replaced the use of the deductive Aristotelian syllogism in theology with an inductive search for living biblical witnesses to validate one's experience of reconciling grace in Christ.[6] The focus on promise and fulfillment in covenant theology, first developed at Herborn, went hand in glove with the Ramist pedagogy, and laid the basis for reading the Old Testament and the history of Israel as a guide to the history of the Spirit's movement in the church and world to the present time.[7]

The upshot of this background to the Long barn breakthrough moment is this: when Otterbein (1726-1813), as a young missionary pastor from Herborn, met the Mennonite Boehm at that place, he was positioned to interpret that moment in light of the prophetic reading of Scripture and history in which he was schooled. That he did so is shown in a personal letter he left on the subject of the millennium, in which he wrote, "there is in prospect a more glorious state of the church than ever has been, and this we call the millennium....the prophecies will be fulfilled, and they are fulfilling from day to day". He adds, "the best we can do is to make our calling and election sure".[8] This is done, he believed, by fulfilling the order of salvation according to the covenant of grace in Christ, which is a progression from the call to regeneration to the sealing of the covenant in the perfection of holiness. That way of living led to the outcome of participation in a movement of revitalization, birthed in an unsectarian, Pietist-driven barn meeting, that opened the door for the successors of Otterbein and Boehm to remain attentive to opportunities for extending the work of reconciling, covenantal grace through the ministry of the Spirit.

Indeed, the course of salvation history was dependent on that trajectory being continued. United Brethren went from movement to nascent institution by organizing in 1800 with a constitution and elected leaders. But their roots as a spiritual brotherhood lived on in their new name. They were the United Brotherhood in Christ Jesus, and so they persisted until the prefix "church" was at last prefixed in 1889. Until that time, they remained at heart a revitalization movement, and one that was becoming international with the extension of overseas missions to Africa and the Orient. Features of their Spirit-led, "unpartisan" focus included (1) the acceptance of women preachers in the movement a century before Methodism did so -- the Spirit makes no distinction between male and female (Joel 2:28-29) -- and (2) their uncompromising opposition to slavery among members that led them to initiate an early African-American led mission to Sierra Leone in West Africa. That mission had as its focus inter-tribal reconciliation among indigenous tribes decimated by slave trading. When their bishop explained the rationale for that activity, he appealed to the Long Barn precedent, asserting that here was a renewed opportunity to extend the new reconciled humanity announced at Pentecost to the African continent.[9] It may also be the case that their adoption of ecclesial language and enhanced clerical standards near the close of the nineteenth century signaled their demise as a spontaneous revitalization movement.[10] Before that time, they grew by holding "big meetings" among those seeking revival and they organized societies. In the process they became the nation's ninth largest religious denomination by 1906.

For this historical revitalization movement to have present-day impact within the community of those who stand in its legacy, the enduring aspect of its message would need to be reappropriated at critical points in the present life and mission of that community – be it a local church, a mission initiative, or an ecclesial institution. With respect to the United Brethren narrative, the core message has been identified as the capacity to find reconciliation among estranged people groups—such as adversarial faith traditions (as in the case of the Long Barn encounter) or intertribal conflict among peoples ravaged by external colonial powers (as in Sierra Leone). When a movement of revitalization breaks open within such a context, in the form of reconciliation, we may sense that we have found the trajectory of the Holy Spirit in history, at a given point in time and space, breaking down the dividing wall of hostility, and bringing creation a step closer to liberation from "its bondage to decay and brought into the glorious freedom of the children of God" (Romans 8:21b).

If the narrative of the United Brethren in Christ is invoked in contexts where reconciliation is struggling to break through the impasse of human incorruptibility, this initiative may result in one of at least three consequences.

First, if that story is intentionally used to advance the interests on one party in a self-justifying way of giving attention to a forgotten tradition, the outcome is likely to be demonic. Then remembering the past becomes an idolatrous affair, no better than the amnesia of having no historical memory whatsoever.

However, there is a second possible consequence of invoking this memory of past moments of reconciliation. If the outcome is to awaken the impulse to exercise reconciliation at crucial points of estrangement—as in the case of Bishop Mills' appeal to the Long Barn event to incite missionaries to build b ridges between estranged tribal cultures in Sierra Leone--then that narrative is given new lease on life and may become a force for igniting revitalization anew. Then there may be the sense of authentic participation if the initiatives of the Holy Spirit in bringing to life new expressions of revitalization in unexpected times and places, and thereby advancing God's sovereign trajectory of claiming the kingdoms of this world for the Kingdom of Christ.

Of course, there is also a third option: God is sovereign to raise up new agents of reconciliation in new crises, even as God has done in the past, without those new agents realizing they stand in any particular historical trajectory. Then, finding the links between the seasons of revitalization becomes the task of the historian or the missiologist seeking to develop a comprehensive narrative that documents God's redemptive footprint in the odyssey of humanity on planet earth.

The second approach has been implicitly at work through much of this revitalization project, as fresh expressions of revitalization have been examined and their import discerned. Since we also recognize that new revitalization movements often occur apart from intentional awareness of precedents in which they stand, the prospect of realizing this third option may become a long term outcome of the discussion begun at the revitalization consultation that convened at Edinburgh in the centenary year of the historic World Missionary Council of 1910. To God be the glory.

Notes

1. A historical precedent for this line of thought is found in John Calvin, where he writes that being in the image of God is to be integrated holistically in one's inner being, in relation to one's God, rather than fragmented in that integrity of body and soul, or of will, mind, and emotion. – John Calvin, *Institutes of the Christian Religion* (1559/1960: Library of Christian Thought, 22), I.15.

2. In this vein, John Wesley declared that Methodists were persons who sought not the "form but the power of godliness..." – John Wesley, "Thoughts upon Methodism," in *Wesley's Works, XII, Letters and Essays* (August 14, 1786), XIII, 258.

3. These lines are taken from "The Task", a poem by Gerhard Tersteegen (1697-1769), in *Sermons and Hymns* II, Harvey and Tait, ca 1991, 9.

4. "*unparteiisch*" was the name given this unsectarian fellowship among those attracted to the Otterbein-Boehm movement.—Protocol of the United Brethren in Christ, 1800-1812, in Arthur Core, *Philip William Otterbein: Pastor, Ecumenist* (EUB Board of Publication, 1968).

5. Unlike the polemical confessions of these two religious parties, the Lutherans and Reformed, the Heidelberger began by posing an ecumenical query: "what is your only comfort in this life and the next?" Answer: "That I belong to my faithful Savior Jesus Christ..." *The Heidelberg Catechism* (United Church Press, 1963), Part One.

6. Ramus, a Hueguenot martyr of the St. Bartholomew's Day massacre in Paris

(1572), had objected to Aristotle for developing argumentation that was logically precise but morally irrelevant, as practiced by the polemicists of Protestant Orthodoxy. His devotees at Herborn preferred to use reason to "draw...one matter out of another, thereby discovering the state and condition of his auditors". The Bible was not a source of proof texts for doctrinal polemics between rival confessional parties. It was to be a source of witnesses from which the religious seeker seeks a fitting testimony to illumine his/her experience of saving grace. See Hendirk Visscher in T.J. Frelinghuysen, *A Clear Demonstration of a Righteous and Ungodly Man* (1731).

7. The father of federal (covenantal) theology, the celebrated Dutch biblical theologian Johannes Cocceius (d.1669) was mentored by two Herborn teachers, Martinius and Crocius. For further discussion of these important scholarly breakthroughs in revitalization thinking, see Hans Schneider, *German Radical Pietism (2007)*, 27, and H.R. Ward, *Christianity under the Ancien Regime* (1999), 85.

8. Philip William Otterbein, "Letter concerning the millennium," in Core, *op.cit.,* 102f.

9. See John S. Mills, *Mission Work in Sierra Leone, West Africa* (1898), 114.

10. The same trajectory may be traced among a parallel German-American revival denomination, alias movement, the Evangelical Association of North America (*Evangelische Gemeinschaft*) which long retained use of German preaching, hymnody, and publications, producing the longest-running German religious periodical in American history, *Die Christliche Botschafter* (1839-1946).

Appendix A

The Pentecostal Renewal of the Church; A Biblical-Historical Inquiry into the Theme: Pentecost and the New Humanity

[Keynote Address for Consultation One (October 2009)]

HOWARD SNYDER
DISTINGUISHED PROFESSOR OF WESLEY STUDIES, TYNDALE SEMINARY

Introduction

Pentecost did not begin at Azusa Street in 1906—nor, for that matter, on the New Testament Day of Pentecost recorded in Acts 2. Pentecost traces back to the Hebrew Scriptures and Hebrew religious practice. The biblical theme of Pentecost however has been a theme and dynamic throughout Christian history in a wide variety of ways.

Our consultation theme, "Pentecost and the New Humanity," arises not from a focus on twentieth-century Pentecostalism, important as that is, but initially from reflection on Radical Pietism and the way the Pentecost and new humanity themes functioned within Protestant revitalization movements in the seventeenth and eighteenth centuries. Pentecost and its connection with revitalization has been around for a long time.

My address asks: What is the meaning of Pentecost, understood biblically and historically? I will trace the Pentecost theme in the Bible and church history, exploring the inner dynamics of Pentecost and its relevance for revitalization movements today. The aim is to show how Pentecost illumines the dynamics of church revitalization (renewal movements) and perhaps gives us a basis for a broad understanding of revitalization today, including the role of the Holy Spirit in both renewing the church and renewing all creation.

The rise of Pentecostalism after 1900 brought the themes of Pentecost, the Holy Spirit, and spiritual gifts to the church's consciousness as never before. As is often the case with renewal movements, Pentecostalism has served to reawaken the church to biblical and theological themes that had been neglected for centuries.[1]

Our question here is this: What is the essential meaning of Pentecost, and how has this functioned in church history, particularly with regard to currents of renewal and revitalization?

The Idea of Pentecost

Pentecost comes straight out of Scripture—first of all, the Old Testament. The internal logic (as it might be called) of Pentecost derives from the Hebrew Scriptures, then is expanded and deepened in the New Testament. As we will see, it also ties in with the theme of New Humanity.

Five Dimensions of Pentecost

Several themes are inherent in the biblical idea of Pentecost, and all are theologically rich. Unpacking the biblical meaning of Pentecost opens up several fruitful dimensions and leads, I suggest, to a model of Pentecost consisting of five key elements.[2]

"Pentecostal" movements of various sorts typically stress one or two of these themes, but I will argue that all are important and contribute to the dynamic of revitalization. The five interrelated biblical themes are: (1) harvest of firstfruits, (2) time and history, (3) peoplehood and witness, (4) sovereign action of the Holy Spirit, and (5) the eschatological promise of New Creation. We will look briefly at each.

1. Harvest of Firstfruits. Historically speaking, Pentecost is first of all a harvest festival commemorating the first ingathering of the wheat harvest, the firstfruits. In the Old Testament, Israel's three great festivals were Passover (celebrating the barley harvest), the Feast of Weeks (called Pentecost in the New Testament), associated with the wheat harvest and firstfruits, and Tabernacles (associated with the grape harvest and commemorating Israel's wilderness wanderings).

Pentecost—that is, the Festival of Weeks—is the middle festival. It is above all the festival of firstfruits.[3] The Feast of Weeks begins in fact with "the day of the firstfruits," as it is called in Numbers 28:26. Firstfruits is thus a key element in the biblical understanding of Pentecost.[4]

Note here the very earthiness of Pentecost. In ancient Israel, the Feast of Weeks was not *symbolic* of a *spiritual* harvest. It was a celebration of a real physical, edible harvest. Of course, as such it signified and symbolized God's faithfulness. But Pentecost first of all is deeply rooted in Israel's dependence on the land; deeply woven into the Old Testament economy of *God – People – Land*, the covenantal relationship between Yahweh, his people, and his property—the earth, upon which Israel was dependent and for whose rest and well-being she was responsible.[5]

The Feast of Weeks thus celebrated God's gracious provision of the land and the harvest. Israel's well-being depended upon God's blessing of the land and upon Israel's fidelity in serving God and nurturing, and being nourished by, the land. So Moses says to Israel, "When you have eaten and are satisfied, praise the Lord your God for the good land he has given you" (Dt. 8:10 TNIV).

In the Old Testament, then, Pentecost is not a parable. The Feast of Weeks is not an earthly drama with a heavenly meaning. Rather, it is a celebration of the proper relationship between Yahweh, Yahweh's people, and Yahweh's land; the proper *shalom* interrelationship of earth and heaven.

So we find no dualism here. The Feast of Weeks is not symbolic of some "higher," "spiritual" (as opposed to material), truth. Pentecost is precisely a periodic celebration of the covenant of *shalom* between God, his people, and his land.

Further, by its very nature Pentecost as a harvest theme points to the future. Pentecost links past and present with God's yet-to-be-realized promises. It celebrates God's goodness in the past in providing seed and land. It celebrates God's goodness now, as the harvest is reaped. And Pentecost looks to both the near-term and the longer-term future—near-term, for the firstfruits anticipate the full harvest; longer-term, for the harvest provides the seed for future harvests in the succession of seasons. Fruitfulness, and ever-increasing fruitfulness, is part of the promise of Pentecost. Already we begin to sense the link with eschatology.

This is what Pentecost would have meant to Jesus. Much had changed, of course, and Israel was now under Roman domination. Still, seedtime and harvest were still basic to the Jewish economy and identity, as is obvious from the Gospels.

And yet, interestingly, the Feast of Weeks itself is scarcely mentioned in the New Testament. Jesus as recorded in the Gospels never refers specifically to Pentecost; the term "Pentecost" does not occur in the four Gospels. It is found only three times in the whole of the New Testament, in fact—twice in Acts and once in 1 Corinthians 16:8.[6] John 5:1 says, "After this there was a festival of the Jews, and Jesus went up to Jerusalem," but does not specify which festival this was—though some early church traditions identify it as Pentecost (as did John Wesley). *Which* feast it was seems unimportant in the narrative. Nothing in the ensuing narrative (John 5) clearly connects this feast to the Feast of Weeks, unless the healing at the pool (Jn. 5:1-15) is seen as a kind of "firstfruits" of Jesus' later healings, or unless Jesus' cryptic references to his own ministry and authority (and perhaps resurrection) are taken to point to Jesus himself as the firstfruits (1 Cor. 15:20, 23). Such associations seem clearly beyond the intent of John or the meaning of the text, however.[7]

In contrast to John 5, John 7 has an extended narrative about Jesus' attendance at the Feast of Tabernacles, the third of the great Jewish festivals. John records, "On the last day of the festival, the great day, while Jesus was standing there, he cried out, 'Let anyone who is thirsty come to me, and let the one who believes in me drink. As the scripture has said, "Out of the believer's heart shall flow rivers of living water"'" (John 7:37-38). John explains that Jesus "said this about the Spirit, which believers in him were to receive; for as yet there was no Spirit, because Jesus was not yet glorified" (Jn. 7:39). If in Jesus' day the Feast of Weeks (Pentecost) had been closely associated with the Holy Spirit, these references to the Spirit might more pointedly have been offered at the earlier festival (John 5) rather than at the Feast of Tabernacles.

In sum, Pentecost as a festival of firstfruits does not have as prominent a place in the New Testament as in the Old. In the Gospels, almost all the references to Jewish festivals or feasts are to the Passover. The few New Testament references to Pentecost seem to underscore how much less prominent this middle feast or festival was compared with Passover. Within the New Testament narrative, Pentecost seems to serve as much as a calendar marker as anything else (e.g., 1 Cor. 16:8).

But then comes the Day of Pentecost after Jesus' resurrection, recorded in Acts 2! Now something new happens that in effect completes the dramatic events that began with Jesus' crucifixion at Passover and his resurrection three days later. Pentecost forever takes on new meaning, at least for Christians.

The obvious reason why in the New Testament the harvest of firstfruits is not more closely associated with Pentecost is that sowing and harvesting is a much broader theme than is Pentecost itself. All Judaism's great festivals were in some way tied to agriculture, and thus to seedtime and harvest.

Although the firstfruits harvest is more prominent in the Old Testament than in the New, yet this festival is an important component of the larger biblical economy. It testifies to the materiality and goodness of the creation, both human and nonhuman, and it witnesses to God's covenant relationship with his people and the earth. Seedtime and harvest, sowing and reaping, is thus a key biblical theme, even if not tied specifically to Pentecost in the New Testament.

Jesus' teaching is significant here. Jesus said, "The harvest is plentiful, but the laborers are few; therefore ask the Lord of the harvest to send out laborers into his harvest" (Mt. 9:37-38). He spoke of sowing and reaping especially in his parables—most crucially in the parable of the sower in Mark 4. Jesus implies that this parable is key to all others, for he tells his disciples, if you don't understand this one, "how then will you understand any parable?" (Mk. 4:13 TNIV). Jesus says this parable has to do with the "secret [or mystery (*musterion*, musth/rion)] of the kingdom of God" (Mk. 4:11). Some of the seed reproduces extravagantly—"thirty and sixty and [even] a hundredfold"—the key, apparently, to kingdom fruitfulness (Mk. 4:20; cf. Mk. 4:27-29).

Some of Jesus' seedtime and harvest references are clearly eschatological: "Let both of them grow together until the harvest; and at harvest time I will tell the reapers, Collect the weeds first and bind them in bundles to be burned, and gather the wheat into my barn" (Mt. 13:30). "The harvest is the end of the age" (Mt. 13:39). Similarly, in Revelation 14:15 one of the angels is told, "Use your sickle and reap, for the hour to reap has come, because the harvest of the earth is fully ripe."

New Testament writers speak of a "harvest of righteousness" (1 Cor. 9:10, Phil. 1:11, Jas. 3:18), referring to spiritual character growth among Christians. Paul uses the image also in the sense of evangelistic fruit when he tells the Romans that he hopes to "reap some harvest among you as I have among the rest of the Gentiles" (Rom. 1:13).

In Paul's theology, sowing and reaping is a fundamental principle: "You reap whatever you sow. If you sow to your own flesh, you will reap corruption from the flesh; but if you sow to the Spirit, you will reap eternal life from the Spirit" (Gal. 6:7-9). For "the fruit of the Spirit is love, joy, peace, patience, kindness, generosity, faithfulness, gentleness, and self-control" (Gal. 5:22-23). Then in 1 Corinthians 15 sowing and reaping becomes a key metaphor for the Christian's physical resurrection: "You do not sow the body that is to be, but a bare seed. . . . But God gives it a body as he has chosen. . . . So it is with the resurrection of the dead. What is sown is perishable, what is raised is imperishable" (1 Cor. 15:37-42).

Paul ties sowing and reaping directly to the work of the Holy Spirit when he writes (in the passage cited above), "If you sow to the Spirit, you will reap eternal life from the Spirit" (Gal. 6:9). And of course the agency of the Spirit is directly related to resurrection: "If the Spirit of him who raised Jesus from the dead dwells in you, he who raised Christ from the dead will give life to your mortal bodies also through his Spirit that dwells in you" (Rom. 8:11).

What we see in the New Testament, then, is that seedtime and harvest is a prominent theme, though not associated specifically with Pentecost. There is however a link between sowing and reaping and the agency of the Holy Spirit.

It would be a misreading to say that the New Testament "spiritualizes" the Old Testament seedtime and harvest theme in any dualistic way. Rather—as with many of Jesus' parables—the New Testament assumes the interrelationship between things spiritual and things material. The same principles and dynamics are at work, because all comes from the hand of the Creator. The Old Testament focus on actual physical seedtime and harvest is not canceled out in the New but rather underlies and informs the New. God's purposes and kingdom still involve his people and his land. Thus a fully biblical model of Pentecost will affirm and explore the way God's plan or economy (*oikonomia*, Eph. 1:10, 3:2, 3:9) involves both God's people and the land—in other words, all the physical creation. Here is one of several places that the theme and dynamic of renewal links the present creation with the New Creation.

Harvest of firstfruits is thus fundamental to the biblical meaning of Pentecost. Although the Pentecost link is not explicit in the New Testament, it helps form the background of the work of Jesus and the renewing work of the Spirit.

2. Time and History. In Scripture, Pentecost is more than a harvest festival because of who God is and how he has revealed himself. The theme of time and history is basic to the biblical understanding of Pentecost, so a fully biblical "model" of Pentecost will weave the biblical conception of time and history into its essence.

Harvest festivals can of course be understood in purely cyclical or even pagan ways. Ancient Near Eastern religions, and other religions of the world, provide plenty of examples. Harvest festivals were often associated with fertility and the cyclical dying and rising of the gods.

In the Old Testament, things are different. We find the call of Abraham, the sojourn and bondage in Egypt, and the Exodus. Captivity to the cycle of seasons is broken. Though the seasons continue (Gen. 8:22), they have fallen to second place behind the larger fact of narrative history. Israel follows a God of "mighty acts," not just of seasonal cycles. Seasons are still important, not least because Israel lives in covenant relationship with the land as well as with God (Gen. 9:8-17). Her livelihood depends in large measure on the land. But the larger truth is that God has instituted a historical process, or rather a journey, toward a larger goal of universal *shalom*. The cycles of nature have been stretched into a line, or have become as it were a horizontal spiral that is really going somewhere in history, in time and space.[8]

So Pentecost both celebrates God's bounty in the cycle of the seasons and points ahead to richer and more comprehensive bounty in the future. This then informs the function of Pentecost in the New Testament. Though the Feast of Weeks is not prominent in the New Testament, as noted, the basic narrative structure of God's unfolding promises punctuated by key annual festivals celebrating God's faithfulness underlies the whole New Testament.

The point here is that Pentecost signals God's work in time and history. Christianity is a historical faith with a historical narrative, both explicit and implicit. We shall see how this later becomes part of the renewing dynamic inherent in the Pentecost theme.

A genuinely biblical model of Pentecost, then, will engage the biblical understanding of time and history. The Christian faith is historical because it concerns what God has done in the past, is doing now, and will do in the future—in actual spacetime history. A biblical conception of Pentecost will be sensitive to the way revitalization, while bringing renewal, also ties in with what God has done and is doing in history.

3. Peoplehood and Witness. What was obvious to Old Testament Israel and the early church has not always been obvious to renewal movements since, especially in the West: Namely that Pentecost is a corporate experience, not a private or primarily individual one. It is however the nature of movements to create a sense of group identity and solidarity, and therefore a sense of corporate witness. God has raised up this movement, its adherents believe, as a witness to what he is now doing in history.

In the Old Testament, Pentecost, together with other festivals, bound Israel together as a people. Identity as God's people was doubly reinforced by remembrance of God's liberating, redemptive acts in the past and by festivals, rituals, and ceremonies that recalled the past and renewed the present sense of covenant identity—implying also a future.

This is the background for the New Testament communal sense of the church as the people of God. "You are a chosen race, a royal priesthood, a holy nation, God's own people, in order that you may proclaim the mighty acts of him who called you out of darkness into his marvelous light" (1 Pt. 4:9). Peoplehood and witness go together. Witness is given to the whole people of God, not just to the few; not solely to "religious professionals." Through the great High Priesthood of Jesus, the church has become "a holy priesthood" (1 Pt. 2:5), "a holy priesthood" (1 Pt. 2:9), "a kingdom and priests serving our God" (Rev. 5:10; cf. 1:6). Here is the New Testament accent on the priesthood of believers, which in turn relates to the fullness of the *charismata* in the church. The Spirit gives a diversity of gifts to the church so that it may effectively be God's priest-ly people on earth.[9]

And so of course a biblical model of Pentecost will stress not just individual experience, but what God is doing in forming a missional people for his own purposes.

4. Sovereign action of the Holy Spirit. The Old Testament celebration of Pentecost was a recurring reminder of who God is, what he had done, and how Yahweh is different from the gods of the nations. As we have noted, Pentecost was a reminder not just of God's goodness in providing another harvest, but that this year's harvest stands in continuity with God's gracious and powerful acts in the past, going back to Abraham, Isaac, and Jacob, and even before. And of course it also foreshadowed God's guidance and covenant faithfulness into the future.

For Christians, Pentecost and the Holy Spirit are closely connected because of the outpouring of the Spirit at Pentecost as recorded in Acts 2. The link be-tween Pentecost and the Spirit in the Old Testament is less obvious. It is of course Yahweh who calls, guides, blesses, and judges Israel, and the Old Testa-ment does not really distinguish between Yahweh and the Spirit of Yahweh. Hence there is no explicit association of God's Spirit with the Feast of Weeks.

Israel's later prophets promised that God would pour out his Spirit and re-store Israel. The key promise is of course Joel 2:28-29, "Then afterward I will pour out my spirit on all flesh; your sons and your daughters shall prophesy, your old men shall dream dreams, and your young man shall see visions. Even on the male and female slaves, in those days, I will pour out my spirit." Here there is no explicit connection with Pentecost, but the implicit connection has to do with God's promise to bless and sustain his people and eventually bring uni-versal *shalom.*

In other words, Pentecost is about the sovereign God's action, his promise and fulfillment. The Holy Spirit is the Spirit of God, of Yahweh, not some other god or spirit.

From a Christian standpoint it would be a mistake to so link the Holy Spirit with Pentecost that we forget that salvation is the work of the Holy Trinity, and that the mission of the Holy Spirit is to testify to Jesus Christ, to lift him up and make him real in our experience, the focus of our discipleship, and the basis of our ethics.

Pentecost concerns the complete dependence of God's people on his sove-reign action —and his people's openness to that action and their willingness to be witnesses of and for the divine purposes.

5. The eschatological promise of New Creation. From what is been said so far, it is clear that Pentecost in both its New Testament meaning and Old Testa-ment roots *points ahead* to the future. The grounding in present and past is not lost, of course. Peter at Pentecost points back to the prophet Joel. But the point of the Joel 2:28-32 passage is eschatological: "I will pour out my spirit on all flesh; your sons and your daughters will prophesy, your old men shall dream dreams, and your young men shall see visions. . . . Then everyone who calls on the name of the Lord shall be saved."

The outpouring of the Holy Spirit is promised—and effected at the first Pentecost—but to what end? Peter and the book of Acts link the Spirit's filling specifically to witness (Acts 1:8, 2:32, 3:15, 10:39). But from the beginning this witness is connected with the full coming of God's kingdom (Acts 1:2-8, 8:12-19, 20:22-25) and with the final, full "restoration of all things" (Acts 3:21 ASV).

Note especially Peter's statement in Acts 3:19-21. Here we have what might be called the double action of Pentecostal fulfillment. Addressing a crowd at the Jerusalem temple, Peter urges the people, "Repent therefore, and turn to God so that your sins may be wiped out, so that times of refreshing may come from the presence of the Lord, and that he may send the Messiah appointed for you, that is, Jesus, who must remain in heaven until the time of universal restoration that God announced long ago through his holy prophets" (Acts 3:19-21). Note the two key phrases: "times of refreshing" now and eventually the long-promised "time of universal restoration," linked with Jesus' return to earth.

This is typical of biblical prophecy in both Testaments—an immediate, initial fulfillment and a final, complete fulfillment. These two "phases" or "stages" are not unrelated. They are doubly linked: First, in the sense that the initial fulfillment is a *sign* of the later fulfillment, and second, that the initial fulfillment actually *leads to, prepares the way for,* and in some sense actually *begins to effect* or accomplish the final fulfillment. In this sense the initial fulfillment is a kind of sacrament of what is to come.

This double, interrelated aspect of the Spirit's working becomes most explicit in Paul's writings, where it is specifically tied to the role of the Holy Spirit and to the Pentecostal theme of firstfruits. We read: You who have "believed in him, were marked with the promised Holy Spirit; this is the pledge of our inheritance toward redemption as God's own people, to the praise of his glory" (Eph. 1:13-14).[10] Similarly in 2 Corinthians: "But it is God who establishes us with you in Christ and has anointed us, by putting his seal on us and giving us his Spirit in our hearts as a first installment" (2 Cor. 1:21-22) of what is to come. The presence of the Spirit is the "first installment" of the full inheritance to be received, which is eventual bodily resurrection and the full New Creation God has promised.

Note here the resonance that "pledge of our inheritance" (aÓrrabw»n thvß klhronomi÷aß hJmw◊n) and the "Spirit . . . as a first installment" (to\n aÓrrabw◊na touv pneu/matoß) has with *firstfruits*—a resonance in fact made explicit in other passages. The most explicit New Testament passage is in Romans 8. We read, "the creation itself will be set free from its bondage to decay and will obtain the freedom of the glory of the children of God. We know that the whole creation has been groaning in labor pains until now; and not only the creation, but we ourselves, who have the first fruits of the Spirit, groan inwardly while we wait for adoption, the redemption of our bodies" (Rom. 8:21-23).

Here the "redemption of our bodies" (not souls) and the larger context of Romans 8 make clear that God's promise is that all creation will be renewed as an integral part of Christians' own full redemption. The New Testament does not promise resurrected bodies in a disembodied heaven. It promises a renewed, restored heaven and earth.

Both the Holy Spirit and Jesus Christ are described as "firstfruits," consistent with a robust Trinitarian theology. More precisely, it is in his resurrection that Jesus Christ is the "firstfruits" (1 Cor. 15:20, 23), and it is the Spirit's indwelling presence in the church and in Christians personally that Paul calls "firstfruits." Thus "firstfruits" suggests both that Jesus in his resurrection and the indwelling Spirit are the firstfruits of which the church is the (partial) harvest, and that the church now (and in any time and place?) is the firstfruits of the ongoing growth (and renewal?) of the church and in fact of the healing restoration of all creation. So Paul can speak of the first Christians (i.e., the first harvest of Christians) in a new area as "firstfruits" (Rom. 16:5, 1 Cor. 16:15). In a remarkable passage, James says the church itself is "a kind of firstfruits of all [God] created" (Jas. 1:18). The resonance between Paul and James here is striking.

In a particularly key passage, the book of Revelation speaks of those who "were purchased from among the human race and offered as firstfruits to God and the Lamb" (Rev. 14:4). Although commentators debate just who is meant here, the reference clearly pictures the church, or some part of the church, as the firstfruits of God's larger *oikonomia*—the firstfruits of the New Creation, the renewed heaven and earth. Taking in view the whole of Scripture, in fact, *firstfruits* is a key theme linking the two Testaments. It carries the most eschatological freight, tying together the seedtime and harvest theme with the larger promise of New Creation.

This fifth dimension of Pentecost—the eschatological promise of New Creation—is obviously the most explicitly eschatological dimension of the five we are exploring. Eschatology is implicit in the other four aspects, and but is explicit in the fifth. This is coherent, for the whole idea of Pentecost presupposes the biblical conception of the sovereign God of history in contrast to other views of deities, fate, or destiny. The power of Pentecost as a conception or model is found precisely in its biblical roots. Pentecost is the promise of New Humanity. More than that, it is the promise of the new, restored creation.[11]

The Full Meaning of Pentecost

A fully biblical—we might add, a fully "operational"—view of Pentecost combines these five dimensions synergistically, ecologically. The full meaning of Pentecost thus comes into view. Biblically speaking, Pentecostal fullness is not just a matter of individual persons, or even the church, being filled with the Spirit, or speaking in tongues. Eschatologically speaking, Pentecostal fullness means new heavens and a new earth; the earth "full of the knowledge of the Lord as the waters cover the sea" (Isa. 11:9).

Combining the five dimensions of Pentecost as Scripture does thus leads us to the potent biblical promise of universal *shalom*. Note well that this is neither the Golden Age of philosophical mythology nor a secular optimism. It is not a scientistic view of progress or evolution. Nor is it the view of the soul's, or the church's, ascent from earth to heaven; from body to spirit; from spacetime materiality to eternal spirituality. Pentecostal fullness means in fact the marriage of heaven and earth; the resurrection of the body (an orthodox Christian hope, even if often eclipsed); the fulfillment and renewal and flourishing of "the everlasting covenant between God and every living creature of all flesh that is on the earth" (Gen. 9:17).

In this sense, what Jesus' prayed in Matthew 6:10—God's will done on earth as in heaven—has the same ultimate meaning as the fullness of Pentecost, the fullness of the Spirit, and the fullness of the kingdom of God.[12] To seek first God's kingdom and righteous (Mt. 6:33), and to seek the fullness of Pentecost, are found eschatologically to be the same thing.

The link between the kingdom of God and the Pentecostal fullness of the Spirit is evident throughout the New Testament. After the resurrection the apostles ask about the kingdom of God (as they then understood it), and Jesus responds by speaking of the Holy Spirit (Acts 1:6-8). Was Jesus directing the apostles' attention *away from* the hope of the kingdom? Clearly not, for when Jesus "appeared to them over a period of forty days" he "spoke about the kingdom of God" (Acts 1:3 TNIV). Rather Jesus was saying, in effect: Do not be concerned about "times or dates," but rather be witnesses to Jesus and his reign "to the ends of the earth" (Acts 1:7-8) in the present and immediate future. In Samaria Phillip, apparently filled with the Spirit, "preached the good news of the kingdom of God [literally, *evangelized* the kingdom of God] and the name of Jesus Christ" (Acts 8:12). In Ephesus after the Holy Spirit was poured out, Paul argued "persuasively about the kingdom of God" (Acts 19:8). The book of Acts closes with Paul boldly proclaiming God's kingdom (Acts 28:23, 31).

In sum, the biblical Pentecost theme combines these five dimensions: harvest of firstfruits, time and history, peoplehood and witness, sovereign action of the Holy Spirit, and the eschatological promise of New Creation.

The next question is: What is the relevance of this Pentecostal fullness to church history and renewal? Which if any of these five dimensions are found in the various revitalization movements that have reenergized Christian witness from time to time? If we take this five-dimensional view of Pentecost as a model, do we find it embodied anywhere in history?

Pentecost and the History of Revitalization

Time and space do not permit much elaboration, so my comments here are more research suggestions than detailed analysis. The five dimensions of Pentecost have indeed played a role in church history and renewal and help illuminate that history.

Harvest of Firstfruits

Sowing the gospel seed and reaping a harvest of souls has been a prominent theme in many Evangelical missionary and evangelistic movements. In my own experience I remember Psalm 126:6 often being applied evangelistically: "He that goes forth weeping, bearing precious seed, shall doubtless come again with rejoicing, bringing his sheaves with him."

The gospel song "Bringing in the Sheaves," popular in the early and mid-twentieth century, captures the sentiment:

> Sowing in the morning, sowing seeds of kindness,
> Sowing in the noontide and the dewy eve;
> Waiting for the harvest, and the time of reaping,
> We shall come rejoicing, bringing in the sheaves.[13]

Contrast this with William Fullerton's magnificent missions hymn, "I Cannot Tell," also from the early twentieth century:

> I cannot tell how He will win the nations,
> How He will claim His earthly heritage,
> How satisfy the needs and aspirations
> Of East and West, of sinner and of sage.
> But this I know, all flesh shall see His glory,
> And He shall reap the harvest He has sown,
> And some glad day His sun shall shine in splendor
> When He the Savior, Savior of the world is known.[14]

Fullerton affirms that Jesus Christ "will reap the harvest He has sown," eventually winning "the nations," claiming his "earthly heritage," and satisfying all the world's "needs and aspirations"—not merely reaping a harvest of souls.

Among Evangelicals this harvest theme, though prominent, was not specifically linked with Pentecost, whether in the biblical or the modern Pentecostal sense. And it certainly was not meant in the literal sense of tilling the ground and reaping a harvest of wheat in order to feed the world's poor. The image was spiritualized; the literal, physical harvest was symbolic or parabolic of a spiritual harvest of souls, or perhaps of eternal life.

Literal seedtime and harvest was of course built into the life of many of the settled monastic communities, such as the Benedictines, who in fact contributed much to productive and sustainable agriculture during the Middle Ages. Monastic communities at their best seem to have combined the physical and spiritual dimensions of seedtime and harvest. And then there are the mendicants: Perhaps it was St. Francis of Assisi who best interwove the spiritual and material dimensions of seedtime and harvest, though however with an extreme view of poverty.

To my knowledge, few if any movements throughout history have intentionally combined the Old Testament literal seedtime and harvest theme with Pentecost as a theme of renewal and revitalization in the church and in society. This theme can however add rich dimensions to a comprehensive conceptual model (and practice) of revitalization today. It seems to me that modern Pentecostal and Charismatic movements, to the degree they have employed seedtime or harvest language, have done so in a fairly exclusively spiritual (as opposed to physical or literal) sense—though this also is something that might be worth researching, along with the question of the degree to which seedtime and harvest are found in other movements, such as the Social Gospel.[15]

Time and History

Time and history have been key accents in most revitalization movements, for fairly obvious reasons. Renewal movements generally see themselves either as the fulfillment of time and history (prophetic and eschatological accents), or a major rupture with history (apocalyptic accents). The degree of historical continuity or discontinuity varies according to the ideology and the social-political-economic context of such movements.

Historically, Pentecostal movements have had a troubled relationship with history. Often history is seen to represent dead tradition, or the church's unfaithfulness or even apostasy. Sometimes renewal movements therefore tend to stand against history, seeking not historical continuity but discontinuity. God is doing a new thing—a rupture, a break with history to a greater or lesser degree. At one extreme renewal movements are apocalyptic, believing that history "as we know it" has ended and a new age has begun. Other renewal movements see themselves as more continuous with history—as prophetic, perhaps, without being apocalyptic. External factors (politics, economics, war, natural disasters) as well as internal factors (theology, leadership, biblical interpretation) push renewal movements toward either continuity or discontinuity with history—as often becomes clear in hindsight.[16]

In general, monastic movements have been more prophetic than apocalyptic in their view of time and history. Monastic orders are committed to the long haul. They often have been involved in agriculture, long-term scholarship, and painstaking manuscript copying and illumination, for example.

The Pentecost theme in relation to time and history does appear, interestingly, in the rise of Cluny in the tenth century and the great reform of the Benedictine Order that followed. A key figure was St. Odo, the second abbot of Cluny (927-944), who was instrumental in the rise and spreading influence of the monastery. Odo, ironically, though he was building for the long term, believed "the end of the world and the Day of Judgement were at hand. For the great mass of mankind which was enslaved by concupiscence there seemed to be little hope. The only safe way to salvation lay through repentance and conversion and entry into the monastic life. The monks were the Pentecostal Church created and renewed by the Holy Spirit," as C. H. Lawrence summarizes. The silence of the cloister was already a participation in paradise. "This conviction that the restored Benedictine life was the only authentic fulfillment of the Christian vocation was at the heart of the appeal Cluny made to the society of its time."[17]

In the late nineteenth and early twentieth centuries, the Social Gospel movement generally was friendly toward history. History and historical processes were to be taken seriously. Actual, present history was the plane upon which salvation was to be worked out and the kingdom of God demonstrated. As we know, the split between the Social Gospel and premillennialism, and between Modernism and Fundamentalism, had much to do with conceptions of time and history. Much the same could be said for the differences between Latin American liberation theology and twentieth-century Evangelicalism.

Here "classical" Pentecostalism contrasts with the charismatic movements and renewals of the second half of the twentieth century, which often saw the charismatic emphasis as renewing and leavening the historic churches immediately and over time. Early Pentecostalism, due in large measure to the earlier rise if dispensational premillennialism and end-of-century apocalypticism, embodied a more discontinuous view of history.[18]

For our purposes, the point is that a biblical "model" of Pentecost will seek an understanding of time and history that is consistent with the biblical narrative and worldview (not a totally undisputed question). As I view it (and as argued earlier) this means a sense of a long-term historical trajectory within which the cycles and seasons of the created order, and perhaps even of culture to some degree, are recognized, celebrated, respected, and leavened by the good news of the kingdom of God. "Therefore every teacher of the law who has been instructed about the kingdom of heaven is like the owner of a house who brings out of his storeroom new treasures as well as old" (Mt. 13:52).

Peoplehood and Witness

The sense of being a distinct people called to be witnesses to a new, inbreaking reality seems also to be a constant in revitalization movements, though in varying ways. It certainly has been a part of Communist movements—which underscores the fact that the nature of the community, the character and ethic of the foreseen future, and the permissible means of getting there are crucial considerations. Communism had a sense of peoplehood and witness, but unfortunately not one shaped by the character and ethic of Jesus.

Within Christian movements, peoplehood and witness have of course meant some form of the church and some kind of evangelization. The book of Acts sets the New Testament pattern. Generally Christian revitalization movements have seen the church in Acts as either precedent or pristine model, normative for the church and therefore key to its renewal (primitivism, restitutionism, restorationism).

In the long sweep of church history, Roman Catholic and Eastern monastic orders have perhaps best perfected the models and mechanisms of peoplehood and witness—so much so that present-day Protestant renewal communities speak of "a New Monasticism" and "new friars."[19]

A key issue here of course is *community.* A rediscovery of the central importance of community and new forms of community are a constant in all renewal movements.[20] The degree of self-conscious, defined community and countercultural tension with the larger society (or church) is of course a key variable in renewal movements and has been a major topic in the sociology of religion.[21]

Renewal communities see themselves as embodying witness—witness to a better way of life, a better society, and the better future to come. Renewal communities are "contrast societies." Their sense and practice of witness vary, partly in function of the openness or repressiveness of the larger society. Many renewal communities, including some monastic and Anabaptist-type communities, see their witness as being largely passive—witness by example. Other renewal communities, such as early Pentecostal congregations and groups like the Jesuits and Youth With A Mission (YWAM) have understood and practiced witness in a much more aggressive, activist way.

This also is where the gifts of the Spirit and the priesthood of believers play an essential role. The key *theological* point is that all believers are priests and witnesses, each one endowed uniquely with spiritual gifts "for the common good" (1 Cor. 12:7) empowering the church's witness in the world. The key *sociological* point is that this universal "mobilization" of all members in behalf of a movement's mission is key to its renewal dynamic, its revitalizing impact. Someone has said that the most socially revolutionary teaching in the Bible is the doctrine of spiritual gifts, because in principle this suggests that *anyone*— women, the poor, the uneducated, the young—may be lifted by the Spirit to a place of leadership, irrespective of official status or ecclesiastical authorization.

For our purposes here, the broader point is that culturally-transforming movements must have a clear sense of peoplehood and of witness. If biblically grounded, this will be tied to the biblical meaning of "people of God"—a people in reconciled relationship with God and with the land—and effective witness to this reality in its present and future dimensions, tied to the full hope of New Creation.

Sovereign action of the Holy Spirit

The question of God's sovereignty in movements of renewal and revitalization is a contested one. Views on the matter cover a wide spectrum. Secularists and many academics discount claims of God's action in revitalization movements, preferring explanations that can be more empirically studied—social, political, economic, or ecological factors, for instance. To some degree this is in reaction to too-easy explanations that attribute renewals and revivals almost exclusively to God's sovereign intervention in history (*deus ex machina*).

Even within Christian theology we find a spectrum of views concerning God's agency in bringing renewal. As I have noted in my book *Signs of the Spirit,* interpretations of great revivals in Christian history range between the view that revivals are due exclusively to God's sovereign intervention (perhaps in response to repentance and prayer) and the view that revivals are simply the fruit of human obedience to what God has already revealed or promised (the view of Charles Finney, for example).[22]

In the biblical perspective, the sovereign action of God's Spirit and human agency are both part of one picture. As I noted in the earlier discussion, Pentecost concerns the complete dependence of God's people on his sovereign action as well as the people's openness and response to that action; their willingness to be witnesses of and for the divine purposes. In the Old Testament it is God who provides the harvest and guides his people, but it is the people who do the actual work of sowing, reaping, and gratefully worshiping God. In the New Testament, clearly Pentecost comes upon the early community of disciples as God's intervention in response to their obedient waiting:

When the day of Pentecost had come, they were all together in one place. And suddenly from heaven there came a sound like the rush of a violent wind, and it filled the entire house where they were sitting. Divided tongues, as of fire, appeared among them, and a tongue rested on each of them. All of them were filled with the Holy Spirit and began to speak in other languages, as the Spirit gave them ability (Acts 2:1-4).

It is natural therefore that Pentecostalism, especially in its earliest phases, would emphasize God's sovereign intervention. "This is that which was spoken by the prophet Joel" (Acts 2:16 KJV)—the pouring out of the Holy Spirit. Those within the church who opposed Pentecostalism also thought they saw supernatural agency at work. Tongues-speaking was a Satanic deception.

Within new movements, we often find this dynamic: In the earliest stages, the participants are conscious of and emphasize the sovereign agency of God's Spirit. In later phases, later generations begin to unpack the human and cultural factors that also played a role. Presumably most new Christian revitalization movements have believed that in some way God's Spirit was at work in birthing and initially guiding the movement.[23] Perhaps the more "Pentecostal" or "charismatic" a movement is, the more it stresses God's sovereign action. Yet all down through history Christians involved in leading revivals and revitalization movements have generally felt they were being led by, or at least were cooperating with, God's Spirit, who was working to embody his purposes.

For our purposes here, the point is that the biblical model of Pentecost recognizes God's sovereign agency, is fully open to the work of the Holy Spirit, and seeks to be obedient and faithful to God's leading. A fully biblical Pentecostal movement will seek to discern where God is leading and to be faithful to that vision.

This leads naturally then to the fifth and final dimension of Pentecost:

The Eschatological Promise of New Creation

Biblically speaking, Pentecost points to the future, as we have seen. Every Pentecostal renewal is eschatological.

In more secular "revitalization movement" theories this dynamic is understood as some new vision for society, some "new mazeway Gestalt" (Wallace) for the culture.[24] From a biblical standpoint however we are dealing with the promise of New Creation—a vision for the full manifestation of the kingdom of God, however that is understood.

Every revitalization movement has its eschatological vision. The extensive literature on millenarian, communistic, and utopian movements and communities shows this clearly,[25] as does the history of renewal movements all down through Christian history, from monasticism to "new monasticism" and "emergent churches." Every movement expects some different and better future. A key question, of course, is the degree to which this eschatological vision is thought to be possible or realizable within present history, or is expected only after the end of the present order of things.[26]

For our purposes, the key question is the degree to which the new movement faithfully embodies the biblical promise of New Creation, a renewed heaven and earth. My thesis is that the full Pentecostal renewal of the church means a vision for, and a commitment to, the full manifestation of the kingdom of God in all its dimensions—both as a future hope and as a present agenda because of the present agency of the Holy Spirit and the present ethical pressure of the promised future.

By way of conclusion of this section, then: A vision for the full Pentecostal renewal of the church involves learning from the history of revitalization movements down through history. More broadly, it means seeking to understand and embody the full biblical promise of Pentecost in our churches and cultures today. The study of revitalization movements can illuminate the historical questions. The faithful study of Scripture and the living out of the gospel within vital communities today, seeking to embody the full Pentecostal hope, is necessary however if the study of revitalization movements is to be more than an academic exercise only. (Hence this series of consultations.)

Biblically speaking, "New Humanity" is not separable from New Creation—the kingdom of God in its fullness, heaven and earth healed and renewed. Because of Jesus' resurrection, Christians believe, God's Spirit "will give life to [our] mortal bodies" (Rom. 8:11), not just enliven our spirits. What we are waiting for in the New Creation, ultimately, is "the redemption of our bodies" (Rom. 8:23), not our non-material souls. We are reminded here of the very materiality of Jesus' resurrection: "Look at my hands and my feet; see that it is I myself. Touch me and see; for a spirit does not have flesh and bones as you see that I have" (Lk. 24:39). And he ate some fish (Lk. 24:43). Jesus' resurrection was as literal and physical as were the firstfruits brought to the temple at the Old Testament Pentecost.

Romans 8 as well as other passage make clear that God's intent in creating New Humanity is the liberation of all creation; that God intends to save humanity *with* their environment, not *out of* their environment (Rom. 8:19-25). New Humanity and renewed creation are inseparably part of the same picture.

Pentecost and New Humanity Today

All the foregoing discussion leads, finally, to this thesis statement: The most culture-transforming embodiments of Pentecost are those that most fully embody all five of the biblical dimensions of Pentecost. The most prophetic renewal movements are those that are most fully "Pentecostal" in this multidimensional sense. In other words, the most socially and spiritually transformative expressions of revitalization are those that interweave in ecological harmony the dynamics of *harvest of firstfruits, time and history, peoplehood and witness*, reliance upon the *sovereign action of the Spirit*, and the *eschatological promise of New Creation*.

Three implications for our theme of Pentecost and the New Humanity today can be identified here:

1. *It could prove useful to study particular renewal movements, historic and contemporary, through the lens of these five dimensions.* How does the presence or absence of these dimensions illuminate each movement? *Why* are these five elements present or absent? Which are most dominant, or best explain the core dynamic of the movement? Which are more peripheral? My guess is that most movements could be mapped according to their "take" on these five dimensions.

(See Appendix.)

For example, the sense and experience of community—the shared, corporate experience of Pentecost—clearly is fundamental in any biblical conception of Pentecost. In the Old Testament, this meant the sense of being the covenant people of God; in the New Testament, the Body of Christ, the community of the Spirit, and the renewed and now expanded people of God. Community is essential to the meaning of Pentecost, and thus becomes a key element in a comprehensive template for mapping and assessing the validity of contemporary revitalization movements. What are a particular movement's sense, depth, and forms of community as church or as *ecclesiola* within the church?

This schemata could serve as a useful tool also in comparing revitalization movements from the past with those of the present.

2. Relatedly, *this fivefold model could prove useful as an diagnostic or heuristic tool within existing movements*—a tool for self-analysis and visioning. If this fivefold model really is biblical, what does it show us about the blind spots and the potential of our movement? Could our movement be strengthened, in fact, by giving attention to dimensions that are missing or anemic?

To take a fairly obvious example: If a movement is interpreting itself only in terms of present spiritual renewal but not in terms of the full biblical promise of New Creation, more emphasis on this dimension could give the movement a larger hope, a more culturally-transformative role, and perhaps a broader appeal.[27] Another example: A movement might discover, under the peoplehood and witness category, that it has been giving inadequate attention (or even too much attention) to community and practical structures for community or witness.

3. *Theology and revitalization theory should explore further the Old Testament background of Pentecost* and its implications for the possibilities and potential of revitalization today.

Here some insights from the late Dutch theologian Arnold Van Ruler in his book *The Christian Church and the Old Testament* are much to the point. Van Ruler notes (quoting H. Bergema), "Just as the New Testament keeps us from interpreting the Old Testament legalistically, so the Old Testament prevents us from understanding the New Testament idealistically or mystically after the Greek manner."[28] The Hebrew Scriptures, properly attended to, can guard the church from over-spiritualizing the New Testament message.

Van Ruler speaks of the "faithfulness to the earth and time" that marks the Old Testament, but notes that this theme is less obvious in the New Testament. In this respect at least "we have to speak . . . of the greater value of the Old Testament as compared with the New."[29] Van Ruler argues:

The Old Testament has a more positive concern with creation and the kingdom, with the first things and the last, . . . with sanctification and humanity, with ethos and culture, with society and marriage, with history and the state [than does the New Testament]. These are precisely the matters at issue in the Old Testament, [which embodies] a profound confidence in the goodness of the world, the serviceability of man, and the possibility of sanctifying the earth.[30]

Van Ruler contends that the "church has spiritualized" this very earthiness of the Old Testament, or perhaps "brought it into its own liturgy or used it as a witness to the message of Golgotha or simply said that it has been superseded by Christ."[31] Such spiritualization undercuts or ignores however

> the social ideal of the Old Testament, a just society, the brotherhood of all [people], the king or authority who is the true shepherd . . . . For centuries the Christian church has ignored these things or acted as if they were adequately achieved in the fellowship of the community, as though the harsh realities of social and economic life, of domestic and foreign politics, could be kept off the horizon of the Christian church and its God, as though the cross of Christ were not and did not have to be set up especially in these realities.[32]

Van Ruler concludes: "To put it even more sharply, the New Testament is not enough. It leaves us in the lurch in respect of life in society on earth and in time. . . . what is really needed is to go back to the Old Testament. This is where the Old Testament has its own independent significance for the Christian church. . . . the quintessence [of the Old Testament] is to be found in politics in the broadest sense of the term: the state, social and economic life, culture—in a word, the sanctification of the earth."[33] What is required is that the Christian church "see and acknowledge the Old Testament . . . not merely as background but . . . as horizon."[34]

Van Ruler does not refer specifically to Pentecost in this connection. His book in fact makes little or no reference to Pentecost. Instead he is pointing to a basic hermeneutical issue that should color the way we view Pentecost. As I have emphasized throughout this paper, Pentecost is first of all an Old Testament festival, and we miss its full meaning if we ignore or underplay or overspiritualize the Old Testament meaning.

This mining of the Old Testament meaning of Pentecost could be particularly significant for a theology of revitalization and church renewal today. I have already hinted at some of the ways this might be true. (Of course, the same applies to other Old Testament themes, as well.[35])

Behind the specific question of the role of the Old Testament in understanding Pentecost and revitalization today is a larger is a worldview question: The relationship between spirit and matter, heaven and earth, time and eternity, history and eschatology. We misunderstand the New Testament and the Christian gospel, I argue, if we read it through an alien lens, whether that lens is Neo-Platonism, Enlightenment rationalism, Postmodernism, or socio-biological determinism.

Reprise: A Vision for Full Pentecostal Renewal

I end with a vision for *full* Pentecostal renewal. Combining all that has been said, we come to a Pentecostal vision way beyond anything earth has yet seen. Perhaps all the genuine revitalization movements of history are mere pointers and signposts, firstfruits of an eventual great Pentecostal renewal that fulfills and embodies all that has been promised—much as, in C. S. Lewis' vision, all genuine myths point to the one great and true Myth.[36]

As Christians, we believe this can come only by the Spirit of God—the same Spirit who raised Jesus Christ from the dead, now dwells within and beyond the church, and is at work now to bring New Creation in its fullness.

The Bible contains many visions of this New Creation, from the great poetic promises in Isaiah and other biblical prophets to the picture in the last two chapters of Revelation.

Can we envision a full Pentecostal renewal where all five dimensions of Pentecost become visible not only in the church, but in all peoples and all the earth? Where earth brings forth abundantly, resiliently, grain and grapes, fruit and flowers, and all have enough to eat. Where history is a friend as we celebrate God's providence in the journey, and now the full fruitful meaning of the fullness of time. Where God's people are a light to the nations, and the nations walk in the light of the Lamb. Where the Triune God is honored and served; where everyone has "fellowship . . . with the Father and with his Son Jesus Christ" (1 Jn. 1:3) through the Spirit and all are "participants of the divine nature" (2 Pt. 1:4). Where God leads and guides his people is green pastures; where New Creation truly has begun and continues to grow and develop and blossom, with the full abundance of human creativity now flowing to the glory of God and the blessing of all people and all creation. Where all evil and death itself has been judged and destroyed.

We read in Revelation 21 and 22,

> Then I saw a new heaven and a new earth; for the first heaven and the first earth had passed away, and the sea was no more. And I saw the holy city, the new Jerusalem, coming down out of heaven from God, prepared as a bride adorned for her husband. And I heard a loud voice from the throne saying,
> See, the home of God is among mortals.
> He will dwell with them as their God;
> they will be his peoples,
> and God himself will be with them;
> he will wipe every tear from their eyes.
> Death will be no more;
> mourning and crying and pain will be no more,
> for the first things have passed away.
>
> And the one who was seated on the throne said, "See, I am making all things new." . . .
>
> Then he said to me, "It is done! I am the Alpha and the Omega, the beginning and the end. To the thirsty I will give water as a gift from the spring of the water of life. . . .
>
> [Then I saw] the holy city Jerusalem coming down out of heaven from God. . . . I saw no temple in the city, for its temple is the Lord God the Almighty and the Lamb. And the city has no need of sun or moon to shine on it, for the glory of God is its light, and its lamp is the Lamb. The nations will walk by its light, and

the kings of the earth will bring their glory into it. Its gates will never be shut by day—and there will be no night there. People will bring into it the glory and the honor of the nations. But nothing unclean will enter it, nor anyone who practices abomination or falsehood, but only those who are written in the Lamb's book of life.

Then the angel showed me the river of the water of life, bright as crystal, flowing from the throne of God and of the Lamb through the middle of the street of the city. On either side of the river is the tree of life with its twelve kinds of fruit, producing its fruit each month; and the leaves of the tree are for the healing of the nations. Nothing accursed will be found there any more. But the throne of God and of the Lamb will be in it, and his servants will worship him; they will see his face, and his name will be on their foreheads. And there will be no more night; they need no light of lamp or sun, for the Lord God will be their light, and they will reign forever and ever (Rev. 21:1-6, 9-10, 22-27, 22:1-5).

This is the picture of the New Jerusalem, and in fact of all creation healed. There is "no temple in the city"—no religion or cultus; no more distinction between church and society, no more split between earth and heaven, discipleship and politics, stewardship and economics. Creativity and the arts are freed to show the truth in breathtaking beauty which all can enjoy.

"They will not hurt or destroy on all my holy mountain; for the earth will be full of the knowledge of the Lord as the waters cover the sea" (Isa. 11:9).

And finally, everyone will live shalom under their own literal, physical, but renewed "vines and their own fig trees, and no one shall make them afraid; for the mouth of the Lord of hosts has spoken" (Mic. 4:4).

Notes

1. Ironically, Pentecost has functioned as a powerful renewal theme in history, but not much in theology. In doing research for this paper, my first surprise was how little material there is on Pentecost in standard works and encyclopedia on the Bible, mission, and church history. There is for example no article on Pentecost in the *Dictionary for Theological Interpretation of the Bible,* ed. Kevin J. Vanhoozer (Grand Rapids: Baker, 2005), though there is one for Sacrament.

2. The connection between the number five here and the fifty days from which the term Pentecost derives is merely coincidental.

3. Lev. 23:15-16 instructs regarding the Feast of Weeks, "…you shall count off seven weeks; they shall be complete. You shall count until the day after the seventh sabbath, fifty days; then you shall present an offering of new grain to the Lord" (NRSV). Here the Septuagint uses *penteconta* for "fifty." The Greek term *pentecostos* itself means "fiftieth." Lev. 23:16 is the only place in the OT where fifty days, rather than seven weeks, is specifically associated with the Feast of Weeks.

4. Later Judaism associated Pentecost with the giving of the law under Moses, but that development apparently came after the destruction of the Jerusalem temple in 70 A.D. For Jesus, the meaning of Pentecost is its Old Testament meaning. For this reason it

is hermeneutically dubious to link Pentecost with Jesus as a "Second Moses" who gives a "new law" for his new people, the church. Jesus may fulfill that role, but this has no direct connection with Pentecost.

5. Proper care (stewardship) of the land/earth is a major theme throughout the Hebrew Scriptures. The Sabbath and Jubilee years were parts of, but not the full extent of, this basic biblical theme. I deal with this matter at some length in my forthcoming book, *Salvation Means Creation Healed*.

6. It occurs twice in the Apocrypha. Tobias 2:1 says, "At our festival of Pentecost, which is the sacred feast of weeks, a good dinner was prepared for me and I reclined to eat."

7. As a matter of biblical hermeneutics, it is a curious thing also (especially in light of later Pentecostalism) that the Bible does not make a very specific link between the Old Testament Pentecost (Feast of Weeks) and the Holy Spirit. Even in the New Testament, the only explicit link between Pentecost and the Spirit is in Acts 2. When Jesus tells his disciples to "stay…in the city until you have been clothed with power from on high" (Lk. 24:49), he doesn't specify how long.

8. Cf. N. T. Wright, *The New Testament and the People of God* (Minneapolis: Fortress, 1992), 233-34.

9. I elaborate on the interrelationships between the priesthood of believers, the *charismata*, and the call to be servants of Jesus Christ in *Liberating the Church: The Ecology of Church and Kingdom* (Downers Grove, Ill.: InterVarsity, 1983), especially Chap. 8, "The Ministry of All Believers."

10. Or as Markus Barth translates it: "After you came to faith you, too, have been sealed with his seal, the promised Holy Spirit. He is the guarantee of what we shall inherit [to vouch] for the liberation of God's own people, to the praise of his glory." Markus Barth, *The Anchor Bible: Ephesians 1-3* (Garden City, N.Y.: Doubleday, 1974), 76 (brackets in original).

11. New Testament scholar William Webb notes that since the New Creation in Scripture is eschatological, it is for that very reason also key to the present. "The new society 'in Christ' is rooted in the eschaton," Webb writes. "Even so, its redemptive aspects and social modifications are to be realized as much as possible in the way we live now. Perhaps if anything transcends culture, it should be the theology of ultimate new creation." In his attempt to develop a "hermeneutics of cultural analysis" Webb argues, "If any [biblical] patterns should be granted ongoing significance, it should be those found within the new-creation material" in Scripture. While many aspects of the biblical material that is grounded in the original creation "have culture-locked components within them," this is not true of "the 'in Christ' new-humanity texts" in the New Testament. "In fact, the counterculture dimensions to these texts underscores their predisposition toward a transcultural framework." The eschatological promise of New Creation is thus at once biblical, eschatological, and transcultural. William J. Webb, *Slaves, Women and Homosexuals: Exploring the Hermeneutics of Cultural Analysis* (Downers Grove, Ill.: InterVarsity, 2001), 146-48.

12. The New Testament language of "fullness" (plh/rwma, *pleroma*) is relevant here.

13. "Bringing in the Sheaves," by Knowles Shaw; music by George A. Minor. *Light and Life Songs No. 4* (Chicago: Light and Life Press, 1928), No. 229.

14. "I Cannot Tell," by William Young Fullerton (1857-1932) in *Hymns for Today's Church* (London: Hodder and Stoughton, 1982), No. 194. The content and style of these two songs is quite suggestive of the split then developing between a narrower premillennialist theology of mission and a more optimistically comprehensive one.

15. The Social Gospel mined a number of OT themes for their social-ethical significance, as has liberation theology. Examples are themes of Jubilee, *shalom*, and the exodus.

16. For example, the French Revolution of 1789 was a factor in the rise of dispensational premillennialism, and the U.S. financial panic of 1857 helped trigger the revival of 1858.

17. C. H. Lawrence, *Medieval Monasticism: Forms of Religious Life in Western Europe in the Middle Ages* (New York: Longman, 1984), 77-78; F. L. Cross and E. A. Livingstone, eds., *Oxford Dictionary of the Christian Church*, 3rd ed. (New York: Oxford University Press, 1997), 1174.

18. Biblically speaking, Pentecostalism and apocalypticism are not inherently inextricably linked—something Pentecostal denominations eventually come to wrestle with.

19. Scott A. Bessenecker, *The New Friars: The Emerging Movement Serving the World's Poor* (Downers Grove, Ill.: InterVarsity, 2006).

20. See Howard A. Snyder, *Signs of the Spirit: How God Reshapes the Church* (Grand Rapids: Zondervan, 1989).

21. I have in mind here particularly the large sect-church discussion and the work of contemporary sociologists such as Rodney Stark.

22. Snyder, Signs of the Spirit, 42-48.

23. Even new secular and political movements often affirm that some force beyond their immediate human agency is at work in bringing about, or accounting for the direction of, their movement—some form of evolution or progress or historical dialectic, as in early Communism.

24. Anthony F. C. Wallace, "Revitalization Movements: Some Theoretical Considerations for Their Comparative Study," *American Anthropologist* 58 (April 1956), 264-75.

25. E.g., Norman Cohn, The Pursuit of the Millennium: Revolutionary Millenarians and Mystical Anarchists of the Middle Ages, rev. ed. (New York: Oxford University Press, 1970); Mark Holloway, Heavens on Earth: Utopian Communities in America 1680-1880, 2nd ed. (New York: Dover Publications, 1966); Donald E. Pitzer, ed., America's Communal Utopias (Chapel Hill, N.C.: University of North Carolina Press, 1997).

26. I explore this dynamic in my book *Models of the Kingdom* (Nashville: Abingdon, 1991, and reprints), giving examples.

27. A counter-argument might also be made—that a movement's appeal and dynamic depend upon a rather specific and limited agenda, and that broadening the agenda dilutes this dynamic. Yet the motivating appeal of most movements seems to be the large overarching vision and hope that the movement embodies. In the case of successful movements, the trick seems to be holding together a transcendent (sometimes rather vague) vision and a very specific present agenda.

28. H. Bergema, quoted in Arnold A. Van Ruler, *The Christian Church and the Old Testament,* trans. Geoffrey W. Bromiley (Grand Rapids: Eerdmans, 1971), 99.

29. Van Ruler, The Christian Church and the Old Testament, 88.

30. Van Ruler, 88-89.

31. Van Ruler, 89.

32. Van Ruler, 90.

33. Van Ruler, 91.

34. Van Ruler, 56-57.

35. I have elsewhere suggested the importance of the themes of *shalom,* land, house and city of God, justice for the poor, and sabbath and Jubilee for a fully biblical theology of the kingdom of God. Howard A. Snyder, *A Kingdom Manifesto* (Downers Grove, Ill.: InterVarsity, 1985); also published as *Kingdom, Church, and World: Biblical Themes for Today* (Eugene, Ore.: Wipf & Stock, 2002), with updated Preface.

36. C. S. Lewis, "Myth Became Fact," in *God in the Dock* (Grand Rapids: Eerdmans, 1970), 66-67.

Postscript: Five-Dimensional Model of Pentecost

The five dimensions of Pentecost discussed in this paper may be visualized as follows. The continuum for each dimension suggests the range within which revitalization movements tend to fall, or embody themselves, with regard to that dimension. Revitalization movements could thus be "scored" or "mapped" according to these dimensions. The numeric scale is intentionally biased toward an ecological, synergistic combination of the range of options, in keeping with the thesis of this paper. (See the somewhat similar schemata comparing eight models of the kingdom of God in Snyder, *Models of the Kingdom,* 121-26).

Harvest of First fruits

1 —— 2 —— 3 —— 4 —— 5 —— 4 —— 3 —— 2 —— 1

Literal, Physical   Ecological, Spiritual-Physical   Spiritual only; Neo-Platonic

At one extreme, firstfruits has reference only to agriculture; actual harvesting; emphasis on harmony with the land. The other extreme totally spiritualizes the concept; ultimate goal is spiritual harvest only; land ultimately irrelevant. The biblical conception: Both physical and spiritual meanings in interrelationship (ecological).

Time and History

1 —— 2 —— 3 —— 4 —— 5 —— 4 —— 3 —— 2 —— 1

Prophetic - Continuous   Biblical narrative, Teleological   Apocalyptic - Discontinuous

Revitalization movements understand and experience history in different ways. Prophetic movements see continuity; apocalyptic movements see themselves embodying a radical break with history. Pentecost in its biblical conception sees God's economy within the context of time and history, involving both "the present age" and "the age to come."

Peoplehood and Witness

1 —— 2 —— 3 —— 4 —— 5 —— 4 —— 3 —— 2 —— 1

Visible counterculture   People of God, Community, Kingdom witness   Spiritual community/mission only

Renewal communities tend either to be visibly separatist, embodying high tension with surrounding culture, or integrationist, seeking to permeate and leaven culture, but with less intense and deliberate forms of community; witness varies accordingly. Pentecost envisions a visible people of God proclaiming and seeking to embody God's reign within the present order.

Sovereign Action of the Holy Spirit

1 —— 2 —— 3 —— 4 —— 5 —— 4 —— 3 —— 2 —— 1

Human agency primary   Humanistic synergism   Evangelical synergism   God's agency only

How is God's hand at work in the movement? One side emphasizes human action in obedience to God; the other attributes all causes and effects to God. Various sorts of synergism lie between. Evangelical synergism (compatible with the biblical view of Pentecost) attributes primary and ultimate agency to God alone ("by grace through faith") but emphasizes responsive and responsible human agency (discipleship, witness; "to will and to do") as well.

Eschatological Promise of New Creation

1 —— 2 —— 3 —— 4 —— 5 —— 4 —— 3 —— 2 —— 1

Earthly society perfected   Present-Future, New Heaven-Earth   Disembodied souls in heaven

The revitalization movement announces and seeks to effect or model the coming New Creation—understood either as the perfecting of earthly society in all dimensions, or as forming a spiritual communion of saints, a foretaste of immaterial eternity in heaven. On one side, New Creation encompasses all creation; on the other, human spirits only. Biblically, Pentecost is the future prophetically present now; no spirit-matter dualism.

Appendix B

"How Do You Spell Revitalization?" Definitions, Defining Characteristics, Language

EUNICE L. IRWIN, PHD
ASSOCIATE PROFESSOR OF MISSION AND CONTEXTUAL
THEOLOGY, ASBURY THEOLOGICAL SEMINARY

Introduction

This chapter introduces the language of revitalization, and the associated complex web of words, being utilized in current twenty-first century mission discussions. Christian scholars and practitioners from around the world gathered to engage new acts of God through the lens of global Christianity at the Edinburgh, May 2010, consultation, "Exploring the Dialectic between Revitalization and Church." This research consultation was sponsored by a Luce funded grant through the Center for the Study of World Christian Revitalization Movements (CSWCRM). Consultation participants were assigned to construct a new definition of revitalization with the expectation that: focused deliberation on current examples of the Spirit's vitality would produce fresh articulations; new movements would be highlighted; and, most importantly, the question "What is Christian revitalization today?" would be answered.

The consultation deliberations explored both descriptive and prescriptive dimensions revitalization phenomena. The research project first sought to recover phenomena and then describe as a way to establish meaning and stimulate new definition. They sought language from which to generate definition emerged during conversations held among delegates around four conference tables. Participants brought attention to instances or seasons when persons or whole communities experienced God's presence in exceptional ways, bringing "awakening" and giving new life.

Table groups constructed definitions based on data from the first October 2009 research consultation as well as presentations, case studies and personal stories included in the second, Edinburgh, consultation. Participants listened and spoke, observing words, meanings, usages, and contexts. They described defining characteristics, plotted scenarios of revitalization for reflection, and each table group wrote definitions after reaching consensus on the evidence. The concluding task of the three-day research consultation involved designing a plausible model of revitalization by imaginative engagement and portrayal of the synergy present in existing revitalization situations. This work of giving definition moved to a higher level, beyond merely accounting for separate or clustered characteristics of revitalization. The task of defining the term "revitalization" moved from descriptive to prescriptive by calling for table groups to identify a truthful replica, or a model that ideally would be one suitable for current use when examining revival or renewal phenomena on the ground, or when discerning appropriate criteria for Christians to use in engaging or responding to movements of the Spirit in the global church.

Revitalization Terms Used in this Project

Updating definitions, the goal of the Edinburgh consultation, aligned with CSWCRM's mission to study phenomena and issues related to Christian revitalization. "The Center for the Study of World Christian Revitalization Movements contributes to the vitality of Christian mission and local congregations by synthesizing learnings from past and present revitalization movements worldwide."[i] Working definitions of three key terms historically associated with special Christian movements of the Holy Spirit provided prior to the consultation include:

Revivalism: is intended to mean in biblical/theological terms a movement of spiritual awakening, both personal and social, within exiting faith communities which are perceived to be deficient or lacking signs of a living faith. This movement proceeds by appeal to the Holy Spirit, working through human instrumentality, in manifesting vitality or vivification through the grace of Jesus Christ for persons and communities of faith, resulting in personal regeneration and transformation of human society and creation.

Revitalization, as a corollary, denotes a process or movement marked by a sense of divine intervention that not only gives new life but breaks spiritual and temporal principalities and powers of human bondage, including conditions of injustice against humanity and the natural order, found within and without the prevailing forms of organized religion. The outcome of that intervention is typically perceived as effecting a renovation of the image of God within humanity and the release of creation from its bondage to decay (Romans 8:18-

23). It is often associated with the modern awakenings within Protestant Christianity, dating from the late sixteenth through the twentieth century.

Revitalization: is **a more inclusive term used in this project** to denote the activities of spiritual awakening described in revivalism, that pertains not only to evangelical Protestantism but also to other major communities of global Christianity, including mainline Protestant denominations, Pentecostals, Roman Catholicism, Orthodoxy, and the indigenous Christian movements now being manifested in the Global South. It is a **term that has a basis in the social sciences**, as applicable to the behavior of social groups, and as popularized in the work of Anthony F C Wallace. Revitalization in its social science context, as defined by Anthony Wallace: Revitalization movement is a "deliberate, organized effort by (some) members of a society to construct a more satisfying culture," centered in a sacred message enunciated by a prophet or maximum leader, stating what is wrong with the society now, what it should be like in the future, and how to get from now to utopia." Awareness of this process is viewed as a "useful antidote to over reliance on rational decision-making models for predicting the behavior of societies in the throes of social movements." -- from Anthony CF Wallace, in "Recurrent Patterns in Social Movements", September 23, 1990

Renewal: in our context, this term references efforts to achieve more programmatic or institutional changes in a group (or church body) that are perceived as improvements for or by the members of the groups in which it is applied. ."

Data gathered at the Edinburgh consultation aimed to answer the broad question, "Do definitions developed [by the table groups] clarify or expand prior understandings of Christian revitalization?" The inductive research approach assured that the data emerging from each table discussion would be captured as table members talked about their lived traditions, studies, and memories of God's work. Members from diverse backgrounds, academic training, traditions of Church, and personal experience brought depth and texture to discussions. Although the inductive approach allowed for depth and diversity, the need to analyze and report data limited the breadth of each table discussion. Table groups offered current replicas of revitalization but with new language and insights. Not surprising, results from all four tables do not harmonize fully. Yet many realities and characteristics appear consistently.

Critical questions challenged and refined the research process: "How will norms for revitalization be found?", and "What system of reporting will do justice to group work and the task itself?"

First, the table data indicates four aspects in valid definition of revitalization. These aspects are dynamically engaging one another in the process of revitalization. They consist of interactions between: 1) the Trinity, 2) the Church, 3) The Salvation of God, and 4) Human Life and Hope.

Several theological points are important: 1) The Trinity is fundamental to revitalization since explaining the character of God [Father, Son and Holy Spirit] and spiritual encounter with God [new life, renewal, revival] is essential to defining revitalization; 2) The Church is a significant part of revitalization since ecclesial understandings and practices shape definitions of revitalization;

3) The Salvation of God is vital to framing the broadest explanation of the full and complete way in which revitalization has occurred, being realized in the Reign of God, yet expressed in the particular context-specific, content-particular ways; 4) Human Life and Hope is a significant part of defining revitalization since the promise of God's life abundant must be realized; it must touch the human experience and transform the human situation.

Thus, the fitting comment from table notes: "Theology provides the normative framework for revitalization."

Table Definitions

Second, we turn now to the Table definitions.

Table A

Table A's Definition of Revitalization: "To make a collectivity of people that is a congregation, more the complete locus of God's presence and action in the world, the body of Christ working. Revitalization is a societal shift that includes social awakening; conversion or new birth (affirming Christian identity), counteracting apathy or sterility; a fresh, creative expression or production of new religious knowledge; and education in terms of identity formation). The latter includes equipping the saints, ferreting out heterodoxy, providing meaning to what they are doing, and upward mobility. Its corollary: "Christianity is a text-based faith tradition."

Language and Experience: "We are missing something!"— a felt need, a sense of anxiety or despair a willingness to risk; visionary leadership capable of replicating the same experience in others.leadership that may be official or de facto, even as bishops were once acclaimed by the vox populi. An outcome of revitalization is re-appropriation of the core values of the Christian tradition, including the recovery of Scriptural holiness in the Wesleyan tradition. Implicit is a sense of "breakthrough", internal or external. This phenomenon may be expressed as a positive response, a new walk, a seminal change of behavior, or a sense of participation in salvation history, giving a momentum for boundary crossing. Revitalization may also be precipitated by having a tradition with an unfulfilled promise [tradition/promise of fulfillment/sense of fulfillment). By analogy, we think of being anchored, leaving anchor, and being re-anchored. Related phenomena include a sense of reconciliation in relationships, or making things whole. Revitalization may also be precipitated by an event that leads to or can lead to reconciliation; and re-imaging of Christianity and of God (marked by joy and holy affection), and as a consequence, leading to an opposition and resistance as well as a positive outcome.

Table A's Setting for Defining Revitalization: The congregation. The point of departure for exploring revitalization is the local fellowship of followers of Christ. Revitalization operates via the "collectivity of people", the body of Christ.

The strength of this definition is its articulation of the Trinity's role in en-livening the church. The scriptures become the Word of God by the Spirit.

Together these become the instrumental means of vital encounter with God. The Son, Jesus Christ is made real and present by the Spirit through the Word. Members receive edification and instruction by the preaching and teaching of the Word. They are guarded against false doctrine. They are "awakened" to realization of their identity and responsibility through image of the incarnated Son who follows the Father's will and acts on his behalf to fulfill bringing salvation to the world. The role of the Spirit is weak, acting but recognized more instrumentally. Two comments from table data are relevant here. "The Trinity is the Achilles' heel of Protestants." "The Pentecostal movement is a reaction to an absence of the Holy Spirit."

Ecclesiology operating in this definition is its focus on the members. Definition and language seem to rely on Protestant understandings of the nature of the church as local congregation. One finds a strong sense of a common journey, with the members participating in activities of the Spirit that are the privilege of the people of God in mutually life-giving and life-receiving fellowship. Little attention is given to institutional leaders or structures. Emphasis features "visionaries", inspired lay leadership, formation and flourishing through Word, Spirit and Christian disciplines. Hunger for God is expressed in quests for a restoration of Christ's image in the community, a call for personal holiness through discipleship, a restoration of members to one another, the growth of the fellowship and joy in the community. The weakness of this definition may be in its narrowness of focus, perhaps leading to divisiveness in not accepting the churches having different understandings of the work of the Trinity or holding other ecclesial traditions.

The hope for abundant life as expressed in the definition might be over-spiritualized, although the "journey" motif in which movement is sensed in "breakthroughs" and "boundary-crossings", shows sensitivity to the human quest for "experiencing an unfulfilled promise being realized", and the sense of "making things whole." Response of the Son to the human situation is a role model to guide social responsibility.

Table B

Table B's Definition: Revitalization originates from and is rooted in the Triune God; it takes place where people in specific (historical, cultural, social and spiritual) contexts experience God's enlivening and reawakening Spirit leading to a fresh encounter with the living Christ. This gives rise to repentance, new life, spiritual revival, healing, reconciliation, love, hope and holistic salvation. It often takes place amid dissatisfaction with the status quo, vulnerability, suffering and pain, deep yearning, radical discipleship including persistent prayer, scripture study, worship and an unquenchable anticipation of God's renewing presence. It is the rejuvenated partnership of God and the people of God towards life, faith and justice. It is the prophetic impulse for social and spiritual transformation in every generation.

Language and Experience: New emphasis is given to the doctrine of the Trinity, and the Church participates with God to broaden and direct the move of the Spirit. Revitalization is a fresh encounter with God which allows for returning to God and moving forward; Revitalization is an inclusive term that embraces such different terminology, reflecting in distinctive ecclesial traditions, as revival and renewal. Use of the terms "awakening" suggests an impact on culture. Revitalization also makes space to receive new things, it is linked with hope; the fullness of the gospel comes from all members of the Trinity and this sparks revitalization. The desperation of people seeking God requires messages of hope and blessing. Prayer in the power of the Spirit brings revival, which comes when the Holy Spirit works through brokenness and pain. An important outcome here is a fresh encounter with the living Christ and not merely an encounter with faith. The presumption beforehand is that it is about life, but life linked to the Kingdom of God. Revitalization entails the emergence of a new humanity. Dimensions of that humanity include an encompassing of this worldly and an otherworldly ethos, bringing hope of a new heaven and new earth. Here is a receiving and channeling of new life that is biblical, historical, and contextual. It embodies God's creativity, flattens hierarchy, and gives rise to status changes. Pilgrimage is an important motif in revitalization. While a sect has control at heart, community has a journey at its heart. Its accompanying evidences are gifts in the Church, joyful singing, and a capacity for education (catechesis).

Table B's Setting of Revitalization: "The Encounter with God." Discussions here center on revitalization as it is sustained by the "Triune God" who chooses to work in and through the Church, the locus of the Spirit who makes Jesus known and through whom comes the energizing of relational encounter amid the blessings of awakening and renewal movements. The Spirit is at work in the world.

Participants began with an inquiry into the Trinity to gain theological orientation as well as historical insights regarding the dynamics of revitalization. Each member of the Trinity has a fundamental role resulting in a continuous participation in revitalization. Similarly, the view of Church as the Body of Christ and agent of mission [via *missio Dei*] calls its members and positions its structures instrumentally to participate in renewal. This ecclesial view of the Church stimulates movements of renewal, healing and reconciliation to arise within churches, drawing together Spirit-inspired persons alongside believers from other Christian traditions.

The strength of this definition is its emphasis on the Trinity. It affirms that churches must be fully Trinitarian to prepare for revitalization. God's nature is fundamentally relational as seen in fellowship shared among Persons of the Trinity—Father, Son and Holy Spirit. Revitalization then continues the pattern to create instances and occasions of divine and human encounter. Teaching about the Triune God preserves the mystery of encounter, yet balances how doctrinal and practical expressions of the encounters are understood and experienced.

The ecclesiology exhibited is very open, following the Spirit across boundaries. Greater awareness will promote ecumenical harmony between traditions. This table group expresses sensitivity to Pentecostalism, manifested as a corrective reaction to the lack of consideration of the Holy Spirit.

Revitalization may occur amid a discovery of the unity of the Spirit among diverse expressions of the one Body of Christ. Ecumenism is an avenue for renewal when it encourages fellowship and the flourishing of multiple expressions of meeting God and manifesting the arrival of God's Kingdom. Participation in this broader dimension is en-livening by the Spirit.

Concepts of the renewing of God in revitalization movements are shaped by a vision of the Spirit working to renew all things, which is the theological basis for a comprehensive understanding of salvation. The overflowing blessing of God brings abundance and joy. The nature of encounter with God must be studied through Trinitarian eyes to gain awareness. Scripture acts to norm expectations regarding specific roles of members of the Trinity, and highlights the collaboration of human and divine agency at work in the phenomena of revitalization. It is the work of the Holy Spirit that elicits a fresh encounter with Christ, and brings repentance, healing, reconciliation and restoration.

Awakening and renewal occur across history and through the ages. It happens when people are hungry and desire God with all their heart. It occurs when there is a united call for God's presence, when there is radical discipleship, accompanied by humility. Effects of some movements of revitalization last for centuries. Agents of revitalization are: the Triune God, the people of God and whomever God decides to work with. The Holy Spirit moves in specific places with specific people. Renewal enables, energizes and rejuvenates the Church to function effectively and efficiently as the body of Christ.

Observations: Concepts of revitalization are shaped by the Church's vision of the Spirit's work in renewing all things, which is the theological basis for a comprehensive understanding of salvation. Conversely, too broad a vision of the Spirit's work through and beyond the Church may be alienating for Pentecostal churches that must choose between ecumenism or identifying with an evangelicalism that shows little warmth for charismatic exuberance and one that disenfranchises them on the basis of hermeneutics and the doctrine of the Spirit. Pentecostal and charismatic churches as the fruit of a renewal movement have potential to elicit revitalization across of plethora of Christian traditions. These churches maintain fellowship with some independent churches. They are a stream within nearly every Christian tradition, particularly the Protestant wing, and leaving occasionally due to the reaction of evangelicals who have excluded them from affiliation. They express vitality and joy through vibrant worship, praise, and manifestations of the Spirit, as well as powerful prophetic preaching, and giving continual witness to the power of God in their daily lives. Fellowships grow rapidly because of a willingness to enjoy encounter with God on a daily basis and rich discovery of the power of the Holy Spirit as the source of power, sustaining the vitality of abundant life in human situations.

In summary, the ecumenical movement itself is paradoxical because it draws such a mixture of churches and groups into its wide tent. Its strength is inclusiveness and its weakness is generalization and lack of consensus about theological claims of normativity regarding the nature of human encounter with God.

Table C

Table C's Definition: A Christian revitalization movement is a group of people shaped by a complex matrix of interpretations and agencies generated by dissatisfaction and/or motivated by a better future and pulled into that future by a vision of the reign of God.

Table C's view of revitalization is highlighted by cycles of deliverance and blessing. Conversation focuses on revitalization that gives priority to anthropology over theology. This discussion creates a typology that will answer questions related to the environment of social dynamics in the lives of persons being changed. Christian understanding of human response to divine "moments" of encounter with God can also be viewed through the lens of social movement theory. Essentially borrowed from Wallace,[iii] the definition is an "applied" use of the anthropologist's revitalization theory, simplified to be useful as a typology of dynamics and forms of revitalization movements. The typology can explain why renewals occur, and when a movement waxes and wanes in vitality.

The approach of table C does not account for theological content per se, but examines divine and human elements as "interpretations" and "agencies". These are applicable to Christian revitalization because they can add to theology key background information in which to evaluate a movement's view of God.. These interpretive elements bring to fore interactions among leaders and members of revitalization movements that aid in viewing the relationship of the community to Jesus Christ and the Holy Spirit. This approach can investigate sources of salvation and human hope, including deliverance and blessing, as expressions of soteriology and eschatology. These contributions are presented alongside the essential components needed in Christian revitalization. Given these factors, analysis of a particular revitalization movement may identify redemptive factors, and be not only described but have its Christian identity discerned as well.

Ancillary to this process, social movement theory gives allowance for trajectories of growth or decline and desperate crises or blessed contentment and peace. It is useful in observing the significance of messages, including use of scripture, visions, and the place given to prayer, prophecy, and healing, each of which functions among Christian groups manifesting the desire for intimacy with God.

The approach to definition leads to "grassroots" consideration of multiple contextual and circumstantial factors that have a "pushing" and "pulling" effect on a social movement's form of community, faith, or the hope they have in the world These factors influence its identity and ability to carry credibility in its current expression as a movement. Variables among movements of revitalization include how a group deals with such factors as dissatisfaction, radical discipleship, and adaptability. Dissatisfaction creates pressure either to become radical in discipleship, to become demoralized, to return to the past, to be re-formed into a new movement, or to disband. Radical Discipleship raises the possibility of a rising individualism, a new movement, or revolution within the context of the present one. Adaptability measures ability to maintain the status quo, reach a breaking point, re-appropriate existing tradition, or reach the capacity to step outside that tradition.

In combination, variables lead to insightful inquiry about many phenomena and functional aspects of new movements within the church that would be otherwise ignored. The matrix suggested by this table group is especially helpful in recognizing key moments when breakthroughs occur that involve new messages connecting groups to normative theological elements of Christian revitalization. Having content-specific and context-relative messages are significant to engaging and discovering an appropriate relationship with new movements. The approach affirms one of the essential theological components in the theology of revitalization. It shows high value for human life with its hope in struggle, acted out by persons seeking a better fullness of life. The arena of social movements becomes the place for churches to journey alongside the movements to discover their identity and to influence them toward a fully Christian encounter with God. This life is filled with uncertainty and experiences that show human frailty and lack of power. Relationships in the world are disappointing and transient, and bring feelings of hopelessness, abandonment, futility. The human quest is to discover how to have "life in its fullness"—blessings of healing, reconciliation, provision, or peace with contentment. It is no less than what they envisioned—salvation realized, and fulfillment for themselves, others and the earth. Movements occur in cycles, with special opportunity for renewals, while the inspiration of founders gets normalized eventually.

Table D

Table D's Definition. "It is finished!" Comprehensive renewal of all creation has already occurred by the act of the Father in the life, death, and resurrection of the incarnate Son by the Spirit. The Church's revitalization is participation in that reality as gift and promise, through the life of the Spirit, now.

Language and Experience. Evangelization is related to Christian initiation. There is need for deep reconnection between revitalization, mission and Church discussion across traditions. Bringing together grace and nature by the Word is a puzzle or mystery, requiring openness to the Spirit that is critical. Whatever revitalization model, community is called to an ongoing life of the Spirit that promotes conversion inspired by repentance, lament, and self-denial. Where the Spirit is, there is the Church; where the Church is there is the Spirit and fullness of grace. Renewal fits a complex cycle of life that stretches back to Abraham and Sarah and spans the history of the Church. Likewise, Mother church can sometimes take in all movements and smother them

Table D's Setting for Revitalization: Sacraments. Discussion centers on theological positions on the salvation of God. Debate concerns conflicting positions regarding how the church understands its role and function with regard to offering God's gift of grace to human beings. Catholic and Pentecostal traditions differ enormously regarding how to offer the "the Body of Christ broken for you". Tension among Christian traditions has been severe, leading some groups to consider others as not yet having experienced vital encounter with God.

Opposing views of how properly to re-present the risen Christ who has authority over the church, and places his representatives as mediators or agents of grace, and uses ordinances, particularly baptism and communion, as instruments of grace, is more than a mere symbolic debate. This discussion discloses core issues that touch all essential components of theology related to revitalization.

Theological understandings that differ, at varying levels, involve the Trinity, the church, the salvation of God, and human life and hope. However, these are integrally connected by simultaneous presentations in myth and ritual that announce the offer of revitalization in a theologically comprehensive portrayal through the Mass. To Catholics this is the central place of encounter with God— for repentance, faith, hope, and renewal.

While some Protestant churches do recognize the real Presence of Christ in the Eucharistic meal, other groups in this tradition argue that it is a fellowship meal, a communion of believers with Christ. Sacramental and memorial views contrast immensely, leading to banter about the potential of Protestant idolatry in the search to maintain the sovereignty of the Word. The theology of revitalization, using a sacramental view, privileges the clergy over the laity. This point applies when evaluating what is meant by any mediating and intercessory role of Christ and priests in their work for the Church. Implications for evangelization are huge. Although scriptures and the Spirit are freely accessible to all members, there remain limitations on the laity in official capacity. They may be viewed as lesser valued in the ministry. Ecclesial representation in the church is relegated to a hierarchy of leaders of the church. Ordination is a sacrament. Reformation is a long process if it waits for the structure to respond. A danger is that Mother Church sometimes takes in all movements and smothers them.

The sacramental theology of offering Christ through ministries of incarnation by the laity holds promise for revitalization. Through practical actions the meaning of salvation touches lives of missioners and those in communities where they go. The radical choice to "follow Christ", bear of the image of Christ in and to the world—even to martyrdom—is a sacramental posture marked by refreshing social change and personal renewals that follow. To witness until death places the image-bearer, peace-keeper, and preacher of the gospel into opposition and suffering. Its focus is upon the way of sinners where issues of justice and truth are needed. The pain of sin is experientially a part of witness. It becomes a moment when the power of the Spirit brings en-livening faith and hope.

<u>Quotes and Implications:</u>

"And we who with unveiled faces all reflect the Lord's glory are being transformed into his likeness from one degree of glory to another which comes from the Lord who is the Spirit." (2 Cor. 3:18) "The joys and hopes, the grief and anguish of the people of our time, especially of those who are poor or afflicted, are the joys and hopes, the grief and anguish of the followers of Christ as well."[iv]

"First, an authentic revitalization movement will bring the Church to acknowledge its own poverty. Through the power of the Spirit such a movement will enable the Church to bring the liberating presence of Christ for the healing of human brokenness."

"Second, a flourishing of fresh and surprising theological reflection will emerge from all corners of the globe to enrich and enliven the credal faith of the Church." [Quoted from Table Conversation notes]

Provocative Questions and Statements from the Data

- Divergent Christianity exists in new groups and churches. How should we judge them?

- Is revitalization always good? All want it, but what sort? Individual or communal?

- Are individual or communal forms problematic to revitalization?

- How do we know what is being revitalized? Dynamics complex.

- What cannot or should not be revitalized because it is just a refreshment of old religious ideas?

- What ecclesiology dominates the revitalization movements?

- What is the ecclesiology of a revitalized congregation?

- Revitalization creates change in the dynamics of the status quo—some people win and some lose. How do we assess these dynamics?

- If revitalization depends on social and spiritual relationships, what is the substance of these relationships?

- Revitalization that is noted operates most frequently and powerfully at the level of the laity. What is implied by this realization?

- Revitalization touches all dimensions and areas of human existence, even the earthly environment that sustains it. Is environmental theology an important supplement, and is revitalization as Christian environmentalism needed?

- Revitalization is related to an individual or local fellowships of people, based on developing relationships and discipling, in terms of collectivity (a whole tribe) and among people at the margins.

- Revitalization also occurs in studied, devotional isolation of retreats.

- Revitalization movements are very specific, with unique features.

- Revitalization is related to human markers of "time" and "place", seasons and centers. It has a temporal and a geographical rationale, including crossing boundaries of eternity and time, as preeminently embodied in the life of Jesus Christ.

- Do renewals show similar marks across time and traditions? Yes, these similarities can be traced, but their patterns are unpredictable.

- Can standards be set, or may standards, models, and examples be used as guidelines?

- It is not feasible to evaluate Christian movements early on, but only much later. Issues of change are to be factored, and the tendency of movements to morph into new forms..

- Revitalization is cyclical. The vitality is recurring, yet impossible to last.

- Revitalization is not a new burst of strength. It is a "new birth"!

- The world is the locus for the relationship of God's revitalizing activity in human life.

- Sacrament is a visible sign of an invisible grace--an interactive dynamic activity, socially constructed.

- The church is the Christocentric presence of God in the world.

- The church is also an imperfect, growing body.

- Do movements have to move outside the church in order to take root? Can we accept new movements within existing structures, or are they created by moving outside of structures?

- For whom, what, and what purpose is revitalization? Revitalization of the church for the church, or the church for the kingdom of God?

- Asymmetries of gender, economics, and ethnic groups should be considered seriously in evangelism, but these have been largely unmentioned so far in revitalization discussion.

- Christians are "renewalists", according to Todd Johnson.

- There is a rise in renewal movements at the beginning of the 21st century, according to Todd Johnson.

- A new term, "vitalization movement" refers to a movement of persons first hearing of encounter with God and Christianity.

- It may be better not to use a model, and a typology is difficult. Try to think of a Christian revitalized church by characteristics.

Defining Characteristics of Revitalization
[from compilation of data]

- Profound reorientation of life
- Creating new spaces
- Breakthrough, changing of lives
- Humility
- Fruitful change
- Re-imaging of God
- Flattens hierarchy
- Human flourishing
- "new thing", "grounded in diffused past, a re-appropriation of prior tradition

Conclusion

Are prior definitions of revitalization and renewal challenged and updated by this data from the table group discussions? Is it possible to propose a new model of revitalization that will provide a way to better understand and engage the new Christian movements emerging today? The answer to the first question is a resounding "yes".

Concerning the use of models of revitalization: We find credible data to show that revitalization is possible in every ecclesial structure that exists. This affirms whatever model we employ. The community is called to ongoing discernment of the Spirit that promotes conversion inspired by repentance, lament, and self-denial. Such renewal provokes radical opposition, demonic activity, and fear. A revitalized model provides the possibility for the appropriation of the gifts of the Spirit that is "context specific and person-relative. Renewal fits into a complex cycle of life that stretches back to Abraham and Sarah and spans the history of the Church."[v]

The challenge will be to study but also move beyond analysis of single movements one at a time, and to discover broader and more universally recognizable ways to understand and articulate revitalization as it has been observed, while avoiding the reduction of findings to any type of uniformity. Todd Johnson's suggestion of employing an approach of examining characteristics rather than devising models or taxonomies has merit. Using this descriptive approach would be done alongside the preservation of biblical and normative components of theology, as recognized and shared in the traditions of all communities of the Christian faith.[vi]

Our task is to prepare tools to enable response to the proliferation of new communities of Christians in the Global South, which are unquestionably in some remarkable way the fruit of the gospel, consisting of those chosen, called, and given "new life" by the Triune God, Accepting the expressions of the Spirit's power and joy within these communities, and at the same time engaging and extending the conversation about the meaning of the lessons of what sustains revitalization will be essential. Further, engaging these new communities in interpretive dialogue to discern the gracious presence of the Spirit at work among them will be necessary. To alert Christians in established churches of these cutting edge movements will in itself be revitalizing. This clearly fits with extending knowledge of "new Christianities" which speaks to the global focus of the Center's purpose to publish information on revitalization movements.

The next step in this research project should be to engage in fresh descriptive and analytical interpretation of revitalization movements by examining cases in recent memory, where participants in them and analysts looking on could review understandings and press for new interpretations. Consultation Three in 2011 will have cases as their focus, whereby the data from this consultation may be tested and extended in light of twenty-first century realities. Prevailing categories still follow a Western epistemology of knowledge. Use of this tool may not be helpful in comparing categories of non-Western thought in terms of a content-specific and context-relative analysis of the experience of revitalization in the new movements found in the Global South and East.

Reframing and Updating Essential Components of Theology

1.   Scripture and tradition provide norms for grounding investigation of subsequent movements of renewal or revival. NORMING DEVICE 1 refers to the experience and testimony from past generations of Christians described in scriptural accounts. These traditions remain available as tools to challenge and correct the present analysis of the work of God among local groups. NORMING DEVICE 2 refers to a focus of analysis on the dynamics of spiritual awakening as recorded in the Bible where accounts of the "fresh wind of God" move upon leaders and Christian groups

2.   The focus on culture asks how can the inbreaking of God in revitalization be recognized among new believers in previously unreached areas of the world? Further, will such breakthroughs be recognizable and accepted by other Christian groups on the basis of their own knowledge of Christian spiritual vitality, which is both divinely and humanly sourced? If so, how might this occur? Of concern here is the question of how much heterodoxy among culturally diverse groups will be identified? This is a question for the future of Christianity. Indeed, its answer may determine how fragmentation occurs within the Christian traditions.

3.   "New faces around the table": The global perspective in revitalization asks whether there can be found any universal language for revitalization? Evidence for this may be found in

testimony and fellowship in the Spirit, and affirming the fruit of revitalization as bearing "marks" of authentic Christian spirituality?

4. Christian and Local Identities. The dialectic between revitalization and church brings us back in terms of social theory to a new point: that all revitalization movements must negotiate expression via language and concepts that are indigenous to the historical, social and cultural location of their local community. At the same time they must remain faithful in expressing their Christian identity by aligning with biblical and theologically-recognizable patterns that connect them to the wider global community of churches claiming to be Christian. The transition from systematic to narrative theology will be welcoming to communities of oral learners. The mysteries of God are too great for reduction to explanation, but they can be captured in stories (gospel as narrative) and metaphors (theology as profound "faith-bounded" analogies), both of which are sacramental in many cultures.

The data from these table discussions, with the distinctive definitions of revitalization each table formulated, have provided the source for the perspectives on Christian revitalization in the twenty-first century, which comprise the chapters of this study.

The data from Edinburgh, concerned with exploring the dialectic between revitalization and church, has presented distinctive responses to the theme of the relationship between revitalization and church. Each has nuanced the meaning of revitalization in distinctive ways. Latent within the data, a number of themes were identified for further development of the meaning of Christian revitalization for twenty-first century global Christianity. The essays in this volume offer perspectives on the themes from Edinburgh, from the standpoint of scholars and practitioners of revitalization from the church around the world.

Notes

1. CSWCRM's Bulletin, "Revitalization", Vol. 18, No. 1, Spring/Summer 2011. 1.

2. Terms here are quoted from the document: "Definitions of Terms related to the research project of the Center", distributed from J. Steven OMalley by email attachment. on March 11, 2011.]

3. See the discussion of revitalization theory in the address by Michael Rynkiewich, found in the Appendix to this volume.

4. See Glauben und Spes, 1. Gaudium et Spies, Part 1 "The Pastoral Constitution on the Church in the Modern World." Second Vatican Council, 1965.

5. Howard Snyder, Consultation One paper and table group notes.

6. Todd Johnson, presentation notes.

Appendix C

Catechesis and Revitalization

[Plenary Address for Consultation Two (May 28–June 2, 2010)]

William J. Abraham, PhD
Albert Cook Outler Professor of Wesley Studies
and Altshuler Distinguished Teaching Professor,
Perkins School of Theology,
Southern Methodist University, Dallas, Texas

Proposals about renewal invariably offer or assume the following: a description of the problematic state of the church, a diagnosis of what has gone wrong, and a prescription for putting it right. Consequently, efforts are renewal or revitalization can go wrong at any or all of these levels. The description can be false, the diagnosis can be misguided, and the prescription can be inappropriate. It should not surprise us that renewal is a thoroughly difficult enterprise. Given the complexity it can take a lot longer to sort through what needs to be done, not to speak of actually doing it. Even then it can blow up in our faces.[1]

I am deploying here a medical analogy. However, it is interesting to work this analogy back to front, as it were. In the medical arena it is obvious that a single prescription can be used to tackle a number of different diseases. This suggests another angle from which to look at revitalization. We can identify some medicine and work backwards to see what it might do; or, stated more aptly, we can think of applying the same medicine to address a network of challenges in the church. In this strategy rather than starting from above, say, with a vision of the disease that needs to be cured, or with a vision of the church that should be implemented, we begin more modestly with materials and practices that we can all recognize to be healing in their effects. This does not mean we are indifferent about the soteriological and ecclesial issues that inevitably crop up in debates about the revitalization of the church; there is a time and place for deploying our best insights on these topics. However, there is also a time and place for beginning where we are and working more intuitively, informally, and pragmatically.

In this paper I want to highlight the place of catechesis in renewal by suggesting that catechesis could well be vital for addressing an important range of problems that demand attention in the revitalization of the church today. I am by no means arguing that catechesis is a panacea; my claim is the more modest one that properly understood and rightly administered serious experiments in catechesis could well enable us to make significant progress in ecclesial renewal. I shall prepare the ground for this by noting that there are interesting historical precedents that connect catechesis and renewal. After clarifying and illustrating what is involved in catechesis I shall then explore its potential place in revitalization.

"Catechesis" is not exactly an exciting term. It is perhaps the last kind of thing that we would envisage as medicine in the life of the church. The word "catechesis" is not commonly known in most Protestant churches; and it readily summons up musty ideas of catechism, rote learning, and boring teaching. In my own history, I suspect I was still part of the last generation that actually used a series of catechisms, graded according to age and capacity. I can actually remember being excited about learning the various Methodist catechisms that were used in Irish Methodism in the sixties. I do not recall very much from them; my only regret is that I did not pay more attention and make better use of them. Catechism was swept away, as memory recalls, by a wave of enthusiasts who rejected them in favor of child-centered education. Appeal to learning by doing and learning by experience became the watchword; these were the equivalent of the rage for outcomes education that we know today. We might say that catechisms suffered the same fate as the use of Articles of Religion of Confessions of Faith within the United Methodist tradition. In the latter case students were urged to make up their own creeds and confession, perhaps according to the Wesleyan Quadrilateral of scripture, tradition, reason, and experience.[2] The net result has been disastrous: generations have come up through the church without any internalization of the central concepts or basic doctrines of the faith. They do not have the scaffolding for developing a serious version of the Christian faith intellectually; they do not have the basic concepts needed to identify and speak of spiritual experience; when they arrive at seminary they are functionally illiterate doctrinally.

It is tempting at this point to turn the tables and call for the retrieval and redeployment of catechisms in the contemporary church. We can be sure that such a call would evoke astonishment, if not aggressive hostility. This move, however, would probably be a mistake. As John Henry Newman once noted, some things can only be said after other things have been said. The bigger problem here is the need for intellectual and spiritual formation; and catechesis fits neatly into this wider arena. Originally, catechesis simply meant instruction by word of mouth. As mentioned in the *Chambers Encyclopedia* of 1753, "In the ancient church catechesis was an instruction given, viva voce, either to children, or adult heathens, preparatory to their receiving baptism."[3] It is here in the early church that we find the paradigm for catechesis. At its heart it was the handing over of the faith of the church to those who were entering as new members and believers. As such it was intimately related to evangelism and spiritual formation.

Under no circumstances should it be seen as a perfunctory exercise; it was a vital corporately for the health of the church and for the spiritual welfare of the individual.[4] Would-be members were taken through a complex process that could last as long as three years. The operation as a whole involved exorcism, the development of spiritual discipline, the learning of the doctrinal content of the faith, baptism, and the illumination of the Holy Spirit. What we now call "Lent" was effectively the penultimate stage of an arduous process that sought to ground the catechumen in the faith in a serious manner. Gavrilyuk's summation of what was at issue is worth noting.

> For many believers through the centuries, this process has meant a profound reorientation of life. It was this in process that souls wounded by sin received their first cure; repentant hearts were opened to the accept the love of God and share it with others; humble minds were enlightened by the Holy Spirit to comprehend the Word of God; docile bodies were trained to become vessels of holiness; spiritual senses were attuned to discern the hand of God in all things; and the lifelong journey toward deification began.[5]

The production of catechisms in magisterial Protestantism represents a truncation of this wider process of catechesis. The Reformers rightly grasped that they could not leave the formation of their peoples to chance; the rejection of Roman Catholicism left a vacuum that had to be filled. It was not enough to hand believers a bible and hope for the best; they needed guidance on the core elements of the faith and the freshly discovered vitalities of justification by faith. Catechisms were in turn complemented by the development of Articles of Religion and Confessions of faith, material that clearly stood in continuity with the early creeds of the Church.[6] In the case of The Church of England these were further supplemented by various volumes of canonical homilies.[7]

The Books of Homilies of the Church of England were in turn the model for John Wesley's canonical Sermons on Several Occasions.8 Read as a whole they are effectively a manual of spiritual direction that divides nicely into three sections. The first group (1-15) sets out to describe what is involved in becoming a Christian; the second (16-28), focusing on the Sermon on the Mount, delineates what it is to be a Christian; the third (29-44) are really a form of parenesis, addressing the kind of spiritual challenges involved in remaining a Christian. A contrasting handbook of spiritual direction was furnished in the ensuing century by the great revivalist Charles Grandson Finney. In his *Lectures on Revivals of Religion,* after analyzing what a revival is (1-3), he turns to exploring the place of prayer in the revival of persons (4-8), the role of testimony and of the preacher (9-16), and finally the role of the sinner in coming to terms with the gospel (17-22).[9] It is in this last set of lectures where Finney shows his clear grasp of the importance of catechesis in renewal. Contrary to popular stereotype Finney insists that it is the truth, not the cultivation of emotion that is vital to the instruction and spiritual vitality of new converts.[10] Wesley and Finney taken together provide ample proof of the natural and essential connection between catechesis and revitalization.

Insufficient critical attention has been given to the content of catechesis as it relates more generally to Christian initiation. Working in a temporal framework that fits with contemporary practice in my own context, and presupposing that the heart of the Gospel is the inauguration of the kingdom of God in the life, death, and resurrection of Jesus Christ, I have suggested that the following list of items are critical: the gospel, the Nicene Creed, Christian experience, love of God and neighbor, membership in the church, the gifts of the Holy Spirit, and the spiritual disciplines.[11] The central move here is to think of Christian initiation as first and foremost initiation into the kingdom of God. Minimally this will then involve a clear grasp of what the gospel is in itself and as contrasted with the counterfeits that inhabit the airwaves and flit through the church at large. Beyond that initiation into the kingdom will involve coming to terms with and internalizing the intellectual content of the faith as summed up the Nicene Creed, its moral requirements as represented by the Great Commandment, its characteristic experiential elements as captured in such critical concepts as justification and new birth, its ecclesial dimensions as represented by baptism, its spiritual disciplines as represented by, say, study of scripture, fasting, and regular participation in the Eucharist, and its operational mode as recognized in the great wealth of gifts of the Spirit. One could readily shift the orientation by conceiving of the horizon of initiation into the church and then making entry into the kingdom a dimension of ecclesial existence, but I think that this is mostly a verbal or secondary issue.[12] What really matters is that contemporary forms of catechesis take seriously the roundedness and richness of Christian initiation.

My goal here is less to insist on one way of delineating my own take on the content of catechesis, much less articulating the logistics involved, and more to draw attention to the kind of enterprise I have in mind. I am in fact currently working on a radically different way of proceeding in the local church where I teach. In this instance I propose to take the canonical sermons of Wesley, make them available in book form in accessible contemporary English, and develop an accompanying workbook for their use. The plan is to experiment with immersion in this material in small groups over the course of a year. Using Wesley's material as a baseline, I intend to integrate the other elements of initiation outlined above into the process as a whole. The strategy in this instance is to tap into the originating spiritual vision of Methodism and into the observed effectiveness of the Wesleyan material across the years in local churches and in my teaching in seminary.

There are a variety of ways to identify the goal of such catechetical experiments in my ecclesial setting. Thus one can think of it as the making of genuine disciples, as providing an exercise in fundamental (as opposed to ongoing) spiritual formation, or as grounding new believers in the faith for the first time. It is helpful to identify what is not going on here. Thus this is not an exercise in theology, or training in ministry, or preparing people for church membership, or offering an elective in Christian education, or filling a gap in current church life.

The primary concern is to develop a form of catechesis that will establish converts in the faith and give them a fighting chance of becoming serious followers of Jesus Christ who can survive in their contemporary culture. It is an effort to take serious baby steps in a wider journey that could lead to the creating of a raft of catechetical options that would be genuinely effective in the years ahead.

It is worth pondering why catechesis went under in the modern period in the West. I think of a host of reasons. On the mundane level, catechesis is hard, grinding work, so sustaining it requires diligence and tenacity. In many places we did not invest the energy needed. At another level, it fell out of fashion because it was seen as intellectually and pedagogically primitive; it was construed as an insult to ask people to learn by rote that which was not worked out by themselves; it was a deep denial or personal integrity and a barrier to the virtue of rationality. At yet another level, catechesis was replaced by the learning of scripture; scripture was the Word of God, while catechetical material was at best a portable summary of scripture and at worst the teaching of mere human tradition. In these circumstances the learning of scripture (a great good in itself) marginalized or eliminated the development of good catechetical materials and practices.

I suspect that the really deep reason for the demise of catechesis was a massive failure of intellectual nerve in the leadership of the church in the West in the late nineteenth century. The concerted attack on the faith of the church in the late Enlightenment period left the church between a rock and a hard place. On the one hand, the move to revise the faith to fit modern sensibilities (both rational and romantic in nature) left the churches without an agreed account of the faith to hand over to a new generation and to new believers. On the other hand, Christian intellectuals became captivated with issue of epistemology; knowing how we know trumped knowing, so much so that the kind of materials and practices that are essential to catechesis were sidelined and then simply lost. This has not changed in the shift to postmodernity in that the encounter with the latter leaves the primacy of epistemology unchallenged. To be sure, the turn to postmodernity can create space for the retrieval of lost Christian materials and practices; the old confidence that triumphalistically dismissed Christianity as incredible and superstitious has faded somewhat; however, the actual result tends to be more of a lucky-dip approach to the past which changes kaleidoscopically over space and time. The deep underlying problem in both modernity and postmodernity is the pedagogical privileging of epistemology over the substantial content and practices of the Christian faith.[13]

What we need now are well-thought out, road-tested proposals in catechesis that will provide comprehensive formation for children brought up in Christian families and for new believers. Such a development would address three challenges in the contemporary church that deserve attention.

First, this strategy would address the problem of nominalism and thin formation already present in many churches in the United States. Happily, there is still a residual level of Christian commitment right across the culture that provides a generally positive disposition towards the Christian faith. Some of this stems from the potent place of civil religion in the culture; some of it stems from the unique forms of Christianity that were either imported or invented in North America; some of it stems from the influence of the market mentality and of the market state on religion. To be sure, there are deep pockets of resistance to robust forms of Christianity in the elite media and in the academy as a whole. However, it is a matter of speculation rather than fact that the United States will go the way of Europe in the loss of faith. However we read the situation, a concerted commitment to serious forms of catechesis could play an important role in strengthening and deepening the significant if thin commitment to Christianity that is evident across much of the country.

Second, this development would provide a vital link to connect work in evangelism with the journey into full church membership. The surest way to argue this case would be to incorporate catechesis into the conception and practice of evangelism as a matter of principle. However, one need not go this far (one I would favor) to see the vital place that catechesis has in the neighborhood of evangelism. In the recent past this place has often been named as follow-up, especially where evangelism has been construed in terms of proclamation. Thus all committed to this particular vision of evangelism have at a minimum paid lip service to the danger of ephemeral commitment by insisting that local churches find ways to connect new converts to the life of the local church. However, this is really a placeholder for catechesis. So catechesis turns out to be the vital link between proclamation and initiation into the faith as a whole.

Third, implementing robust forms of catechesis could help develop the kind of mature disciples who could become genuine salt in the culture as a whole. Consider just one example, in this regard, namely, the place of Christians in the political order at the highest level of government. Contemporary political life is something of a blood sport. The mixture of populist anger, corrupt funding interest, party spirit, and the demands of the logic of electioneering operate to undermine basic human virtues like transparency, honest disagreement, and informed discernment. If Christians are to be other than the mirror of the forces that drive the Hobbesian reality we all know, then they will need to be given enough formation that will provide an initial bulwark against temptation and the platform for sustained faithfulness in the political arena.

There are, I suspect, other challenges related to revitalization that would be partially met by the development of healthy forms of catechesis. Suffice it here to set the ball rolling and then wait and see where in the providence of God others might take it.

1. I have discussed a raft of proposals at length in my *The Logic of Renewal* (Grand Rapids: Eerdmans, 2005).

2. I constantly hear of confirmation classes in local United Methodist Churches where the confirmands (generally around the age of twelve) are writing and presenting their own credos. No doubt the intentions behind this are good, but the spiritual and intellectual consequences strike me as ludicrous; at the very least young Christians need to learn and internalize the faith of the Church before they try their hand at making up their own. This whole way of thinking is the legacy of nineteenth Liberal Protestantism recast to fit the needs of the contemporary culture. Its deleterious effects constitute a massive problem for contemporary mainline Christianity in the USA.

3. See the Oxford English Dictionary entry for catechesis.

4. For a splendid overview see Paul L. Gavrilyuk, "The Healing Process of Initiation: Toward the Retrieval of Patristic Catechumenate," in Paul L. Gavrilyuk, Douglas M. Koskela, and Jason E. Vickers, eds., *Immersed in the Life of God, the Healing Resources of the Christian Faith* (Grand Rapids: Eerdmans, 2008), 21-41.

5. Ibid, 38.

6. For a magisterial study see Jarisolav Pelikan, *Credo, Historical and Theological Guide to Creeds and Confessions of Faith in the Christian Tradition* (New Haven: Yale University Press, 2003). Unfortunately, Pelikan takes as the paradigm of confession the confessions of the Reformation; this leads to a reading-back of the Reformation sensibility into the creedal developments of the early period.

7. Most notably the *First and Second Books of Homilies* published in 1562.

8. London: Epworth Press, 1944. For various reasons this important edition of Wesley's sermons is rarely seen in the United States of America.

9. A fine critical edition has been furnished by William G. McLoughlin and was published by Belknap Press of Harvard University in 1960.

10. In causal terms Finney insists that there are three agents (God, the one who brings the gospel and the sinner) and one instrument in revival. See Lecture 1, section 3. This point is completely lost on the devastating critique offered by the immigrant Scotch-Irish theologian John Williamson Nevin. I have great sympathy with many of Nevin's observations but he failed to take the full measure of what Finney was doing. See, for example, *The Anxious Bench, Antichrist, and The Sermon on Catholic Unity* (Eugene, Oregon: Wipf and Stock Publishers, n.d.). Finney's *Reflections on Revival* (Minneapolis: Bethany Fellowship Inc., 1979), compiled by Donald Dayton, is essential reading to get a rounded picture of Finney's work and theory.

11. I provide an extended discussion of these in *The Logic of Evangelism* (Grand Rapids: Eerdmans, 1989), chapters 5-7.

12. See my discussion in paper in Carl Braaten and Robert Jenson, eds, *Marks of the Body of Christ* (Grand Rapids: Eerdmans, 1999).

13. I am not here committed to the epistemic privileging, say, of the doctrine of the Trinity so ably championed by Bruce Marshall in his *Trinity and Truth* (Cambridge: Cambridge University Press, 2000). For my own most recent take on the epistemology of theology see *Crossing the Threshold of Divine Revelation* (Grand Rapids: Eerdmans, 2006).

Appendix D

Church as Sacrament

Judith M. Kubicki, PhD

Associate Professor
Department of Theology
Fordham University

Introduction

It is a joy and a privilege to be here to share with you some ideas on the notion of Church as sacrament from my own Roman Catholic tradition. It is topic of great interest in my own research and in my teaching at Fordham University. Therefore, I look forward to a stimulating exchange of ideas regarding this model for describing the Church.

The simple phrase "church as sacrament" is, in reality, a theological mouthful, so to speak. It involves theological assumptions and a particular way of interpreting the Scriptures and the Christian tradition. In order to make sense of this model for understanding church, I would like to begin with a brief consideration of the notion of "sacramentality."

Sacramentality

The basis for understanding "sacrament" is the broader and perhaps more illusive notion of "sacramentality." Simply stated, sacramentality can be described as having one's eyes and ears attuned to the intimations of a benevolent God inviting us into a transforming relationship. [By "us" I mean every human person.] Sacramentality requires an openness of the imagination to being surprised by God's presence in the mundane experiences of everyday life. In this way, ordinary created realities serve as symbols or windows into the divine. A sacramental perspective enables us to view the world as the locus where God reveals God-self to us and where we respond to that revelation. It is difficult to per-ceived the presence and action of God in human life—and even more in the ri-tuals or in the Church—without this ability to see the fundamental structures of sacramentality within ordinary human existence.

Sacramentality is expressed in the New Testament with the Greek word *mys-terion*, meaning "hidden" or "secret." St. Paul uses the word to speak about the hidden wisdom of God revealed through Christ's death and resurrection (1 Cor 2:7). The early Christian Church used *mysterion* to speak about a variety of rites, symbols, liturgical objects, blessings, and celebrations. But by the Middle Ages, the Latin translation for *mysterion* was *sacramentum* and this term was used to refer only to the official sacramental rites of the Church.[1]

Sacramentality is a particular way of looking at the world and at life. Be-cause of that, it provides a framework not only for the way we live in the world and with each other, but also for the way we understand the mystery of the church and its sacred rituals.[2] A sacramental imagination involves having a pro-found awareness that the invisible divine presence is disclosed through visible created realities. In other words, it takes seriously those everyday experiences the church appropriates to celebrate its life in God through liturgy or worship.[3] The sacramental world view perceives the sacred manifested in the secular; God is perceived as present and active within the world.

When we speak of sacramentality, however, we cannot limit the notion to an experience of God's presence. No matter how much the experience of God's presence may be mediated through the mediation of symbolic activity, no reve-lation of God can ever be complete on this side of the grave. So there is, along-side the experience of God's presence, a corresponding experience of God's absence—in our personal lives, in the church, and in the world. This experience of the hiddenness of God is also a dimension of sacramentality. The more we discover the presence of God in the here and now, the more our desire for God results in a yearning for the fullness of God's presence, a fullness that can only be attained in eternity.[4] This is part of the eschatological dimension of sacramen-tality. In other words, while God's creation offers glimpses of God's loving presence to those who have the eyes to see, this experience is balanced by a longing for what can only be realized when God is encountered face to face. But the experience of God's absence is nevertheless a positive thing. It serves as a promise that what is glimpsed but dimly in the present time is but a shadow of what will be revealed to us when the need for sacraments shall cease.[5]

Definitions

Let us then hold on to this general notion of sacramentality as we consider the notion of Church as sacrament. To make clear the perspective from which I am speaking, I would like to offer some brief definitions and/or descriptions of church and sacrament as I understand them within my own Roman Catholic tradition. First then, let's consider sacrament.

Sacrament

The traditional definition of sacrament in Catholic theology is derived from Augustine's understanding of sacrament as an outward sign of an invisible reality. The outward sign or symbol bears witness to the inner reality of grace. But when Christian churches speak of sacraments, they generally mean either the two or seven special events of grace officially recognized as "sacraments." This has not always been the case. In the early Church, the concept of sacrament was broader, reflecting a keen awareness of the sacramentality of human experience. The number of sacraments was more fluid. Augustine's definition of sacrament as a sacred sign represents the Patristic viewpoint that understood countless objects and actions as "sacraments."[6]

So the traditional definition of sacrament sees it first of all as a sign of grace. As Paul Tillich has pointed out, a sign can merely point to something that is absent or point to something without participating in the reality to which it points. But a sacrament is a symbol or full sign of something that is really present because the symbol participates in the reality to which it points. It is a visible sign of an invisible grace.

Furthermore, the Christian tradition has never understood the sacraments to be merely individual transactions. Nobody baptizes herself. Rather, sacraments take place in an interactive dynamic that permits people together to achieve a spiritual breakthrough that they could not achieve alone. Therefore we can say that a sacrament is a socially constituted or communal symbol of the presence of grace coming to fulfillment.[7] Such an understanding naturally leads to a consideration of the notion of both Jesus Christ and the Church as sacrament.

Twentieth Century Theological Perspectives

Jesus Christ as Primordial Sacrament

As Christians, we share the belief that the Risen Lord is present in his Church. Twentieth century theologians, particularly Henri de Lubac, Karl Rahner, Edward Schillebeeckx, and Louis-Marie Chauvet, have contributed to an understanding of Church as the primary location of Christ's presence in the world. This is the basis for speaking of the Church as sacrament. Their writings include the notion of Jesus Christ as primordial sacrament and the Church, therefore, as foundational sacrament.

Henri de Lubac argued that the divine and the human in the church can never be dissociated. An excessively spiritual and individualistic view of the life of grace, he cautioned, leads to a merely secular and sociological understanding of the Church as institution. The notion of sacrament, he suggests, harmoniously combines both aspects.[8]

De Lubac maintains:

> If Christ is the sacrament of God, the Church is for us the sacrament of Christ; she represents him, in the full and ancient meaning of the term, she really makes him present. She not only carries on his work, but she is his very continuation, in

a sense far more real than that in which it can be said that any human institution is its founder's continuation.[9]

Building on the work of de Lubac, Karl Rahner constructs his theology of church and sacraments on a similarly strong Christological foundation. He begins by describing Christ as "the historically real and actual presence of the eschatologically victorious mercy of God."[10] In other words, in the Word of God, that is, in Jesus Christ, God's last word is uttered into the visible public history of humankind. Jesus is this word of grace, reconciliation, and eternal life. No longer does God's grace come down from on high, from an absolutely transcendent God. Instead, this grace is permanently in the world in tangible historical form, established in the flesh of Christ as a part of the world, of humanity, and of its history.[11]

Edward Schillebeeckx presents this same idea in a similar way, referring to Christ as primordial sacrament. He points out:

> The dogmatic definition of Chalcedon, according to which Christ is "one person in two natures," implies that one and the same person, the Son of God, also took on a visible human form. Even in his humanity, Christ is the Son of God. The second person of the most holy Trinity is personally man; and this man is personally God. Therefore Christ is God in a human way, and man in a divine way.[12]

This line of reasoning is the foundation for Schillebeeckx's understanding of Jesus as sacrament: the humanity of Jesus is sacrament of the Divine Logos. He explains it this way:

> Because the saving acts of the man Jesus are performed by a diving person, they have a divine power to save, but because this divine power to save appears to us in visible form, the saving activity of Jesus is *sacramental*. For a sacrament is a divine bestowal of salvation in an outwardly perceptible form which make the bestowal manifest; a bestowal of salvation in historical visibility. . . The man Jesus, as the personal visible realization of the divine grace of redemption, is *the* sacrament, the primordial sacrament, because this man, the Son of God himself, is intended by the Father to be in his humanity the only way to the actuality of redemption.[13]

By "actuality of redemption," Schillebeeckx means God's redemptive love for all of humanity. But after the resurrection and ascension, Jesus is no longer visible or perceptible in his bodiliness. It is at this point that the Church begins to function as sacrament or symbol of God's redemptive love for all of humanity.

Viewed from this perspective, the Church becomes the continuation and perpetual presence of the task and function of Christ—that is the historical and human Jesus Christ—in the economy of salvation.[14] Rahner describes the Church as Christ's presence in the world when he explains:

> The Church is the abiding presence of that primal sacramental word of definitive grace, which Christ is in the world, effecting what is uttered by uttering it in sign. By the very fact of being in that way the enduring presence of Christ in the world, the Church is truly the fundamental sacrament, the well-spring of the sacraments in the strict sense.[15]

In this citation Rahner provides a convincing argument for describing the Church as the primordial sacrament, that is, as *Ursakrament*. Christ's presence as God's mercy and grace is found in all the other sacraments because of this presence *first* in the Church.

In the sacramental theology of Louis-Marie Chauvet, the Holy Spirit is understood to be the agent of God's embodiment. This embodiment involves the threefold body of Christ: the historical Jesus, the eucharistic Lord, and the ecclesial body of Christ, that is, the Church.[16] The Spirit's role is *"to write the very difference of God in the body of humanity*, and first of all in the body of the church, which was its first visible work after the resurrection. . . .*[17] In fact, it is only possible for humanity to become the sacramental locus of God's embodiment through the power of the Spirit. Chauvet explains:

> This sacramental locus where in some way the risen One withdraws through the Spirit in order to be "rising," that is, to raise for himself a body of new humanity, is the church, "body of Christ" in the process of growth "to the measure of the full stature of Christ" (Eph 4:13). In its historical visibility, the church is the promise and pledge of the transfiguration to which humankind and, in connection with it, the whole cosmos are called (Rom 8 and theme of "new heaven and new earth").[18]

However, Chauvet leaves no doubt that this Church, even as the embodiment of Christ, is an imperfect body straining to grow into the fullness of Christ. Nevertheless, the scandal [perhaps even more surprising than the scandal of the cross] is that the weak and sinful Church is the body that God has chosen to continue his presence in the world.

Church

The English Word "church" (and its equivalents in the other Germanic languages) derives from the Greek word *kuriakos* which means "belonging to the Lord." It was probably a shorthand version of *kuriakon doma* or *kuriakos domos* which means "the Lord's house." In its early usage, the word referred to the building in which Christians met for worship. However, the word *kuriakos* was always used to translate the Greek word *ekklesia* in versions of the scriptures. And the first meaning for *ekklesia* was not a building, but an official assembly of the people. The Greek word *ekklesia* is derived for the verb *ekkaleo* which means "to summon" or "to call out." Hence, the English word "convocation." [19]

The word "assembly" has roots in the ancient worlds of both Israel and Greece. Its theological usage can be traced to the Hebrew Scriptures where the term *qahal* is translated, like the Greek *ekklesia*, as a summons to an assembly or the act of assembling. More specifically, this assembly of persons was gathered by the Lord in order to live in his presence.[20] This sense of the assembly of Israel convoked by God and expressed by the word *qahal*, appears in Deuteronomy 5:19, 23:2-9, 1 Chronicles 28:8, Numbers 16:3, 20:4, and Micah 2:5. These passages focus on the divine initiative of the call and how that initiative constitutes the assembly. They also portray the divine call as the source of the people's unity.[21]

The assembly, and in particular the worshiping assembly, is key to understanding the Church as sacrament or as the locus of the presence of Christ. In fact, it is the key tenet of the sacramental theology of Louis-Marie Chauvet. Indeed, Chauvet asserts that it is impossible to have church without a worshiping assembly. Referring to the etymology of the word "assembly," Chauvet insists that the gathering, called or convoked by God or Christ, is *the* major characteristic of Christians. In other words, Christians are a people who gather as an assembly of brothers and sisters in the name and in memory of the Lord. Chauvet calls such an assembly the "fundamental sacrament" of the risen Christ.[22]

This church or assembly of people called by God has become, throughout history a visible and social presence in the world to which it has been missioned by Christ. As an organized people of God, it has evolved through many institutional forms, and none of them—including the excessively centralized papacy of the Roman church of the present time—may be regarded as definitive. In this regard, as institution, the church does not differ essentially from other institutional structures of nations or states. What does distinguish the church from other empirical societies (at least in the estimation of the Roman Catholic Church) is that it is also a mystery or sacrament. Such a designation points to its unique relationship with God and also a unique relationship with the world that God created.[23]

Edmund Hill explains it this way:

> As the Church, the fulfillment of Israel, the people God has taken for himself from all nations (Acts 15:14), it enjoys a quasi-divine filial relationship with the Father by being identified with his Son, by being the body of Christ endowed with the Spirit of the Father and the Son. Thus the mystery of the church is inseparably linked with the mystery of the Trinity, and indeed is the concrete, visible effect of the revelation of the supreme divine mystery.
>
> This derivation of the church from the revelation of the mystery of the Trinity through the divine missions of the Son and the Holy Spirit means that the mission of the church is an element in its aspect of mystery, and derives from the mission of the Son and of the Spirit.[24]

Lumen Gentium, the Second Vatican Council's *Dogmatic Constitution on the Church*, says this about the mystery of the church in its opening paragraph: . . . the church, in Christ, is a sacrament—a sign and instrument, that is, of communion with God and of the unity of the entire human race . . . (art. 1) We understand, of course, that this communion with God and unity of the human race will only be perfectly realized when Christ comes again. Therefore, both the nature and mission of the church have an essentially eschatological dimension. Like all the sacraments, the church has a future reference to eternal glory and a past reference to the saving paschal events of Christ's death, resurrection, and Pentecostal gift of the Spirit. Its mission to proclaim the good news of the kingdom must be understood as preparing humankind for its ultimate destiny and leading it toward that destiny.[25]

This way of describing the church as mystery and sacrament is closely related to another description of the church to which *Lumen Gentium* devotes an entire chapter. The title, "people of God," can be traced not only to the Hebrew

Scriptures, but also to the New Testament. The early Church appropriated this image as is evident in Peter's words: "You, however, are a 'chosen race, a royal priesthood, a holy nation, a people he claims for his own to proclaim the glorious works' of the One who called you from darkness into his marvelous light. Once you were no people, but now you are God's people. . ." (1 Peter 2:9-10).[26] Richard McBrien connects this people of God image to the Body of Christ image when he explains that

> If the People-of-God image underlines the Church's intimate connection with Israel and with God's call to a covenant relationship, the Body-of-Christ image underlines the Church's intimate connection with Jesus Christ and with God's call to a communal relationship, one with another in Christ. . . The Church of the New Testament is the People of God, but a people newly constituted in Christ and in relation to Christ. . . In principle, both images are rooted in the Old Testament idea of corporate personality.[27]

As Kenan B. Osborne has pointed out, "in the documents of the Second Vatican Council, the word "church" has a multivalent reference, even though Roman Catholic Church is the basic referent. These many references complicate the hermeneutical import of the phrase 'the church as a foundational sacrament.'"[28] Even though there is some ambiguity or circumspection in the passages in the Vatican II documents that speak of the church as a foundational sacrament, it is clear that when the bishops discussed the mystery and essence of the church, they wanted to indicate that by its very nature, the church is sacramental.[29]

But recall that when we were speaking of the nature of sacramentality, we spoke of both presence and absence. The Church is a "pilgrim" church, as *Lumen Gentium* describes it in chapter seven. From a theological standpoint, a pilgrim church can be sacrament only in an incomplete way. If, however, the pilgrim church possesses its sacramental character only partly and in a historical way, then the church can manifest its sacramental nature only incrementally or imperfectly. Even with the incarnation and the paschal mystery of Christ's life, death, and resurrection, there remains an incompleteness to the pilgrim church so that, with its ecclesial divisions, the elements of both holiness and truth are scattered or diminished. In this way, the disunity of the church affects sacramentality so that one must consider whether there is a disunity in the very sacramentality of the church itself, a disunity not only of individual Christians, but of corporate groups of Christians as well.[30]

Implications or Significance of Understanding Church as Sacrament

The church participates in the mystery of God. Christ who acts through the church, gesturing forth the love, mercy, and forgiveness of the Father, through weak and sinful humanity who live their lives "in the Holy Spirit." In his farewell discourse, as recorded in the Gospel according to John, Jesus prays:

I ask not only on behalf of these, but also on behalf of those who will believe in me through their word, that they may all be one. As you, Father, are in me, and I am in you, may they also be in us, so that the world may believe that you have sent me. The glory that you have given me I have given them, so that they may be one, as we are one, I in them and you in me, that they may become completely one, so that the world may know that you have sent me and have loved them even as you have loved me (Jn. 17:20-23).

Christ understands this unity for which he prays to be a sign to the world of Christ's mission and the love of the Father for all humankind. In other words, we as church become that sign or sacrament of the presence and love of God when we strive to be one in Christ and with each other.

Perhaps that sign becomes more clear when we gather for worship, "for where two or three are gathered in my name, I am there among them" (Matt. 18:20). This presence of Christ when we gather for worship is an anticipatory presence that foreshadows the universal transformation of all humankind into Christ. That, after all, is the purpose of sacraments. But we also need to keep in mind, that we are not called to be the sacrament of Christ or the Body of Christ, so that we can glory in God's election of us as his dwelling place. Rather, our call to unity is meant to be a witness to the unity and love of God that is being poured out for the life of the entire world.

In this way, the Church's vocation to be sacrament of the presence of Christ in the world provides the Church with a strong sense of mission. As God is a God "for us," as Christ was a person "for others," so too the Church is committed to "being for others." We do this, always, in the name of the Lord, whose coming again we long for in joyful hope.

Notes

1. Thomas P. Rausch, *Catholicism at the Dawn of the Third Millennium* (Collegeville, MN: Liturgical Press, 1996), 81.

2. Judith M. Kubicki, *The Presence of Christ in the Gathered Assembly* (New York: Continuum, 2006), 16.

3. Kevin Irwin, "A Sacramental World—Sacramentality as the Primary Language of Sacraments," *Worship* 76 (2002): 197-199. See also Rausch, *Catholicism*, 80.

4. Ibid., 203.

5. This sentiment is eloquently expressed in the last stanza (1881) of William Turton's hymn text, "Lord, Who in This Eucharist Didst Say." Some contemporary hymnals have dropped this verse.

6. Kubicki, 89-90.

7. Avery Dulles, *Models of the Church* (Garden City, NY: Doubleday, 1974), 71.

8. Dulles, 67.

9. Henri de Lubac, *Catholicism: A Study of Dogma in Relation to Corporate Destiny of Mankind*, trans. Lancelot C. Sheppard (New York: New American Library, 1964), 29.

10. Karl Rahner, *The Church and the Sacraments*, trans. W. J. O'Hara (New York: Herder and Herder, 1963), 14.

11. Ibid., 15.

12. Edward Schillebeeckx, *Christ the Sacrament of the Encounter with God* (New York: Sheed and Ward, 1963), 13-14, [Original published as *Christus, Sacrament van de*

Godsontmoeting, Bilhoven, H. Nelissen, 1960].

13. Ibid., 15.

14. Rahner, 13.

15. Ibid., 18.

16. Louis-Marie Chauvet, *The Sacraments: The Word of God at the Mercy of the Body* (Collegeville, MN: Liturgical Press, 2000), 166.

17. Ibid.

18. Ibid., 167.

[19] Edmund Hill, "Church," in *The New Dictionary of Theology*, ed. Joseph A. Komonchak, Mary Collins, and Dermot A. Lane, 185-201 (Collegeville, MN: Liturgical Press, 1991), 185-186.

[20] John Gallen, "Assembly," in *The New Dictionary of Sacramental Theology*, ed. Peter E. Fink, (Collegeville, MN: Liturgical Press, 1990), 71-80. See also Kubicki, *The Presence of God in the Liturgical Assembly*, 38.

[21] Ibid., 38.

[22] See Kubicki, 46.

[23] Hill, 197-198.

[24] Ibid., 198.

[25] Ibid.

[26] Richard P. McBrien, *Catholicism*, study edition (San Francisco: HarperCollins, 1981), 593-594.

[27] Ibid., 595-596

[28] Kenan B. Osborne, *Christian Sacraments in a Postmodern World: A Theology for the Third Millennium* (New York: Paulist Press, 1999), 114-115.

[29] Ibid., 116.

[30] Ibid., 117. See also the explicit statements in this regard in the *Decree on Ecumenism, Ad Gentes*, no. 1.

Appendix E

"We Are Here to Heal": Revitalization Movements as Charismatic Communities in Africa

Kwabena Asamoah-Gyadu, PhD
Vice President and
Professor of Religion and Pentecostal Studies
Trinity Theological Seminary, Ghana

This essay, in line with the focus of Consultation II on 'the dialectic between revitalization and church,' attempts to show how Christian revitalization has worked within the African Christian context. This is a context that believes in a physically and spiritually precarious world and in which people are constantly searching for religion that works and that delivers power. It is the reason for the popularity of revitalization movements. Much of what was said in Consultation I related to the work of the Holy Spirit who is himself a source of power. I will seek to make the point that the single most important reason given for the rise of revitalization movements in Africa is also the experience of the Holy Spirit. In a simple but very important methodological statement for the study of revitalization movements, Harvey Cox observes that, 'knowing the gods and demons of a people and listening to their prayers and curses tell us more about them than any graphs and statistics one could assemble.'[1] The observation was made in the context of a study on Pentecostalism but it is relevant for our purposes because African Christian revitalization movements have always had a pneumatic character even if they do not consciously describe themselves as such.

That pneumatic orientation resonates very much with traditional religious piety in which through the presence of spirits and spirit possession communications and interventions are sought from the supernatural realm of health and salvation. In one of the earliest studies of revitalization in sub-Saharan Africa, Christian G. Baëta of Ghana pointed to how these churches adopted the adjective 'spiritual' to define their brand of churches. The expression 'spiritual' as he explained was 'intended to signify that, in their worship, the groups concerned engaged in various activities which (by their own assertion) were either meant to invoke the Holy Spirit of God, or were to be interpreted as signs of his descent upon worshippers. These "activities and 'signs'", Baëta described as:

> [Rhythmic] swaying of the body, usually with stamping, to repetitious music (both vocal and instrumental, particularly with percussion), hand-clappings, ejaculations, poignant cries and prayers, dancing, leaping, and various motor reactions expressive of intense religious emotion; prophesying, 'speaking with tongues', falling into trances, relating dreams and visions, and 'witnessing', i.e. recounting publicly one's own experience of miraculous redemption.[2]

In other words issues, experiences and exercises of aggressive and *glossolalic* prayer, prophecy, healing, deliverance, visions and revelations, and other such pneumatic phenomena are cherished in African Christian revitalization movements but are seen as neglected in the historic mission churches. So for example, such movements usually starts with a calling through an experience of the Spirit but the mission churches do not create the religious space for such beliefs. When in the early 1920s a Methodist catechist started manifesting experiences such as speaking in tongues and healing, his Superintendent minister simply described them as belonging to the occult and instigated his dismissal. The result was the formation of the 'Army of the Cross of Christ Church' led by the dismissed catechist, William Egyanka Appiah.

Even without reference to any statistical data, it is clear that the various forms of Christian revitalization movements that have developed in Africa since the beginning of the 20th century account in large measure for the emergence of Africa as a major heartland of Christianity today. What Christian revitalization movements have emerged within the last century? How are we able to define models of revitalization within African Christianity looking at their main religious tendencies and emphases? In what ways have the rise of revitalization movements contributed to new African understandings of church and what do these say about the central themes of Christian revival in Africa?

Types of Christian Revitalization Movements

Writing on Christianity and African initiatives, Andrew Walls notes that, the sheer size of its professing Christian community must be one reason for taking seriously the significance of Africa.[3] This significance I contend has come through Africa's revitalization movements. There are at least four main

Christian revitalization movements that have emerged in Africa since Edinburgh 1910. There are internal variations and some that are syncretistic and eclectic, but broadly, the well known ones are:

1. Independent itinerant charismatic prophets who led revivals with massive conversions of people from traditional African religions to Christianity from about 1910. They include William Wadé Harris of Liberia; Garrick S. Braide of the Niger Delta; Simon Kimbangu of the Congo and Isaiah Shembe of South Africa. This is what Ogbu Kalu says of their historical influence: "These prophets tilled the soil on which modern Pentecostalism thrives. They were closer to the grain of African culture in their responses to the gospel and so felt the resonance between the charismatic indigenous worldviews and the equally charismatic biblical worldview."[4]

2. African initiated churches that emerged as a direct result of the work of the indigenous prophets listed in (i) above. The churches concerned emphasized the charismatic triad of prayer, prophecy and healing. Healing is a fundamental quest in African religious practices and so it is not surprising that it has become a central concern of Christian revitalization on the continent. The hugely popular ministries of the AICs led to emulative action on the part of the historic mission churches culminating in a different type of revitalization movement, that is, charismatic renewal movements within the older churches.

3. Renewal movements within historic mission denominations. Through these 'local charismatic movements' the renewal and revitalization that was drawing people into the African initiated churches were introduced into historic mission Christianity. It did not stop the hemorrhage but it definitely stemmed the drift and loss of membership from the older churches to the newer AICs.

4. Neo-Pentecostal movements and ministries that have been burgeoning in Africa since the late 1970s. These are indigenous movements but the influence of American prosperity-style televangelism on their ecclesiology is undeniable. African neo-Pentecostalism is similar to those churches that Donald E. Miller refers to as 'new paradigm churches' within the North American Context. With their very modern outlook, relaxed dress codes, internationalism, innovative use of modern media and contemporary forms of worship, the neo-Pentecostals have proven very attractive to Africa's upwardly mobile youth.

In the revitalization movements mentioned here, we find what African Christians consider important to their faith. The older AICs are known as 'Spiritual churches' in Ghana but in Nigeria, they were mainly called *Aladura*, meaning, people of prayer. On account of the importance of charismatic personalities and their ministries of healing within the AICs, Harold W. Turner chose to refer to them as 'Prophet-Healing' movements. What we find then is that the charismatic triad of 'prayer', 'prophecy' and 'healing' are present in all the forms of African revitalization movements listed here. This underscores an observation by Andrew Walls that except for the differences in outlook—and this is unavoidable because they emerged within different historical circumstances—the different streams of African revitalization movements share the same religious characteristics. Writing with direct reference to the similarities between the prophet-healing churches and the neo-Pentecostals, Walls observed:

> Like the prophet-healing churches, they proclaim the divine power of deliverance from disease and demonic affliction, but the style of proclamation is more like that of American Adventist and Pentecostal preaching. ...All the new movements share with the prophet-healing churches a quest for the demonstrable presence of the Holy Spirit and a direct address to the problems and frustrations of modern African urban life.[5]

The theological emphasis, styles of worship and the ecclesiology of these movements reveal certain underlying themes that help to define revitalization within the African Christian context. The most important of these is the experience of the Holy Spirit, which Walls also refers to as Baëta did earlier. Turner's summary of the key theological emphases of the AICs, I have argued elsewhere, are equally present in the revitalization movements that emerged in Africa during the 20th century and into the 21st. He notes that the prophet-healing movements stressed two aspects of the totality of Christian belief:

> Pneumatological emphasis: 'the Godhead is envisaged as present and powerful through the Holy Spirit, who reveals the will of God and the destiny of the individual, guides through dangers, and fills men with new powers of prophecy, utterance, prayer and healing.

> Soteriological: the movements consisted of 'those who have rejected both the spirits and deities of the traditional pantheon, and the medicine-man with his magical powers and techniques, have turned to the Christian God for their salvation when in trouble, and for their protection from the host of evil forces that surround them. Salvation has been interpreted in an extremely practical this-worldly fashion.[6]

This suggests that the streams of Christianity that have appealed to Africans most are those that have placed considerable emphases on the power of Jesus Christ as experienced through the Holy Spirit. The belief in the experience of the Holy Spirit is the reason for the oral nature of revitalization theology and their effective inculturation and innovative gender ideology. Almost eighty years before any mainline Protestant denomination ordained women, the independent churches of African had already recognized the Holy Spirit experiences of women who were functioning as founders of African churches.

The founder of an African Christian revitalization movement is first and foremost a 'receiver' of revelation from the Spirit. It is from him or her that those who choose the Christian alternative come to seek God's intervention in their problems instead of visiting the 'demonized' traditional religious shrine. The power of the Holy Spirit is especially deployed in situations of crises and ill health. Within African cultures, concepts of illness and health are usually more social and cultural than biological. Etiology and diagnoses in the context of traditional African thought, Masamba ma Mpolo rightly points out, poses the following basic question: 'Who is the cause of my illness? In this context spiritual causality, organically manifested symptoms are always the result of some external aggression.' [7] The world of the traditional African is an 'intentional' one in which nothing happens by chance and 'the unseen powers are held to be active also in the natural order.' [8]

Defining Christian Revitalization in the African Context

The papers and discussions on Consultation I, 'Pentecost and the New Humanity' generated certain words and expressions associated with Christian revitalization that resonate with the nature of the African versions. Christian revitalization, wherever it appears, defines itself in terms of a recovery of the activity of the Holy Spirit for the church. Thus a number of Pentecostal movements, for example, talk about their existence in terms of the Spirit pouring out the 'latter-rain' upon the church. Since the Holy Spirit is associated with the 'power of God in action', or 'anointing' as the newer movements refers to it, a revitalized Christian community is an empowered community. He brings the word of God to life and return power to the church in the same way that we read about in the post-Pentecost apostolic era.

The stirrings of the Spirit lead to certain developments including inspiration, renewal, revival, transformation, enthusiasm, ecstasy, health and wholeness, and restoration. Within the African Christian context in particular, it is normative to view 'revitalization' in terms of supernaturally-inspired attempts to rescue religion from suffering a moribund fate at the hands of some traditional representatives of its belief systems and practices. In Christian revitalization, as evidenced in the work of African revitalization movements, revivalism replaces denominational formalism, exuberant worship replaces dry denominationalism, spontaneity replaces routine religion, faith replaces doubt, prosperity replaces poverty and deprivation, and holiness replaces carnality. When a church is renewed charismatic experiences are normalized in its worship and the dichotomy between body and soul is bridged in rituals of healing. Additionally, there is an ardent desire to experience the immediacy of the *Presence* of God in personal and communal Christian lives. That sort of religious experience breaks the monopoly of patriarchal clergy over religious affairs because individuals including women receive dreams and visions through which they are also called to minister through their *charisms*.

All this is to suggest that in both its older African initiated church and contemporary neo-Pentecostal forms, revitalization movements in Africa define their ministries in terms of the zeal, activity, power, experience and work of the Holy Spirit. The experience of the Holy Spirit is considered as 'missing', 'neglected', 'marginalized' or 'down-played' in the life of the historic Western mission-related churches. For example, in the mid 1960s, the Presbyterian Church of Ghana established a Committee to look into the drift of their members into the burgeoning Spiritual churches. Five out of the eight reasons given by the Committee as it tried to explain the attraction of the Spiritual churches to its historic mission church patrons are most instructive for understanding models of the church for revitalization in Africa. They were that:

1. A large number of Christians join them because they are disappointed with their former Churches. They complain that the worship there is dull, that there is no 'spiritual power', that Church agents are hypocrites, and that there is not sufficient prayer in the old churches. They therefore seek a younger, more zealous and more 'spiritual' fellowship.
2. Pagans find their way more easily into these churches [because] worship is less intellectual…
3. Their worship is appealing, and people take an active part in it and obviously enjoy it.
4. Divine healing plays a prominent role in all these churches and obviously satisfies a great desire for giving due attention to the spiritual side of sickness and healing

The references to 'dull worship', 'lack of spiritual power', 'intellectual worship', and 'lack of divine healing' are important as indicators of what Africans expect a revitalized church to look like. Unlike in the historic mission denominations in which such ideas were dismissed as nonsensical and occultic, revitalization movements take primal worldviews of causality seriously and create ritual contexts within which appropriate responses may be made to the anxieties and fears that they generate. Thus revitalization movements in Africa, as elsewhere, are meant to be movements of restoration of life to the church and this through the *Presence* of the Spirit. In effect, that is why African Christian revitalization movements generally tend to have a pneumatic orientation. Historically, they were formed and grew largely because of the failure of western mission-founded churches to accept or to integrate 'charismatic experiences', especially healing, into their faith and practice. As a Ghanaian pastoral theologian notes:

> Foremost in the faith and practice of these churches is divine healing. In many respects, their practice of divine healing is phenomenologically similar to the activities of the traditional priest healers. This renders them culturally and religiously very amenable to the masses of people who find in them a congeniality and familiarity absent from the staid, silent, 'orderly' form of worship and liturgy in the western mission-founded churches with their non-interventionist theology.[9]

This is often evident in the 'charismatic triad' of prayer, prophecy and healing but even these are based on particular understandings of the work of Jesus Christ. It is said of Prophet Braide, who worked in the Niger Delta around 1915 that 'he mobilized masses of the citizenry in a bid to make Christianity more relevant to contemporary needs.'[10]

Model of Revitalized Church

Lamin Sanneh for example draws attention to the importance of prayer in an African revitalization movement and points out how its emphasis on prayer related directly to the African religious worldview:

> Prayer was understood in two specific ways. First, it was the means whereby the individual received certain benefits, including the fulfillment of wishes and desires; secondly, it was the obtaining of guidance. In this way personal need and control, which used to form a prominent part of traditional religious life and practice, acquired a new lease of life in a Christian setting.[11]

Christian G. Baëta studied the African independent church movement in the early 1960s. Observing how important prophecy was to the Spiritual churches, he wrote of the prophetic in religion as being 'a perennial phenomenon of Africa life.' He explains how this works as follows:

> Powers credited to such persons, of healing, of revealing hidden things, predicting the future, cursing and blessing effectually, etc., will be attributed to him whether he claims them or not. Some will make a more successful showing than others. Such things as the above-mentioned endowment, inward illumination, a sense of divine vocation, spontaneous enthusiasm (in the original sense of being in God, experiencing ardent religious zeal) are facts of life and have their effects on Africans society.

Writing on the neo-Pentecostal forms of revitalization André Corten and Ruth Corten to the book *Between Babel and Pentecost,* refer to how the newcomers have shifted the emphasis from 'speaking in tongues' and 'retreat from the world' that characterized the theology of the classical Pentecostal denominations. In contemporary African Pentecostalism, they note, the emphasis is now on miracles of prosperity and 'divine healing'. Divine healing is 'understood in the broadest sense of alleviating the causes of suffering, be they physical, financial, spiritual or social.'[12] In this new type of African revitalization movements, 'salvation is now resolutely this worldly and the evidence of new life has become as much material as spiritual.'[13] The point here is that there is clear continuity between the two sets of revitalization movements in Africa—the AICs and the neo-Pentecostals—and this gives us an indication of what Africans consider important as far as a revitalized Christianity is concerned.

The issue of translation of the Scriptures has been identified as being 'absolutely pivotal' to the rise of 'reform, renewal and revivalism' in Africa. The vernacular principle was supposed to be 'the pulse of the revival movements' that swept across sub-Saharan Africa in the early decades of the 20th century.[14] I take that for granted in this work because accessibility to the Scriptures in mother tongues betrayed the gaps between what came to be understood as Biblical Christianity and the staid, silent and liturgically straight-jacketed forms that mission agencies made available. Through the vernacular Bibles, God who revealed himself in Jesus Christ came to be understood as the one who, by the power of the Holy Spirit, became our healer.

The efforts of Prophet Harris in particular led to the formation of the 'Church of the Twelve Apostles' by two of his most prominent converts—John Nackabah and Grace Tani—both of whom were former custodians of powerful traditional shrines. A third member of the group, John Hackman, got converted through the ministry of Nackabah. In his seminal work on these churches as they formed in Ghana, Baëta refers to all three persons as having had 'gifts of "prophecy" and spiritual healing.'[15] He proceeds to provide the following apt summary of what the Church of the Twelve Apostles stood for in terms of what these new movements brought to African Christianity as revitalization movements:

> Emphasis is laid, to the exclusion of all other matters, upon the activity of the Holy Spirit in enabling certain men and women to predict future events, warn of impending misfortunes, detect evil-doers and, above all, to cure illnesses. Asked to put in a nut-shell what their Church stood for, Mr. Nathan [an important leader] had no hesitation in exclaiming: "We are here to heal".[16]

Healing, one would say, has been central to the work of the revitalization movements in Africa. It is always related to prayer because the source of health is divine and healing is related to prophecy because like divination in the traditional setting, it is through prophecy that destinies and the sources of predicament are revealed. Healing in this context would encapsulate something more than just the cure of ailments. It includes all those divine interventions made possible by such spiritual disciplines as 'waiting', 'fasting' and 'prayer' and through which health and fortunes are restored and deliverance received from one's enemies. In healing divine resources are deployed to provide release for the sick, demon-possessed, demon-oppressed, broken, disturbed and troubled persons, in order that victims may be restored to proper functioning order and that means, health and wholeness, that 'they may enjoy God's fullness of life understood to be available in Christ.[17]

Revitalization and the Life of the Church in Africa

Christian revitalization in Africa therefore, one would say, constitutes indigenous attempts at answering a basic Christological question. J.V. Taylor, himself a former missionary to East Africa, succinctly articulated this question as follows:

> Christ has been presented as the answer to the questions a white man would ask, the solution to the needs that Western man would feel, the Savior of the world of the European world-view, the object of the adoration and prayer of historic Christendom. But if Christ were to appear as the answer to the question that Africans are asking, what would he look like?[18]

The idea of religious movements 'implies an organized attempt to introduce change in religion' and such change 'is normally accompanied by strain and conflict between religious movements and their competitors or opponents.'[19] In this context the competitors or opponents of African Christian revitalization movements have been the historically older and more administratively and doctrinally firmly established historic mission denominations. Their vision of Christ was the one who saved people to take them to heaven. The revitalization movements took a different approach. Thus when a member of the Church of the Twelve Apostles said 'we are here to heal', it was supposed to be an indirect indictment on their older compatriots for being closed to those experiential aspects of the Christian faith that allowed for such charismatic experiences as healing to take place within the context of Christian worship.

Religious movements, like social movements, usually attempt to cause change in a system of beliefs, values, symbols, and practices concerned with providing supernaturally based general compensators.[20] For the movements under study here therefore, the provision of ritual contexts—prayer places and healing camps—for the purposes of providing supernatural interventions for people seeking help in times of need was key to their religious and theological identity. That the worldview of supernatural causality within which they functioned resonated with traditional religious ideas served to underscore their importance within the African Christian religious landscape.

Conclusion

When Edinburgh 1910 was constituted, no one foresaw the emergence of a vibrant Christian presence in Africa, let alone the emergence of a distinctly African experience of Jesus Christ.'[21] It was just around 1910, the year that European Missionary leaders gathered in Edinburgh to map out the future of mission in Africa and the rest of the world that Wade Harris trekked from Grebo Island through the Ivory Coast to the Gold Coast, baptizing, healing, teaching new choruses, and charismatizing the religious landscape. The charismatic fire that he lit, it has been said, became more important for the future of Christianity in Africa than the grand Edinburgh Conference of 1910 that shut out African voices.[22]

When the Conference reconvened in Le Zoute, Belgium in 1926, there was a recommendation for the setting up of mission boards, committees and agencies to provide resources to African missionaries in terms of recognized courses at home and on the field so they can take an effective approach to mission. By then, Africans had already taken their spiritual destiny into their own hands. Through the translated scriptures and openness to pneumatic activities, African Christians had acquired the means to make their own responses to the Christian message, and in terms of their own needs and categories of meaning. Through these revitalization movements, Lamin Sanneh noted:

> A process of internal change was thus initiated in which African Christians sought a distinctive way of life through mediation of the spirit, a process that enhanced the importance of traditional religions for the deepening of Christian spirituality. The Charismatic churches, therefore, combined the two fundamental elements of Christianity and African culture in a way that advertizes their Christian intentions without undervaluing their African credentials. Biblical material was submitted to the regenerative capacity of African perception, and the result would be Africa's unique contribution to the story of Christianity.[23]

This essay has shown how revitalization movements have served as new communities of health and wholeness and continued to serve as places of restoration for those who are broken or disturbed by the difficulties of life. Although their primary intention is usually biblical, healing has become important to African Christianity leading to the institutionalization of healing camps because the underlying ideas or worldviews that move people to look for religious interventions are also present within traditional religions. Healing in this context, is understood broadly to include supernatural interventions in situations of ill health, demonic afflictions and other obsessive behaviors and emotional disturbances affecting the fullness of life that God makes available in Jesus Christ.

Notes

1. Harvey Cox, 'Foreword', in Allan H. Anderson and Walter J. Hollenweger ed., *Pentecostals after a Century: Global Perspectives on a Movement in Transition* (Sheffield: Academic Press, 1999), 12.

2. Christian G. Baëta, *Prophetism in Ghana: A Study of Some Spiritual Churches* (London: SCM, 1962), 1.

3. Andrew F. Walls, *The Missionary Movement in Christian History: Studies in the Transmission of Faith* (Maryknoll, NY: Orbis Books, 1996), 83.

4. Ogbu Kalu, *African Pentecostalism: An Introduction* (Oxford: Oxford University Press, 2008), x.

5. Walls, *Missionary Movement*, 93.

6. Harold W. Turner, *Religious Innovation in Africa: Collected Essays on New Religious Movements* (Boston, MA: G.K. Hall, 1979), 98.

7. Masamba ma Mpolo, 'Perspectives on African Pastoral Counseling', in Masamba ma Mpolo and Wilhelmina Kalu ed., *Risks of Growth: Counseling and Pastoral Theology in the African Context* (Geneva: WCC, 1985), 9.

8. Kwesi A. Dickson, *Theology in Africa* (Maryknoll, NY: Orbis, 1984), 49.

9. Emmanuel Y. Lartey, 'Healing: Tradition and Pentecostalism in Africa Today', *International Review of Mission*, vol. lxxv, 297 (January 1986), 75.

10. Lamin O. Sanneh, 'Translatability in Islam and Christianity in Africa: A Thematic Approach' in Thomas D. Blakely, Walter E.A. van Beek and Dennis L. Thomson ed., *Religion in Africa: Expression and Experience* (London: James Currey; Portsmouth, NH: Heinemann, 1994), 41.

11. Lamin O. Sanneh, *West African Christianity: The Religious Impact* (Maryknoll, NY: Orbis Books, 1983), 191.

12. André Corten and Ruth Marshall-Fratani ed., *Between Babel and Pentecost: Transnationalism in America and Latin America* (Bloomington and Indianapolis: Indiana University Press, 2001), 5

13. Corten and Marshall-Fratani, *Babel and Pentecost*, 7.

14. Sanneh, 'Translatability', 42.

15. Christian G. Baëta, *Prophetism in Ghana: A Study of Some Spiritual Churches* (London: SCM, 1962), 9.

16. Baëta, *Prophetism*, 15.

17. J. Kwabena Asamoah-Gyadu, *African Charismatics: Current Developments within Independent Indigenous Pentecostalism in Ghana* (Leiden: E.J. Brill, 2005), 165.

18. John V. Taylor, *The Primal Vision: Christian Presence amid African Religion* (London: SCM, 1963), 16.

19. James A. Beckford (ed.), *New Religious Movements and Rapid Social Change* (London: Sage, 1986), x.

20 .   Rodney Stark and William Sims Bainbridge, *The Future of Religion: Secularization, Revival, and Cult Formation* (Berkeley, Los Angeles, London: University of California Press, 1985), 23.

21. Kwame Bediako, *Jesus in Africa: The Christian Gospel in African History and Experience* (Akropong-Akwapim, Ghana: Regnum Africa, 2000), 4.

22. Ogbu Kalu, *African Pentecostalism: An Introduction* (Oxford: Oxford University Press, 2008), x.

23. Lamin O. Sanneh, *West African Christianity: the Religious Impact* (Maryknoll, NY: Orbis Books, 1983), 180.

Appendix F

Atlas of Global Christianity and the Global Demographics of the Pentecostal/Charismatic Renewal

TODD M. JOHNSON, PhD

RESEARCH FELLOW IN GLOBAL CHRISTIANITY

GORDON CONWELL THEOLOGICAL SEMINARY

The *Atlas of Global Christianity* is the first scholarly atlas to document the shift of Christianity to the Global South. It features contextual maps of world issues and major religious traditions, including global coverage of religious freedom and religious diversity. It is the first atlas to map Christian affiliation at the provincial level. It is a unique Christian publication in the sense that it contains ecumenical and global coverage, including all Christian traditions in every country. Full-color maps of Christian affiliation in every United Nations region in the world partner with historical essays on Christianity 1910–2010 by sixty-four scholars *from* every region of the world to highlight the 100-year history of Christianity in each region. Included with the atlas is an interactive presentation assistant on CD of all maps and graphics for classroom use.

To understand the context of global Pentecostalism and world evangelization as we lead up to the 100th anniversary of the World Missionary Conference held in Edinburgh in 1910 we will consider trends both inside of global Christianity and outside of global Christianity.

Trends inside Global Christianity

One major trend within global Christianity is that Christianity has shifted dramatically to the South. There has been little change in the status of global Christianity over the past 100 years. For the entire 100-year period, Christians have made up approximately one third of the world's population. This masks dramatic changes in the geography of global Christianity—a process stretching back to the earliest days of the world Christian movement.

The 1910 Edinburgh World Missionary Conference was placed directly in the center of this Western-focused Christianity. As recounted by Ken Ross,

> the delegates were, overwhelmingly, British (500) and American (500). Representatives from continental Europe were a small minority (170). Even fewer were the delegates from the 'younger churches' of India, China and Japan (17). There were no African participants, nor were there any from Latin America. No delegate was invited from the Roman Catholic or Eastern Orthodox Churches. While the participants were struck by the diversity of participants, from a longer historical perspective it is striking how limited was their range.[1]

The shift in demographics by continent from 1910 to 2010 most clearly illustrates the shift of Christianity to the global South. While 66% of all Christians lived in Europe in 1910, by 2010 only 25.6% lived there. By contrast, less than 2% of all Christians lived in Africa in 1910 skyrocketing to almost 22% by 2010. The Global North (defined as Europe and Northern America) contained over 80% of all Christians in 1910 falling to under 40% by 2010.

Western influence extended far beyond just the Christian world; Western overconfidence in science and technology was also a major factor throughout the twentieth century. Daniel Jeyaraj notes that

> Unprecedented Western discoveries in science, technology, medicine, information communication, dissemination of knowledge, and transportation predicted not only progress and prosperity for all peoples, but also the end of poverty and other miseries. People hoped for a mutual sharing the earth's resources. They anticipated equal access to knowledge, opportunities, just global markets and politics.[2]

Simultaneous to the shift of Christianity to the South was the decline of Christianity in the North. Moonjang Lee notes with irony,

> it was through the modern missionary movement that Christianity became a worldwide phenomenon, and in that process Christianity came to acquire the image of a Western religion. The subsequent globalisation of the image of Western Christianity poses a problem for non-Western Christianity. Though we talk about a post-Christian West and a post-Western Christianity, the prevailing forms of Christianity in most parts of the non-Western world are still dominated by Western influences.[3]

The transition of Christian leadership from North to South has been anything but smooth. Daniel Jeyaraj notes that

> When World War II broke out, Western missionaries had to hand over power to the native Christians, whom they had failed to train for leadership tasks, and thus

these could not manage the vast landed properties, huge buildings, and money- and time-consuming administrative structures the missionaries left behind. In order to generate money, many church properties were sold. Greed led to court cases, competitions and betrayals.[4]

One way of illustrating the shift of Christianity is to map the statistical center of gravity of global Christianity over the past 2,000 years. One can readily see that in the modern period there has been a decisive southern shift. At the time of the 1910 Edinburgh conference the statistical center of global Christianity was near Madrid, Spain. In fact, at that time, over 80% of all Christians were European. In 2010 the statistical center will have shifted well south of Timbuktu in Mali. This 100-year shift is the most dramatic in Christian history.

Tracking the statistical centre of global Christianity, AD 33–2100

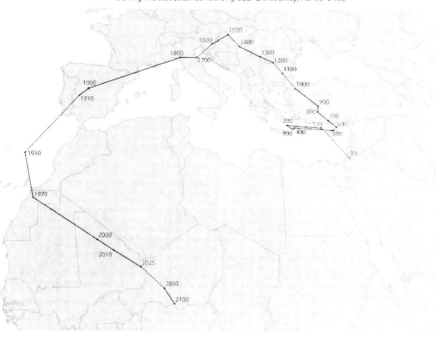

The southern shift can also be put in context of the entire history of Christianity. Christians of the Global South were in the majority for the first 900 years of Christian history. European domination of global Christianity can be seen as a recent phase of world Christianity that has now passed. Since 1981, Southern Christians are, once again, in the majority.

It is obvious to see from the various maps in the atlas that Christianity in 1910 was largely a Western phenomenon—including a strong European Roman Catholic presence in Latin America, where few church leaders were Latin Americans. By mapping the same phenomenon by province 100 years later, it is clear that the global situation has changed. The most dramatic difference between these two dates is in Africa—less than 10% Christian in 1910 but nearly 50% Christian in 2010, with sub-Saharan Africa well over 70% Christian.

The top 10 countries with the most Christians in 1910 and 2010 are presented below, where the southern shift can be quickly perceived. Nine of the top 10 countries in 1910 were in the Global North, whereas seven of the top 10 in 2010 are in the Global South. The fastest growth over the past 100 years or over the past 10 years has all been in the Global South (over the past 100 years, the top five fastest Christian growth was in Burkina Faso, Chad, Nepal, Burundi, and Rwanda. Over the past ten years, the countries include Afghanistan, Cambodia, Burkina Faso, Mongolia, and Timor). In terms of language, Spanish (the top global language with the most Christians) and Portuguese (ranked third) reflect the numerical strength of Christianity in Latin America.

Largest population of Christians by country, 1910 and 2010

	1910	*Christians*	*2010*	*Christians*
1	USA	84,800,000	USA	257,311,000
2	Russia	65,757,000	Brazil	180,932,000
3	Germany	45,755,000	Russia	115,120,000
4	France	40,894,000	China	115,009,000
5	Britain	39,298,000	Mexico	105,583,000
6	Italy	35,330,000	Philippines	83,151,000
7	Ukraine	29,904,000	Nigeria	72,302,000
8	Poland	22,102,000	DR Congo	65,803,000
9	Brazil	21,576,000	India	58,367,000
10	Spain	20,357,000	Germany	58,123,000

A second trend within global Christianity is the fragmentation of its adherents. Christians are now found in 41,000 denominations. These range in size from millions of members to less than one hundred members and are listed for each of the world's 238 countries in the *World Christian Database.*[5] Moonjang Lee observes that

Christianity has become too fragmented. Existing in a fragmented world, churches fail to show a united front. There are so many divisions within

Christianity that it is an intriguing task to clarify a Christian identity. At the beginning of Christian history, the designation of a person as a 'Christian' was sufficient to tell about his or her social, religious and cultural identity. Today, however, we have to supply subcategories to tell about who we are as Christians, for there are many different and conflicting forms of church life.[6]

The chart below shows these enumerated by major tradition. Note that the vast majority is in the Independent and Protestant traditions. Note as well that Orthodox and Roman Catholic congregations are much larger because they are based on parish models. By 2025, there will likely be 55,000 denominations.

Christian major traditions by denominations, 2010

	Denominations		Congregations	
	Total	Average size	Total	Average size
Anglican	169	514,000	103,200	840
Independent	27,010	14,000	2,496,100	150
Marginal	1,800	19,000	157,800	220
Orthodox	1,030	268,000	120,320	2,280
Protestant	10,840	39,000	1,404,900	300
Roman Catholic	239	409,000	568,200	2,030

A third trend is the unprecedented renewal occurring globally across the faith. There are many forms of renewal within global Christianity including Evangelical movements, liturgical renewal, Bible-study fellowships, and house church movements. One of the most significant is the Pentecostal/Charismatic Renewal which coincides with the 100-year period that we have been reflecting on. A part of this Christian renewal around the world is the changing role of women in Pentecostal churches. Daniel Jeyaraj observes,

> Another major player in this period was Pentecostal Christianity with its modern beginnings in the USA. It promotes the ideals of Spirit-filled holy life, apostolicity and catholicity. It incorporates practical ways of leadership, training and mission that draw much inspiration not only from Western business models, but also from local socio-religious customs, hierarchies and practices. Its emphasis on tithing of financial resources and time, using personal talents in mission, and accountability to the Holy Spirit make it mostly self-sufficient and self-propagating (although its view on material wealth and good health as symbols of God's blessings is critiqued).[7]

We will return to this subject in more detail.

Lastly, the unequal distribution of Christian resources worldwide is another trend within global Christianity. A serious aspect of suffering for Christians of the Global South is the paucity of resources, especially compared to the Global North. Christian in the South represent 60% of all Christians worldwide but receive only about 17% of all Christian income. This puts them at a disadvantage in many areas including health, education, communications, and overall quality of life. This imbalance is one of the great tragedies of global Christianity that could not have been easily predicted by our colleagues in Edinburgh in 1910.

The disparity is highlighted in global partnerships such as the World Alliance of Reformed Churches, World Council of Churches, and World Evangelical Alliance. Moonjang Lee notes, "The churches in the non-Western world are mostly conservative, evangelical and spiritual. As Tan Kang San has observed, Christians in the non-Western world differ from their Western counterparts by 'their belief in the Bible as authoritative, their proclamation of Christ as the only way for salvation, and their reliance of the power of the Holy Spirit to bring renewal'."

Contextualization as a Global Concern

Dana Robert states that, "Although most Western missionaries remained trapped in colonial mindsets and structures, for both Catholics and Protestants the most significant new development in the period between the World Wars was the idea that the gospel should adapt to the forms of each culture."[8] This line of thought encourages Christians to reconsider the cultural "norms" that have been attached to the faith. A comparison of northern and southern cultures reveals that it is actually southern cultures that are sometimes more aligned with the culture in which Jesus lived and ministered to. The worldview of Christians in the global South might actually better align with the way of life outlined in the Christian scriptures. Could the shift of Christianity to the global South upon up new possibilities for the life and health of Christianity around the world? And likewise, is the future of Asian Christianity one of bananas where Asian Christians are yellow on the outside but white on the inside (southern Christians trained by northern) or one of mangoes where Asian Christians are yellow on the outside and yellow on the inside (southern Christians with a southern worldview)?[9] Is the demographic shift of Christianity good news if it is not accompanied theological reflection from fresh cultural perspectives of more recent members of the global body of Christ?

Trends outside Global Christianity

One might have the impression today that what is needed is more evangelism to reach the world for Christ. But, in sheer quantity, there is already enough evangelism in the world today for every person to hear a one hour presentation of the gospel every other day all year long. This amounts to over 1,136 billion hours of evangelism generated by Christians every year ranging from personal witnessing to television and radio broadcasting. When broken down by UN region, it is easily seen that Asia and Northern Africa have the lowest amount of evangelism but the largest non-Christian populations.

The churches of the Global South are notable for their dynamic nature. Daniel Jeyaraj observes,

> Yet non-Western Christianity shows signs of vitality, authenticity and hope. It is far from perfect but moves towards better manifestations of Christian beliefs in word and action. The ethos of the Euro-American Enlightenment does not constrain non-Western Christians. They do not see Jesus Christ of the Bible reflected in Western theologies centered on God and God's rule. They constitute suffering minorities in anti-Christian settings. They carry the burden of past Euro-American political colonialism and contemporary forms of economic and military neocolonialism. They seek to interpret their Christian beliefs and practices among the peoples of other living religions and ideologies who too are engaged in purposeful missionary activities. The interventions of Christians on behalf of the poor and neglected have socio-economic repercussions. Their discipleship is often a costly affair.[10]

Another startling reality is that most Christian outreach never reaches non-Christians—over 85% of all Christian evangelism is aimed at other Christians. Close examination of virtually any Christian evangelistic activity reveals this massive imbalance. Part of the explanation is the unanticipated success of Christian missions in the twentieth century. Much missionary deployment is trying to keep up the growth of the churches in Africa, Asia, and Latin America. What is surprising today is how missionaries from the Global South have also been drawn into mission primarily to other Christians. Deployment studies in Nigeria and India have shown this to be the case, although there is a perceptible shift in the past decade toward work among non-Christians.

A current trend affecting global Christianity is the opposing views of what Moonjang Lee has described as secularization and spiritualization.[11] In an age of church buildings being renovated into apartment buildings, some may wonder if Christian, or any religious faith can survive at all. The post-modern era, however, is proving to be quite interested in religious adherence, evidenced by a religious revival that was thought impossible by many throughout the twentieth century. At the same time, Western intellectualism is also sprouting forth a fierce secularization that poses a serious and consistent threat to Christian faith.

The *Atlas of Global Christianity* also views the world by majority religion by province in 2010. It is important to note that Christianity and Islam seem to have the greatest geographical reach, and indeed, together represent about 55% of the world's population. Recent research reveals that as many as 86% of all Muslims, Hindus, and Buddhists do not personally know a Christian. This is tragic in light of the strong biblical theme of incarnation which is at the heart of Christian witness. Christians should know and love their neighbors! In the twenty-first century it is important to realize that the responsibility for reaching Muslims, Hindus, and Buddhists is too large for the missionary enterprise. While missionaries will always be at the forefront of innovative strategies, the whole church needs to participate in inviting people of other faiths to consider Jesus Christ. Note that Muslims, Hindus, and Buddhists are increasingly found living in traditionally "Christian" lands. Lastly, the most responsive groups appear to be in the least-Christian areas.

> Innovation in mission in the past was spurred by understanding a holistic ministry, such as that of women medical missionaries in the Punjab in 1900. Over the course of the century, missionaries realized the need for a new understanding of Christian mission, much like those at the 2010Boston meeting are doing the same for the next century. The twentieth century raised doubts about not only missionary methods, but also doubts regarding particular "Western" theologies, approaches to personhood, and activities of governments worldwide. Mission gradually moved outside the context of colonialism, and in doing so lost the institutional support it once had.[12]

The biblical text (Rev. 5:9, 7:9) leads us to a world where all peoples have access to the gospel message. The body of Christ will not reach its full stature until all peoples are worshipping at the throne of God. The cover of the *Atlas of Global Christianity* features artwork from Chinese Christian artist He Qi. Here Jesus is depicted as the resurrected Lord with the peoples of the world looking on. This is the ultimate destination of both global Christianity and its global mission. It is crucial for the Christian to always remember the reality of the global human family. Moonjang Lee comments,

> Andrew Walls has observed that Christianity lives by crossing cultural frontiers and suggests that in the twenty-first century the new players of non-Western Christianity will have to cross cultural boundaries, even Western cultural boundaries, for the continued life of the Christian faith. However, once the era of Western Christendom is replaced by the era of world Christianity, a further shift in the centre of Christian gravity might no longer be anticipated, as the 'centre-periphery' division within world Christianity would no longer be considered relevant. From now on, global Christianity will either live or die as a whole depending on its success in worldwide evangelisation.[13]

Renewal in the Global Context[14]

The case for the Pentecostal and Charismatic Renewal as a single interconnected movement can best be made by considering how the movement starts and spreads in any area, from the days of the earliest Pentecostals to those of current Charismatics and Independent Charismatics. The start of the movement anywhere has always been an unexpected or unpredictable happening rather than the result of any human planning or organization. First individuals (at random across the existing churches), then groups, then large numbers in semi-organized movements become filled with the Spirit and embark on the common Charismatic experience. All of them, originally, can collectively be termed Renewalists. All these Renewalists find themselves living initially within existing mainline non-pentecostal churches and denominations. There, they have been labeled as Charismatics, revivalists, enthusiasts, spirituals or Pentecostals. Though often they have been dismissed as cranks, fanatics, sectarians, heretics, schismatics or worse, all of them initially attempt to stay within, and work within, those churches. But before long evictions begin, and ejections, withdrawals and secessions occur in varying degrees. In a pattern recapitulating their start, individuals, then groups, then whole movements are forced into schism, or opt for it, and so begin separate ecclesiastical structures and new denominations.

When mapped by province, Renewalists and global Christianity as a whole look similar in many ways. They are different, however, in that the Renewal in Europe is weaker than Christianity as a whole, with higher percentages of Christians in the Global South in the Renewal. The distinction between global Christianity and the Renewal can be seen in maps that show higher concentrations of Renewalists in the Global South. Almost 27% of all Christians worldwide are now part of the Pentecostal/Charismatic Renewal (614 million out of 2,292 million), up from 24% in 2000 (483 million out of 2,004 million). In 1910 the three largest Renewalist populations were in South Africa, Nigeria and the USA. In 2010 China, Brazil, and the USA are the three largest.

South Africa contained a much higher concentration of Pentecostal Christians than any other country due to the large numbers of indigenous African movements with Pentecostal characteristics in the early twentieth century. Wherever Christianity reached during the twentieth century, to a large extent the Renewal did as well. Countries where large populations held to animistic and spiritist traditions generally embraced the Renewal due to its emphasis on signs, wonders and miracles—phenomena compatible with those in their former tribal religions. One example of this is sub-Saharan Africa, which moved largely from ethnoreligions to Christianity in the past century. Today, countries with the highest percentages of Renewalists are found in the Global South, with a preponderance of countries in southern Africa.

By 2010 the centre of gravity of global Christianity had moved southward, but the centre of gravity for Christian Renewalists actually moved toward the Global North. This is due to concentrations of Pentecostals, Charismatics and neocharismatics growing in regions outside of South Africa. Many regions saw up to 15–17% annual growth rates where both Christians and nonbelievers embraced this form of Christianity. In 1910 there were just over one million Renewalist Christians worldwide, but by 2010 there are upwards of 614 million. This huge influx of adherents comes from a variety of ethnicities and Christian backgrounds.

If one considers the Renewal from the standpoint of where Renewalists are currently growing the fastest, then the leading countries in the world are those in which Christianity is relatively new, such as Laos, Afghanistan, and Cambodia. The fastest growth rates over the entire century reveal those countries that now have some of the largest Renewalist populations, such as Brazil, Philippines, and DR Congo.

The Renewal continues to grow in Africa, Asia and Latin America while slowing in Northern America and Europe. Exceptions to this trend can be found among Independents in the USA (still growing) and Charismatics in Europe (some growth among Roman Catholics). Another significant trend is the migration of Renewalists from the Global South to the Global North. Thus, some of the largest congregations in Europe are African neocharismatic in origin. In the USA, many recent Hispanic arrivals, legal or illegal, are either Catholic Charismatics or Pentecostals.

Three Types of Renewal

From its beginnings in this way, the Renewal can be conceived as expanding in three surges, waves, or types though the genesis of each of these is only approximately sequential. The demographics of the Renewal are best understood by its constituent parts, namely, the three types: Pentecostals, Charismatics, and Independent Charismatics. Each of these types has different strengths in various countries around the world. Thus one finds that while Renewalists are numerous in China, Brazil and the USA, there are relatively few Pentecostals in China; Charismatics dominate in Brazil; and Independent Charismatics (neocharismatics) are most numerous in China and the USA.

The first type consists of Pentecostals. These are Christians who are members of the explicitly Pentecostal denominations whose major characteristic is a rediscovery of, and a new experience of, the supernatural, with a powerful and energising ministry of the Holy Spirit in the realm of the miraculous that most other Christians have considered to be highly unusual. This is interpreted as a rediscovery of the spiritual gifts of New Testament times, and their restoration to ordinary Christian life and ministry. They number 94 million in mid-2010.

Pentecostalism usually is held to have begun in the USA in 1901. For a brief period Pentecostalism expected to remain an interdenominational movement within the existing churches without beginning a new denomination, but from 1909 onward its members increasingly were ejected from all mainline bodies and so forced to begin new organised denominations.

Pentecostal denominations hold the distinctive teaching that all Christians should seek a post-conversion religious experience called baptism in the Holy Spirit, and that a Spirit-baptised believer may receive one or more of the supernatural gifts known in the Early Church: instantaneous sanctification; the ability to prophesy, to practice divine healing through prayer, to speak in tongues (*glossolalia*) or to interpret tongues; singing in tongues, singing in the Spirit, dancing in the Spirit, praying with upraised hands; dreams, visions, discernment of spirits, words of wisdom, words of knowledge; miracles, power encounters, exorcisms (casting out demons), resuscitations, deliverances, signs and wonders.

From 1906 onward, the hallmark of explicitly Pentecostal denominations, by comparison with Holiness/Perfectionist denominations, has been the single addition of speaking with other tongues as the 'initial evidence' of one's having received the baptism of the Holy Ghost (or Holy Spirit), whether or not one subsequently experiences regularly the gift of tongues. Most Pentecostal denominations teach that tongues-speaking is mandatory for all members, but in practice today only a third of all members have practiced this gift, either initially or as an ongoing experience. Pentecostals, then, are defined here as all associated with explicitly Pentecostal denominations that identify themselves in explicitly Pentecostal terms, or with other denominations that as a whole are phenomenologically Pentecostal in teaching and practice.

The largest Pentecostal denomination in the world is the Assemblies of God. Countries with large numbers of Pentecostals but not as many Charismatics or Independent Charismatics include Indonesia, Ghana and Angola. First type (Pentecostal) denominations depend mainly on foreign missions and church planting as means of growth. Interestingly, Pentecostals make up the highest percentage of all Christians in Cambodia, a country where the church has been built up recently.

The second type of the renewal consists of Charismatics. These are defined as Christians affiliated to non-Pentecostal denominations (Anglican, Protestant, Catholic, Orthodox), who receive the experiences described under Pentecostals in what has been termed the Charismatic Movement. The Charismatic Movement's roots go back to 1907 and 1918, but its rapid expansion has been mainly since 1950 (later called the Charismatic renewal). Charismatics usually describe themselves as having been 'renewed in the Spirit' and experiencing the Spirit's supernatural and miraculous and energising power. They remain within, and form organised renewal groups within, their older mainline non-Pentecostal denominations (instead of leaving to join Pentecostal denominations). They demonstrate any or all of the *charismata pneumatika* (Greek New Testament: gifts of the Spirit) including signs and wonders (but with *glossolalia* regarded as optional). They now number 207 million, a majority of which are Roman Catholic.

Charismatics (or, until recently, Neopentecostals) usually are defined as those baptised or renewed in the Spirit within the mainline non-Pentecostal denominations, from the first mass stirrings in 1918 in Africa on to the large-scale rise from 1950 of the Charismatic Movement (initially also termed Neopentecostalism to distinguish it from Classical Pentecostalism) who remain within their mainline non-Pentecostal denominations. The Movement was later called the Charismatic Renewal. Note that many individuals and groups in the mainline churches already had been receiving baptism in the Spirit without publicity for many years before the usually quoted beginning dates.

Note the somewhat unusual example of the Coptic Orthodox Church in Cairo, where in 1974, a young schoolteacher (Brother Simon), decided to work among the poor where all the garbage in the city was collected and sorted. Now, thirty years later, after many documented miracles, including people raised from the dead, the church has seven chapels carved into the mountain.

In terms of Latin America, Catholic Charismatics in the Philippines, Brazil, Colombia, Mexico and Argentina comprise the largest proportion of Renewalists in each of those countries. Charismatics grow by recruiting new members within existing denominations. Research among these denominations (especially Roman Catholics) has shown that some countries have stagnant or declining numbers of Charismatics (USA), while others continue to grow rapidly (Brazil, Philippines).

The last type of the Renewal is defined as Neocharismatics of Independent Charismatics. Since 1945 thousands of schismatic or other independent

Charismatic churches have come out of the Pentecostal and Charismatic movements; these independents now number more than the first two types combined. They consist of evangelicals and other Christians who, unrelated or no longer related to the Pentecostal or Charismatic Renewals, have become filled with the Spirit, or empowered or energised by the Spirit, and have experienced the Spirit's supernatural and miraculous ministry (though usually without recognising a baptism in the Spirit separate from conversion); who exercise gifts of the Spirit (with much less emphasis on tongues, as optional or even absent or unnecessary) and emphasise signs and wonders, supernatural miracles and power encounters; and who leave their mainline nonpentecostal denominations but also do not identify themselves as either Pentecostals or Charismatics. In a number of countries they exhibit Pentecostal and Charismatic phenomena but combine this with rejection of Pentecostal terminology. These believers frequently are identified by their leadership as Independent, Postdenominationalist, Restorationist, Radical, Neo-Apostolic or the 'Third Wave' of the twentieth-century Renewal. Because they constitute a major new revitalising force, we also term the movement the Neocharismatic Renewal.

Also largely Pentecostal or semipentecostal are members of the 250-year-old Independent movement of Christians, primarily in the Global South, or churches begun without reference to Western Christianity. These indigenous denominations, though not all explicitly Pentecostal, nevertheless have the main phenomenological hallmarks of Pentecostalism (including Renewalist spirituality; oral liturgy; narrative witness/theology; dreams and visions; emphasis on filling with the Holy Spirit; healing by prayer; atmospheric communication [simultaneous audible prayer]; and emotive fellowship). The case for enumerating adherents of these movements as Renewalists has been fully made by W. J. Hollenweger, in 'After twenty years' research on Pentecostalism,' *International Review of Mission* (April 1986), and *Pentecostalism* (1997). Examples (all over 50 million) include Chinese house churches, African Initiated Churches, and the white-led movements such as the Vineyard.

The latest development among Independent Charismatics is the rise of hidden believers in Christ. One type is insider movements—defined as "movements to Christ where the Gospel flows through pre-existing communities and networks, and believing families remain inside their socio-religious communities, retaining their natural identity while living under the Lordship of Jesus Christ and the authority of scripture." Muslims, Hindus, and Buddhists around the world are following Christ while remaining within their own communities.

While found in many of the same countries as Pentecostals and Charismatics, neocharismatics are proportionally larger in South Africa, DR Congo, India and Zimbabwe. Third Wavers (neocharismatics) experience growth by planting new churches and by schisms from traditional denominations. Of the three waves, neocharismatics are most strongly concentrated in the Global South.

Summing up, the Renewal can be viewed in three waves, surges, or types. The Renewal can be viewed by United Nations region by the absolute number and percentages of Renewalists in 1910 and 2010. It can also be viewed by the growth rates in the same regions from 1910 to 2010 and from 2000 to 2010. Each method of evaluation reveals the stunning reality of a fast-growing movement over the course of the twentieth century.

Waves of Christian renewal

Renewalists by major tradition

	1910		2010		1910-2010
	Adherents	*%*	*Adherents*	*%*	*Rate*[+]
Anglican	1,000	0.1	19,267,000	3.1	10.18
Catholic	12,000	1.0	139,210,000	22.7	.67
Independent	1,164,000	96.8	313,048,000	51.0	5.46
Marginal	0	0.0	3,000	0.0	5.80
Orthodox	0	0.0	4,817,000	0.8	11.21
Protestant	26,000	2.2	137,665,000	22.4	8.65

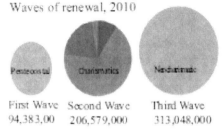

Waves of renewal, 2010

Pentecostal   Charismatic   Neocharismatic

First Wave   Second Wave   Third Wave
94,383,00   206,579,000   313,048,000

▲ Waves and traditions of Christian Renewal
The Christian renewal movement expanded in three waves or surges. The first wave is known today as Pentecostalism. The second wave is the Charismatic movement and the third wave consists of neocharismatic renewal outside the Pentecostal and Charismatic movement.

Edinburgh University Press, 2009

Notes

1. Kenneth R. Ross in *Atlas of Global Christianity*, Todd M. Johnson and Kenneth R. Ross, editors, Edinburgh: Edinburgh University Press 2009, xvi.

2. Jeyeraj in *Atlas of Global Christianity*, 54.

3. Lee in *Atlas of Global Christianity*, 104.

4. Jeyeraj in *Atlas of Global Christianity*, 54.

5. See www.worldchristiandatabase.org published by Brill Online (Leiden, Netherlands).

6. Lee in *Atlas of Global Christianity*, 104.

7. Jeyeraj in *Atlas of Global Christianity*, 54.

8. Robert in *Atlas of Global Christianity*, p.258.

9. See Hwa Yung, *Mangoes or Bananas: The Quest for an Authentic Asian Christian Theology*, Oxford: Regnum, 2009.

10. Jeyeraj in *Atlas of Global Christianity*, 55.

11. Lee in *Atlas of Global Christianity*, 104.

12. See Robert in *Atlas of Global Christianity*, 258-9.

13. Lee in *Atlas of Global Christianity*, 105.

14. See full-length treatment in Todd M. Johnson, "The Global Demographics of the Pentecostal and Charismatic Renewal," in *Society*, Vol. 46, No. 6, November/December 2009.

Appendix G

Revitalization Amid Secularity: New Religious Communities in Ukraine

CATHERINE WANNER, PhD
PROFESSOR OF HISTORY
PENNSYLVANIA STATE UNIVERSITY

After the collapse of the Soviet Union, a commitment to religious pluralism was incorporated into the very idea of the Ukrainian nation, at a minimum to accommodate the various Orthodox churches and the Ukrainian Greek Catholic Church, all of whom claim to be indigenous national institutions. The various splits and divisions among the three competing Orthodox churches in Ukraine, the Ukrainian Orthodox Church-Kyiv Patriarchate, the Ukrainian Orthodox Church-Moscow Patriarchate, and the Ukrainian Autocephalous Orthodox Church, means that there is not a single "national" church that can lay claim to a privileged status protected by the state, as is the case in most other highly secularized European and Eurasian countries. As a result, a comparatively tolerant legal and political climate has emerged in Ukraine toward minority religious communities and foreign religious organizations, allowing them to establish a formidable presence in Ukraine.[1]

Many religious organizations have even made Ukraine a base for missionizing the former USSR. From small bureaucratic concessions, such as eliminating the need for foreigners to obtain visas, to allowing religious organizations to receive humanitarian aid directly from abroad and distribute it to the recipients of their choice without state regulation and monitoring, the Ukrainian government has consistently demonstrated an atmosphere conducive to developing and strengthening indigenous religious institutions. A 2006 bill paved the way for religious-based instruction to be integrated into all levels of education, from preschool to higher education, claiming "providing religious organizations with the opportunity to set up schools in the world, where alongside standard educational disciplines the basics of religious values will be taught, will give Ukraine not only educated and aware but also highly moral and spiritual citizens, which will further the spiritual revival of the Ukrainian nation."[2] This is one of many initiatives that have been adopted on the heels of 74 years of state-sponsored promotion of atheism.

Since the collapse of communism, Ukraine, unlike the other former Soviet republics turned countries, has even become a center of publishing, seminary training and missionary recruiting for a multitude of faith groups.[3] Currently, hundreds of Ukrainian missionaries travel to Russia and throughout the former Soviet Union annually to evangelize.[4] Ukrainian believers possess the cultural capital to effectively missionize among former Soviet citizens and they are able to elude state policies designed to stem the flow of "foreign" missionaries proselytizing "non-traditional" faiths.

By analyzing the social ministries and missionizing activities of two transnational megachurches that have firmly established themselves in Ukraine, I wish to consider how these churches are revitalizing religious life in a highly secular society. A profile of these churches and their activities also begins to suggest what it means for believers and governments in Eurasia to have Ukraine develop as a base for missionary and clerical training.[5] Both of these churches are committed to the twin goals of reversing the rampant secularism they perceive in Eurasia and to alleviating social suffering, inequality and violations of biblical understandings of justice as they understand them.

The networks and activities of these two churches illustrate the interrelated dynamics of saving souls from a communist atheist upbringing in the "east" as well as from European secularism in the "west." Most religious communities in Eurasia are barely able to financially sustain themselves, let alone finance missionaries and social ministry outreach initiatives. So, missionizing successes in Europe finance charitable outreach activities in Eurasia. In this way, Ukraine has become a central node, a hub, if you will, of networks for these two churches, and for a multitude of others, that links Ukraine via the global networks of religious organizations and via the missionizing efforts of individual believers to Eurasia every bit as much as it links Ukraine to Europe and even to believers elsewhere. In this way, Ukraine, which means "borderland", lives up to its name as a border zone bridging Eurasia and Europe, linking them and drawing them closer together.[6] By considering the dual dynamics of individual Ukrainians missionizing others and their religious organizations forging links with communities throughout Eurasia and Europe, we see how religious organizations connect Ukraine to Eurasia and its socialist past as well as how they forge new links to other parts of the world.

Secularism and its Legacies

Thinking about the current religious landscape in Eurasia has obliged me to think about the secular, for the two are intricately related. Theoretically, I have taken inspiration from Talal Asad, who has gone against the dominant theoretical debates on secularism that have largely centered on a conceptualization of secularism as a diminishing role for religion in public life and a dwindling respect for religious authority and a religious basis of various forms of knowledge. Rather, he has suggested that we should think of secularism as a concept that produces political subjects of a certain kind through the promotion of distinctive practices, knowledges and sensibilities. This strikes me as a perspective that yields richer insight, especially when considering, as I am here, the efforts of some religious groups to undo Soviet secularism by promoting charitable inclinations, a willingness to assist unknown others, and a commitment to alleviating social suffering. By looking at the practices embedded in the social ministries of the two churches to be examined, which are targeted to young people, we see how new political arrangements are part and parcel of the religious renaissance that is clearly underway in Ukraine and elsewhere in the world.

Conversion and Nominal Orthodoxy

One of key reasons all forms of religious groups descended in droves upon the former Soviet Union beginning in the late 1980s was that many Slavs were thought to be non-believers or, at best, "nominally Orthodox". In other words, many thought that Soviet citizens had no faith, no sense of religious identity, and no church membership and therefore, having been denied religious knowledge, were now ripe for harvesting. However, religious identity in Orthodox countries largely hinges on who one is, more so than on what one does. Among many other religious groups, it is the other way around. That is to say, in Eastern-rite Christianity cultural, linguistic, national and territorial identities are meant to coalesce organically with confessional identities and ideally synthesize into a single national-confessional identity. This creates an allegiance to Orthodoxy that is often opaquely described as "nominal".

Nominal allegiance is most vividly manifest in a multitude of survey and ethnographic research that illustrates the often paradoxical categories that individuals commonly have used to describe their religiosity: Orthodox non-believer, Christian pagan, and, as Belarussian President Aleksandr Lukashenka infamously declared himself recently, Orthodox communist.[7] These categories demonstrate an allegiance to the Orthodox Church based on an ascribed nationalized identity (however defined) and on a recognition and respect for the contribution of Orthodoxy to national historic, artistic and intellectual achievements.[8] An embrace of Orthodoxy often does not include religion. Although the allegiance to the Church is often real and heartfelt, it often has little to do with religious practice in the transcendental and doctrinal sense of the term. One does not have to do anything, not even believe, to consider oneself Orthodox. In other words, for some the relevance of Orthodoxy over time has become gutted of its religious content but this has not eviscerated the popularly held reverence for the achievements of those associated with the institution of the church. Hence, much to the frustration of social scientists, survey data is routinely peppered by responses of individuals who self-identify as "Orthodox" and "non-believer" in the same breadth.[9] Such respondents understand Orthodoxy to be more than religion. Rather, it symbolizes culture, community, a particular sensibility, a worldview and even a form of spirituality in the broadest sense of the term.

A similar dilemma was faced by Soviet ideologues who expected that once they inculcated non-belief, indifference, ignorance, or some other cognitive vacuum in their citizens, religion and its sacred symbolism and pageantry would cease to hold sway over individuals. This was clearly not the case, although the social weight of non-belief, indifference and ignorance of religion are undeniable in Ukraine and elsewhere in the former Soviet Union.

This compendium of unusual factors, which creates selective affinities with Orthodoxy and culminates in what is often referred to as "nominal" allegiance or a form of "invisible religion", "civil religion", "privatized religion" and so on, is in part attributable to the flexible and frequent use of secularizing and sacralizing dynamics over the course of the twentieth century by the Soviet state. The push to secularize Soviet society, which often resorted to mobilizing sacred means, resulted in large sectors of the population becoming ignorant or indifferent to doctrine and the meanings of religious symbolism at the same time that it sensitized them to sacred experiences involving reverence, awe and the like. This yielded individuals who still maintained some empathy for religion and religious experiences and therefore were extremely open to all forms of proselytizing once overt and public forms of religiosity became possible once again. This explains the vast numbers of missionaries who arrived in the former Soviet Union with high hopes of converting the masses of non-believers and the varying degrees of success they achieved.

It was in the midst of this post-Soviet fever that the two churches profiled below were founded. These two churches provide some of the most vivid and unexpected illustrations of churches currently working to revitalize religious and social life after the collapse of communism. Their visions for personal and social transformation have thus far met with remarkable success and merit our attention.

Faith in Action

The first church I would like to consider is the Blessed Kingdom of God for People of all Nations, or the Embassy of God, as it is known to its followers. With 25,000 members, this church is currently the largest evangelical megachurch in all of Europe. Founded in 1994 by a Nigerian self-taught Pentecostal pastor, the Embassy of God now has 38 churches in Ukraine and 18 abroad, including five in the U.S., four in Russia, two each in Belarus, Germany and

Holland, as well as others in less common places such as the United Arab Emirates and India. Although the Church has faced enormous challenges, it still is very much of a force driving social change.

The second church, Hillsong, is the largest church in Australia with 20,000 members. After creating a base in London, Hillsong opened a church in the center of downtown Kyiv in 1992 with hopes of using that as a gateway to Eurasia and particularly to Russia. Since opening the Kyiv church, Hillsong planted a church in Paris and on March 1, 2007, it's newest European church opened in Moscow.

The two churches share several features in common. Both are charismatic Pentecostal churches that feature expressive, even ecstatic, forms of worship. Doctrinally, they advocate beliefs in an inerrant Bible as the literal word of God and basic tenets of Pentecostal theology, such as prophecy, faith healing and the vitality of the Holy Spirit as manifest by speaking in tongues, for example. Both are run by husband and wife "preaching teams" but now have a plethora of Ukrainians, both men and women, serving in a multitude of leadership positions. In contrast to almost all other Soviet-era communities, including Pentecostal and Orthodox ones, they support a relaxation of the general suspicion of worldliness, the strict codes of personal morality and ascetic lifestyle that characterized the beliefs and lifestyles of longstanding believers and their religious communities in Ukraine and elsewhere in the former Soviet Union. Yet, these two churches retain an overall conservative slant on a variety of social issues, especially homosexuality. Both of these churches promote a belief that financial and professional success is a sign of God's favor.[10] Indirectly, such a principle endorses the virtues of neoliberal economic values by encouraging commitments to individual responsibility, initiative and charitable giving. Both churches masterfully exploit the media to advance and spread their visions for personal and social transformation. In sum, both of these churches offer much more that a set of religious beliefs. They offer an alternative lifestyle, replete with the social structures to support the emergence of alternative moralities, communities and practices. They foster new self-conceptions that celebrate empowerment and fulfillment.

Love Rehab

Among the differences that separate these communities, however, are the important ones of race and class. Both of the churches display their foreign influences, associations, and connections in their names. However, when the Nigerian founder of the Embassy of God speaks of "peoples of all nations," it signifies that this church is a particularly receptive to minorities, immigrants, and people of color.[11] Caribbean and African-American visiting preachers are interspersed in a steady stream of visiting white evangelical Americans.[12] At nearly every service foreign delegations visiting the Embassy of God are presented to the congregation.

One of the reasons why they know of this church is that Sunday Adelaja originally came to Soviet Belorussia in 1986 to study journalism, demonstrating his early preoccupation and savvy when it comes to media and communication. His church has its own publishing house where Adelaja's more than forty books have been published (some in English), and its own television studio, which allows the church to use televangelism as a source for attracting religious seekers.

The Embassy of God's missionizing strategy centers on its drug and alcohol rehabilitation program, which champions faith healing and the efficacy of prayer as a means of remedying addiction. Its healing programs and the accomplishments of its rehab centers are showcased in an annual march in downtown Kyiv. The Church's beginnings with drug addicts and alcoholics mean that its core membership and nearly half of the pastors serving in the church are former addicts who claim to have simultaneously experienced physical and spiritual restoration as part of their involvement with the Church's Love Rehabilitation Program. An additional component of the church's membership is grateful family members of former addicts. Although the leaders of the church's Love Rehabilitation Center are not adverse to medical intervention, few of their clients can afford it.[13] On the other hand, prayer and fellowship are offered free of charge to all. When addiction is positioned as a spiritual problem mandating a spiritual solution, indeed the church's programs gain credibility. The Embassy of God's faith healing programs mirror in many ways the twelve-step healing programs embraced by such groups in the U.S. as Alcoholics Anonymous that include surrender to a higher force.[14]

So far the Kyiv based Love Rehab model has been replicated in Minsk, Belarus and Vladimir, Russia. In 2001 the Embassy of God sponsored the March for Life, renamed in 2005 the March for Jesus, as a proselytizing forum to showcase the liberating effects of belief. From its inception, these marches were presented as broad ecumenical actions involving Orthodox priests and other clergy. These marches, as orchestrated, coordinated events involving a broad cross-section of clerical leadership in Ukraine, represent important precursors to the united front religious communities mounted in opposition to the falsified election results that led to the Orange Revolution in 2004. With the notable exception of the Ukrainian Orthodox Church-Moscow Patriarchate, all religious groups supported the Orange Camp and about 4,000 members of the Embassy of God were on the *Maidan* everyday in late 2004 to protest.

Official Russian hostility to Adelaja and his vision for transforming the post-socialist order was manifest on 31 May 2006 when the Russian FSB refused to grant Adelaja entrance, claiming that he was "a threat to the security of the country" when he arrived in Moscow to appear on the television show *"Pyst' Govoriat."* He lost a legal appeal to revoke his entrance visa. But it is too late to try to close the door. The Embassy of God Church has been actively missionizing among the most vulnerable populations in Russia since 2000 and has already created what is officially referred to as a "sectarian Russian cell." Alexander Dzjuba, the head pastor of the Moscow Embassy of God Church has been quite vocal in his assertions that he would like to see an Orange Revolution in Russia. As they have done in Ukraine, the Embassy of God's strategy in Russia to affect change by offering "spiritual solutions" to social ills and actively proselytizing to entrepreneurs with the hopes of putting godly people in public office. So, although it is possible to shut out the foreign face of the Embassy of God in Russia, in so many places it already has a native face beckoning people of all nations to join.

Rock 'n' Roll Religion

Hillsong's experiences in Australia have tremendously affected the way in which they present themselves in Ukraine and pursue missionizing in Eurasia. Institutional religious participation in Australia has been steadily waning for decades, suggesting that it is on a path to European-like secularization.[15] Yet, Hillsong members who participate in charitable initiatives are often motivated by a faith-in-action type of calling, even if they are entirely non-practicing religious believers. In other words, Hillsong uses participation in social service initiatives as an opening to middle class young people who perhaps have little inclination toward membership in what they might perceive to be a centralized, hierarchical traditional institution, but who nevertheless are willing to join charitable initiatives because of their concerns for justice, fairness and morality.

In Australia, two-thirds of the church's 20,000 members are under 30 years of age. In Kyiv, three of the seven services offered every weekend are specially designed to appeal to the 2,000 young people who attend. Music has been the signature vehicle that Hillsong has used to deliver its message of salvation to young people. The house band of the Sydney church, the Bayca Boys (Believe And You Can Achieve), has released CDs that have topped the music charts in Australia and given the church enormous visibility -- and profits.

Hillsong Kyiv features a series of Saturday night Christian rock concerts, called *Vybukh* (Ukr. explosion), celebrating personal empowerment and fulfillment, as its main means of outreach. These concerts are recorded live and sold in CDs and cassettes at weekly services. Hillsong Kyiv meets in a rented theater in the historic center of the city, wedged between a Chinese restaurant and a kickboxing studio. The head pastors of the church, Zhenia and Vera Kasevich, both 30 years old, assert that sermon-based services are ineffective for reaching youth. So, they use the appeal of rock music as a first step to introducing young people to the numerous "blessings" that flow from faith.

Sixty percent of the church's budget is spent on social ministry, with "Teen Challenge" as its most successful initiative. Hillsong operates on the principle that Europe is one of the most unreached parts of the world. Outreach is oriented to the most vulnerable members of society who, not surprisingly, because of feelings of powerlessness and isolation, are often the most open to supernatural experiences and to conversion. Hillsong Kyiv offers such initiatives as the "Tribe X" youth movement to evangelize the over 100,000 orphans in state institutions via a "volunteer army" to help Orphans live in "freedom and excellence." A 2006 Tribe X CD entitled "Salvation," featured such hits as "Awesome God" and "Shout Unto God," all performed in "passionate Euro-styled worship." In this way, via music Hillsong draws in young people and celebrates the glories of becoming a person of faith and of participating in charitable endeavors to help other young people as a means of becoming a better, more moral person.

The missionizing of the Embassy of God is equally as performative, but in a public proselytizing street format. Whereas the Embassy of God's missionizing is multidirectional, oriented to the U.S. as much as to Europe as well as to other locales, Hillsong operates on the principle that Europe is one of the most un-reached parts of the world. One of Hillsong's goals is to have its "European churches" in London, Kyiv, Paris and Moscow use a variety of media, especially "praise and worship music" to make Russian language churches "champions in ministry"[16]

Just as Adelaja's commitment to the land of his birth, Nigeria, sparked charitable outreach programs there financed by the Embassy of God, the Hillsong Sydney church's long-standing commitment to missionizing in Africa, has prompted its Kyiv church to launch charitable outreach programs in Uganda among "child soldiers." Working through an international organization, the Australian church sponsors and supports over 3,000 children that all live within close proximity to one another. The Kyiv church launched an initiative to sponsor the orphans in a neighboring village to complement the efforts of Hillsong Sydney. Both of these churches, therefore, tie Ukrainians and Ukraine to other parts of the world where there has historically been limited economic or political engagement.

Conclusion

The activities of the two transnational megachurches I have described here oblige us to question, if not discard, such common tropes as "core" and "periphery," "East and West " and even dynamics that are assumed to be ongoing between "colonizer-colonized" when discussing religion. For, as I have suggested, through the impulse to missionize, members of these two churches have embarked on their own "civilizing mission" to their former colonizer, to Europe, and to the U.S. Just as local Ukrainian congregations furnish missionaries who travel the world, they also tie these local congregations into global organizations, thereby bringing the world to Ukraine. These globalized and globalizing tendencies enhance the appeal of membership in these communities, especially for peoples who perceive themselves to have been "behind the Iron Curtain," on the forgotten margins of the world.[17] The charitable impulses and missionary activities of these communities connect their members to fellow believers on multiple continents. In doing so, these local religious communities become the sites of social relations that span great distances and increasingly interlock the local and the global in powerful ways to shape the consciousness, everyday practices, and identities of individual believers.

In closing, I would like to suggest that the spectacular and rapid success of global religious organizations such as these promoting a charismatic renewal of religious life, which includes a commitment to providing charitable services to the needy, pressures traditional religious denominations in Eurasia and Europe to change. Many of these denominations are founded on the principle of serving a particular nation in partnership with the state. This renders the state part of a trinity, a provider of services to the population and to the religious institution itself. Charismatic churches, such as the two profiled here, shift the burden of caring for the needy away from the state and recast it as a moral obligation of believers, as a means of witnessing their faith and demonstrating conviction. These charismatic megachurches challenge the patterns of church-state interdependence and self-limiting outreach that have historically dominated in this part of the world. Transnational charismatic megachurches have become a formidable force transforming the lives of individual believers. Their missionaries are committed to delivering equally formidable levels of social transformation through revitalization and dismantling secularizing tendencies wherever they find them, be it Eurasia, Europe, or the U.S.

Notes

1. For a complete breakdown of the number of registered communities as well as a listing of infractions against their rights, see the U.S. Department of State's "International Religious Freedom Report 2002" at www.state.gov/g/drl/rls/irf/2006/71415.htm for Ukraine and www.state.gov/g/drl/rls/irf/2006/71403.htm for Russia, accessed 26 March 2007. For an in-depth comparison of the politics of religion in Ukraine and Russia, see Serhii Plokhy. 2002. "State Politics and Religious Pluralism in Russia and Ukraine: A Comparative Perspective," in P. G. Danchin and E. A. Cole, eds., *Protecting the Human Rights of Religious Minorities in Eastern Europe*. New York: Columbia University Press and Myroslaw Tataryn. 2001. "Russia and Ukraine: Two Models of Religious Liberty and Two Models for Orthodoxy," *Religion, State, and Society* 29, no. 3 (September 2001): 155-72.

2. See www.risu.org.ua. 16 February 2007, last accessed 26 March 2007.

3. Evangelical groups have become particularly prominent. For example, Kyiv alone currently has four Baptist and three Pentecostal seminaries, all of which have internet-based distance learning programs in Russian that, along with clerical training, offer instruction in a variety of lay leadership spheres from choral direction to "Christian counseling," or biblically-based psychotherapy. See Catherine Wanner, *Communities of the Converted: Ukrainians and Global Evangelism* (Ithaca: Cornell University Press, 2007).

4. Patrick Johnson and Jason Mandryk. 2001. *Operation World: 21st Century Edition*. Waynesboro, GA: Paternoster Publishing, pp. 644-45.

5. Currently, one-third of the world's Christians are either Pentecostal or Charismatics. See Martyn Percy. 1997. "The City on a Beach: Future Prospects for Charismatic Movements at the End of the Twentieth Century" in Stephen Hunt, Malcolm Hamilton, and Tony Walter, eds. *Charismatic Christianity: Sociological Perspectives*. New York: St. Martin's Press, p. 207.

6. Given the global reach of these megachurches, a second aspect of this research project explores how religious communities contribute to an overall despatialization of identity. When feelings of belonging, commitment and identity are so tied to beliefs and practices that are mobile, does this result in a deterriorialization of identity or simply a reterritorialization that defies the boundaries of nation-states?

7. Larissa Titarenko, "On the Shifting Nature of Religion during the Ongoing Post-Communist Transformation in Russia, Belarus and Ukraine" *Social Compass* 55(2) (2008): 237-254. This article is in dialogue with the following two: Irena Borowik, "Orthodoxy Confronting the Collapse of Communism in Post-Soviet Countries" *Social Compass* 53(2) (2006) : 267-278 and "Between Orthodoxy and Eclecticism: On the Religious

Transformation of Russia, Belarus and Ukraine" *Social Compass* 49(4) (2002): 497-508.

8. The charged and judgmental nature of the category "nominally Orthodox" prompts me to suggest that we use the term "culturally Orthodox", rather than nominally Orthodox to refer to those who have a hybrid form of allegiance to the Orthodox Church.

9. Borowik, "Between Orthodoxy and Eclecticism" p. 504

10. Some of the risks in contemporary Ukrainian economic life and how they are understood and experienced are illustrated in Catherine Wanner, "Money, Morality and New Forms of Exchange in Ukraine" *Ethnos*. 71(4) (Winter 2005): 515-37.

11. Although many Ukrainians continue to outmigrate in search of economic opportunities, other immigrants are settling in Kyiv, creating unprecedented levels of diversity as Ukraine emerges in the post-socialist aftermath as an immigrant sending *and* receiving country. See Blair A. Ruble, *Creating Diversity Capital: Transnational Migrants in Montreal, Washington, and Kyiv*. (Baltimore: Johns Hopkins University Press, 2005).

12. Miles Monroe from Jamaica as well as Benny Hinn and Creflo Dollar from the U.S., all strong proponents of prosperity theology, have been guests at anniversary celebrations.

13. Although the core membership shares a history of overcoming addiction, it would be wrong to conclude that the church appeals uniquely to the down and out. Some members of the church are so wealthy that they single-handedly finance entire charitable endeavors, such as homeless shelters or business counseling centers.

14. For an extended discussion of the Embassy of God's faith healing programs, see chapter six of Catherine Wanner. 2007. *Communities of the Converted: Ukrainians and Global Evangelism*. Ithaca: Cornell University Press.

15. Philip Hughes of the Christian Reasearch Association claims that 9% of the Australian population attended church in 2001. Because the number of attendees over 60 years of age is so high, within twenty years the percentage of the population attending church is expected to drop to six. See "We've got to have faith" Barney Zwartz, *Sydney Morning Herald*, 13 April 2006.

16. http://www.hillsong.com.ua/transforminglives/index.php?pageLang=en.

17. Anthony Giddens refers to the overall phenomenon of bringing people from disparate places together as the creation of "distanciated relations." Anthony Giddens. 1990. *The Consequences of Modernity*. Stanford: Stanford University Press, p. 87.

CPSIA information can be obtained
at www.ICGtesting.com
Printed in the USA
LVOW11s0446030817
543668LV00001B/29/P